THE POLITICAL SYSTEM OF BRAZIL

INSTITUTE OF LATIN AMERICAN STUDIES · COLUMBIA UNIVERSITY

The Political System of Brazil

⌒〰⌒ ⌒〰⌒ ⌒〰⌒

EMERGENCE OF A "MODERNIZING" AUTHORITARIAN REGIME, 1964–1970

⌒〰⌒ ⌒〰⌒ ⌒〰⌒

RONALD M. SCHNEIDER

Columbia University Press · New York and London · 1971

Ronald M. Schneider is Professor of Political Science at Queens College.

Copyright © 1971 Columbia University Press
Library of Congress Catalog Card Number: 75–154860
International Standard Book Number: 0–231–03506–3
Printed in the United States of America

To my parents, who started me out on the road, and whose confidence in what I have chosen to do has provided support when my own doubts have risen

AND

To my wife, for two decades of affection and companionship, patience with my impatience, encouragement when the road seemed rough and rocky, and invaluable collaboration in the most important job of all, the raising of our children.

The Institute of Latin American Studies of Columbia University was established in 1961 in response to a national, public, and educational need for a better understanding of the contemporary problems of the Latin American nations and a more knowledgeable basis for inter-American relations. The major objectives of the Institute are to prepare a limited number of North Americans for scholarly and professional careers in the field of Latin American studies and to advance our knowledge of Latin America and its problems through an active program of research by faculty, by graduate students, and by visiting scholars.

Some of the results of this research program are published from time to time by the Institute of Latin American Studies. Professor Schneider gathered most of the research materials presented in this book during the period 1963–1969 when he was Associate Professor of Political Science at Columbia University and a member of this Institute. He spent the summer of 1965, a major part of 1966 while on leave from Columbia, and the summer of 1967 doing research in Brazil. This volume provides not only interesting conceptual insights within the discipline of political science but, for Brazilianists, it documents the intricately involved processes and events which determined the political evolution of Brazil during the turbulent period since World War II. Professor Schneider has shown convincingly how Brazil simply does not fit neatly into the more conventional typologies of political systems. Social scientists who have been interested in Brazil will profit from his comprehensive portrayal of Brazil's recent political life.

Since 1969 Professor Schneider has been Professor of Political Science at Queens College of the City University of New York.

We are grateful to the Ford Foundation for financial assistance which has made this publication program possible.

Preface

MY RESEARCH on the Brazilian political system has roots going back more than fifteen years to my undergraduate study of Latin American politics, which spanned the 1951–1954 period during which Getúlio Vargas was apparently attempting to govern Brazil within the limits of the democratic Constitution of 1946. Although my interests were drawn more strongly to the Guatemalan crisis which, in the United States as well as most of the world, overshadowed developments in Brazil at the time, by mid-1958 I had turned my attention systematically to Brazil. In keeping with the state of the comparative politics field at that juncture, bolstered by the general optimistic image of a Brazil moving toward political as well as economic development, my attention focused upon the interest groups, which seemed a critical element in the political processes, given the weaknesses of the Brazilian party system.

The breakdown in 1964 of the system which, as late as 1960, had appeared to be functioning relatively well required a shift in my research priorities. It became necessary to analyze the Brazilian military's decision in March, 1964, to oust President João Goulart and to describe the evolution of the crisis that led the reputedly legalistic Brazilian Armed Forces to intervene so decisively in the political life of the nation. An examination of the secondary sources available soon led me to the reluctant conclusion that analyses of the relevant aspects of Brazil's political modernization and development were inadequate to serve as the basis for a monographic work concentrating upon the evolution of the 1961–1964 crisis, the coup itself, and its lasting impact upon the Brazilian political system. Thus, I was forced to broaden the scope of my original inquiry. The result is the present study of the emerging political system since 1964, as well as a second book that will examine Brazilian political development and crisis politics from the late nineteenth century through the impasse of the early 1960's.

While Thomas Skidmore's history of the 1930–1964 period provides answers to many crucial problems concerning the crisis of the early 1960's, systematic examination from the perspective of political science is still necessary.[1]

Skidmore's excellent volume contributes greatly to our understanding of the pre-1964 era with admirable attention to the interplay of politics and economics. But in addition to the fact that it essentially ends with the 1964 military-civilian revolt and does not analyze the fundamental changes that followed, Skidmore's work does not go back sufficiently far in time. Although the year 1930 afforded a convenient, plausible, and accepted benchmark, a truly useful examination of the emergence of the military as a major political factor needed to begin considerably earlier with a systematic examination of the process of Brazil's political development. For, as closer examination revealed, scholarship on the political processes of the first three decades of the twentieth century, both North American and Brazilian, was inadequate and often inaccurate. Yet the existence of Skidmore's and, to a lesser extent, Reisky's books, which give the interested reader at least a good beginning in his quest for understanding developments to 1964, contributed to my decision to publish this analysis of the post-1964 political system before that covering the earlier period.

The second study, *Modernization and the Military in Brazil, 1889–1964,* will contain a more comprehensive discussion of the conceptual gap between the political development and the civil-military relations

---

[1] Consult Thomas E. Skidmore, *Politics in Brazil, 1930–1964: An Experiment in Democracy* (New York, 1967). The only relatively comprehensive study of contemporary Brazilian politics since Karl Lowenstein's 1943 *Brazil under Vargas* was Vladimir Reisky de Dubnic's *Political Trends in Brazil* (Washington, D.C., 1968), and it concentrated almost exclusively upon parties, their programs, and foreign policy, not the factors of greatest import in comprehending the transformation Brazil was undergoing after 1964.

subfields of comparative politics than is possible here. For the purposes of this study, attention will be focused only upon certain specific propositions relevant to an adequate understanding of the process whereby an authoritarian military regime of a decidedly developmentalist, if not necessarily modernizing, orientation emerged out of the structural crisis of the early 1960's. Its central focus is the systems boundary change catalyzed by the April, 1964, replacement of a populist, albeit essentially reconciliationist, regime by the military's first experience with direct exercise of governmental authority and political power since the 1889–1894 period.

There are three general questions concerning the events of the 1960's in Brazil with which the lay reader might be concerned: (1) Why did a crisis develop in Brazil during the early years of the decade? (2) What is and has been the character of the Brazilian military institution? and (3) What has been the evolution of the Brazilian military regime in power since 1964? This book is addressed primarily to the last of these interrelated concerns and secondarily to the intermediate one, with analysis of the breakdown of the pre-1964 system treated only as necessary background for the comprehension of subsequent developments. Thus, while sufficient information for intelligibility will be provided on the role of the Armed Forces within the traditional system up to 1964, comprehensive exploration of this area is not within the province of the present book. However, Chapters 2 and 3 are put forth as a selective summary of the chronological argument of the second book, but without the full development of many of its interpretations and excluding treatment of themes not immediately germane to the focus of this study. The supporting evidence, documentation, and discussion of sources, which have been all but omitted in these background chapters, will be found in *Modernization and the Military in Brazil.*

As was the case of my *Brazil Election Factbook 1965* and *Brazil Election Factbook Supplement,* published by the Institute for the Comparative Study of Political Systems in 1965 and 1966, this study is both a by-product and an integral part of my broader and continuing study of Brazilian politics. As such, it draws upon well over a decade of intensive investigation, which includes a series of eight research trips to Brazil. These opportunities to observe Brazilian political life at firsthand embraced a critical period of the Kubitschek administration, five months' residence during the Goulart government, and annual visits totaling more than a year in Brazil since the 1964 "revolution." In 1959, 1962, 1965, 1966, and 1967 these research trips involved all the major cities from Belém to Pôrto Alegre, providing me with a chance to discuss events and developments with a wide range of regional scholars and spokesmen as well as individuals active on the national scene. While full acknowledgment to many of the Brazilians and U.S. scholars and observers who have contributed to my efforts to gain an understanding of Brazil must await publication of my more inclusive studies, I would like here to make a downpayment on my debt to those individuals whose assistance has been directly linked to this particular project.

Cândido Antônio Mendes de Almeida has been a close friend as well as a constant source of insights and inspiration, and the other Brazilian scholars who have graced the halls of Columbia University's Institute of Latin American Studies in recent years have all added significantly to my comprehension of their country's affairs. Florestan Fernandes, Fernando Pedreira, Afrânio Coutinho, Antônio Olinto, Octavio Ianni, Julian Chacel, and Hilgard O'Reilly Sternberg provided me between 1963 and 1968 with a fairly representative cross section of Brazil's intelligentsia to serve as a sounding board for my tentative interpretations of their nation's affairs. Among Brazilian political scientists, Hélio Jaguaribe, Alberto Guerreiro Ramos, Orlando Carvalho, Luiz Navarro de Brito, Nélson de Souza Sampaio, Victor Nunes Leal, Leonidas Xausa, and Francisco Ferraz have repeatedly gone far beyond the requirements of both professional courtesy and Brazilian hospitality to facilitate my research efforts. My debt to Brazil's talented political journalists is also great, with Pedreira, Luiz Alberto Bahia, Carlos Castello Branco, and Oliveiros S. Ferreira meriting special appreciation. Senhora Helosia Dunshee de Abranches very kindly facilitated my archival inquiries at the *Jornal do Brasil*. Among the many participants in the events herein who were willing to discuss them with me, special gratitude goes to José Jeronimo Moscardo de Souza, former private secretary to the late President Castelo Branco; Commander Paulo Castelo Branco, the Marshal's son; Colonel Francisco Boaventura Cavalcanti, an officer with the courage not only to express his convictions but to fight for their implementation; General (Ret.) Golbery do

Couto e Silva; and Minister Paulo Egydio Martins. These five individuals not only patiently endured multiple and protracted invasions of their precious leisure time to satisfy my unceasing questions, but also generously facilitated my efforts to enter into dialogue with many of their associates. Among the numerous other Brazilian public figures whose cooperative attitude was particularly important for this book, I would like to acknowledge my gratitude to Minister Roberto Campos, Minister Luiz Gonzaga do Nascimento e Silva, Minister Octavio Gouveia de Bulhões, Minister Jarbas Passarinho, the late Brigadier Faria Lima, General Carlos de Meira Mattos, General Antônio Carlos da Silva Muricy, General Reinaldo de Almeida, General Alfonso Albuquerque Lima, General Rafael de Souza Aguiar, Lt. Brigadier Nélson Freire Lavanère-Wanderley, General Lyra Tavares, and General Jurandir da Bizzaria Mamede.

My colleagues in Columbia University's Latin American program have consistently provided stimulation and support as well as useful suggestions from the perspectives of their disciplines and professional viewpoints. Charles Wagley, until recently Director of the Institute of Latin American Studies, has patiently and sympathetically dealt with my requests concerning research needs and given encouragement to my every effort. Kempton E. Webb, Gregory Rabassa, Douglas Chalmers, Ralph della Cava, and more recently Nathaniel Leff and E. Bradford Burns have been excellent companions both at the Institute and in the field. Maria Yolanda Umburanas, now of the University of Toronto after several years on the faculty of Columbia, proved a perceptive and resourceful research assistant in her native Brazil as well as an informed critic of my interpretations of current developments.

The students who have undertaken research in Brazil under my supervision have all contributed to my knowledge concerning its modernization and current political processes. Alfred Stepan, now of Yale University, has provided expert, imaginative, and highly creative reactions to a number of my ideas since he first entered my classroom in 1964. Kenneth Erickson's very thorough dissertation research on the political role of labor has contributed to my comprehension of the interaction of the urban workers with other political forces in the post-Vargas period. Robert Myhr's detailed analysis of the political role of Brazilian students and Riordan Roett's thorough exploration of the political relationships involved in development programs in the northeast of Brazil helped clarify my views on a number of relevant aspects of Brazil's political development. Richard Foster's research in the summer of 1968 on the contribution of the Escola Superior de Guerra to the recent course of events provided clues to the workings of the Brazilian military mentality.

Other veterans of my spring, 1968, doctoral seminar on "The Political Development of Brazil" whose papers provided interesting ideas at least tangentially germane to this study include, in addition to Secretary Moscardo de Souza, Jeffrey Wheeler, Miss Natalia Udovik, John Rogers, Miss Linda Lee, and Dale Nelson. Among the members of my 1965 seminar on this subject who have contributed ideas of some utility to my understanding of Brazil then or subsequently, mention should be made of Susan Kaufman, David J. Goodman, Roger Garcia, and Harry Weiner. The other members of these two highly stimulating seminars also aided in the sharpening of my judgments as well as the caulking of some of the intellectual seams which were apparent in my preliminary hypothesizing. Professors Brady Tyson of American University and Jordan Young of Pace College stand out among involved "Brazilianists" with whom one can always profit from dialogue on contemporary developments.

My warmest appreciation goes to my wife, Anita L. Schneider, for her valiant efforts to transcribe a nearly illegible manuscript into a clear and clean typescript while at the same time completing her own graduate study. I am even more grateful to her for cheerfully assuming the formidable burdens resulting from the many dislocations arising from the frequent travel that was necessary during the researching of this book. Without the sustained cooperation and understanding shown by her and our children, both here and while resident in Brazil, with regard to the manifold restrictions on normal family life while the head of the household was caught up in the throes of authorship for protracted periods, this study could not have been completed. Professor Karl M. Schmitt of the University of Texas read the first draft of the over-all study and made useful suggestions for revision as did Mr. Bernard Gronert, of Columbia University Press, and Miss Marcia Case, a most sensible and constructive editor.

An NDFL-Fulbright Hays Faculty Fellowship made possible my extended stay in Brazil during 1966, and together with grants from the

Institute of Latin American Studies and Columbia's School of International Affairs, allowed me to return to the field in 1967 and 1969. The Institute's Mrs. Lilia Guerra and Mrs. Carol Ann Ramsour provided important secretarial assistance and logistic support during the period of drafting and revision, while Mrs. Patricia Nagykery greatly facilitated administrative matters.

For errors of fact and interpretation that may remain in this study, I assume exclusive responsibility and invite the informed reader to join me in their extirpation. A great deal of basic research concerning Brazilian politics remains to be done. Fortunately, a new generation of scholars—including a significant number with excellent disciplinary training in political science in U.S. and European universities—will be available to staff Brazil's faculties and research institutes during the 1970's. With full confidence that the research they undertake will greatly improve the depth and sophistication of political analysis in and on Brazil, I offer this study as an interim contribution. As such, its conclusions should often be taken as hypotheses to be empirically examined and further tested. Thus I hope to provoke constructive criticisms and efforts to investigate more thoroughly some of the factors and phenomena treated tangentially in the pages which follow.

RONALD M. SCHNEIDER

Queens College, CUNY
December, 1970

Contents

THE POLITICAL SYSTEM OF BRAZIL

CHAPTER ONE

Political Decay and Military Intervention

To THE SUPPORTERS of representative democracy in the Western Hemisphere the Brazilian military's seizure of power was in many respects the most serious and painful blow of the whole 1962–1964 period, during which governments were overthrown by force in no fewer than nine of the American republics. Not only was Brazil by far the largest and most populous country of Latin America, and the one moving toward general acceptance as an emerging international power, but the Brazilian Armed Forces were noted for their adherence to constitutionalism and legality. Although in fact they had played a decisive role in previous political crises in 1945, 1954–1955, and 1961, the Brazilian military officers had apparently done so reluctantly and shown no desire to hold on to power, in each case promptly placing the reins of government in the hands of the constitutional successor. Indeed, a leading United States student of Latin American military, writing only a few months before the 1964 coup, quite properly singled out the Brazilian Armed Forces as playing a unique role compared to those in the Hispanic American countries.[1]

Johnson accurately detailed the developmental role of the Brazilian

[1] See John J. Johnson, *The Military and Society in Latin America* (Stanford, 1964), pp. 175–243.

Armed Forces and the favorable public image this had created, but failed to note the continuity of an interventionist current in the military from the time of their supposedly rather selfless renunciation of power in 1894 until the Revolution of 1930. While relatively sound on Army influence under Getúlio Vargas (1930–1945) and during the period up to 1960, Johnson's interpretation of subsequent trends led him to conclude that "the army's response to the growing power of the masses had resulted from a conviction that those groups must be given a greater voice" and to predict that the younger officers "will be far more sympathetic than the present generation to the demands of the historically oppressed masses." [2]

Thus the surprise and shock at the Armed Forces' intervening to oust President João Goulart was much greater than they had been in the cases of Argentina, El Salvador, Peru, Guatemala, Ecuador, Honduras, and the Dominican Republic, or were to be seven months later in Bolivia. Moreover, for the first time in history the Brazilian military appeared ready, even determined, to control the national government directly. It therefore became necessary to analyze the process by which the Brazilian political system lost its ability to reconcile pressures for change with demands for stability, to explain why and how an institutional crisis developed that could be resolved only by a revolt led by officers, most of whom had been considered democrats and legalists.

Recurrent crises and disturbances have subsequently served notice that all is not progressing smoothly in a Brazil under the guidance of the military. The kidnaping of the United States Ambassador in September, 1969, and the prolonged quest that began at the same time for a viable successor government to that of the late Artur da Costa e Silva were only the most recent and dramatic in a series of developments that underlined the continuing political malaise in Latin America's one potential world power.

1. THE BRAZILIAN SETTING

Brazil is, among the nations of the world, an adolescent giant in severe trouble. With a population exceeding that of the next three most populous countries of Latin America combined, and nearly ten times that of Chile or Venezuela, Brazil is obviously pivotal as far as the

[2] *Ibid.,* pp. 218 and 243.

region's development is concerned. Within the boundaries of this diverse and poorly integrated country are found major areas manifesting most of the problems associated with the incomplete process of modernization in other Latin American nations. In the case of Brazil, however, the scale and magnitude is much greater. Both problems and opportunities, needs and resources are much more significant in this land of the future, which some skeptics doubt will ever achieve the progress or fulfill the promise long predicted by a series of foreign observers.

The Brazilian political system and decision-making process, among the most complex extant, involve an interaction of overlapping political parties, a rich variety of interest groups, and a very large and diffuse bureaucracy. Tremendous regional imbalances in political as well as economic development and the division of responsibility and power among the three levels of Brazil's federal structure further complicate the political process. The Brazilian political system cannot be understood, or its developmentally critical elements identified, without some examination of its evolution over the past forty years and consideration of the wide variety of factors affecting its present and future development. While it is necessary to analyze the various components of the political system separately, the most important aspect by far is their interaction—a subject to which little attention has been paid.

Brazil's complexity and diversity are such as to render generalizations about its problems difficult and to forbid the working out of solutions applicable to all parts of the subcontinent. For several decades, Brazil has been increasingly caught up in the process of transition from an agricultural country dominated by a near oligarchy to an economically diversified nation with a broad base of popular participation in its political life. This process of modernization has been retarded not only by physical obstacles to national integration but also by structural weaknesses in the country's political and social endowment, such as a high proportion of illiteracy, serious educational deficiencies, widespread health problems, intractable regionalism, and the dominance of entrenched special interests. In spite of these, Brazil has made uneven progress toward modern nationhood and the development of a viable representative political system—at least until the collapse of 1964.

Acutely conscious of the country's vast economic potential and its remarkable rate of demographic expansion (with a population expected to reach 100 million by 1973), Brazilians have come to view the world from the point of view of an emerging major power. At the same time, their awareness of how far Brazil must yet travel has added urgency to their aspirations for rapid economic development.

Sustained industrialization during the last three decades in southern Brazil has served to accentuate the differences between the relatively rich and advanced states (São Paulo, Rio de Janeiro, Guanabara, Minas Gerais, Rio Grande do Sul, and Paraná) and the rest of Brazil. Industrial development has been marked by chronic balance of payments difficulties and progressive inflation, which successive governments proved reluctant to curb for fear of restraining business expansion and slowing the rate of economic development. Thus, while the process of modernization has carried Brazil part way along the road toward becoming an urban, industrialized nation, it has also produced acute socio-economic dislocations and serious strains on the political system.

New groups have been brought into the political arena, diversifying and expanding the electorate. Urban industrial, commercial, and financial elements have largely won national political control from the conservative landowners (who, however, still dominate the internal politics of many states, particularly in the north and the interior). A rapidly growing urban middle class is gaining in political strength through its capacity for political leadership, its importance in the burgeoning bureaucracy, and its dominant position in the communications media. Urban labor is also an increasingly important element on the political scene, although its significance rests as much in its susceptibility to political manipulation as in its yet minimal capabilities for independent action.

The traditional power of the large landowners has declined steadily since the 1930's as industrialization has replaced expansion of agricultural exports as the impetus for economic growth. Large landowners, however, still retain sufficient political power in many regions (especially the more traditional Northeast) to obtain essential favors and privileges. Some elements of the landowning class, especially the coffee barons, have diversified their interests over the years and are powerful in both urban and rural politics. Small commercial farmers are not significantly represented in the influential commodity institutes and semipublic agencies at the national level, but are gaining in political effectiveness in

*Brazil and Neighboring Countries, Showing States
and Territories of Brazil and Their Capitals*

some southern states. There are significant indications that the coffee growers are becoming less potent in forming government policy. For decades, the federal government depended on coffee to finance industrialization; however, this policy, which led to the building of enormous surplus stockpiles, is now conditioned by official desires to reduce the deficits and inflationary pressures caused by subsidies and to diversify agricultural output to provide cheap food for urban consumers. Nevertheless, the coffee growers still constitute a significant group, whose ability to sway the government is reinforced in a number of cases by their position, or that of related interests, as investors in industry, banks, and other urban activities, especially in São Paulo. Not since 1930, however, have the planters been dominant politically on the national level, and in the postwar period they have been eclipsed by industrialists and business interests within their former stronghold of São Paulo.

The fundamental social, economic, and political changes which have taken place since 1930, so noticeable in the cities, have not yet penetrated into the rural areas where the majority of the Brazilian population continues to live. In the cities, political participation is theoretically open to all except the relatively few who are excluded by a literacy requirement for voting whereas, in large areas of rural Brazil, effective participation in politics is still restricted to a small number of landowners and local party chiefs. Thus Brazil's rural laboring population is largely excluded from an effective role in normal political activities. With improved communications the discontent of urban laborers and of the awakening rural workers has been manifest in a tendency to listen to (if not necessarily follow) those who offer radical solutions to the nation's problems. Even the traditionally moderate middle sectors have grown restless in recent years. For, during the postwar period, there has been a revolution in the aspirations of the Brazilian people. Although most of the population enjoys—albeit to widely varying degrees—material and social advantages previously unknown, a climate of frustration has stemmed from the widening gap between what they have and the mode of living to which they feel entitled.

Under the Goulart regime (1961–1964), the growing forces of the left tried to wrest control from the dominant center-conservative elements, while improved political communications and radical agitation aroused strong pressures for sweeping changes in the established order.

Although the increase in the number of radical leftists in policy-making positions in the Goulart regime led to great concern on the part of conservatives and United States observers, much of this development could be viewed in terms of redressing a balance that had long been heavily overweighted in favor of the traditionally dominant elites. Peaceful incorporation of emerging groups in the past helped Brazil avoid violent political upheaval, and gradual, but fairly rapid, broadening of the political base (there was a doubling of the Brazilian electorate between 1950 and 1962) could not help but bring in its wake a change in the composition of the policy-making elite. The purges of the leftist and progressive elements from legislative bodies in the wake of the 1964 *coup d'etat* disrupted an already discontinuous process of leadership renovation. Hence a new political generation may well push to the fore during the early 1970's; indeed its emergence cannot be delayed far beyond that date. For Brazil's unparalleled phenomenon of the political "influence life" of a single military generation spanning a half century (1920–1970), with one civilian political generation—that which came to power with Vargas in 1930—lasting four decades in high governmental offices will soon end as mortality takes its steady toll.

The 1964 hybrid "revolution-counterrevolution" was in a very real sense but another step in the zigzag chain of political abnormalities and military interventions that extends from the 1930 Revolution that brought Getúlio Vargas to power, through the 1945 revolt that ousted the dictator, the 1964 *golpe* that led to his suicide, the "countercoup" of 1955 that paved the way for the return to power of his political heirs, and the succession crisis of August–September, 1961, precipitated by Jânio Quadros' abrupt resignation. Mistrust of Goulart, as well as exasperation with the political class as a whole, lay at the root of each of the four military interventions into politics in the 1954–1964 decade. Indeed, it may be helpful to view the 1954–1964 period as a continuous crisis broken by an "artificial" stability during the Kubitschek years (1956–1960).

The five chapters that make up the body of this book are devoted to exploring the course of developments since 1964, one in which the initial seizure of power by the Armed Forces has been followed by a series of "coups within the coup" and pronounced movement away from the originally announced goal of a reformed representative system toward an increasingly repressive regime. In these chapters, as well as in the background chapters on the functioning and breakdown of the pre-1964 political system, a conscious effort has been made to avoid recourse to disciplinary jargon and excessive use of technical political science terms. Yet while couching the analysis in as clear expository language as the complexity of events permits, I am convinced that systematic explanation of the emergence of an authoritarian political order requires utilization of a number of concepts not part of daily discourse for many readers, and certainly absent from the vocabulary of informed journalistic interpretation. Introduced and explained in the pages that follow, these concepts will be utilized both in focusing the inquiry and in formulating its conclusions. The reader whose interests center upon what has happened rather than why may be tempted to skip much of this initial chapter; to minimize this temptation, most of the considerations important for the scholar, but not essential for the general reader, have been relegated to an appendix.[3]

The ensuing two sections of this introductory chapter serve distinct but closely related purposes. The first sets forth the objectives of the study as well as its conceptual framework: the propositions from the literature on comparative politics that will be used in analyzing the problems and events selected for critical examination. The second section provides crucial factors for an interpretation of the complex process of modernization in contemporary Brazil, focusing on the development of its political system and the nature of its recurrent crises.

2. A FRAMEWORK FOR ANALYSIS

The character of the present study has been largely determined by both the unreliability of historically oriented investigations of the military as an important part of the political system and the absence of an adequate analysis of Brazil's political development. Given the magni-

---

[3] The lay reader who wishes to relate the Brazilian experience to the broader Latin American scene might refer to Jacques Lambert's perceptive *Latin America: Social Structures and Political Institutions* (Berkeley, 1967) or Luis Mercier Vega's provocative *Roads to Power in Latin America* (New York, 1969). Those interested in broadening the scope of comparison beyond the Western Hemisphere should consult W. Howard Wriggins, *The Ruler's Imperative: Strategies for Political Survival in Asia and Africa* (New York, 1969).

tude of the task, priority has been accorded to extracting the maximum of data and insights from the vast body of relevant, albeit often ill-focused, literature available, supplemented by discussions with Brazilian scholars concerned with many of the questions involved and interviews with participants in some of the crucial and partly clouded events. A large number of significant topics have been all but omitted in order to focus on the examination of events and the interpretation of developments critical to the emergence of the present political system and the crisis in which it was born.

A consistent effort has been made to relate this study of Brazilian crisis politics to the theoretical propositions of the discipline, and to lift it out of the realm of "incomparable" uniqueness that has so inhibited the contribution of configurative monographs to comparative politics. In this respect, it hopefully may approximate Verba's concept of a "disciplined configurative approach." [4] Many aspects of Samuel Huntington's recent broad-gauged comparative study of political modernization and development have proven particularly useful in relating Brazilian experience to the range of global generalizations.[5] Not only in the 1961–1964 crisis, but in those that preceded it and even during the 1920's a major factor in Brazil's political instability was the gap between the rate of social change and mobilization of new groups into politics on the one hand, and the very slow development of political organizations and institutions on the other. With appropriate adaptation to the time difference involved, this factor holds for the 1884–1889 crisis as well.

In addition to several military interventions and coups, Brazil has encountered three "crises of regime" during the nearly 150 years of its existence as an independent country. The first developed in the 1880's and led to the establishment of the Republic; the second unfolded during the 1920's and resulted in the Revolution of 1930; the most recent took form during the 1960's and had as its outcome the 1964 assumption of power by the Armed Forces. In addition to the matter of timing—the 41-year life of the "Old Republic" and the 34-year span of the "demo-

[4] Sidney Verba, "Some Dilemmas in Comparative Research," *World Politics,* XX, No. 1 (October, 1967), 114.

[5] Samuel P. Huntington, *Political Order in Changing Societies* (New Haven, 1968).

cratic experiment"—these crises, which resulted in major reshaping of the nation's political institutions, share many structural similarities as well as common contextual features. Through utilization of several analytical categories introduced in this section and empirical substance presented in subsequent chapters, systematic comparison of these processes of regime breakdown and replacement will be possible.

Modernization, the concept utilized in this work most open to substantial ambiguity, is consistently used in the fundamental and "clean" sense adopted by Dankwart Rustow, as denoting "rapidly widening control over nature through closer cooperation among men." [6] "Modernization" has been chosen as more analytical and less normative than "development" and more precise and circumscribed than "change." It also has the merit of emphasizing attitudinal changes rather than essentially modifications in the tangible realm of the material world. As heavily stressed in the writings of Eisenstadt, the extension of state authority and broadening of political participation are the two facets of political modernization central to the concerns of this study.[7] Eisenstadt's propositions concerning the "breakdown of modernization" have been utilized, particularly with regard to their focus upon "change-absorbing institutions" as the critical variable, but in the strictly political sphere preference has been given to Huntington's formulations (since Eisenstadt provides no distinct concept of political development, substantially autonomous, if highly interdependent with modernization in general). Social mobilization is used in Karl Deutsch's widely accepted definition as the process whereby "major clusters of old social, economic and psychological commitments are eroded or broken and people become available for new patterns of socialization and behavior." [8] With regard to "political development," a term used in a wide variety of overlapping meanings by different authors, Huntington's definition, "the institutionalization of political organizations and procedures," appears most

[6] Dankwart A. Rustow, *A World of Nations* (Washington, D.C., 1967), p. 3.

[7] Samuel N. Eisenstadt, *Modernization: Protest and Change* (Englewood Cliffs, N.J., 1966), pp. 4, 12–15, and 84–98, and "Political Modernization: Some Comparative Notes," *International Journal of Comparative Sociology,* V, No. 1 (March, 1964), 3–24.

[8] Karl W. Deutsch, "Social Mobilization and Political Development," *The American Political Science Review,* LV (September, 1961), 494.

useful, in large part as a result of the distinction thus made from modernization as social mobilization and participation.[9]

Huntington has pointed out that in the postwar era "throughout Asia, Africa, and Latin America there was a decline in political order, an undermining of the authority, effectiveness, and legitimacy of government." [10] Certainly this was the case in Brazil, which in light of its size and developmental potential merits close attention in the elaboration and validating of comparative theoretical propositions concerning these regions of the world.

Huntington's basic proposition is eminently applicable to Brazil, where the "lag in development of political institutions behind social and economic change" is a critical element in the "instability and disorder" that has characterized the past quarter century of national life. Urbanization and industrialization progressed apace during this period, while— as will be amply illustrated in this study—political institutionalization made relatively little headway.

A notably complex and heterogeneous society, in Huntington's use of the term, the fragility of Brazil's political community resulted primarily from an inadequate level of institutionalization. Accepting Huntington's definition of institutionalization in terms of adaptability, complexity, autonomy, and coherence of both organizations and procedures, Brazil's development was intermittent and discontinuous throughout much of the last one hundred years compared to economic and social changes. When rates of mobilization were high and participation significantly expanded, the degree of institutionalization achieved frequently proved insufficient, with political order being undermined as a consequence. Political organizations have been characterized by low adaptability, particularly in a generational sense. Thus, for example, the political leadership that entered with the Revolution of 1930 maintained a dominant position into the 1960's, and the political parties that came into existence in 1945 were in most cases under the control of their founders at the time of the 1964 crisis and coup. The major parties demonstrated very little functional adaptability, either in terms of a

[9] These semantic and terminological difficulties are discussed in Lucian W. Pye, *Aspects of Political Development* (Boston, 1966), pp. 31–48.

[10] Huntington, *Political Order . . .*, p. 4.

changing constituency or a successful transition from government to opposition, or the reverse. In terms of complexity and autonomy, where Huntington is least precise and his concepts most difficult to operationalize, the Brazilian picture is quite mixed, but organizations and, to a somewhat less marked degree, procedures have been lacking in coherence.

Huntington's dictum that "modernity breeds stability, but modernization breeds instability" appears useful in understanding Brazil's recurrent crises.[11] Similarly, Brazilian experience tends to bear out his contention that the degree of political instability varies directly with the rate of social and economic modernization, while the major political challenges are faced simultaneously rather than sequentially.[12] The postulated relationships between social mobilization and economic development, social frustration and mobility opportunities, and political participation and institutionalization are supported by the course of Brazilian developments.

Huntington's model of a "praetorian" polity provides a convenient starting point for analyzing the Brazilian political system. It can be argued that at a low level of participation under the Empire, institutionalization was sufficient that Brazil developed a civic polity, but that the task of adaptation to the beginnings of middle class participation led to an institutional crisis. Again, Brazil may have moved from a praetorian to a civic polity around the time of World War I, but a similar lag of institutionalization behind the entrance of the urban middle class into national politics intervened. This problem largely overcome by the end of World War II, Brazil's evolution toward a civic polity foundered on the incapacity of its institutions to adapt to expansion of participation by the urban working class and the political awakening of the peasantry.

In the case of Brazil, which after all is far from a new nation, having achieved its independence just under a century and a half ago, Huntington's scheme can be used to advantage in analyzing the "political decay" that marked the collapse of three structurally distinct political-governmental regimes: a monarchical system, which persisted until 1889; a representative republican system with very limited participation which developed and deteriorated from the 1890's through the 1920's;

[11] *Ibid.,* p. 41.
[12] *Ibid.,* pp. 45–46.

and a rather tumultuous experience with a more broadly based and increasingly representative system embodying more advanced representative institutions and evolving democratic procedures. The crises that led to the demise of each of these regimes involved an essentially similar process, the basic components of which were industrialization and the concomitant social change leading to modifications in the patterns and extent of mobilization and participation beyond the capacity of the country's political institutions for an adequate response.

Huntington has pointed up the fact that "a society which develops reasonably well organized political parties while the level of political development is still relatively low . . . is likely to have a less destabilizing expansion of political participation than a society where parties are organized later in the process of modernization." [13] This, as will be shown, is patently true with regard to Brazil's experience. Indeed, party organization was quite retarded even during the post-1945 period of rapid expansion of the electorate, sustained industrialization, and massive urbanization. Thus, the Brazilian case does not contradict his assertion that "the stability of a modernizing political system depends on the strength of its political parties." [14] A single case cannot of course establish even the presumptive validity of a proposition such as "the susceptibility of a political system to military intervention varies inversely with the strength of its political parties." [15] It will, however, be established in the course of examining Brazil's political crises over a span of some eight decades, during which the country passed through different stages in the process toward modernization, that the parties were particularly weak at the time of crises that led to military intervention.

The tendency of political leaders to shift from one party to another, which is relatively unusual in developed political systems, has been common in Brazil down to the present.[16] Parties have been unable to move effectively from expansion to institutionalization, in many cases hardly passing the polarization threshold from factionalism to the process of expansion. From the Brazilian case, Huntington appears correct in stating that "the precondition of political stability is a party system

[13] *Ibid.*, p. 398.
[14] *Ibid.*, p. 408.
[15] *Ibid.*, pp. 408–409.
[16] See my *Brazil Election Factbook, Number 2* (Washington, D.C., 1965), pp. 41–47 and 58–71.

capable of assimilating the new social forces produced through modernization" and that "a multi-party system is incompatible with a high level of political institutionalization and political stability in a modernizing country." [17] The reasons for this are, however, somewhat different from those he adduces in support of these comparative generalizations.

With regard to parties and the cleavage between urban and rural interests, Huntington's argument is quite different from Brazilian reality. The major national parties in Brazil were not born in the city to mature in the countryside, but rather created on the basis of local and provincial bifactionalism with deep traditional roots. Their challenge was not to "reach out for rural support" but to reach into the cities for mass support, adopting a more modern stance at the cost of modifying their rather traditional goals and values.[18] This process was quite the reverse of that postulated by Huntington, except insofar as the populist movements tried to pick up some electoral strength in the countryside, and this was accomplished more by deals with dissident factions of the established parties than on a programmatic basis. It is in this respect that Huntington's framework for understanding political modernization is weakest, for it contains no consideration of populism as a force and style as distinct from an older and narrower brand of personalism. Yet the departure from Huntington's rule may well be a major explanation of the weakness of national parties in Brazil.

Huntington maintains, in counter-distinction to a number of analysts of civil-military relations, that neither external military aid nor foreign military training affects the inclination of the military to play a political role. Nor does he accept the premise that the social composition of the officer corps and internal structure of the military are major factors in determining whether the Armed Forces of a country will intervene in politics or not.[19] Generalizing for the entire world, he is probably correct in the sense that experience in these regards is ambiguous and the evidence contradictory. Yet these propositions deserve to be examined in the case of individual countries, as will be done in this study, with comparison over time adding a dimension to the investigation. The Brazilian case does, however, bear out Huntington's basic contention, that "the most important causes of military intervention in politics are

[17] Huntington, *Political Order* . . ., pp. 420–21 and 423.
[18] *Ibid.*, pp. 433 ff. contains Huntington's reasoning.
[19] *Ibid.*, p. 193.

not military but political and reflect not the social and organizational characteristics of the military establishment but the political and institutional structure of the society." [20]

Although Huntington's basic division of politics into civic and praetorian provides some insights into the analysis of Brazilian political modernization, it has already been pointed out that Brazil represents a borderline case, one that has crossed and recrossed the boundary at something approximating generational intervals. Thus there are significant discrepancies between his model, or ideal type, of praetorian polity and the realities of Brazil's political system. As a description of the present regime, the fit is relatively close, with "all sorts of social forces" directly engaged in general politics and an absence of "effective political institutions capable of mediating, refining, and moderating group political action." [21] On the other hand, there is substantial if incomplete agreement on "legitimate and authoritative methods for resolving conflicts."

Thus Brazil does not fit into any of the six types of political systems Huntington has defined: with a medium ratio of institutionalization to participation, it falls between his Whig civic and Radical praetorian. It is sufficiently distinct from either (exemplified by Chile and Egypt in Huntington's scheme) to warrant a separate classification, perhaps as a middle class ambivalent system. (Indeed, the variations within Latin America indicate that a three by three, nine-category typology would be considerably more meaningful than that which Huntington has chosen to employ. If participation can be treated as high, medium, or low, there appears to be no inherent reason why the ratio of institutionalization to participation must be dichotomous.) As previously indicated, Huntington's analytical scheme is weakened by its relative inflexibility in dealing with variations concerning patterns of urban-rural sector relations in modernizing polities. An intermediate model between civic and praetorian is needed to cover cases such as Brazil; "borderline" is inadequate.

Huntington's formulation concerning the relationship of the military's orientation in politics and the stage of the modernizing process transcends the rigidity of his civic-praetorian dichotomy and is congruent with Brazilian experience:

[20] *Ibid.*, p. 194.
[21] *Ibid.*, pp. 194 and 196.

As society changes, so does the role of the military. In the world of oligarchy, the soldier is a radical; in the middle-class world he is a participant and arbiter; as the mass society looms on the horizon he becomes the conservative guardian of the existing order. Thus, paradoxically but understandably, the more backward a society is, the more progressive the role of its military; the more advanced a society becomes, the more conservative and reactionary becomes the role of its military.[22]

As the politicization of the military is in large part a function of the institutional weakness and the incapacity of civilian leadership to resolve major issues of public policy, orientation toward change varies with the expansion of participation. From cutting edge for the middle class's effective entrance into politics, the Armed Forces may evolve toward a role as their shield against the surge for power by the working class, unless the process of broadened participation has been accompanied by a relatively high degree of political institutionalization. From "breakthrough" coup they may thus move with passage of time to mount one or more "veto" coups. Characteristically, the military will perceive of its mission as guarding the country's "democratic" institutions from a threat of mass-based dictatorship rather than as thwarting modernization. In this sense, their inculcation with a highly developed sense of an internal security mission disposes them to view demands for radical change as "subversive." In part this is a reaction to the anti-militarism of the reformers, whose views on the proper role of the Armed Forces conflict with its determination to retain a capability for acting as guardian of national interests and institutions. In general terms, this corresponds to the course of developments in Brazil. The military interventions of 1889, 1930, and, in a qualified sense, 1945 were of the breakthrough or "reformist" variety; those of 1954 and 1964 were increasingly of a veto or "conservative" nature.

Huntington's scenario for the divisions following a veto coup corresponds in its basic outlines to the process in Brazil analyzed in subsequent chapters of this study. The size of the Brazilian officer corps relative to that of any of the other countries under consideration gave rise to a somewhat more complex situation, but the basic lines conform to the general pattern. Thus, the more perceptive of the Brazilian military might agree with Huntington that

[22] *Ibid.,* p. 221.

The guardian role of the military is based on the premise that the causes of military intervention arise from temporary and extraordinary disruptions of the political system. In fact, however, the causes are endemic to the political system and are the unavoidable consequence of the modernization of society. They cannot be removed simply by eliminating people.[23]

Indeed, one of the four options open to a regime resulting from a veto coup, that of "restrain and restrict," is patterned by Huntington on that followed by the Castelo Branco government in 1964–1966.[24]

In one very significant respect, the Brazilian military in power appeared to diverge from the attitudes postulated by Huntington. Rather than manifesting hostility toward political parties as such, as distinct from certain parties and many politicians, the leaders of the first "revolutionary" administration seemed aware of the functions of parties in modern political systems. Largely owing to the investigations and deliberations previously carried on within their institutions of higher education, one important element of Brazil's military leaders was acutely conscious of the need to reform the country's political institutions, particularly the parties, to make them more effective vehicles for interest aggregation. Indeed, some of Brazil's more intellectual officers have viewed their dilemma very much in the same realistic terms as Huntington's sober diagnosis.

Military leaders can be effective builders of political institutions. Experience suggests, however, that they can play this role most effectively in a society where social forces are not fully articulated. The tragedy of a country like Brazil in the 1960's was that it was, in a sense, too developed to have either a Nasser or an Ataturk, its society too complex and varied to be susceptible to leadership by a military regime. Any Brazilian military leader would have had to find some way of striking a balance between the regional, industrial, commercial, coffee-growing, labor, and other interests which share power in Brazil and whose cooperation was necessary for the conduct of government. Any government in Brazil has to come to terms, one way or another, with the São Paulo industrialists. Nasser did not have such a problem, and hence he could be Nasser; so also Ataturk dealt with a relatively small and homogeneous elite. Modernizing military regimes have come to power in Guatemala, El Salvador, and Bolivia. But for Brazil it may be too late for military modernization and too late also for the soldier as institution-builder. The com-

---

[23] *Ibid.*, pp. 232–33.
[24] *Ibid.*, pp. 235–36.

plexity of social forces may preclude the construction of political institutions under middle-class military leadership.[25]

Other of Huntington's formulations will be re-examined in the concluding chapter, qualified or refined in light of Brazilian experience, and amended if necessary. There, too, propositions bearing upon the present situation and the possibilities of the military's playing a modernizing role in the future will be assessed.[26] While most of the critical evaluation of the literature on civil-military relations as it relates to this study has been left to the appendix, one limited-scope comparative formulation that complements Huntington's basic scheme bears discussion here as an essential element of our analytical framework: José Nun's perceptive and creative conceptualization of the "middle class coup." [27] Concerned primarily with the nexus between the social origins of the Latin American officer corps and their political behavior, Nun rejects both the notion that militarism victimizes the emerging middle classes and the proposition that, through their developmental role, the Armed Forces can contribute to the political rise of the middle class and hence facilitate the democratization of Latin America. The first Nun finds uncritically transferred from nineteenth century European antimilitarism, while the second is inappropriate borrowing from the experience of the Afro-Asian "new" nations.[28] His quest for a valid explanation of the reasons for military intervention in Latin America and variations in its orientation leads him to postulate that "given certain circumstances, in certain Latin American countries, sectors of the middle classes induce and/or favor military interventionism" and that the contradictory orientation of such interventions from one country to another is a reflection of the "ideological contradictions of the middle classes." In the industrializing

[25] *Ibid.*, p. 261.

[26] For a perceptive critique of Huntington, which points out a number of inconsistencies and ambivalences, see Dankwart A. Rustow, "The Organization Triumphs Over Its Function: Huntington on Modernization," *Journal of International Affairs,* XXIII, No. 1 (1969), 119–32.

[27] José Nun, "A Latin American Phenomenon: The Middle Class Military Coup." in University of California, Institute of International Studies, *Trends in Social Science Research in Latin American Studies* (Berkeley, 1965), pp. 55–99. This is reprinted, with a modifying note, in James Petras and Maurice Zeitlin (eds.), *Latin America: Reform or Revolution?* (New York, 1968), pp. 145–85.

[28] *Ibid.*, pp. 63–64.

countries of the region the middle class confronts a mobilized working class, may have ties to foreign interests, and the newer elements often have very different attitudes from those of longer or more secure standing at this social level. Thus, the greatest certainty concerning the middle class is its "basic lack of cohesion and homogeneity" at the stage of its consolidation as well as before, accompanied by a lack of its own organizations.[29] In this type of situation the Army, as the institution most representative of the middle class—reflecting its cleavages as mediated by its own institutional values and interests—will step in to "rescue" the middle class when its interests are jeopardized by the two-front competition for power with an entrenched upper class and an aggressive working class.[30]

Amplifying his original work, Nun has recently suggested even more explicitly than before that existing theories of military intervention are inadequate for Argentina and Brazil.[31] Focusing upon the "more developed" countries of Latin America, he concerns himself with the causes of the very different patterns of civil-military relations in Argentina and Brazil on the one hand as compared with Chile, Mexico, and Uruguay, where civilian supremacy has been established and maintained. In a judgment that is clearly applicable for Brazil as well as Argentina, Nun points out that, while of middle-class origin, the military possesses a degree of cohesion and "institutional solidarity" that its civilian counterpart so markedly lacks. If professionalization is seen as the means by which the Armed Forces are "incorporated into a determined place in the structuralization of society as a whole," then the difference between a pattern of "early" professionalization combined with late organization and industrialization in Latin America and the reverse sequence in Western Europe should not be surprising.[32] With the Armed Forces as one of the few, if not the only important national institution controlled by the middle class in a preindustrial society in which the hegemony of the bourgeoisie was not yet established, the claims of the middle class upon the state were limited to participation rather than radical change,

---

[29] *Ibid.,* pp. 79–83.
[30] *Ibid.,* pp. 90–91.
[31] "The Middle-Class Military Coup," in Claudio Véliz (ed.), *The Politics of Conformity in Latin America* (New York, 1967), pp. 66–118.
[32] *Ibid.,* pp. 75–77.

while the military was viewed by them as a partner more than a restraint or rival.

For Nun, the "hegemonic crisis" of the 1930's in the more advanced Latin American countries should be perceived as the result of an essentially unplanned process of industrialization by import substitution whereby the landowning oligarchy was not necessarily antagonized and many of the political and social effects of the "industrial revolution" blunted.[33] Following a line of analysis of Brazilian development congruent with that discussed in the next section of this study, Nun arrives at the conclusion that the Armed Forces ousted Getúlio Vargas in 1954 in response to the middle class's opposition to his turn toward the left. Similarly, in 1964, unable to understand the structural basis of Goulart's policies or "to give articulate expression to a programme capable of mobilizing the popular sectors," the middle classes "frightened by the populist measures of the government, allied itself with the traditional defenders of the status quo and gave encouragement to the coup." [34]

Refining the formulation of his earlier work, Nun stresses the limiting effects of economic stagnation upon the middle class's "progressive" strategy of offering the popular sectors incentives to seek satisfaction of their demands within the existing structural framework. Thus, in Brazil and Argentina, at least (with Uruguay and Chile perhaps set apart by their bureaucracies),

owing to the absence of an English-style adaptation facilitated by a remarkable economic development, and also of a French-style bureaucracy capable of absorbing the shocks originating from political conflict, it is the armed forces which assume the responsibility of protecting the middle class. It was with their support that the middle class achieved, at the beginning of the century, political recognition from the oligarchy; it was with their protection that it later consolidated itself in power; and now it is with their intervention that it seeks to ward off the threat posed by the popular sectors that it is incapable of leading.[35]

Moreover, with the worsening of the middle classes's relations with the popular sectors, "systematic anti-communism appears as the kind of rationalization most appropriate to its interests." [36] The crux of the crisis in Brazil and Argentina then is the unfortunate coincidence that

[33] *Ibid.*, pp. 86–90.
[34] *Ibid.*, p. 92.
[35] *Ibid.*, p. 103.
[36] *Ibid.*, p. 111.

Just at the moment when the loss of the dynamic impulse of the import-substitution model is creating the objective conditions for ending the agrarian-industrial pact, free elections are becoming an essential instrument of political bargaining, which makes possible the gradual union of the progressive groups. This possibility is, however, eliminated by the fears of the upper and middle classes; it is for this reason that both the Brazilian and the Argentine military governments have lost no time in suspending the electoral process, and are tending to search for forms of functional representation which avoid the risk inherent in normal elections.[37]

The application of basic concepts from Huntington and Nun to the Brazilian scene has provided us with a basic framework for viewing the process of institutional decay and middle-class insecurity that were fundamental factors in the breakdown of the flawed representative system, as well as helping to explain the military's role in that political process. At the same time, a number of distinguishing features of Brazilian political life have been introduced: the weakness and heterogeneity of the political parties, whose center of gravity is in the stagnant countryside rather than the developing urban centers; the relatively cohesive Armed Forces, which have tended to fill the vacuum existent at critical junctures owing to the inadequacy of political institutionalization and fragility of governmental legitimacy; the increasingly conservative nature of the military's political orientation as the pace of change accelerated and threatened the newly established position of the middle class; and the defensive outlook of the civilian middle class as political competition between entrenched elites and a no longer docile working class has resulted in political polarization. In the remainder of this chapter, additional salient features of the Brazilian political experience will be defined and delineated to provide a coherent conceptualization of the system whose functioning and demise will be summarized in Chapters 2 and 3 as the crucible in which the post-1964 authoritarian regime was initially forged.

3. THE BRAZILIAN STRUCTURAL CRISIS

It was indicated in the last section that a blend of the conceptual formulations of Huntington and Nun provided the most meaningful framework for viewing the developments within the Brazilian polity that

[37] *Ibid.*, pp. 112–13.

are the central concerns of this book. A parallel effort to relate Brazil to approaches for the comparison of total political systems reveals the partial inappropriateness, although not total irrelevance, of much of the work in this field at its present stage of refinement.

Gabriel Almond, in his widely influential typology of political systems, classifies Brazil as the prototype of a "modernizing authoritarian" system.[38] This categorization, based on the degree of structural differentiation and cultural secularization, places Brazil among the "modern" systems that possess differentiated political infrastructures (that is "input" structures such as parties and interest groups as well as communications media) along with some form of "participant" political culture. Within the broad range of modern systems, Brazil falls among the "mobilized" stratum that includes most of the world's industrialized or significantly industrializing nations. Relative to Mexico, Brazil is considered authoritarian rather than "democratic with low subsystem autonomy," while it is distinguished from Spain by the allegedly modernizing as against conservative nature of its authoritarianism (which is defined as lack of subsystem autonomy and prevalence of a mixed subject-participant political culture).

Interestingly, and highly relevant to the point already made concerning the absence of analytical studies of the Brazilian polity, Almond and Powell include four-or-five-page summary sketches of the prototype or illustrative country in each of the other fifteen cases within their interpretative scheme. Only with regard to Brazil is the pattern broken and no effort made at all to describe the political system and explain how and why it demonstrates the basic features of "modernizing authoritarian" type polity.

It should also be stressed that Almond pays virtually no attention to civil-military relations as a significant variable for comparative studies and rules them out as a dimension for his classificatory scheme. All that is said concerning the salient characteristics of a modernizing authoritarian political system is that "there is a limited responsiveness to the more modern elements in the society, such as Western-trained army officers, technically trained elements in the bureaucracy, and perhaps some of the components of the modern economy such as business

[38] Gabriel A. Almond and G. Bingham Powell, Jr., *Comparative Politics: a Developmental Approach* (Boston, 1966), pp. 217 and 256.

entrepreneurs, managers, and technicians." [39] As an analytical tool this is a very blunt instrument indeed.

Since the general comparative literature fails to deal adequately with Brazil, we must introduce the essential elements of an analytical model. Two of the most important tools for understanding the Brazilian system are Hélio Jaguaribe's concept of the "cartorial" state and his description of "clientelistic politics." [40] The cartorial state is one in which public employment is used to provide positions proportional to the political needs of the elite, rather than to the requirements of effective public service. Since appointments are exchanged for electoral support, the result is an infinite pyramid of positions where innocuous papers are circulated and where the only activity is the feeding of the bureaucracy through self-benefiting practices. Such an administratively dysfunctional means of providing for the economically marginal, but politically significant, middle class contributes to this element's undue weight in public opinion, on political matters, and in the making and execution of policy decisions. In this bargain, the dominant class, through its taxes, indirectly subsidizes the "leisure" of the middle sectors; it is amply repaid, however, since "the state served to foster and protect the existing regime while providing the necessary sinecures to insure the political support which the ruling class would otherwise have lacked, and which it needed in order to preserve its economic and political control of the country." [41]

Largely the product of the substantial urbanization that preceded significant industrialization, the Brazilian middle class exceeded the

---

[39] *Ibid.,* p. 311. In his essay on "Political Development: Analytical and Narrative Perspectives," *Comparative Political Studies,* I, No. 4 (January, 1969), 447–70, Almond calls for both viewing the environment as the independent variable with the political system as dependent and the system itself as the independent variable with its impact upon the environment as dependent. More important, he recognizes the need to blend leadership and problem-solving models with his system-functional concepts.

[40] The Essay on Sources contains a full discussion of the impressively wide and varied series of publications in which his useful constructs have been developed and polished over a period spanning the last two decades. Citations here will be limited to readily available English language publications.

[41] Hélio Jaguaribe, *Brazilian Nationalism and the Dynamics of Its Political Development* (Washington University, St. Louis), *Studies in Comparative International Development,* II, No. 4 (1966), 59.

country's limited needs for technical and administrative personnel during the early stages of economic development. While a minority of its members found a career in the Armed Forces, most bargained with the ruling strata of plantation owners and export-import merchants for bureaucratic positions in exchange for their vote and political support. This style of clientele politics existed at all levels as "pacts of mutual interest," which were formed in the municipalities and then progressed to the provincial capitals and the federal bureaucracy. Although it had roots in the Empire, this system did not fully flourish until the establishment of the Republic had demonstrated a threat to the dominant class. For Jaguaribe, the interaction of clientelistic politics and the cartorial state, the second both the product of the first and the vehicle for its perpetuation, explains how the oligarchy was able to stage political comebacks after the elimination of the monarchy and the 1930 Revolution. The middle class, more concerned with its patronage positions than any radical changes in the system, failed to fulfill a revolutionary role in the 1930's and permitted consolidation of democratic forms without correlative social policies in the postwar period.[42]

With the rate of urbanization and growth of the middle class outstripping the absorptive capacity of the "clientelistic-cartorial" system, both its civilian and military components acquiesced in Vargas's imposition of a semi-fascist regime. Realizing that electoral democracy under the existing socio-economic system would lead to a return to power by the landowning-export merchant class whose rural dependents greatly exceeded the urban middle class vote, the latter submerged their liberal ideals and accepted a regime without parties or elections, but one in which they would play a major role in a rapidly expanding bureaucracy. (In a different context, they adopted a similar stance after 1964.) In 1930, as in 1889, the Army was the vehicle for the middle class's overturning of the old governmental institutions, but when the military returned to the barracks the civilian middle sectors could not hold on to political power in an essentially patrimonial society. Yet the changes

---

[42] An expansion of this argument to cover the past decade is included in Jaguaribe's *Political Strategies of National Development in Brazil* (Washington University, St. Louis), *Studies in Comparative International Development,* III, No. 2 (1967–1968).

of the 1930's went deeper than those of the 1890's.[43] Through a largely unconscious process accompanying the import substitution stage of industrialization, the middle class took control of the "cartorial state" but did not come to control the political system as a whole. "The apparatus of government continued to service the class that controlled the economy, while it looked after the needs of the middle class, which asked no more than guaranteed State-employment."[44] During this period, however, an industrial bourgeoisie developed as a potentially significant political factor, and Vargas began to turn toward the strategy of an industrialist-working class political base for his increasingly developmentalist and nationalist policies. Jaguaribe views Vargas' ouster in 1945 as an instinctive reaction by the old landowning and mercantile elite in alliance with the middle class against this process of change.[45]

Jaguaribe perceives the middle class as itself undergoing a transformation at this juncture, with the entrance of a new generation of technical and administratively oriented personnel and a "new intelligentsia" concerned with development problems. Yet the insecure elements of the middle class still feared their possible proletarization as much as the rise of the working class. Thus, although the governments from the reelection of Vargas in 1950 through the overthrow of Goulart in 1964 were all based more or less upon a loose coalition of industrialists, the commercial sectors linked to the internal market, the "technical" elements of the middle class, and the urban working class, the military, with the support of more traditional elements of the middle class as well as conservative interests, would intervene repeatedly when the process of development threatened to bring with it significant socioeconomic changes. The progressive forces failed to create a new party, resting instead on the inadequate basis of the Vargas-forged alliance between the PSD (strong in Congress) and the PTB (with popular support in urban areas).

Juscelino Kubitschek, the "amiable man" whose political centrism and conciliatory style made few enemies, avoided the type of confrontation that cost Vargas his office (and life) in 1954 and lead to Goulart's

---

[43] *Ibid.*, pp. 29–30.
[44] Jaguaribe, *Brazilian Nationalism . . .*, p. 59.
[45] *Ibid.*, p. 61, and *Political Strategies . . .*, p. 32.

downfall a decade later by a tacit alliance with the landowning forces so powerful within his PSD. "He would keep unchanged the conditions of the countryside, preserving the economic and political interests of the landowners in exchange for a free hand in promoting industry." In adopting a policy of "strategic postponement," Kubitschek assumed that a forced-draft program of industrialization would indirectly bring change to the countryside. The validity of this assumption, and the fact that the painless economic growth of his years in office (1956–1960) could not be duplicated owing to the limits reached on import substitution and inflation, meant that successor regimes had to face hard and politically divisive choices he had been able to avoid.[46]

Thus the "structural crisis" that impeded Brazil's modernization and development and underlay the 1964 military intervention was inseparably economic and political, involving the framework of societal structures and political institutions. The first component is the dualism between the urbanizing and industrializing "modern" South and the rural and backward Northeast which has long been noted. While Jaguaribe comments perceptively on both the regional and sectoral imbalances involved, the most sophisticated political analysis of "the two Brazils" is contained in the work of Glaúcio Soares.[47] This Brazilian political sociologist, trained at Washington University and the University of California, attempts to demonstrate the existence of two "entirely different political cultures." Contrasting the nine states of the rural Northeast with the six industrializing Southeastern states (and omitting such key "border" states as Minas Gerais and Goiás) Soares finds that the proportion of urban population is nearly one-half in the latter, as against slightly over one-fifth in the former region, while the difference in percentage of the labor force in manufacturing is one of 20 per cent compared to only 7 per cent. The average per capita income is four times as great in the Southeast as in the Northeast, with the maximum

[46] Jaguaribe, *Political Strategies* . . ., pp. 33–37 discusses the Kubitschek development plan and its implementation.

[47] Glaúcio Ary Dillon Soares, "The Politics of Uneven Development: The Case of Brazil," in Seymour M. Lipset and Stein Rokkan (eds.), *Party Systems and Voter Alignments* (New York, 1967), pp. 467–96. Soares amplifies his work in "The New Industrialization and the Brazilian Political System," in Petras and Zeitlin, *Latin America* . . ., pp. 186–201.

contrast in polar states being of the magnitude of twelve to one. Literacy rates of roughly two-thirds of the adult population in the more developed states compare with only 30 per cent in the Northeast.

Hypothesizing that in the economically and socially backward regions "there exists widespread nonideological, instrumental use of political parties" with traditional dominance of landowners and small-town economic elites, Soares postulates that the politics of the more urban and developing areas is characterized by "class cleavage and the increasing role of ideology." [48] Rapid urbanization and industrialization in two Northeastern enclaves, the major cities (with about 1 million inhabitants each) of Recife and Salvador, have introduced a modernizing influence into the politics of the two most populous states of this region. But since industrialization has not kept pace with urban growth, particularly in Recife, the underemployed and unemployed masses experience a marked gap between heightened aspirations and their nonfulfillment, thus providing the basis for radical political movements as contrasted to the lower middle-class populism of the great urban centers of the Southeast.

With regard to the factors shaping the politics of "developing" Brazil, that is primarily the Center-South, Soares quite correctly points out that the industrializing process under conditions of borrowing twentieth century capital-intensive technology allows for the possibility of achieving a relatively high level of productivity without a massive expansion of industrial employment.[49] The dramatic growth is in non-manual employment, with "middle-classization" a concomitant of this "new" industrialization, in contrast to that of the United States and Western Europe. Brazil's following of the older developmental strategy, Soares postulates, has contributed to a situation in which the proportion of the labor force in manufacturing and in the secondary sector as a whole did not increase between 1950 and 1960, while the tertiary sector rose from one-fourth of the total labor force to one-third.

The rapid expansion of the middle class and the urban unemployed or seriously underemployed population relative to the slow growth of the employed working class gives rise to increasing conflict

[48] "The Politics of Uneven Development," pp. 476–77.
[49] "The New Industrialization . . .," pp. 189–90.

between the interests of the middle class and the "reserve army of un-employed workers." [50] In an interpretation highly congruent with that of José Nun as well as Jaguaribe, Soares views the crisis of 1964 as stemming from the unwillingness of a "politically and militarily power-ful" middle class to see its privileges reduced by governmental policies favoring the working class and lumpen-proletariat.[51] Since the middle class is sufficiently powerful to resist a revolutionary movement based upon the working class, and industrialization is not providing employ-ment opportunities for a growing urban mass, "serious political turmoil of revolutionary character" can be expected as the outlet of voting for a party or even individual politicians representative of their interests has been closed off by the present military regime.

To Jaguaribe, socio-economic dualism and its political ramifica-tions account for survival of patronage politics in the face of modern-izing influences that might be expected to give rise to "interest group" if not ideological politics. With parties rendered incapable of repre-senting group interests, they turned to their respective "class" organiza-tions, unions, and commercial associations. Inadequately organized in this respect, the middle classes turned toward the Army as defender of their basic interests, leading to a breakdown of the "developmentalist" coalition of forces that had functioned effectively during the Kubitschek era.[52] In this environment Quadros' valiant effort in 1961 to switch from "national capitalism" to "national laborism" as a model and strategy for development foundered on the impossibility of playing a Bonapartist role "in the service of a reformist design, but without the control and support of Bonapartist armies."

In an effort to conceptualize the evolution of the crisis that led to Goulart's ouster in 1964, Jaguaribe places very heavy emphasis on the "positive or developmentalist left" and "negative or statist left" experi-ments of 1963. The first, under the guiding hand of San Thiago Dantas and Celso Furtado, he sees as "the most conscious and deliberate at-tempt at execution of national laborism ever tried in Brazil." [53] Unfor-tunately the negative left, by their insistence upon socialism and an

---

[50] *Ibid.*, p. 196.
[51] *Ibid.*, pp. 200–201.
[52] Jaguaribe, *Political Strategies . . .*, pp. 39–40.
[53] *Ibid.*, p. 45.

anti-United States foreign policy as against social justice measures and an "independent" international stance, drove the "national bourgeoisie from the progressive camp into that of the reactionary forces." [54] As he summarizes the process:

It was precisely because the negative Left, under Brizola's irresponsible adventurism, could address to the masses the most revolutionary promises and appeals, that the viable compromise offered by the positive Left was made to look irrelevant, if not disguising a social treason. Correspondingly, the fallacious appeal, by the Right wing conservatives, to unrestricted advantages for the bourgeoisie, could mislead the national entrepreneurs and make them believe that the viable compromise offered by the positive Left was not worth its price.

Goulart opted by early 1964 for an attempt at a social revolution from the top, although as events demonstrated the requisite revolutionary cadres and mass organizations were lacking.

The "statist Left," mobilizing the best organized sectors of the people— trade unions, students, the lower echelons of the armed forces, peasant leagues, newspapers and, despite the opposition of their leaders, the rank and file of the Brazilian Communist Party—achieved a clear predominance over the "developmental left" which it virtually stripped of popular support. Deputy Brizola, aside from his undoubted powers of organization and leadership, was also the brother-in-law of President Goulart, in which happy capacity he was able to manipulate the machinery of State to his own ends without restraint.
Given such a set of circumstances, President Goulart, party leader but no statesman, excellent tactician but poor strategist, gifted with keen political intuition but bereft of practical know-how, showed himself incapable of controlling events and reconciling short-term advantages—which he was always adroit in securing—with the longer-term interests of his Government, which he was prone to sacrifice to the expediency of the moment. [55]

As useful as Jaguaribe's systematization of Brazilian politics is, it pays relatively little attention to several factors that will be demonstrated in this study to be critical aspects of the process of political modernization. First in this respect is populism, which by 1960 had come to be as significant a feature of political life as clientelism.

---

[54] Jaguaribe, *Brazilian Nationalism . . .*, p. 65. The quotation that follows is from his *Political Strategies . . .*, p. 45.
[55] Jaguaribe, *Brazilian Nationalism . . .*, p. 65.

Jaguaribe does, however, provide a meaningful definition of this phenomenon.

Populism represents a non-traditional direct relationship between the masses and a leader, bringing to the latter the allegiance of the former and their active support to his bids for power, based on his charismatic capability of mobilizing the hope of the masses for, and their confidence in, the quick realization of their social expectations by the leader if only given enough power. It is typical of populism, henceforth, that the relationship between the masses and the leader are direct, without the mediation of intermediary echelons and that they are founded on the expectation of rapid attainment of the promised goals, provided only that the leader is given appropriate power.[56]

The crucial concept of populism in Brazilian politics is still very much understudied. The most systematic work has been done by Francisco Weffort.[57] As Weffort interprets Brazil's modernization process, "classic anticipation" by the dominant groups has kept the masses from having a significant role. With a faction of the elite presuming to speak for the interests of the people, the latter have not yet been a direct factor in any of the political crises. Even very strongly antagonistic elements have sought formulas for accommodation and compromise in order to avoid radicalization of the political process. While some changes have taken place in the composition of the elite, the new groups share in its "oligarchic spirit." [58]

The urban middle classes—including the military as well as the liberal professions and public employees—took a leading part in the 1930 Revolution, but lacked the independence to formulate a political program for Brazilian society as a whole or even to establish their autonomy from the dissident oligarchies who participated in the movement or quickly aligned with the new regime. Instead of a pluralist democracy, the popular authoritarian regime of Getúlio Vargas emerges, building up the urban working class as a potential power factor under a corporative institutional structure. Thus, even with the 1945 re-

[56] Jaguaribe, *Problemas do Desenvolvimento Latino Americano* (Rio de Janeiro, 1967), p. 168.

[57] *State and Mass in Brazil* (Washington University, St. Louis), *Studies in Comparative International Development,* II, No. 12 (1966).

[58] Francisco Weffort, "Política de Massas," In Octavio Ianni et al., *Política e Revolução Social no Brasil* (Rio de Janeiro, 1965), pp. 161–62.

establishment of representative politics, "all the important organizations functioning as mediators between the State and the individual are really entities annexed to the State itself rather than effectively autonomous organizations." [59] In a framework of direct contact between the state and urban masses through the intermediary of populist leaders, personalities take precedence over ideologies.

During the postwar period, the problem of political absorption of the growing urban masses was a factor in all crises, since the realities of the electoral process and influence of established interests led to a situation in which the President was generally faced with a cabinet and Congress much more conservative than the voters to whom he owed his election. The basically conservative orientation of the major political parties and the heavy if not predominant rural influence in their leadership prevented the urban voter from any close identification with them. Thus, while "nationalists" proclaimed the era of ideological politics and were followed by the relatively highly politicized leadership of unions and "popular" organizations, the masses turned to a direct link between their vote and a political leader with some significant degree of charisma. [60]

Clientelism, which served as the basis for holding much of the middle class to the established political leadership and the parties in terms of exchange of a vote for employment or a specific favor, could not work for the urban masses as a whole as the electorate expanded far beyond the patronage potential of even the cartorial state. (From roughly 1 million in 1908 and 2.7 million for the 1934 balloting, the electorate had expanded to 7.4 million in 1945 and 18.6 million by 1962.)

Quadros, with "an arrogant and distant attitude toward the parties and an authoritarian-charismatic position toward the masses," represented the ultimate in the populist style, unadulterated by vestiges of clientelism. [61] His appeal was relatively greater to the more satisfied sectors of the urban masses than was that of Adhemar de Barros, a "patriarchal" populist who promised direct benefits rather than moralization of the system. While Weffort ignores this consideration, the

[59] Weffort, *State and Mass in Brazil*, p. 190.
[60] *Ibid.*, pp. 163–75.
[61] Weffort, *State and Mass in Brazil*, p. 192.

fact that Adhemar de Barros had the support in 1962 of his own party
—a political machine built up carefully on the basis of patronage over
a period of more than fifteen years—takes his electoral performance
out of the realm of populism per se, by introducing a significant component of clientelistic politics.

As Weffort analyzes the developments of the Goulart period:

> Structural problems become aggravated; since none of the dominant groups
> has hegemony, they all turn to the State conceived as an independent entity,
> awaiting its initiatives. But the State becomes practically paralyzed as possibili-
> ties of compromise between the different groups decrease, thereby increasing
> the pressure. As a result, the possibility that populism, through manipulation,
> should keep functioning as an agent conferring dynamism upon the political
> structure is correspondingly reduced. In this situation, popular pressure be-
> comes increasingly ideological, resulting in the alteration of the traditional
> model of mass manipulation. . . . Nationalism, aside from concealing the
> State's inefficiency in practice, establishes as a reality the myth of a demo-
> cratic State of the whole people, independent of class distinctions.

> Thus the actions of both the State and the popular political organizations
> become increasingly guided by the belief in a sovereign State able to control
> any possible reaction on the part of the conservative groups. These groups
> (not only the agrarian sectors but the industrial entrepreneurs as well) look
> upon the State as revolutionary, and therefore radically oppose it.

> It would be premature to define the road followed by the Brazilian political
> process after Goulart's fall. Nonetheless, we might tentatively suggest that,
> with the military's rise to power, the democratization of the State through
> populism has reached an end.[62]

The view of the urban populace as a mass to be manipulated by
leaders who frequently come from the dominant groups is crucial to
the Brazilian concept of populism, although most such politicians appear in fact to be middle class in origin.[63] This is related to the fact
that the brokerage and clientelistic nature of the Brazilian political-
governmental system reflects, in large part, the pervasive role of the

---

[62] *Ibid.,* p. 195.

[63] Paulo Singer, "A Política das Classes Dominantes," in Ianni et al., *Política e
Revolução Social no Brasil,* pp. 65–125, and Juarez R. B. Lopes, "Some Basic
Developments in Brazilian Politics and Society," in Eric N. Baklenoff (ed), *New
Perspectives of Brazil* (Nashville, 1966), pp. 59–77, provide useful discussions of
the types of Brazilian professional politicians and their relationship to patronage
and populist political styles. See also Nathaniel Leff, *Economic Policy-Making and
Development in Brazil, 1947–1964* (New York, 1968), pp. 118–31.

so-called *panelinha,* an informal group of a relatively closed nature, bound together by common interests as well as personal ties and including members in a variety of complementary positions in the socio-political-economic structure. *Panelinhas* exist at all levels from the local to the national. Of the variety of personal links which maintain connections between various organizations, agencies, and interests, the *panelinha* is one of the more difficult to trace out. Kin relationships can be established with relative ease (and are worthy of study if one is to understand the inner workings of Brazilian politics), but the informal groupings based on mutual interest are much harder to uncover, particularly since there are usually a number of alternative or parallel *panelinhas* in existence among which an informal but generally recognized (by the insiders) pecking order usually exists.[64]

Against the background of Jaguaribe's discussion of clientelism as enriched by the concept of the *panelinha,* the role of the industrialists in politics becomes clearer. Thus, Leff's emphasis on the limits of their influence takes on a new perspective, that of the fragmentation of this major element of the entrepreneural strata.

Industrial interests have had several ways of pressing their views upon the government. The oldest and most traditional is through representation by congressmen speaking for their interests. . . . As soon as we mention this mode of interest articulation, however, one important feature immediately shows itself—the fragmentation of industrialist interest articulation. While some congressmen speak for the Confederation of Industries or individual trade associations, many others speak for individual businessmen or 'economic groups' who constitute part of their political clientele.[65]

In the broader setting of the political system:

Brazil's industrialists have also been hampered by certain conditions stemming from the historical pattern of the country's industrialization. For one thing, they have not enjoyed the same political alliances with agriculture and with other business and propertied interests which have supported manufacturing interests in many advanced countries. Historically, Brazilian industry emerged in a context of conflict with other business interests, particularly the commercial groups associated with the import trade, who, indeed, were the industrialists' chief political opponents. By way of compensation, the in-

[64] Anthony Leeds, "Brazilian Careers and Social Structure," *American Anthropologist,* LXVI, No. 6 (December, 1964), 1321–47.

[65] Leff, *Economic Policy-Making . . .,* pp. 110–11.

dustrialists have had as political allies the urban middle strata and the intelligentsia, who have stood with them on most questions affecting government support for industry. The absence of a generalized alliance with other propertied interests, however, has menaced that commanding posture. Moreover, since Brazilian industrialization has been concentrated in only a few states, while national politics are organized on a federal basis, the non-industrial states have been able to exercise disproportionate influence at the national level. As a result, the industrialists have often been in the position of a minority petitioning the government rather than a group with sufficient political support to impose its wishes.[66]

Concerned with the ties of the "industrial strata" (a term he prefers to either "bourgeoisie" or "elite," which he finds inappropriate to the Brazilian reality) to other economic sectors, Martins seeks to identify the activities through which entrepreneurs accumulated capital for industrialization.[67] Martins finds that between 1914 and 1938 a heavy proportion of new industrialists came from the financial and service sectors, while between 1938 and 1962 the sources were services and real estate. He accepts the view stemming from Celso Furtado that the process of industrialization in Brazil proceeded without a rupture of the agrarian structure so that the landowners, their commercial and financial allies, and the industrialists coexisted in power.[68] With the tensions resulting from incorporation of the urban middle class and proletariat lessened by such control mechanisms as populism and inflation, an equilibrium was maintained between these social forces in spite of their antagonistic long-run interests. Thus parallel archaic and modern structures contribute to profound political contradictions, and the classic concept of the "democratic bourgeois revolution" has little explanatory value in the Brazilian case.[69] Only after the economic development of the first 15 postwar years had led to substantial if undramatic social changes did Brazil reach a "crisis of power," when, as in 1930, significant decisions with deep political implications had to be taken, with the industrialists in a most ambivalent position, "socially linked to the

[66] *Ibid.,* pp. 114–15.

[67] Luciano Martins, "Formação do Empresariado Industrial no Brazil," *Revista do Instituto de Ciências Sociais,* II, No. 1 (1966), 91–138.

[68] Luciano Martins, "Aspectos Políticos da Revolução Brasileira, *Revista Civilização Brasileira,* No. 2 (May, 1965), 15–37; published in Spanish in *Revista Latinoamericana de Sociología,* I, No. 3 (November, 1965), 390–413.

[69] *Ibid.,* p. 18.

traditional strata and its mechanisms of security, in spite of being economically in opposition to them." [70] The middle classes matched the radicalization of the organized sectors of the masses by moving to the right and calling upon the military to intervene.

Thus essentially through examination of Jaguaribe's analysis of Brazil's developmental process we have arrived at a general model of the pre-1964 political system and interpretation of its demise. Yet several additional points concerning Brazil's peculiarly dysfunctional party system must be understood before entering upon our survey of crisis politics during the "Old Republic" (1889–1930), the Vargas era (1930–1954), and the collapse of a semi-pluralist representative system (1954–1964).

One of the most distinctive features of Brazilian political life has been the multiplicity of parties of recent origin, their relative lack of ideological content or meaningful differences in program, and the highly personalistic nature of their leadership. All the fourteen legally registered parties that existed at the time of the 1964 *coup d'état,* and persist behind the façade of an artificial two-party system even today, were established after 1945, but only three were organized on a truly nationwide basis: the Social Democratic Party (PSD), the Brazilian Labor Party (PTB), and the National Democratic Union (UDN). The others were essentially regional, with the bulk of their membership concentrated in a few states. In virtually every party the personal element predominated over questions of program and policy. Neither the professional politicians nor the voters have as yet developed a strong sense of party loyalty, and they shift allegiance as suits their personal convenience. Consequently, a party's strength or weakness at the polls has usually reflected the popularity of the individual candidate rather than that of the party platform, a fact evident even in the 1966 balloting under the quasi-military regime.

The multiplicity of parties tended to obscure the fact that, at the local level, bifactionalism became the predominant political pattern after 1945. The chief political families accepted either the PSD or UDN labels to cover their traditional rivalries. Multifactionalism gradually emerged as these groups fragmented. Dissident elements and new forces aligned themselves with other parties seeking a foothold in the state or

[70] *Ibid.,* p. 34.

fighting to broaden their electoral base. New parties also developed at the local level, as local PSD or UDN "colonels" (political bosses, so-called because of the national guard rank they customarily enjoyed under the Empire) became dissatisfied with alliances or coalitions urged or forced on them by the state or national directorates. Continued industrialization and urbanization also contributed heavily to the proliferation of parties at the local level. These developments were particularly important in the spread of the PTB into new areas during the late 1950's and early 1960's.

Ideological differences have been less important than historic, regional, and personality factors in shaping the character of these parties, which persist at the local level. They were equally marked by a pragmatic outlook and loose internal discipline. Each has been more a flexible grouping of state political organizations than a unified and centralized entity. All combined elements of traditional, transitional, and modern political structure varying with the region.

The weak, fluid, and fragmented party system contributes to a situation in which the bureaucracy is subject to the buffeting and disintegrative effects of aggressive interest groups. In many cases, the bureaucracy must undertake the major part of the interest articulation and aggregation functions, which are not adequately performed by the Congress and political executives. Thus, Brazil's vast, sprawling, and poorly coordinated bureaucracy, influence-ridden and highly subject to the direct impact of politics, plays a major role in the political decision-making process. It is frequently important as a source of policy even more than as an administrative instrument. Many of its more than 150 autonomous agencies have developed a significant political clientele to whom they appeal for support.

The very limited role of parties as effective vehicles for modernization and political development is an important factor in explaining the repeated emergence of the Armed Forces as a crucial factor in these processes; the often dominant policy-making role of the bureaucracy underlies comprehension of the post-1964 efforts to construct a de-politicized, technocratic governmental system.

᷍᷍᷍

CHAPTER TWO

The "Moderating" Pattern of Civil-Military Relations

THROUGHOUT MOST OF THE nineteenth century, owing to the peaceful attainment of independence and the unifying force of the Empire, the part played by the Armed Forces—indeed its very character—differed greatly in Brazil from that characteristic in the rest of Latin America.[1] Not only was there no major mobilization, but Brazil avoided the authority vacuum—the absence of a ruler and a regime generally accepted as legitimate—that contributed to protracted civil strife in the Spanish American countries and institutionalized force as the ultimate arbiter of their political life. Although the unsuccessful war with Argentina (1825–1828) diminished the relatively low prestige of the military career, it also led to the enforced departure of Emperor Pedro I in 1831, an action for which the Army would take greater credit as time passed. During the ensuing wave of regional revolts and separatist movements that shook the country, no dictator or even military strong man emerged from these conflicts, which remained remote from the center of national power. With the elevation to the throne of the fifteen-year-old Pedro II in 1841, a turbulent decade ended and a prolonged period of consolidation and centralization began. Employing his "mod-

[1] For a concise treatment of this topic, consult Johnson, *The Military and Society* . . ., pp. 177–90.

erating power" *(poder moderador)*, the Emperor periodically dissolved Congress, thus providing for a peaceful alternation in power of two factions of the political elite, who in most other Latin American countries had to resort to force to gain access to governmental office.[2] Moreover, with very considerable authority resting in the hands of the Emperor, partisan political competition was not the all-or-nothing proposition it was elsewhere on the continent; there was much less in the way of power and spoils to fight over.

When opposition to the Empire began to take root among urban groups during the third quarter of the century, Brazil's pre-eminent military hero, Luiz Alves de Lima e Silva, ennobled as the Duque de Caxias after pacifying Maranhão in 1840, lent his full support to the system, and remained personally loyal to Pedro. But forces for change had been at work, particularly since the Paraguayan War of 1865–1870, and a new military generation was emerging from the academy imbued with positivism and favoring a republic as the vehicle for lifting Brazil from economic and social backwardness. Although the civilian republican movement was gradually gaining adherents, it was the Army, not the Republican Party that eventually overturned the monarchy in 1889 and, cognizant of its responsibility for that action, assumed the function of the *poder moderador* even after yielding control of the presidency to civilians following six years of essentially military rule. From 1889 to the present, an "interventionist" current has existed in the Brazilian military alongside a strong legalist tendency.[3] Most of the officer corps, not firmly attached to either of these factions, would decide in a crisis situation on the basis of multiple factors in which the pride and interests of the military institution was a major consideration along with personal ties and regional loyalties. Others would be unable to resolve their

[2] João Camilo de Oliveira Tôrres, *A Democracia Coroada: Teoria Política do Imperio do Brasil,* 2d ed. (Petrópolis, 1964), pp. 118–50 discusses this distinctive feature of the Empire. The entire book provides a detailed treatment of the imperial political institutions. His *O Conselho de Estado* (Rio de Janeiro, 1965) describes the functioning of the cabinet under Brazil's modified parliamentary system of that era.

[3] José Honório Rodrigues, *The Brazilians: Their Character and Aspirations* (Austin, 1968), p. xxiii, argues that the struggle between these two tendencies within the military goes back to the 1830's.

ambivalences, thus not acting at all, a situation which facilitated moves by more militant and decisive minorities.

Since the establishment of the Republic, there have been very few periods in Brazilian history that have not been marked either by military revolts or by heavy Armed Forces tutelage of the government. In the recurrent struggle between legalism and political activism within the Brazilian military, the latter has long been substantially stronger than depicted by most historians and many contemporary observers. Neglect of this fundamental fact, and the corresponding over-emphasis of the role of civilian politicians and political movements, has distorted interpretations of Brazilian political development. While a series of civilians from São Paulo did govern the country with reasonable security after the initial years of military domination under Marshals Deodoro and Floriano, two of these three presidents faced military crises that in the context of the times posed threats to their continuance in office. Prudente de Morais (1894–1898) was plagued by dissatisfaction over his handling of the Canudos "insurgency" problem, and in November, 1897, was saved from assassination by a veteran of that campaign only because War Minister Machado Bittencourt sacrificed his own life to save the President. Following Campos Salles' quite peaceful term (1898–1902), Rodrigues Alves survived the November, 1904, revolt of the Military School at the midpoint of his administration. The first *Mineiro* President, Afonso Pena (1906–1909), died in office of a 'moral traumatism' soon after being thwarted in his preferences for a civilian as his successor and being forced to accept the candidacy of War Minister Hermes da Fonseca. Nilo Peçanha's year in office was little more than an opportunity to preside over the Marshal's election, and Hermes himself was barely settled in the presidency when the naval revolt of 1910 broke out. His regime was also plagued by protracted insurgency in the Northeast and South by dissident politicians. The latter problem extended into the term of Wenceslau Braz (1914–1918), who otherwise enjoyed stability, although the nation's political king-maker, Senator Pinheiro Machado, was murdered (to the ill-concealed satisfaction of some officers). The military's involvement in World War I temporarily reduced its political interference and left Braz a good bit freer than he might otherwise have been.

Military involvement in politics resurged during the interwar period. Epitácio Pessoa (1919–1922) was involved in rather constant friction with the Armed Forces because of his insistence on appointing civilians to head the War and Navy Ministries. By the last year of his term a grave military question had arisen as the Army, behind Marshal Hermes da Fonseca, adamantly opposed the choice of Arthur Bernardes as President for the 1922–1926 term. Indeed, the entire decade of the 1920's was one of repeated military uprisings, culminating in the successful 1930 Revolution. Vargas himself, although heavily backed by, and to a considerable degree dependent upon, the Armed Forces, faced civil war in 1932 and a Communist revolt in 1935, in both of which movements regular Army elements were involved, before staging his own dictatorial coup in 1937. Like Wenceslau Braz, a quarter of a century earlier, Vargas also benefited from the military's concern with its wartime obligations. But with the end of World War II, Vargas was unceremoniously removed from office by the Armed Forces.

The transition from dictatorship to a constitutional, competitive regime after 1945 did not place undue strains upon the political process shaped by Vargas, at least so long as it received predominantly support rather than demands from the Armed Forces. Subsequently, however, the problems of aftermath politics in a period of emerging populism and resurgent traditional clientilism, aggravated by dislocations caused by the external influence of postwar international adjustments, gave rise to increasing tensions and a "revolution of rising frustrations." Under these conditions, Vargas' return to power through popular elections took place in 1950, only to encounter the full brunt of the participation crisis. Governing within the constraints of a constitutional system that had been consciously devised to thwart a president who might try to operate in his old style, Vargas found his tried and true techniques of manipulation and conciliation inadequate. His response involved a shriller demagoguery and intensified exploitation of nationalism rather than evolving a more serviceable substitute political style. In this situation, the majority of the officer corps withdrew their support from his regime.

Thus the military's repeated intervention in the political arena in the postwar era had behind it a substantial tradition. Indeed, the relative political peace under Juscelino Kubitschek (January, 1956–January,

1961) was as long a recess from major political-military crisis as the Republic had yet witnessed. When Kubitschek turned over the presidential office at the end of his full term to an elected successor in a climate of normalcy, he was accomplishing something achieved only by three previous civilian Presidents (Campos Salles, Rodrigues Alves, and Wenceslau Braz). Moreover, three governments fell by force in the single constitutional term between Dutra and Kubitschek, while the five-year presidential period after Kubitschek saw the emergence and decline of three distinct regimes in a process of nearly continual crises that interred the old pattern of civil-military relations and brought the Armed Forces back to the direct exercise of power they had experienced in the infant years of the Republic.

In a very similar sense to the continuity of *tenentismo* (the political militance of the junior officers entering the service after World War I) and even of the *tenentes* themselves from the 1920's through the 1960's, *Florianismo* in the form of advocacy of military rule as practiced by Marshal Floriano, spanned the 1890's to the early 1920's. First with the "Consolidator of the Republic" himself, then through the political career and presidency of his aide and favorite nephew, Marshal Hermes da Fonseca (1910–1914), and finally with the bridge between *Florianismo* and *tenentismo* in the form of the 1921–1922 campaign of the Military Club against the government under Hermes' leadership, this interventionist current left its impact on the military generation born after the establishment of the Republic. Thus, if events before 1910 were just faint memories to the senior officers of the early 1960's, the same was not true of the Hermes da Fonseca administration and the period of World War I. For with few exceptions, the generals of the post-Vargas era were already cadets at this time, enrolled in military preparatory school (Colegio Militar) if not already in the Academy (Escola Militar). Hence, for example, the naval revolt that broke out after Hermes' inauguration appears to have left an imprint that disposed them to react strongly to the Navy insubordination in March, 1964.

While the earlier military interventions and revolts were part of the Armed Forces' historical memory, the developments of the 1920's were directly related—through the Revolution of 1930, the 1937 coup, and the ouster of Vargas in 1945—to the developments of the 1954–1964 decade. For the general officers of the Quadros and Goulart period

were the *tenentes* of the post-World War I years. Not just observers of
the recurring crises of 1922–1937, they were significant participants in
these episodes and thus felt a sense of responsibility for what took place,
as well as for possible sins of omission in subsequent years. A valid
comprehension of their perceptions in this regard is essential for understanding the changing pattern of civil-military relations, as is an analysis
of changes in the political system itself and the Armed Forces as an
institution and actor within this system. The ensuing section is intended
to provide the elements necessary for understanding this process up to
1950, as well as for exploring the conditions that gave rise to the movements in conflict after 1950. (This telescoped discussion corresponds in
a summary fashion to three chapters of my manuscript study of "Modernization and the Military in Brazil: Institutional Crises, Political Instability, and Army Intervention, 1889–1964." In addition to a much
fuller exposition and argument, complete citations and supporting documentation are provided there.)

1. THE ARMED FORCES AND THE "SYSTEM"

Although not apparent to the casual observer, whose attention was
generally drawn to the political debates of the Congress and the articulate expression of views by representatives of civilian interest groups as
carried in the generally free, if conservatively oriented press, the Armed
Forces exerted important influence on national political life throughout
the period of the Old Republic (República Velha). Since their orientation was essentially centrist—neither clearly in support of those opposing all change nor in favor of the still weak radical forces in society—
the Armed Forces tended generally to merge with the dominant political
currents of the day. Not faced until after 1920 with a government
viewed as hostile to their interpretation of the national interest, as well
as to their own institution, the Armed Forces did not appear to be as
aggressively interventionist as in many Hispanic American countries of
the time. But their favorable image—that they were largely above politics, or were at least disinterested watchdogs of the national welfare—
was in part a historical carry-over from the past. It was also, in part at
least, a result of the fact that no competition between national parties
existed in Brazil. Indeed, there was no real electoral competition for
power and office at the national level. Once the system shook down
around the turn of the century in the so-called politics of the governors,

the dominant coalition of forces headed by São Paulo and Minas Gerais, with Rio Grande do Sul, Rio de Janeiro, and Bahia playing secondary roles, selected the next president. With the powerful state machines falling into line behind a choice influenced heavily by the incumbent president and important financial interests, the lesser states were left with little choice but to adhere. On those few occasions when a real contest seemed possible, the military took an active part in the campaign. In 1894 and 1898, a group of military figures who had enjoyed influence in the regime of Floriano and opposed the idea of civilian rule ran a symbolic opposition candidate, and in 1904 they attempted a revolt. They soon imposed their views of the superiority of a military candidate on the government, and with Hermes' election in 1910 the number of civilian and military presidents under the Republic was evened up at three each. Although opposition candidate Ruy Barbosa, one of the nation's most prestigious figures, argued persuasively that renascent militarism along the lines he had witnessed within Deodoro's cabinet was a threat to Brazilian democracy, he went down to a crushing defeat at the hands of the War Minister of the outgoing administration.

Throughout this period, military figures were actively involved in the political life of the states, albeit more often behind the scenes than in the spotlight. In point of fact, between 1900 and 1930 the Brazilian Armed Forces were an even more active factor in the politics of the nation than were their Argentine counterparts—conventional wisdom to the contrary. The Brazilian Armed Forces differed from the Latin American norm during the first three decades of the twentieth century more as a result of the nature of the Brazilian political system as a whole than in terms of their own particular characteristics as an institution. As the system underwent a process of change, so did the military subsystem, in response to many of the same dynamic factors.

With the beginning of the political decay and institutional deterioration of the Old Republic at the end of World War I, the military was at the center of every crisis. The increasing division within the Armed Forces along generational lines, which placed them on both sides of the conflict between the established order and the forces of change, nourished a continued belief, strongest within the military, but accepted by much of the public, that it was national rather than institutional interests or personal ambitions that motivated their political actions, and to a considerable degree this was true. As their predecessors were the mid-wives of the Republic in 1889, the younger officers—those emerging from the Military School toward the end of the war and after—were its gravediggers.

By 1928, the republican regime in its nearly four decades of existence had reached the same point of deterioration, and the oligarchic system a parallel degree of political decay, as had been the case with the Empire in the mid-1880's. Institutions and processes that might have been suitable for the first years of republican self-government had failed to evolve beyond an amalgam with traditional practices carried over from the monarchy. Indeed, they became entrenched through the federal government's willingness to let state power structures alone as long as they cooperated in Congress and created no undue difficulty over presidential succession. The electoral process was highly fraudulent, national parties were nonexistent, and protests against the inequities of the established order were increasingly met with repression rather than compromise and evolutionary reform. The federal executive, while frequently arbitrary, often lacked the compensatory merit of strength and effectiveness. The political representatives of the patriarchal and "oligarchic" regime could not point with pride to outstanding accomplishments to justify their continued stewardship of the nation. Or rather, when they sought to do so, they were convincing only to themselves, while appearing hypocritical and self-seeking to an increasing proportion of the politically conscious public.

As long as elections might lead to change, there was no strong popular base for revolution. But the people were aware that never in the history of the Republic had the government's candidate lost. Moreover, only on two widely separated occasions had the electorate been given even the shadow of a real choice rather than just an opportunity to ratify the decision of the powerful state machines (and this only when the bargaining process among the president and the governors of São Paulo, Minas Gerais, and Rio Grande do Sul had broken down). Indeed, to all intents and purposes, the selection of São Paulo's governor for the 1926–1930 presidential term had taken place in 1919, when the election of Epitácio Pessoa to the presidency was understood within the political class as a temporary "emergency" interruption of the pattern of São Paulo–Minas Gerais alternation which would give the young state executive four more years to mature. In this context, the presidential succession of 1930 turned out to be the last chance for the old republican system to demonstrate significant flexibility or adaptability. But the course of events from late 1928 on demonstrated that Brazil's political crisis was one both of men and of institutions.

The core of the revolutionary movement that eventually triumphed in October, 1930, was composed of the *tenentes,* who had gained conspiratorial experience as well as a degree of popular renown during the four years of their armed struggle against the government of Arthur da Silva Bernardes (1922–1926). During 1928–1929, they were able to win additional adherents to their cause within the officer corps, exploiting the growing dissatisfaction with the regime's policies. The successful revolution became possible only after they formed an alliance with a broad coalition of political forces possessing a significant power base in the key states, but their proselyting and infiltration of military units throughout the country were essential to the achievement of this purpose. Indeed, without the assurance of widespread military adhesions, the generally cautious political leaders would not have risked a revolutionary venture, particularly the coldly calculating Getúlio Vargas in whose name the 1930 revolt was ultimately launched and who had delayed his commitment until the movement was far advanced.

Tenentismo paralleled in many respects the positivistic republicanism of the young officers in the last decade of the Empire. On the intellectual side, its origins can be found in the Military Academy, reopened in 1911–1912 at Realengo after being closed in the wake of the 1904 cadet revolt. There during World War I such future leaders as Eduardo Gomes, Luís Carlos Prestes, Siqueira Campos, Oswaldo Cordeiro de Farias, Stenio Caio de Albuquerque Lima, and Ciro do Espírito Santo Cardoso (to name but one group among several who maintained a significant exchange of ideas) studied and lamented a "Brazil laden with problems, beneath the weight of the crisis and in the hands of politicians inept as well as unscrupulous and instruments of oligarchies." [4] The leaders of the academy made a conscious effort to keep the education essentially technical rather than highly theoretical, with a taste of the humanities, or at least of positivist philosophy, as had

---

[4] Dalcídio Jurandir, as quoted in Glauco Carneiro, *O Revolucionário Siqueira Campos* (Rio de Janeiro, 1966), p. 59.

been the case at the old academy at Praia Vermelha during the years when its instructors were still the disciples of Benjamin Constant. The goal was to develop competent professional soldiers, well disciplined and obedient to constituted authority. This orientation was successful with many. But in light of the lower middle class origin of a large proportion of the young officers, the example of their superiors' often mixing in politics, the siren call of renewed *Florianismo* through the person of Hermes de Fonseca, and the magnitude of national problems (contrasted with the "selfish" interests of the "boss"-dominated political system), it is not surprising that a significant minority questioned the military's institutional role as a support of the established order.[5]

The militants of both the legalist and reformist theses were greatly outnumbered at the time (as they would be three decades later) by the vast majority of officers for whom the two sides of the nation's motto, "Order and Progress," had equal importance. Since the 1891 Constitution enjoined the Armed Forces on the one hand to be "essentially obedient, within the limits of the law" to the President, but on the other hand declared them "obligated to support the Constitutional institutions," it virtually consecrated ambivalence in ambiguous situations when the threat to the Constitution's integrity appeared to come from the executive. Moreover, the increased emphasis upon study and training advocated so vigorously by the champions of professionalism and embodied in the 1920 military regulations, along with the arrival in the same year of a French training mission which was destined to have a heavy impact upon the Army's mentality, appears to have made young officers more aware of national problems than before. Growing numbers came to believe: "On the national scale the Army, and only the Army, was the organized force which could be placed at the service of democratic ideals and popular demands, against the interests of the bosses and oligarchies which increasingly aggravated the burdensome conditions of survival for the unprivileged." [6]

[5] A classic contemporary interpretation of *tenentismo* up to the São Paulo revolt that stands up well under the test of time is Virginio Santa Rosa, *O sentido do tenentismo* (Rio de Janeiro, 1933). Placing rather heavy emphasis upon class conflict, it relates the *tenente* movement to the rise of the middle class. More recent work is reflected in Octávio Malta, *Os Tenentes na Revolução Brasileira* (Rio de Janeiro, 1970).

[6] Glauco Carneiro, *O Revolucionário . . .*, pp. 104–105.

The spread of this reformist-activist sentiment among the military coincided with the increasing alienation of urban progressive groups who found the establishment unresponsive to their demand for a significant voice in policy-making, and not at all disposed to yield to demands for any type of reform, including that of the electoral system. As had been the case forty years earlier, nearly all of the preconditions for revolution existed. Dissension within the political elite over presidential succession, combined with the impact of the world economic crisis, made the regime vulnerable and provided additional impetus to the formation of a revolutionary coalition capable of overthrowing the established order.

The successful revolutionary movement of 1930 was a heterogeneous amalgam of groups desiring sweeping political changes if not a new social order with elements, which although violently opposed to the incumbent administration and the president's hand-picked successor, were devoid of any wish for more than modest political and administrative reforms. In both its civilian and military components—each crucial to its success—the revolutionary coalition was essentially, indeed almost exclusively, bourgeois in nature. The Communists, considering the October, 1930, revolt to be narrowly concerned with regional rivalries within the existing system, refused to participate or support it—a fact that was to have significant implications for the post-Revolution political struggles.

Presidential succession was the issue that coalesced the fragmented opposition forces into a single movement cohesive insofar as its immediate objective—attainment of power—was concerned. In 1929, the world market crisis combined with a record coffee harvest to thwart government price-support policies and trigger an economic recession. Elements linked to industry, finance, commerce, and services began to react strongly against economic policies favoring export-oriented agricultural producers. Against this background, an unusually strong opposition coalition was forged to contest the 1930 presidential election. When outgoing President Washington Luis of São Paulo broke with tradition and sought to impose another *Paulista* as the official candidate, Minas Gerais political leaders threw their support to the "Liberal Alliance" slate headed by Getúlio Vargas, the Governor of Rio Grande do Sul. Júlio Prestes was announced the winner, but the Liberal Alliance refused to accept the allegedly fraudulent results and launched a revolt in October, 1930. Alarmed at the prospect of civil war and impressed with the visible decay of the old regime in the face of this challenge, the high command of the Armed Forces, after a good deal of maneuvering by generals with key commands, stepped in and forced the president to resign in favor of a *junta*, which it was hoped by some participants might prove a viable alternative to the revolutionary forces.

Vargas became provisional chief executive at the head of a very heterogeneous movement. Although the *tenentes* and some "young Turk" politicians desired a real social revolution, they lacked any coherent plan; other groups wished only to correct the evident deficiencies of the old political system. They agreed only upon a new electoral code incorporating the secret ballot, proportional representation, a system of electoral courts, and extension of the franchise to include women. Following an unsuccessful "Constitutionalist" revolt centered in São Paulo in July, 1932, a Constituent Assembly was elected, and in 1934 conferred a four-year presidential term upon Vargas. During this time both the communists and the local fascists (known as Integralists), thriving in a situation where less ideological parties failed to take root, sought Vargas' overthrow by violent means. In November, 1937, Vargas staged a coup with the acquiescence of the Armed Forces' leaders, assuming dictatorial powers and decreeing a semi-corporative "New State" (Estado Nôvo). By absorbing into his regime important elements of the dominant state machines, he was able to bend the existing political system to his wishes and adapt it to his needs. Thus he was able to govern without a formal party structure while maneuvering to neutralize critical military elements.

Vargas' fifteen-year stay in power, although interrupting Brazil's tradition of constitutional government, helped to break the hold of the traditional elite groups and brought new elements into the political arena. Moreover, Vargas gave impetus to social and economic developments that subsequently tended to give a broader base to Brazilian experiments with representative regimes in the 1946–1964 period. Yet more than anything else the Estado Nôvo reinforced authoritarian tendencies and corporatist structures which proved barriers to the development of a pluralist system.

Vargas' economic policies were oriented toward diversification of production, with heavy emphasis on industrialization. Although he safeguarded the principle of private enterprise, he did not hesitate to intervene in various areas of economic activity and to take the initiative in spheres private capital was reluctant to enter. The federal government extended its powers at the expense of local and state autonomy, thus helping, along with improved communications, to break down the strong tradition of regionalism. In an environment of sustained industrialization and urbanization, the civilian elite groups expanded significantly through the addition of industrial, commercial, and professional elements. The bureaucracy grew substantially in numbers in the wake of broadened governmental activities and came to play an important role in the formulation and execution of national policies. Assumption by the federal government of responsibility for the welfare of urban labor gave the group a new interest in politics and established the image of Vargas as the "Father of the Poor."

With the triumph of Allied arms in World War II, pressure grew in Brazil for a return to representative government. Vargas reluctantly called general elections for late 1945, and political parties were allowed to organize. Important political and military groups—including not only the traditional opposition, but many of the Army leaders long associated with the dictator—doubting the sincerity of Vargas' new-found democratic inclinations, brought about his involuntary but peaceful departure from office in October. (The return of the Brazilian Expeditionary Force from the Italian campaign, where it had fought to defend and extend democracy, was a major factor in Vargas' fall.) The candidate Vargas eventually endorsed, General Eurico Gaspar Dutra, his long-time War Minister, was elected in December, 1945, and gave Brazil five years of orderly if uninspired government. The Constitution of 1946, which remained in effect until 1967, recreated a federal system, with a presidential executive and a bicameral national legislature. It included numerous social welfare provisions and institutionalized restraints on arbitrary exercise of power—the former in response to the Vargas experience and the latter in reaction against it. Although Dutra was a career Army officer, it can be said with substantial justice that he strove conscientiously to act as a democratic President, albeit with a strong leaning toward conservative positions.

Thus Brazil's return to constitutionalism began as had the Republic itself and the post-1930 experiments, with the civilian political groups indebted to the military for having ousted the "decadent" regime. Indeed, the striking fact about Brazil in the immediate postwar period is not the Armed Forces' assumption of responsibility for intervening in politics on behalf of the civilian democratic elements, but the latter's acceptance of this as a proper and legitimate function of the military as a national institution—a tendency which was manifested again in less unqualified terms in 1954 and 1964. The selection of military candidates for the presidential succession of 1945 involved questions of political tactics, if not strategy, as well as recognition that the "re-establishment of democracy" required the sponsorship of the Armed Forces. Yet much earlier the liberal constitutionalists began to woo the Army as the republicans had in the 1880's. Rather than manifesting rancor toward the military leadership for rejecting his November, 1937, plea (delivered as opposition presidential candidate in the elections scheduled for the next year) and being party to Vargas' coup, Armando de Sales refrained in exile from disputing the Armed Forces right to act as the arbiter of national life in crisis situations. As titular leader of the democratic opposition, he repeatedly urged the Armed Forces from 1939 on to intervene once again as the only national force not demoralized by the Vargas dictatorship. Thus, for the liberal constitutionalists, the Armed Forces' action to end the dictatorship on October 29, 1945, both justified their institutionalized role as holder of the moderating power and was justified by it.

The nature of the political party system that emerged in 1945 set significant limits on what could be attempted, much less accomplished, during Dutra's administration. At the same time, Vargas' continuance as the potentially dominant figure in two of the three major parties largely inhibited their development along modern programmatic lines or into institutionalized vehicles for political modernization. Anti-Vargism was the unifying factor and guiding principle of the National Democratic Union (UDN), while the power-oriented Social Democratic Party (PSD) remained closely tied to the ex-dictator. Policy differences were thus subordinated to emotional issues of *Varguismo,* while personal and regional differences stemming from the Estado Nôvo epoch would generally override the class and interest similarities between the UDN and PSD and keep the latter in increasingly uneasy alliance with the Brazilian Labor Party (PTB). Only in the wake of the 1964 revolution—a decade after Vargas' death—would a permanent realignment be imposed upon the parties by the military to supplant an alignment along the cleavages of 1945.

The PSD, pre-eminently the party of the *situacionistas,* or political "in" groups, supplied the majority in the 1946–1950 Congress, occupied the largest share of executive positions in Dutra's cabinet, and controlled the greatest number of state administrations. Essentially non-ideological in its orientation, the PSD combined the dominant state machines of the post-1930 period, chiefly rural-based, with the businessmen and industrialists who had benefited under the authoritarian interlude from Vargas' increasing orientation toward economic development. A high proportion of the new bureaucratic elite, whose ranks had multiplied through the steady expansion of government activities during the Vargas era, also leaned toward the PSD, whose ranks were further swelled by those who sought advantage from associating themselves with the administration party in Brazil's patronage-oriented "cartorial state." Essentially, these groups wanted more of what they had been receiving from the Estado Nôvo and pressed Dutra for special favors as well as increased support for programs beneficial to their diverse interests. Indeed, the PSD was more a loose confederation of regional parties than a unified and coherent national organization. In 1946, it bore a striking resemblance to the state-based republican parties of the pre-1930 regime, in spite of the fundamental changes that had taken place in Brazilian society since that time.

In its early years, the UDN was as much an alliance of political "outs" as the PSD was a coalition of the holders of power. With bifactionalism the predominant pattern on the local level in rural areas, the UDN label was often adopted by the political chief or clan that was not linked to the state interventor's power structure. Thus, in much of the country the UDN was not distinctively different in its social base or policy objectives from the PSD. Similarly, in the cities, the UDN was heavily supported by commercial-industrial interests, many of whose members opted for the PSD. While the pro-Vargas center-conservative PSD attracted many middle-class voters linked to the expanding government bureaucracy, the UDN recruited heavily from among professional men and white-collar employees of the private sector. It was also strong among intellectuals and students, who at that time were intensely anti-

Vargas on juridical and libertarian grounds; in the cities, the UDN was a liberal party in the classic sense. As a minority party, it became accustomed to the role of public critic, although various of its component interests negotiated with the government for what patronage and favors they could extract.

The PTB, at the beginning of Dutra's presidential period, was more significant for its potential than its existing strength. It suffered from organizational deficiencies and was an effective electoral force only in the major industrial centers. Yet few politicians could be blind to the fact that with the continued mobilization of urban groups and development of the working class it would almost surely continue to grow. With Vargas at its head, the PTB would be a formidable power contender and hence merited respect beyond its 1945 electoral performance.

The re-establishment of a representative legislative organ and the emergence of political parties would in any case have seriously affected the operations of the policy-making mechanism and administrative machinery. But the undermining of executive authority was accentuated in the 1946–1950 period by the fragmented and factionalized nature of the parties, constitutional provisions and structural modifications designed to decentralize power, and the political style of the new President. Dutra was a military man of previously authoritarian leanings who was so determined to govern entirely within the limits of the recently reinstituted formal democracy that he failed to take a strong role in resolving the difficult adjustments necessary if the representative system of the renewed Republic was to demonstrate the effectiveness required for long-run viability.

Often uncertain in a situation that provided few guidelines for the development of an effective presidential leadership style, Dutra could be resolute when his background and experience were relevant to the problem at hand. While as the dominant military figure of the time and as an exponent of order he could rely on the support of the Armed Forces and thus be free from the necessity to concern himself with the calculus of survival, Dutra was highly conscious of the fact that his every action set a precedent for the new experiment with democratic government. Combined with the absence of an appropriate constitutional framework for most of his initial year in office, this contributed to an appearance of indecisiveness and tendency toward inaction that at times bordered on drift. Indeed, until the promulgation of the 1946 Constitution, Dutra's administration had much of the character of a caretaker regime: even after that time, the President was scrupulous in not infringing on the prerogatives of Congress, the judiciary, or even the parties. Thus, Brazil failed to receive strong and imaginative presidential leadership in the period of transition from a relatively closed discretionary regime toward an open, competitive, and representative system. While characterized by great freedom and exceptional stability, the Dutra years were hence also a period of lost opportunities. Although many of the vices of the Estado Nôvo were eliminated, its major virtues were also lost, and a number of the less desirable features of the pre-Vargas system re-emerged. Instead of liberal democracy being "legitimized" by its achievements in the aftermath of authoritarianism, its shortcomings were too often underscored by a policy of drift and accommodation with retrograde forces. The conservative Republic became a breeding ground for a new brand of populism that would alter the nature of political life and quality of participation without effecting a new synthesis between the forces of tradition and modernization.

2. POLITICAL CHANGE AND INSTITUTIONAL CRISES

As the first postwar administration drew to a close, the Brazilian political scene appeared calm. Yet behind the façade of stability, pressures for change were beginning to build up. While the transformations were not as obvious as in 1945–1946, when political parties emerged and a new constitution was adopted, the early 1950's were to witness a continuance of fundamental adaptations and adjustments in the Brazilian political system, in response to the increased rate of social mobilization and broadened participation in electoral politics. The established parties, suffering from a lack of coherence and inadequate organization as well as from their conservative orientation, were most unsuitable vehicles for the socialization of the new urban masses entering the electorate. Alongside the still relatively effective clientelistic politics, new types of populist leaders and movements emerged, partially filling the vacuum resulting from the elimination of the one ideological party of the left, the Brazilian Communist Party (PCB), outlawed in 1947.

This peculiarly Brazilian form of "populism," combining features of urban machine politics with personalism and emotional appeals with effective performance in the realm of patronage, assumed several distinct forms in the decade after 1948: (1) the labor-oriented nationalism of Vargas; (2) the conservative populism of Adhemar de Barros, which blended massive public works expenditures with demagogic campaigning and large-scale exploitation of graft and patronage for electoral ends; (3) the moralistic messianism of Jânio Quadros, the ascetic underdog who capitalized on the popular desire for an end to the corruption and controversy of Vargism and Adhemarism; (4) the crusading anti-Communist zeal of Carlos Lacerda and his developing mystique of intransigent oppositionism in a system where opportunism and accommodation predominated. After 1958, at least two new varieties of populism were introduced to fill the vacuum left by the death of Vargas. Leonel Brizola modernized the "laborist" (trabalhista) line by adding a more ideological brand of nationalism and, like his arch-rival Lacerda, effectively exploited the new medium of television to transcend the limitations of communication with the masses on the basis of personal appearance. Miguel Arraes, although not gifted as a speaker, began to evolve a mystique as spokesman for the "other Brazil," the forgotten masses of the Northeast. Confronted with the residual strength of *coronelismo,* the traditional system of patrimonial bossism, he adopted the coloration of a dedicated reformer while utilizing the program and organization of the Communist movement, if not necessarily its ideology.

The several strains of populism shared in common an appeal to the poorly assimilated mass urban population, fed by heavy migration from the countryside, plagued with the insecurities of city life, and dissatisfied with its level of living. The restless but largely nonradical middle sectors also gave substantial support to populist politicians. Although this tendency was still not evident during the Dutra years, it grew in importance through the crises of the 1950's and was crucial to the "Jânio phenomenon." Left betrayed and disoriented by Quadros' resignation in August, 1961, the middle sectors would be important to Goulart's early successes before giving support to the movement which overthrew him.

The rise of populism was matched during the 1950's by a reaction within the military, which also helped contribute to the political confrontation that brought about a fundamental system change in the mid-1960's. Thus, these interrelated developments are crucial to an understanding of the collapse of the representative regime. Indeed, to a very considerable degree, the 1964 coup was a reflection, if not direct continuation, of the political crisis and military interventions of 1954–1955, which saw the final elimination of Vargas and a struggle over whether the victors of the 1955 elections should be allowed to take office. What the Armed Forces did and refrained from doing in 1954–1955 had a profound impact upon their actions in 1961 and 1964, and the roles of the main actors in the 1964 crisis are intelligible only against the background of the positions they assumed a decade earlier. For the leaders of the 1964 coup and Goulart's military supporters had not only held key command positions in 1961, but had been junior generals or senior colonels during the 1954–1955 crisis. In fact, many had played consequential roles in the 1945 deposition of Vargas, and their memories of the 1937 coup, the 1930 Revolution, and even the *tenente* revolts of the 1920's were those of participants as well as observers.

This continuity of leadership, which necessitates a close examination of the 1950's for an adequate understanding of the 1960's, was nearly as pronounced on the civilian side, with the physical absence of Vargas after 1954 more than offset by the pervasive influence of his political legacy and the prominent role of his political heirs, particularly Goulart. Among the civilian leadership of the post-1964 governments, Pedro Aleixo, Vice President under Costa e Silva (1967–1969), had been speaker of the Chamber of Deputies during the mid-1930's, government leader under Quadros, opposition leader through the Goulart regime, and majority leader under Castelo Branco. His predecessor as vice president, José Maria Alkmim, had also been active in national politics for over three decades, as had many congressional leaders and holders of ministerial posts in the military-headed administrations. Thus, to the degree that the 1963–1964 crisis was a replay of the 1953–1954 polarization and military intervention, analysis of the demise of the Vargas government is crucial to comprehension of the breakdown of the system itself a decade later.

Vargas' inability to cope with changing conditions, which led to the chain of deepening crises, can be understood only in terms of the situation in which he came to power and particularly the divisions within the Army that developed in the early 1950's. Elections within the influential Military Club had long been one of Brazil's most significant political barometers. The victor in 1948 was the highly professional Salvador César Obino, with General Leitão de Carvalho, one of the most intransigent legalists, as his vice presidential running mate. The salient issue about which military politics had come to resolve in the early postwar years was that of petroleum policy. While the Dutra administration was relatively favorable to the idea of United States participation in the exploration and development of Brazil's inadequate petroleum reserves, an increasingly vocal nationalist current in the Armed Forces opposed foreign investment in and control over such a strategic resource. In large part, the alignment of this question arrayed the pro-United States politicians of the Italian campaign against leftist and pro-Vargas elements. Leitão de Carvalho joined a number of other retired generals in founding the Center for the Defense of Petroleum and the National Economy (CEDPEN), and Obino, who was far from an unconditional admirer of the Dutra government, permitted debate of this question within the Military Club (to which all Army officers belonged). General Júlio Caetano Horta Barbosa and ex-*tenente* leader Juarez Távora were the major antagonists in this dispute, dating back to the time when the former had served as head of the National Petroleum Council under Vargas and adopted a policy contrary to that followed by the latter when he had been Minister of Agriculture.[7] Since basic legislation in this field was under active consideration in Congress during the 1948–1950 period, the matter remained at the forefront of military concern.

The 1950 Military Club elections thus centered on the question that was also one of the major issues in the concurrent presidential campaign, that of economic nationalism. Vargas had placed increasing emphasis upon this theme in his effort to gain broad popular support for a bid to return to power as constitutional president. At least equally important to the ex-dictator as the response of the electorate was the attitude of the Armed Forces, who, as they had been able to oust him from office in 1945, could still effectively veto his candidacy. In this context the victory of a "nationalist" slate in the Military Club balloting in May removed the major threat to Vargas' political comeback. Elements hesitant to commit themselves to a candidacy which might be

[7] Werneck Sodré *Memórias de um Soldado* (Rio de Janerio, 1967), pp. 258–60 and *História Militar de Brasil* (Rio de Janeiro, 1965), pp. 292–304.

aborted by the Armed Forces now forsaw sufficient military support for the ex-president.[8]

Relations with the United States were a factor in all the crises of the postwar period and drew the greatest attention from public opinion. In the eyes of the Armed Forces, however, traditional rival Argentina was an important consideration, and this came to be a major factor in their subsequent hostility toward Vargas and Goulart. In Juan Domingo Perón's quest for continental hegemony—which led him to close cooperation in the early 1950's with the military strong men who came to power at this time in Chile, Colombia, and Venezuela—the Argentina dictator generally viewed Brazil's pro-United States orientation as a major obstacle. From Perón's perspective, Vargas was clearly preferable to other Brazilian leaders, particularly those closely aligned with the United States as were both Dutra and UDN candidate Eduardo Gomes. Getúlio for his part respected the accomplishments of the Argentine dictator in establishing a new type of popular authoritarian regime based upon manipulation of both labor and the military.

The resignation of João Neves da Fontoura as Vargas' foreign minister turned in large part upon the regime's unofficial contacts with Perón, which circumvented Foreign Ministry channels, and the Army's ability to force the dismissal of Batista Luzardo as Ambassador to Argentina in August, 1953, ushered in a period of increasing military pressure on Vargas that culminated in his ouster and death a year later. Not only did the Armed Forces once again suspect Vargas of harboring continuist objectives, but this time they felt he did so with the backing of the Argentine regime, which had never before encountered such a friendly Brazilian administration. Indeed, a major component of the military's hostility toward João Goulart in 1954, when they would suc-

---

[8] In this instance those who won the battle and even the campaign eventually lost the war, for the defeated "anti-Communists" would constitute the backbone of the 1964 movement which overthrew Goulart and took power themselves. Having ousted Vargas in 1945 only to see him elected President in 1950, subsequently driving him to suicide in 1954 only to have his political heirs triumph in the 1955 elections, and finally witnessing the defeat of the Vargista forces at the polls in 1960 only to watch them come back to power the next year, the Armed Forces would act decisively to end this Vargas succession in 1964, destroying in the process Brazil's experiment with a competitive democratic regime and open political system.

cessfully demand his ouster as labor minister, as well as in 1955, 1961, and 1964 (when they would resort to drastic measures in an effort to keep him from power and finally to expel him by force from the presidency), stemmed from his sympathies toward Perón and behind-the-scenes dealings with the Argentine regime. In the wake of Perón's fall in September, 1955, revelations concerning supposed suspiciously large payments to Goulart in 1950 in a pinewood deal with the Argentine regime were to play a major role in the November military-political crisis.

Even in 1964, Carlos Lacerda continued to exploit this alleged scandal, along with the fact that Goulart was Vargas' protegé, to arouse suspicions concerning Goulart's supposed intention to establish a "syndicalist republic" of the Peronist style in Brazil. Hence in 1964, as in 1954, military suspicions concerning the government's favors to the labor movement and emphasis on fundamental reforms and an anti-United States strain of nationalism would be heightened by awareness of the Argentine experience and the Vargas-Goulart ties to Perón.

In the realm of political tactics as well as on these other dimensions the 1951–1954 experience provided a clear fortaste of the deeper crisis of 1961–1964. Returning to office after a decisive electoral victory, Vargas opted at first for an eclectic and generally pragmatic policy that satisfied neither the economic liberals nor the radical nationalists, but laid down the guidelines for the "developmentalist" program and doctrine that were followed with greater success by the Kubitschek administration. Accustomed to governing relatively free from restraints, Vargas was not comfortable operating within an institutional structure designed to minimize his freedom of action. Moreover, as a result of Dutra's quite narrow construction of presidential powers, Vargas' moves to provide strong presidential leadership were often interpreted as an indication of his "dictatorial" tendencies. Thus, frustrations quickly built up, with the opposition suspicious of the motives behind Vargas' every initiative and the President impatient with the obstruction of policies designed for the gradual modernization of the nation and attacks upon his essentially evolutionary approach to broadened social welfare for the urban working class. Cognizant of the fact that Brazil's urban and suburban population had grown nearly three times as fast as that of rural areas during the previous decade, Vargas was increasingly concerned with industrialization and concomitant problems of guided change rather than maintenance of the status quo.[9]

As he entered the presidency, Vargas wished to function as the manipulator of established political interests as well as mediator between these and emergent groups. Preferring to let the contending political forces, especially those associated with his administration, articulate the issues and policy alternatives, Getúlio remained the resourceful conciliator. There were abundant opportunities in 1951–1952 to play this role of the great political broker. With the urban-oriented wing of the PSD basically developmentalist, but more than balanced by the traditional liberal views of the rural-based elements of the party, and the PTB developmentalist with a leftist fringe leaning to radical nationalism, Vargas was obliged to pursue a mixed and often ambivalent policy in order to gain congressional approval of government-sponsored legislation. The UDN's predominant adherence to neoliberal policies, which in the long run cost it substantial middle sector support, and the fact that economic nationalist sentiment extended across an articulate spectrum of public opinion substantially wider than the Communist movement, or even the broader range of Marxist thought, meant that almost all policies adopted by the Vargas administration were subject to attack from both right and left.

Where the Dutra administration had tended to open the petroleum field to foreign investment, at the end of 1951 Vargas submitted a bill calling for the creation of a mixed (government and domestic private capital) corporation to explore and exploit Brazil's petroleum reserves. Thus, the military's running debate on the oil question came to center around the administration's proposal, making the Vargas policy an issue within the Armed Forces. Vargas may well have thought in terms of the 1950 Military Club election and his War Minister's attitude that a nationalistic petroleum policy would win him increased Army as well as civilian political support. In fact, it was to have the opposite effect: a victory within the arena of military politics for the opponents of radical

[9] Skidmore, *Politics in Brazil, 1930–1964*, pp. 82–100, provides a very useful discussion of the policy issues and debates of the 1951–53 period and sources for their further study.

nationalism, whose anti-Communist sentiments were aroused by the leading role assumed by the Communist Party in the "Oil Is Ours" campaign for "national economic emancipation." As would prove the case for Goulart in 1964, Vargas confused a temporary swing in military opinion with the beginning of a basic, long-term shift in orientation.

Even during this period of quite moderate and democratic behavior by Vargas, important military leaders outside the regime's power scheme (with the officers of the World War II Expeditionary Force as the movement's backbone) launched a strong campaign against its pillars, particularly War Minister Estillac Leal. The victory of the nationalist slate within the Army's "class" organization in 1950 had resulted not only from the popularity of their political views, but perhaps even more from their championing of a new promotions law and pay bill. Thus, that election was not necessarily the mandate for radical political positions that the relatively small group of ideological leftists saw in it. The May, 1950, balloting had taken place before the outbreak of the Korean War, an event that rallied the veterans of the Brazilian Expeditionary Force (FEB) to the side of the United States and gave a powerful impulse to anti-Communism among the officer corps as armed conflict in Asia dramatically reinforced "cold war" thinking insofar as an important sector of the Armed Forces was concerned.

In 1951, then, the alignment within the military, which had been relatively favorable to Vargas when petroleum policy was the line of division, shifted markedly over the question of Brazil's attitude toward the Korean conflict. This impingement of international considerations led very directly to a serious deterioration of Vargas' organized military support or *"dispositivo,"* which was built upon the leftist nationalist current within the Army.

As a result of the pressures from the sectarian leftist minority in the Military Club. War Minister and Club President Estillac Leal had found himself pushed toward radical positions, which cost him support from the less exalted nationalist elements. By the end of 1951, the anti-Estillac forces had organized to contest the upcoming elections. Among the founders of the "Democratic Crusade" (Cruzada Democrática), as the movement called itself, were such major figures of the 1964 coup and Costa e Silva regime as Lieutenant Colonel Sizeno Sarmento, Captain Mario David Andreazza, Major Edson Figueiredo, and Lieutenant Colonel João Bina Machado.[10]

In March, 1952, Vargas, under heavy pressure from the center and right, dismissed Estillac and signed a military agreement with the United States that had been fiercely opposed by the left-nationalist faction. In this changed environment the Military Club elections of May, 1952, saw Estillac Leal soundly defeated (8,288 to 4,489) by the strongly anti-Communist Crusade ticket headed by General Alcides Etchegoyen and Nélson de Mello. (Both were ex-chiefs of police of the Federal District; the latter was also a hero of the Italian campaign.) In the aftermath of this blow to the left, a series of Military-Police Inquiries (IPM's, a Brazilian form of quasi-judicial proceedings conducted by the military services) dealt severely with leftist and ultra-nationalist officers. The increasingly dominant faction within the military advocated cooperation with the United States and was highly sensitive to the freedom of action which the Communists seemed to be enjoying under Vargas.

During the latter half of 1953, a polarization if not radicalization of political life took place that was analogous to that of a decade later. A major cabinet reorganization in June saw conservatives João Neves and Horácio Lafer leave, along with centrist Labor Minister Segadas Viana. Neves was regarded as friendly to the United States and hostile to Perón. His departure, and the elevation to the cabinet of Vargas protégé João Goulart, whose admiration for Perón and his labor-oriented regime was no secret, lent substance to opposition claims that Vargas was moving in the direction of the Argentine dictator. Goulart's appointment as labor minister was depicted not as heralding a somewhat more populist policy aimed at undercutting Adhemar de Barros' presidential bid and strengthening the PTB, but as a prelude to an assault by radical forces on Brazil's social order and democratic institutions. No effort was spared by conservative interests linked to the UDN to create a climate of suspicion that would thwart Vargas' emerging strategy of a

[10] Werneck Sodré, *Memórias* . . ., pp. 386–98, covers the 1952 Military Club campaign from a perspective favorable to the Estillac Leal–Horta Barbosa slate; *O Estado de São Paulo,* for the period March to May, 1952, provides the Democratic Crusade's case.

turn to populism and nationalism as the difficulty of continued reconciliation tactics became apparent to the President.

Spearheaded by the biting press and radio attacks of UDN Congressman Carlos Lacerda and his zealous supporters, Vargas' opponents attacked the government for its alleged reopening of the labor movement to Communist penetration. While Vargas was certainly moving to strengthen the PTB's hand in the October, 1954, congressional elections and to realign his political base for the 1955 presidential succession, his opponents were seeking to impute a subversive intent to his actions. Goulart, the rancher turned champion of the urban working class, became the lighting rod attracting their attacks, a role Leonel Brizola was to play vis-à-vis Goulart a decade later.

Vargas' cultivation of labor and appeals to nationalism in the latter half of 1953, like the "independent foreign policy" of Jânio Quadros in 1961, can best be understood as an attempt to offset the unfavorable impact on the working class of a deflationary program of economic stabilization. At the same time, as part of his policy of balancing moves welcome to the right with measures popular among the left, Vargas increasingly voiced anti-imperialist sentiments and advocated statist solutions to problems of economic development.

As would be the case in the early 1960's, inflation served as the catalyst of social tensions and raised the dilemmas of financial policy which the administration had sought to avoid, making it necessary to disappoint the groups it was most seeking to court. Wage restraints and credit restrictions, essential as they might be for economic reasons, seriously undercut Vargas' efforts to build up political support among labor and the new industrialists. The cost of living in 1952 had risen 21 per cent, compared to 11 per cent for each of the preceding two years; in 1953, it threatened to go even higher. The middle class was badly squeezed by the rise in prices, while labor was demanding substantial wage increases rather than kind words and gestures. Thus, wage policy was to prove a critical factor in the collapse of Vargas' conciliatory strategy and the politics of confrontation which replaced compromise in 1954.

Vargas' problems were accentuated by the inauguration of the Eisenhower administration in the United States. Under the influence of Treasury Secretary George Humphrey and Secretary of State John

Foster Dulles, willingness to use public funds to aid Brazil's development programs was replaced by a policy of insisting that United States private investment would do the job if the Brazilian government would create a sufficiently attractive climate. The Joint United States–Brazilian Economic Development Commission, which had made a notable contribution since it began to function in mid-1951, was to be phased out of existence, with no commitment to finance the projects it had agreed were essential to Brazil's development. The new United States government did not conceal its opposition to the Petrobrás law, which established a state monopoly over petroleum exploration and exploitation, while United States private interests were vocal in condemning it as Communist-inspired. Vargas' foes were not loath to exploit this new difficulty. The President reacted by increasing the nationalistic tenor of his public pronouncements. Vargas had already extended his economic nationalism into the field of profit remittances during 1951 and 1952, when the overvaluation of the cruzeiro led foreign firms to send their profits home instead of reinvesting them in Brazil. In December, 1953, he struck back at United States investors' attacks upon the Petrobrás law by denouncing the "sabotage" of Brazil's developmental efforts by private enterprises with international affiliations. This tactic of attributing Brazil's economic troubles to external factors had substantial success in diverting resentment stemming from the economic austerity away from the Vargas administration.

This stress on nationalism, which struck a responsive chord not only among the urban working class but also with a very large proportion of the middle sectors, did not prove at the time to be the unifying force its intellectual advocates expected it to be. The identification of nationalism with basic societal as well as economic changes, caused by the very vocal role of the radical nationalists in championing the causes Vargas espoused for populist rather than revolutionary reasons, led to apprehension among many middle sector elements.

By the end of 1953, in fact, as would be the case ten years later, there was a propaganda war going on between the rightist opponents of the government and those who hoped to turn anti-foreign capital sentiment against the domestic free enterprise system. Polemics largely replaced dialogue as radicalizers of both extremes played upon class interests and the tensions and insecurity produced by the processes of modernization. In particular, the conservative propagandists strove to drive a wedge between the urban middle sectors and the working class by depicting the political rise of the latter as a threat to the former and grossly exaggerating the extent of the "Communist threat."

A situation parallel to that of 1964 arose as Finance Minister Oswaldo Aranha's efforts to implement the leaking anti-inflationary program came into direct conflict with Goulart's desire to raise the minimum wage sharply in response to labor unrest and leftist agitation.

The inadequacies of the party system were also to be a major factor in the 1954 crisis and military intervention. The UDN was not an adequate vehicle for the middle sectors, particularly those elements favoring industrialization and some degree of nationalism. Given their positive orientation toward moralism as a political value, the PSD held no significant appeal to them, and the PTB's brand of labor-oriented populism stressed class interests distinct from those of the urban middle groups. Adhemar's type of electoral populism, overlying a cynical exploitation of opportunities for graft and favoritism to economic special interests, represented the features of Brazilian politics they most disliked. In São Paulo, many of the middle sectors gained a new symbol with the election of Jânio Quadros as mayor, in March, 1953; but it would be a number of years before the dynamic young critic of the clientelistic system would emerge as a national figure. In strategically critical Rio de Janeiro, the middle class was divided between support for the developmentalist policies of Vargas and adherence to the brand of liberalism represented by the local leadership of the UDN; Carlos Lacerda emerged as a leader with whom many of them could identify, at least in their fears and uncertainties, if not in all their aspirations.

More sharply than in 1945 and very much as would be the case in 1964, the backbone of the anti-Vargas movement was an alliance of the UDN with the strongly anti-Communist wing of the Armed Forces. Lacerda had proposed, as he would again in 1955 and as would finally be done in 1964, Armed Forces' establishment of a "state of exception" in which corrupt and subversive elements would be purged from the body politic and political institutions overhauled to prevent the resurgence of another "Vargas-type" regime. While relatively few important figures within the UDN or the military were ready for such a drastic interruption of the democratic process they had restored in 1945, the seeds for a new intervention had been sown.

The victory of the Democratic Crusade in May, 1952, had been in large part a function of many of middle-of-the-road officers reacting against the leftward swing of the Club, which they saw as introducing dangerous divisions into the officer corps. The "nationalist" fringe on the left clearly represented a very small minority current in the Armed Forces. But neither did the neoliberal faction, with its militantly anti-Communist stance in many cases masking a preference for the status quo, represent majority opinion on the proper road to economic development and the socio-political modernization of Brazil. The broad centrist spectrum of the military linked to neither of the more politicized currents, reflected the same ambivalences of the civilian middle class, complicated by varying attitudes on the "constitutional" responsibilities of the Armed Forces and differential perceptions on the nature of past military interventions in the political life of the nation. Moreover, they were concerned with preserving the unity of the Armed Forces. The overwhelming majority of the officers believed that a fundamental consensus capable of supporting discipline must be preserved if the military was to retain its capacity for resolving any major political crisis. Threats to the basic institutional integrity of the Armed Forces could not be tolerated. One element within this centrist majority held that this could best be achieved by a strict adherence to legality; others were more pragmatic. ("Armed Forces" and "military" are used to mean all three services taken together.) At the beginning of 1954, the military was divided much as it would be a decade later, with attitudes on legalism partially crosscutting those on nationalism. The events of the ensuing eight months moved the Armed Forces closer to consensus on the need to exercise the "moderating power" once again, but without resolving differences on major questions of national policy, particularly in the economic and social realms. Thus, once having performed their surgical intervention, the vast bulk of the officer corps would favor leaving these matters to the interim regime headed by the Vice President.

Since most officers turned against Vargas only after the military had been drawn into the crisis by an incident in which one of their colleagues was killed, they were not highly concerned with the outcome of the elections. But the politicized minority, particularly those who had attended the National War College (Escola Superior de Guerra, ESG), was very much involved in the questions of presidential succession. The founder of the ESG, General Cordeiro de Farias, harbored political ambitions, as did his successor as commandant, Juarez Távora. The War College brought together many civilian politicians, journalists, and businessmen with officers of all three services above the rank of colonel. It was the arena for the development of a doctrine of national security that saw Brazil's future as firmly allied with the western Christian world in its confrontation with the Communist bloc. This doctrine held that the rapid emergence of a strong Brazil would best result from cooperation with foreign initiative, technology, and capital. (The ESG and its role is discussed in detail in Chapter 7.)

The military movement that was to result in Vargas' ouster and death made its first overt move in February, 1954, with the issuance of the so-called Colonels' Manifesto. In this rather curious document— which, although bordering on an ultimatum, reflected certain legalist scruples—a group of eighty-two colonels and lieutenant colonels expressed their strong dissatisfaction with the neglect of the Armed Forces' needs for modernization of equipment, their concern over labor agitation, and their disapproval of corruption in the nation's political life. (Among the signatories who were active in future military crises and remained influential after 1964 were Sizeno Sarmento, Alfredo Souto Malan, Jurandir da Bizarria Mamede, Amaury Kruel, Adhemar de Queiroz, Antônio Carlos da Silva Muricy, and Golbery do Couto e Silva.)

Vargas' nearly immediate removal of Goulart as Minister of Labor, rather than satisfying his critics, was taken as a sign of weakness calling for escalation of the offensive. Vargas responded by turning up the volume of his nationalist pronouncements, introducing a bill to create a government power complex (Electrobrás), and, on May Day, proclaiming a doubling of the minimum wage scale. This move, so similar to Goulart's decision to pull out the stops on "basic reforms" in March, 1964, was taken against the advice of Vargas' economic experts and represented a willingness to alienate important groups in order to solidify his leadership of the workers.

The Military Club elections of May, 1954, confirmed the strength of essentially anti-Vargas forces within the Army. The victors were Canrobert da Costa (War Minister under Dutra) and Juarez Távora, by a margin of roughly 7,000 to 4,000 over General Lamartine Paes Leme, who was supported by an alliance between War Minister Zenóbio da

Costa and the remnants of the "nationalist" faction. Many centrist officers had moved over to support the anti-Communists in the wake of the pro-UDN press's campaign against Vargas' alleged plots for a coup to continue in office beyond 1955. At the same time, the propaganda campaign against the Vargas regime was stepped up by the UDN. The diabolically effective "crusader" Carlos Lacerda led the attack through the pages of his daily *Tribuna da Imprensa,* as well as speaking with devastating impact from every available platform. Returning to his apartment in Copacabana from one of these sessions shortly before 1:00 a.m. on August 5, the founder of the militantly anti-Vargas "Popular Alliance against Theft and a Coup" was the object of an assassination attempt—the bungling of which by Vargas retainers would instead cost the President his life. For while Lacerda was merely wounded in the foot, his companion, Air Force Major Rubens Florentino Vaz, was killed.

Colonel João Adil de Oliveira's vigorous investigation undertaken on Air Force initiative—along with the efforts of Colonel Paulo Tôrres, newly appointed Commander of the Military Police (who replaced pro-Vargas General Morais Ancôra, in 1964 one of the few senior generals remaining loyal to Goulart to the end) and Justice Minister Tancredo Neves—soon had the culprits in hand. But since they were linked to Vargas' chief bodyguard, damage done to the President's position was irreparable. Vargas strove to ride out the storm, but his efforts to arouse popular support fell flat, as daily revelations about the 'sea of mud' surrounding the presidency alienated public opinion. War Minister Zenóbio da Costa held the Army in line, although with increasing difficulty, but the Air and Navy Ministers lost control of the situation. All attempts to find a "constitutional" road out of the crisis ran up against Vargas' unwillingness to be disgraced (and later possibly punished) and the opposition's solidifying view that any solution short of his departure from the presidency would be a temporary palliative at best. Air Force brigadiers subscribed to a statement demanding the President's resignation, and opinion in the Naval and Military Clubs moved quickly in the same direction.

Vargas avoided the humiliation of a second deposition by committing suicide on August 24. He left behind a shrewdly designed political testament that immediately transformed him from tragic failure into martyr.[11] Instead of mass demonstrations against his regime, the country was swept by a series of attacks on Vargas' enemies and against such symbols of United States imperialism as the American consulates in several cities.

Although Vargas was dead and most of his close associates pushed out of the center of the political arena, the tension between pro-Vargas, and anti-Vargas forces continued to dominate the political scene. The Café Filho administration, composed of a mixture of nearly all the non-Vargas forces, including the Dutra wing of the PSD, assumed a caretaker role in keeping with the fact that the country was already in the advanced stages of campaigning for the October, 1954, legislative and gubernatorial elections, with the presidential balloting little more than a year away.

The outcome of the elections of October 3, 1954, held only 40 days after Vargas' death and, as Café proudly stressed, without a state of siege having been imposed in the interim, was a relative stand-off between the heirs and the foes of Vargas. The presidential elections a year later gave a slight plurality to Kubitschek and Goulart running on a PSD-PTB coalition ticket, with the former receiving nearly 470,000 votes more than the UDN's Juarez Távora, and Labor Party national chairman Goulart edging Milton Campos for the vice presidency by less than half that margin. On November 8, the military ministers were informed of Café Filho's proposal (allegedly made on his doctor's advice) to turn the presidential office over temporarily to Carlos da Coimbra Luz, who as presiding officer of the Chamber of Deputies was first in the constitutional line of succession. The ties of the new Acting President to the coup-minded officers and their UDN allies were widely believed to be quite close if not truly intimate. Whatever mistrust the supporters of the victorious candidates harbored with regard to the intentions of Café Filho—who consistently guaranteed that they would be inaugurated if confirmed by the electoral courts—their suspicions of the new Acting President were far greater. Many doubted that Café was really ill and saw his hospitalization as a move to clear the decks for those articulating a coup. While War Minister Henrique Teixeira Lott

---

[11] For an insightful analysis by one of his young technical advisors, see "O Legado Político de Vargas," *Cadernos do Nosso Tempo,* No. 3 (January-March, 1955), pp. 44–56.

debated with himself whether or not to turn over the War Ministry to the individual chosen by Luz to replace him, General Odylio Denys, Commander of the Eastern Military Zone (the present-day First Army), organized a powerful military scheme to thwart the Acting President. Only in the pre-dawn hours of November 11 was Lott informed of their plans and invited to join as the movement's titular leader. With his acceptance, the troop movements began, and by morning the capital was securely in their hands. The PSD presiding officer of the Senate was sworn in over UDN protests as the new chief executive, with Café Filho barred by force from reassuming the presidency.

Since no documentary proof was ever presented of plans to mount a coup to keep Kubitschek and Goulart from office—as distinct from a strong desire to do so on the part of Lacerda and some junior officers— the "preventive coup" was to persist as a bone of contention within the military as well as in the broader political arena. Lott and his associates, who considered themselves to have acted to preserve legality, were denounced as having engineered an unjustified coup. In the 1960 presidential campaign, for example, Lott's sponsorship of the "movement to return to existing constitutional means" was criticized as a cover for a naked power grab. The question of "legality" in this episode was never to be clear, but rather to remain highly ambiguous in succeeding crises as assertion continued to take the place of demonstration. While the "August 24" and "November 11" groups in the military (named after the dates of Vargas' ouster and Lott's coup) would be numerically far inferior to the centrist majority, in periods of political polarization the latter would tend to do nothing, leaving the initiative to the more militant minorities.

The policies of the Kubitschek administration (1956–1961) were, in their general outlines, a continuation of those initiated by Vargas, under whom both Kukitschek and Goulart had served their political apprenticeships. In the domestic field, the policies were directed primarily toward accelerated economic developments, with control of the exploitation of natural resources retained in Brazilian hands. Only secondarily were they concerned with improved social welfare programs for the workers, restricted almost exclusively to urban areas. Kubitschek's foreign policy was largely conditioned by Brazil's developmental needs and the changing hemispheric situation. Operation Pan American (Operacão Pan

Americana, OPA), which grew out of an exchange of letters between Presidents Kubitschek and Eisenhower in May and June, 1958, proposed a joint crusade against underdevelopment in the Western Hemisphere. If it did not give rise to new strains and misunderstandings in United States-Brazilian relations, it did at least accentuate and bring into the open existing ones, owing to the manifold difficulties during 1959 in reaching agreement on the form and substance of the new hemispheric policy that was the chief precursor of the Alliance for Progress.

Following the October, 1958, congressional and gubernatorial elections, in which the strength of the various parties in Congress remained relatively unchanged, the Kubitschek administration entered a two-year period distinguished by very marked progress toward fulfillment of its elaborate economic development-oriented "program of goals." This was accompanied, however, by an accelerated rise in the cost of living, increasing evidences of social unrest, chronic financial difficulties, and intensified activity on the international front. Looming ever larger in the background during 1959 and 1960 was the question of presidential succession, particularly acute since under the 1946 Constitution Kubitschek was not eligible for a second term.

In many fields, Kubitschek did give Brazil the "fifty years progress in five" he had promised in his campaign. But his concentration on infrastructural growth, to the detriment of social development and the country's financial solvency, contributed to a growing feeling that it was time for a change. Thus, although Kubitschek continued to enjoy tremendous personal popularity, the Brazilian voters on October 3, 1960, gave a landslide victory to the UDN-backed opposition candidate, Jânio da Silva Quadros, a highly individualistic populist who had correctly diagnosed the mood of the Brazilian electorate. By contrast, the government candidate, Marshal Lott, the sixty-five-year-old career officer who had served as Kubitschek's War Minister, proved an uninspiring campaigner. Thus, for the third time in a row (Gomes in 1950, Juarez Távora in 1955, and now Lott) a military man was defeated by a civilian. Indeed, the only time since 1910 that a military candidate had been elected president was Dutra's defeat of a brother officer in 1945. The Armed Forces, however, were not solidly behind Lott's presidential bid. A significant portion of the military, who had subscribed to General

Juarez Távora's condemnation of the "corrupt" political class during his 1955 campaign, were drawn to Quadros, the "new broom" candidate who promised to be a moralizing force. Others, who could not forget Lott's role in blocking their 1955 efforts to keep Vargas' heirs from returning to power, supported Quadros as a means of denying Lott the presidency. Then, too, the conservatives and neoliberals of the anti-Communist wing within the Armed Forces supported Quadros as the UDN's candidate.

Quadros realized when he took office in January, 1961, that he could not win legislative support from a Congress in which he had only minority political backing. Hence he tried to effect his programs by using his considerable executive powers, appealing for support directly from the majority public that had elected him. Viewed by many as a miracle worker if not a political messiah, Quadros pledged himself to sweep out the corruption and inefficiency of three decades of the Vargas succession while setting Brazil's financial and administrative house in order, maintaining the momentum of its development, and remembering the "little people," whose interests had been largely neglected by Kubitschek's emphasis on infrastructural growth rather than social development. This was a tall order indeed, but, paradoxically, one which the new confidence engendered by Kubitschek led many Brazilians to believe was attainable, given the leadership and inspiration of a providential man. The disappointment if not betrayal of these hopes was to deepen the crisis of the 1962–1964 period and contribute to a radicalization as some sought in a leftist program and ideology the remaking of institutions and practices which the populist leader failed to deliver. Quadros did, however, implement exchange reforms, decree a sounder coffee policy, mount an attack on corruption and contraband, and reduce the costs of running the government machinery.

In both the administrative field and in foreign affairs—where the neutralistic implications of his avowedly "independent" foreign policy alienated many moderates as well as conservatives—Quadros overplayed his hand in his impatience to reshape the country. In August, 1961, Carlos Lacerda, considered by many as Quadros' "great elector" (owing to his role in obtaining UDN support for the political maverick), denounced the President for allegedly planning to place Congress in permanent recess and assume dictatorial powers. On August 25, partially in discouragement but chiefly in an ill-considered effort to gain a free hand, Quadros offered his resignation to the Congress—after only seven months in office. He blamed "terrible" domestic and foreign pressures for his drastic action, much in the style of Vargas' political testament. If Quadros had expected to be recalled to power following a wave of popular demonstrations, he was disappointed; the nation's reaction was one of stunned disbelief followed by disillusionment. The Armed Forces spurned Quadros' suggestion that they constitute a junta and instead oversaw the swearing in of Chamber of Deputies president Ranieri Mazzilli as acting chief executive as provided for in the Constitution.

Quadros' resignation caught Vice President Goulart on a trip to Communist China upon which Quadros had sent him. Top military commanders, including all three service ministers and the Chairman of the Joint Chiefs of Staff, were unwilling to see the Vargas succession back in power so soon, and placed pressure on Congress to disqualify Goulart from taking office. In this effort they stressed his alleged Communist sympathies and dug up the old charges of involvement with Perón. In light of the development of a strong "legalist" movement led by Rio Grande do Sul Governor Leonel Brizola (Goulart's brother-in-law) and eventually backed by ex-President Kubitschek, the country appeared close to civil war before the crisis was resolved in a typically Brazilian manner by the adoption of a modified parliamentary form of government in which presidential powers were significantly circumscribed. Yet the limits of such ingenious solutions were rapidly being reached; future crises were not all to be resolved by such quasi-legal institutional compromises.

CHAPTER THREE

⌒⋙⌒

The Breakdown of a Semi-pluralist System

JOÃO "JANGO" GOULART came to power in September, 1961, in a situation remarkably parallel to that which had confronted Getúlio Vargas when he took office as president little more than ten years earlier. As in 1951, the new chief executive was a highly controversial figure whose accession to the presidency was strongly opposed by significant elements of the Armed Forces and whose past record led to substantial suspicion on the part of center-conservative political elements. Goulart also took office after a period in which the Vargas succession had been temporarily interrupted by an administration generally hostile to the PTB—and although the Quadros regime was short lived, it undertook more measures to shake up the system in the seven months of its existence than Dutra's government had in its longer tenure. Moreover, "Jango" lacked the enthusiastic popular support and electoral mandate that had conferred legitimacy upon Getúlio's return as President.

Although its indices of economic development and social mobility were higher in 1961 than a decade before. Brazil remained essentially the same as far as problems of governing were concerned. Enhanced capabilities stemming from the expansion of the bureaucratic apparatus during the Kubitschek period were offset by the greatly increased demands unleashed concomitantly. Industrialization and urbanization had progressed apace, but the entrepreneurial and bureaucratic groups, in conjunction with the professional politicians, continued to seek to manipulate the system in much the same manner as they had previously, while the middle sectors were as ambivalent and far from united as before. Furthermore, the accelerated rate of inflation and declining pace of economic growth (which began a decline in 1961 which was to reach stagnation by 1963) catalyzed social tensions in such a manner as to offset the material progress of the 1950's insofar as want satisfaction was a determinant of political attitudes or action.

In the political realm, populism rather than ideologically based reform movements or class-oriented parties was still the dominant "new" urban style, interacting with the traditional clientilistic system. The weaknesses of the party structure had been made painfully evident by Quadros' triumph over the PSD-PTB coalition, and his strategy of paying little attention to them in the governance of the nation until they were fundamentally reformed. His diagnosis of their shortcomings as vehicles for political modernization was essentially the same as that made a decade earlier by students of this problem:

One must strengthen the political parties assuring them of a greater voice in the life of the nation and reciprocally imposing upon them greater responsibilities . . . disciplining them through party conventions; assuring them of an independent fiscal life while supervising their finances so that they do not become bound to economic groups nor influenced by the abuse of propaganda or vested interests.[1]

To at least the same degree that Vargas was hampered in 1951 by the need to operate within a new and, for him, strange and uncomfortable constitutional system, Goulart was forced to cope with an untried institutional arrangement alien to his concept of the presidency. His desire to return to the previous arrangement (which basically matched Vargas' tendency to resort as much as possible to his old political style and Estado Nôvo practices) was a major factor in the "unworkability" of the hybrid system. Yet even the Congress was essentially presidentialist at heart and unable to adapt rapidly to the requisite legislative behavior patterns for a viable parliamentary system. Even with a cooperative Prime Minister like Tancredo Neves, who believed in avoiding a

[1] Jânio Quadros, *Mensagem ao Congreso Nacional* (Brasília, 1961), pp. 82–83.

confrontation with the President over their respective powers and authority, there was little prospect of overcoming the fact that the chief of state in a parliamentary form of government must be a symbol of unity, not the country's most controversial political leader.

The sequence and process of political developments in the 1961–1964 period was essentially the same as a decade earlier. The President began with a program designed to unify the divided nation and win the support of the broadest possible coalition of political groups. By 1963, the deteriorating economic situation rendered such tactics no longer feasible. A political polarization, already fed by what had become an executive strategy of making simultaneous paired concessions to opposition from both the left and right, called for a definition of the President's orientation. Constraints imposed by the exigencies of the international economic system led to formulation of a stabilization program, with an easing of the country's pressing foreign payments problem being granted in return for a pledge of anti-inflationary measures at home. In order to maintain some position of political strength. Goulart (like Vargas before him) adopted a reformist and nationalist stance to satisfy his PTB's basic constituency, the working class, and offset the effects of the economic austerity measures. Nonetheless, in the face of clear signs of loss of popular support, combined with a more aggressive attitude on the part of its opponents, the regime found itself in a situation it perceived as untenable.

During the year 1963 in Brazil everyone conspired. Civilians and the military, *udenistas, petebistas,* workers and peasants, all joined in small groups, without schedule and disgused or not. And no one thought of sustaining the legal government; on the contrary, everyone declared themselves disposed to take power, in spite of not knowing how to do it or what to do with it afterwards. There was not a conspiracy. It was a plateful of little conspiracies. . . .[2]

When the chips were down, Goulart and Vargas both opted for retaining and reinforcing their support from the left. The active rôle of the Communists in the organizations toward which the government turned afforded the intransigent opposition an opportunity to unleash a propaganda assault, or counterattack, on the aggressive "revolutionary"

[2] Leoncio Basbaum, *História Sincera da República,* Vol. IV (Rio de Janeiro, 1968), p. 41.

forces. This domestic cold war was fed by conflict over a crucial policy issue, in Vargas' time Petrobrás, in 1963–1964 the extension of economic nationalism to embrace foreign-owned public utilities and many concessions. Remittance of profits legislation took on symbolic significance in both situations. Moreover, in the latter case the polarizing issue of agrarian reform gave added impetus to the radicalization from whence the final crisis sprang. The higher degree of organization, broader extent of participation, and greater mobilization in 1964 only ensured that the confrontation would be massive rather than restrained.

In this context, the October, 1963, censure of War Minister Jair Dantas Ribeiro by Army Chief of Staff Castelo Branco was as unmistakable a sign of the political crisis moving toward military intervention as was the "Colonels' Memorial" of February, 1954. Indeed, the mid-1963 military discontent over the pay raise issue combined in an almost identical manner with security and subversion considerations as had been the operative pattern in 1954. Thus, in the similarly structured situation, all that was needed by March, 1964, to precipitate a move to oust the government was an issue involving the institutional interests, discipline, and pride of the Armed Forces functionally equivalent to the death of Major Vaz in August, 1954. This they would encounter in an act of naval insubordination.

1. THE GOULART REGIME AND THE COLLAPSE OF CONCILIATION

The year following the inauguration of Goulart was essentially one of increasing conflict between Congress and the President over Goulart's efforts to prove the new hybrid system unworkable and to engineer a return to presidentialism. Although the Brazilian gift for compromise brought the country through several serious crises, the very steep price was the neglect of economic and social problems and a deepening mistrust and suspicion. This was aggravated by a polarizing legislative election campaign in which the clash between right and left was greatly intensified. During the period from September, 1961, to the elections of October 7, 1962, Brazil was governed by a series of cabinets. The first of these possessed an extremely broad base, but it was followed by two abortive efforts to form a government and then by two cabinets that could barely survive, much less gain congressional approval for a coherent program. In each case, however, the Prime Minister (President of the Council of Ministers) made no effort to contest with the President for executive power. Indeed, the Prime Minister functioned more as an ally of the President in his struggle with the Congress.[3]

Contrary to widely held views of the period, which tend to emphasize the hostility of the officers who later led the 1964 revolution, the Armed Forces were on balance one of Goulart's most effective allies in his 1962 campaign of pressure on the legislature and the subsequent destruction of the parliamentary regime. In addition to appeals to nationalism, constitutionalism, and "legality," the President made generally skillful use of selective promotions, intelligent assignment policies, wide expansion of personal and social contacts with the military, and sponsorship of measures to improve their rather precarious economic position. Most important, during this first year and a half in office he scrupulously avoided conflicts or policy clashes in which the Armed Forces could find their institutional interests jeopardized. Goulart's quite remarkable success in dealing with the military during his initial eighteen months as President involved a good deal of moderation and restraint on his part, and this would prove much more difficult after the restoration of his full presidential powers. Beyond that juncture, he could not so easily focus the military's anti-politician feelings on a recalcitrant legislature. For the Congress elected in October, 1962, possessed a recent popular mandate, while Goulart was no longer able to trade upon his "victimization" in September, 1961, but was required to make good on his promises of performance as President.

The third quarter of 1962 was marked by a series of monthly political crises punctuating a hotly contested congressional and gubernatorial election campaign. At the end of June, the President seized upon the resignation of the ten-month-old Tancredo Neves cabinet, necessary so that the ministers would be eligible to run for office in October, to attempt to strengthen his hand and the position of his party. The Chamber of Deputies overwhelmingly rejected his nomination of PTB ideologue San Thiago Dantas for Prime Minister. But, disturbed by an attempted general strike accompanied by a food riot, and anxious to return to the campaign trail in mid-July, it reluctantly approved Francisco Brochado da Rocha, a provincial jurist and personal instrument

[3] The rationale for the position assumed by Tancredo Neves can be found in his *O Regime Parlamentar e a Realidade Brasileira* (Belo Horizonte, 1962).

of Goulart with no significant political experience. A month later there was a new crisis, which was settled by an agreement to fix a date for a plebiscite on the question of presidentialism versus parliamentarianism. Between September 10 and 15, the country appeared near the brink of civil strife or a serious rupture of constitutional order, but the Brazilian genius for political compromise came through once again, with ex-President Kubitschek as its chief agent. The executive-legislative impasse was broken by agreement to hold a referendum on January 6, 1963.

After the inconclusive but bitterly contested October elections and the overwhelming vote for presidentialism in the January, 1963, plebiscite, the Parliamentary amendment of September, 1961, was revoked, and Goulart appointed a center-left presidential cabinet led by San Thiago Dantas as Finance Minister and ex-Premier Hermes Lima as Foreign Minister.

The keystone of Goulart's experiment with conciliation in the early months of 1963 was the Three-Year Plan of Economic and Social Development, drawn up after the elections by Planning Minister Celso Furtado and unveiled on December 31 in a move intended to reinforce Goulart's efforts to appear as a responsible and development-oriented leader on the eve of the plebiscite on his presidential powers.[4] Stabilization and development were to be achieved at the same time, together with administrative, banking, tax and agrarian reforms. Rather than an economic plan in the strict sense of the word, this was a statement of government policy objectives. As such, it was more nearly a mix of Kubitschek and Quadros administration aims than a markedly nationalist or socializing program. Indeed, it called for increased foreign investment and was designed in large part with a view toward impressing the United States government with the seriousness of Goulart's intention to pursue Alliance for Progress goals and fulfill Brazil's international financial obligations.

Goulart's commitment to the Three-Year Plan was based on po-

[4] The definitive version of this bulky document is the *Plano Trienal do Desenvolvimento Econômico e Social, 1963–1965: Síntese* (Rio de Janeiro, 1962); the most sharply focused evaluation of the hastily drafted study is contained in a special issue of the *Revista Brasileira de Econômia* (December, 1962). Consult also Robert T. Daland, *Brazilian Planning* (Chapel Hill, 1967), pp. 55–67 and 146–181 for a knowledgeable and detailed analysis of the plan and its political function.

litical convenience more than conviction, and was to crumble with subsequent change in the considerations uppermost in the President's political
calculations. Indeed, the most dramatic development of 1963 was the
growth and increasing assertiveness of the radical left, as manifested
through a variety of political, labor, and student groups. All of these
elements had close ties to Brizola, and in the struggle between the conciliatory and radical advisors of Goulart they threw their full support to
the latter while denouncing and undermining the efforts of the former.
San Thiago Dantas, his intellectual accomplishments and above average
political acumen notwithstanding, was to prove unable to exert effective
leadership over populist political forces. Both Dantas and Furtado lacked
a strong political base and were not sufficiently adept at manipulating
politicians within the Brazilian system to prevail over the more radical
forces.

If the effort to resume a high and sustained pace of development
while achieving financial stability was not in itself unattainable, the
Three-Year Plan centered on the simultaneous undertaking of "basic
reforms," the definition and formulation of which were to entail more
battling than bargaining, within the regime as well as between the government and its conservatively oriented opposition. The best chance for
enactment of the reforms lay in the formation of a coalition of political
interests that would support compromise measures for differing reasons.
Thus, land reform was advocated on economic grounds as a necessary
modernization of an outmoded system of land tenure that blocked increased agricultural production, a view that had some appeal for urban
consumers highly concerned with food shortages and high prices. It was
also put forward as a means for incorporating into the national money
economy the marginal rural populations that currently lacked any significant purchasing power, a line of reasoning in which both industrialists
and industrial workers could find some merit. These developmental arguments for structural reforms struck a responsive chord among centrist
elements, while justification on the grounds of social justice appealed to
the progressive groups.

Extremists of both the left and the right, however, were more concerned with the power implications of the government's proposed "basic
reforms." The radical reformers viewed the moderate measures as inadequate or designed as palliatives to tranquilize the revolutionary im-

pulses of the Brazilian people, while the reactionaries saw them as dangerous entering wedges for drastic changes that would upset the social order and shift political power perilously far to the left. Hence the acerbic polemic of the 1962 election campaign persisted into the following year. The opposition continued to portray the President as essentially in agreement with Brizola and the other PTB radicals supporting "Communistic" measures, while these elements strove to pull Goulart to the left and to transform his administration into a truly "nationalist and popular" regime. Moreover, division of centrist elements as a result of traditional partisan disputes going back to the Estado Nôvo, hardened in the series of crises since 1954 and reinforced by the bitterness of the 1962 political battles, severely handicapped or even hamstrung efforts at conciliation. Then, too, competing political ambitions, including the rival presidential aspirations of key figures within the UDN and PTB in particular, impeded cooperation in support of a program of economic development and moderate reforms.

Formidable radicalizing forces existed on both the left and the right. Within the UDN Carlos Lacerda, his prestige once again on the upswing following defeat of his candidates in Guanabara during the October, 1962, balloting, headed the intransigent faction of the party, a group as convinced of the necessity of Goulart's overthrow as they had been a decade earlier with regard to Vargas. Following his selection as the party's presidential candidate in April, Lacerda once again embarked on a crusade against Goulart and the other heirs of the "corrupt and subversive" Vargas machine.

Within the PTB, the power struggle turned increasingly in favor of the radical wing, and these elements moved steadily toward complete repudiation of the existing institutional structure of the established economic and political order. Goulart had seen the Three-Year Plan as an opportunity to gain centrist support for his program. To the extent that his hopes in this direction were disappointed, his support for the Plan was diminished. With his long-time base of support, organized labor, strongly against the Dantas and Furtado engineered Plan, the President swung to the left, as he had a year earlier, and sacrificed the two ministers to preserve his political position.

In mid-June, yielding to pressure from the left and having decided against trying to implement the stabilization program negotiated by

Dantas with the United States, Goulart reorganized his cabinet, dropping not only the targets of Brizola's attacks but also members of the radical left, such as Labor Minister Almino Afonso, who had appeared to pursue policies not fully in accord with presidential desires. Frustrated by the dashing of his high hopes, Goulart felt that time was ripe to realign both his political and military support, preparatory to a shift to the left without completely abandoning efforts to conciliate centrist groups.

At the same time, however, the opposition had decided to adopt a more intransigent line. In a speech delivered on June 25, and following on the heels of the announcement of the new cabinet, UDN president Bilac Pinto charged on the floor of Congress that Goulart was preparing a *golpe de estado* and reiterated that the country could no longer tolerate the existing state of affairs. During the third quarter of 1963, prices soared to record highs, investment continued to drop, drastic food shortages occurred, noncommissioned officers of the air force and navy mutinied in Brasília, and the number of politically motivated strikes increased. An ill-considered plan to intervene in Guanabara state to remove Governor Carlos Lacerda, an abortive plot to kidnap Lacerda, an ill-considered request for the proclamation of a state of seige, and the resignation of the most respected moderate in the cabinet helped crystallize opposition to the Goulart regime.

By this time, distrust of the government and concern with its alleged undermining of discipline and political exploitation of the grievances and aspirations of the noncommissioned officers reached from the Armed Forces high command to the captains and lieutenants in most immediate contact with the troops. In April, the military's secret services had undertaken a serious study of the problem that led to a confidential report the following month. Alarmed by its conclusions, some officers joined the anti-regime conspirators; many others began to concentrate on strengthening the discipline and morale of their units. They also grew increasingly resentful of those leftist officers who appeared to be fostering insubordination and, since the latter had close ties to Goulart, of the President himself. It appears that organization of the sergeants was counted upon by presidential advisers as an important piece in the Goulart regime's "sandwich" *dispositivo,* which combined a relatively small number of senior officers in the top command positions with strong support from the warrant officers and noncoms. But as events proved, this tactic cost the regime the support of a large proportion of the legalist-centrist majority segment of the officer corps upon which in the ultimate analysis its security really rested, while few sergeants made any significant contribution to the defense of the government when the final crisis came. Moreover, to the politicized currents on the left and right, as well as to the democratic and legality-oriented centrist groups, Goulart's actions smacked too much of the maneuvering preparatory to Vargas' continuist coup of 1937. Not only did Goulart overestimate the influence of his military backers, but he also failed to realize that a perceived threat to the institutional interests of the Armed Forces could override the constitutionalist scruples of the generally non-political middle mass of the officer corps. In their eyes, if Goulart was systematically undercutting discipline and harboring designs to prolong his stay in office, then he constituted the threat to legal institutions and forfeited their support.

Exhilarated by their defeat of the conciliatory policies of Dantas' "positive left," the radical reformers and revolutionaries felt increasingly certain that the established elite had lost control of the situation and that their day was already dawning. Just as in the 1961 crisis they credited the triumph of legalism to their own efforts rather than to divisions within the military and the generally legalist attitude of its numerically preponderant center elements, the leftist groups by the end of 1963 felt that they had brought the President around to a more radical stand. In the eyes of its often self-proclaimed leaders, the coalition of workers, peasants, students, and nationalist military was making great progress during late 1963 and the opening months of 1964. Student-sponsored Popular Culture and Basic Education Movements, given their emphasis on literacy campaigns with a political content, would over time offset the established center-conservative groups' control of the mass media and educational system and add large numbers of newly participant citizens to the ranks of those clamoring for structural changes. Continued organization of the rural workers and agitation for agrarian reform would also over time work against the dominance of the economic and social elite and the established class of clientelistic politicians. With the active encouragement of the government, as Goulart's increasingly leftist stance promised, these changes would come about sooner rather than later, a prospect that deeply disturbed many moderate UDN and PSD elements as well as those intransigently opposed to Goulart and the whole process of reform and agitation.

Within the PTB, Goulart as President represented a center position rather than one championing the interests of the radical wing. His brand of patronage-oriented, rather paternalistic populism was largely devoid of ideological content, and until he became President, Goulart had made life within the PTB uncomfortable for reformers who wished to give the party a coherent programmatic orientation. A true disciple of Vargas in this respect, Goulart felt uncomfortable without room to maneuver and generally felt most at ease in a relatively fluid bargaining situation where he could play off competing interests and follow a some-what zigzag course toward his objectives. Often viewed as a weak personality for a major political leader, he was not prone to run risks for abstruse principles or causes in which he had no great stake. A shrewd political manipulator with no great vision and prone to look for the path of least resistance, Goulart was not, however, lacking ambitions that transcended the mere holding of office and exercising of power. He did not wish to go down in history as a weak and indecisive man, unable to deal effectively with the problems of Brazil. He was not disposed either to become a powerless tool of the established commercial, industrial, and agricultural groups or to be upstaged and superseded by a more authentic and popular figure on the left, even if it should be his own brother-in-law. Once he had been successful in regaining full presidential powers (perhaps his most noteworthy accomplishment), Goulart's indecisiveness was most clearly reflected in his uncertainty over what road to follow in seeking to make his mark as a worthy successor to Vargas. His irresoluteness stemmed from a lack of training in dealing with technical problems and a lack of patience in studying complex matters.

The controversy over Goulart's position on the political spectrum, or supposed ideological orientation, has tended to draw attention away from considerations that may have had greater operational significance. Thus, for example, Goulart's attitude toward and treatment of governors quite clearly reflected the fact that he had never been a governor, or for that matter a state official of any kind, a most unusual situation for a man in his position and a further indication of the degree to which he was manufactured by Vargas as an instant national political figure. That

Goulart had also never been a legislator, could be discerned in his unsuccessful dealings with Congress, where at times his own party contributed to his difficulties.

This hop-step-and-jump career—straight from the ranch to the
cabinet, then on to the vice presidency, and accidental accession to
power—was all too apparent in his relations with the military. After
achieving full presidential authority, Goulart dealt with them in substantially the same manner as he did with labor leaders, apparently ex-
pecting that they would respond as had most union careerists grateful
for their positions of prestige and perquisites. He failed to see that in the
Armed Forces generals felt that the top posts were theirs as a matter of
equity, with promotion reflecting merit and seniority within the military
institution. They would therefore not be especially grateful to the President for formally conferring on them advancement they had earned
through their professional efforts. Although a few colonels who had
been advanced to brigadier by "Jango" over the expectations of their
peers did feel some personal loyalty to him, all but a handful of general
officers saw promotions as ratification of their achievements. On the
other hand, they believed that absence of advancement indicated a lack
of presidential confidence, and a number came to harbor a resentment
for which they found an outlet in conspiracy. In sum, there is considerable justification for terming Goulart a second-rate Vargas and erstaz
Perón, both of whom understood military values and mentality much
better than did the young rancher turned leader of a labor movement
and head of a political party by the will of his mentor rather than his
own efforts. At least this characterization has the virtue of turning the
spotlight on some of "Jango's" major contradictions.

By the end of 1963, the tone and style of the Goulart regime's
public face, if not yet the basic content and direction of its policies, were
being set by those elements dedicated to a new brand of politics with a
much higher ideological content and emphasis on fostering mass organizations that would provide the basis for drastic shifts in the distri-
bution of political power. Much as the Communists and domestic fascists
(Integralists) had misjudged the pace of change in the mid-1930's, these
leftist groups overestimated the impact of their efforts; this time, however, they carried Goulart along with them, whereas Vargas had used
their earlier counterparts in paving the way for his Estado Nôvo. (It is

true that in 1935–1938 there was no Cuba to provide inspiration and assistance to radical organizations within the Hemisphere.)

The radical left of the Goulart period included not only dissident Communists but also the Acão Popular (AP) youth elements who had developed from their original Catholic base into fervent revolutionaries; minority elements within the clergy, many of whom sponsored AP, also were associated with the government-supported efforts at adult literacy training and political socialization (Movimento da Educação de Base, or MEB). Militant albeit often romantic revolutionaries, the Apistas represented the vanguard of Brazil's socially conscious youth as they sought release from the doctrinal fetters of the Church-oriented Catholic University Action (JUC). In view of the crucial role of the militant youth in the radicalization of 1964, and their subsequent re-emergence in the late 1960's as the backbone of opposition to the emerging authoritarian military regime, an examination of their orientation and actions is necessary before the chronological account of system breakdown can be pursued into its final stage in early 1964.

As in many developing nations, intellectuals and students in Brazil have generally possessed political influence grossly disproportionate to their relatively restricted numbers. Heavily entrenched in the bureaucracy, mass media, and educational institutions, they also act directly through political parties and vociferous protests ranging up to mob action. Concentrated in the cities, they have exercised a considerable degree of political leadership over restless labor elements. The intense nationalism of intellectuals and students tends to be highly tinged with anti-Americanism. More acutely conscious than other groups of the country's ills, they have often turned to Marxism in their search for rapid solutions, and the Communists have been quite successful in penetrating the organized elements of these sectors. The impact of this was heavily felt in the early 1960's (and will continue to be experienced as yesterday's student politicians take their place among the policy-makers of the 1970's).

Student political activity is conditioned not only by their view of the historical role of the *estudante,* but also by public acceptance of "the student tradition," a pattern of student behavior that has affected the political and social life of the nation. Students are frequently held up as champions of freedom, reform, and nationalism—a fact that reinforces their high self-appreciation of their worth and capabilities. In reality, effective student participation in politics has taken place intermittently.[5]

The country's university students overwhelmingly supported the 1930 Revolution but were soon alienated by Vargas' dictatorial turn. The National Union of Students (UNE), created in 1937 as the organ for student participation in the semi-corporative structure of the Estado Nôvo, became a focus of demands for a restoration of democracy. After 1946, university students came to adopt increasingly progressive stands on national issues, at least as reflected in the UNE and the "Academic Centers" of each faculty. Since the legal parties afforded no clear-cut political alternatives or apparent potential as vehicles for reform of the traditional socio-economic order, the student movement developed along fundamentally nonpartisan lines, with few ties to established party politicians. Increasingly aware of the availability of several models, the university students enthusiastically joined in the quest for a definition of Brazilian "reality" and "Brazilian solutions" to national problems. The students had come to

consider themselves the educated elite who had the responsibility to act *on behalf of* (and later on—*with*) the rest of the population to change the social, economic, and political structure of the nation; for such action, in their minds and in the minds of other Brazilians, was the traditional role of the student in Brazilian society. In opting for radical changes within the system, the students would consider themselves as modern-day abolitionists, republicans, and democrats in the best Brazilian tradition of their predecessors.[6]

The University and secondary students came to constitute a major sector of the nationalist movement in the late 1950's and during the Goulart regime. As one of the few groups organized on a nationwide basis, the more than 110,000 university students became an important political force, and their influence increased concomitantly with the rise of nationalism. Although less well organized and less politically oriented, the more than 1 million secondary students in the country also repre-

[5] The most useful analysis of the Brazilian student movement's role in the political system is Robert Myhr, "Brazil," in Donald K. Emmerson (ed.), *Students and Politics in Developing Nations* (New York, 1968), pp. 249–85. See also his "Nationalism in the Brazilian Student Movement," *Inter-American Economic Affairs,* XXII, No. 4 (Spring, 1969), 81–94.

[6] Robert Myhr, "The Political Role of University Students in Brazil" (Doctoral dissertation, Department of Political Science, Columbia University, 1968), p. 36.

sented a significant factor. Many students appeared to find in nationalism both a philosophy that corresponded to their basic dissatisfaction with their social and economic position and an outlet for their youthful exuberance. Characterized by emotionalism, intellectual idealism, and restless energy, the students proved susceptible to manipulation by individuals and groups having a vested interest in the adoption of radical and nationalistic solutions to the country's problems. Radical nationalism became the fashion, and for reasons of prestige and ambition as well as conviction, most student leaders followed the line. By the latter stages of the Goulart regime, student leaders came to feel that they were an important part of a powerful "popular" force being welded together out of the workers, progressive politicians, and nationalist military to put over a program of "basic reforms" in the face of intransigent opposition from outdated, but strongly entrenched, reactionary elements. If this feeling that mass mobilization and ideological politics were just around the corner, or perhaps already arrived, caused euphoria on the left, there was another side to the picture not so clearly perceived. Increased political participation, pushed steadily by growing social mobilization, easily outran the very modest gains in the institutional sphere. Although some structural differentiation took place during the 1950's and early 1960's, the development of specialized interest aggregation structures was very limited. Raw, largely unaggregated demands overloaded the decision-making processes at the same time as the system's supports were decreasing, while mechanisms for conflict avoidance and control proved ineffective in the face of changes in the goals and tactics of key groups. This was particularly salient in the case of urban labor, where a new breed of radical nationalist leaders enjoyed considerable success in elbowing aside many of Goulart's highly manipulable *pelegos* (government imposed union leaders) during the early 1960's. By mid-1963 their ability to translate control over strikes into effective power to extract significant concessions from the President injected a fundamentally new factor into the policy-making equations.[7]

[7] Professor Kenneth Erickson of the State University of New York at Stony Brook, in a dissertation, "Labor in the Political Process in Brazil," written under my direction and defended in January, 1970, analyzes in detail "the role of the labor leaders when many of them ceased being instruments of the government and began to act autonomously, using the power which they accumulated through their posts in the para-governmental structures to exact satisfaction of their demands from the governmental leaders."

As for the position of major political leaders, it was still largely determined by their presidential ambitions, even as the crisis deepened. While Adhemar de Barros, whose electoral prospects were not very strong, had opted for revolution, other major contenders were justifiably afraid that a coup would upset the electoral timetable and introduce changes in the rules of the game that could adversely affect their personal prospects. Kubitschek was trying strenuously to hold together the traditional PSD-PTB alliance by pulling Goulart toward moderation and urging his congressional followers to be more receptive to the President's pleas for basic reforms. Lacerda was torn between his virulent opposition to Goulart and his desire not to jeopardize his electoral possibilities. Clearly in most direct opposition to everything for which Goulart stood, Lacerda's presidential bid gained strength among the center and even some moderate left voters as the Goulart regime failed to deal effectively with the nation's pressing problems and as the possibility of a radical PTB candidate loomed larger. Minas Gerais Governor José de Magalhães Pinto, on the other hand, was losing ground within the UDN to Lacerda and sought a base as a conciliation candidate acceptable to those moderate elements of the left who wished to block the election of the violently anti-PTB Lacerda. Suspicion that Goulart intended to stay in office rather than permit a free election of his successor led many other leading politicians to join or condone the conspiratorial movement against the regime.

The political atmosphere during 1963 was further radicalized by accusations and counter-accusations of corruption and unconscionable use of large sums of money to influence the outcome of the 1962 balloting. While the left pushed investigations of conservative "buying" of elections, the Institute of Economic and Social Studies (IPES) founded by Rio de Janeiro and São Paulo businessmen as their political action arm, was channeling its energies and material resources into the growing conspiracy as well as a propaganda campaign in support of Alliance for Progress goals, and giving at least lip service to the principles of the Catholic social encyclicals.

The staff of IPES came chiefly from among the large number of inactive military officers in the Rio de Janeiro area, with General Hector Herrara organizing its secretariat primarily from among graduates of the National War College (ESG), and General Golbery do Couto e

Silva, who had run the National Security Council under the Quadros government, as chief of the "research group." (Closely linked to Castelo Branco, Golbery became the government's director of intelligence services after the 1964 coup.) Under Golbery's able direction, dossiers were established on all groups or public figures considered Communist or otherwise "subversive." The "editorial group" encouraged and subsidized publication of anti-Communist materials on a large scale to counter the heavy outpouring of leftist-ultranationalist works during this period. In terms of support given to anti-Communist worker and student groups, IPES' success may have been relatively limited, at least as compared to its impact on urban middle class opinion, but organizational and financial assistance to women's groups such as the Women's Campaign for Democracy (CAMDE) and Feminine Civic Union (UCF) was to have a significant pay-off during the 1964 crisis.

The "historical" conspirators, whose ranks had been swelled during 1963 as a result of Goulart's leftward drift, at this point badly needed a prestigious senior general on active duty in the Rio de Janeiro area to assume a leadership role if they were to gain the adherence of any significant proportion of the total officer corps. The ideal choice was Army Chief of Staff Humberto Castelo Branco. Castelo was a hero of the Italian campaign who enjoyed a reputation for having avoided involvement in political affairs except when the military was united in exercise of the moderating power. He had developed a large following among the middle-grade officers during his long tenure as Director of Instruction and later as head of the Command and General Staff School, and among the colonels as Subcommandant of the National War College. Marshal Adhemar de Queiroz, a close friend since academy days, and other senior officers committed to the coup worked hard to convince the scholarly general that the military should prepare to block subversion of the country's basic institutions. They reminded him of their joint struggle against leftist elements in the 1950 Military Club elections, when both Castelo and Queiroz, along with Emílio Ribas Rodrigues Júnior, Jurandir Mamede, and Nélson de Melo, had been part of the defeated Cordeiro de Farias slate. These old comrades in arms found that Castelo had been in contact with UDN leader Bilac Pinto since the preceding March over their mutual concern with the direction in which Goulart appeared to be carrying the country. This concern had deepened with the subsequent crises enumerated above, and by late 1963 Castelo had agreed to assume military leadership of the coup.

The moderate Castelo's adherence was, however, not without important conditions. The first of these was that all plans to move against Goulart were to be contingent on the President's violation of the accepted rules of the game. As long as he did not close Congress, show clear indications of attempting to continue in office beyond the expiration of his term, or otherwise act illegally, Goulart would still be considered the legitimate commander in chief of Brazil's Armed Forces. Castelo's early 1964 addresses and circulars expressed an increasing feeling that Goulart was treading on dangerous ground and close to violating these conditions.

By the end of 1964, political polarization appeared to be reaching a potentially perilous level. General Albino Silva, Goulart's former Chief Military Aide, lashed back at Communist control of Petrobrás, as the radical left sought with success to bring about his replacement as head of the state petroleum entity by Marshal Osvino Alves, notorious for his leftist inclinations and self-proclaimed stance as a "peoples general." This development provided grist for the mill of the opposition's newly inaugurated political offensive—a campaign denouncing the existence of a government-encouraged state of "revolutionary war."

Several significant incidents near the end of February testified to the radicalization of the situation. Goulart appeared as guest of honor at a luncheon at the Vila Militar, where there was at least one conspicuous absence—that of General Castelo Branco. A few days later, on the 25th, Brizola, protected by marines, attempted to speak at a Popular Mobilization Front gathering in Belo Horizonte, but large-scale hostile demonstrations dissolved the rally and forced him to beat a hasty retreat from the Minas Gerais capital. Combined with the nearly concurrent episode in which the highly publicized congress of the CUTAL (Single Center of Latin American Workers), a pro-Castro regional labor confederation, had to be transferred from Belo Horizonte to Brasília because of major "anti-Communist" demonstrations by *Mineiro* women's groups, these incidents presaged the troubles ahead. Yet, as attested to by several of its key figures after the regime's collapse, the government felt that its military power structure—which rested on a few leftist officers, the legalist orientation of most of the others, the record of relative avoidance of involvement in partisan politics on the part of Castelo Branco, and the personal ties between General Amaury Kruel and the President—was more than adequate to cope with a yet relatively small group of military conspirators and their civilian allies. In fact, however, the plotters were already far more numerous than the government thought, and the events of March were to strengthen their ranks rapidly while eroding the regime's support. Moreover, the state military forces of both São Paulo and Minas Gerais had been built up numerically by Governors Adhemar de Barros and Magalhães Pinto, and in the former case, partially re-equipped with arms produced by São Paulo industrialists, ready, if necessary, to "double the effort of '32 in '64." With the governors of Guanabara and Rio Grande do Sul also involved in preparing for armed resistence to the Goulart administration, the President was counting heavily on key military commanders to hold these movements in check, a grave miscalculation of the true situation within the military.

2. THE REVOLUTION OF 1964

By the end of February, 1964, articulation of the conspiracy that was to overthrow the Goulart regime was far advanced. Yet it was still a loosely coordinated movement comprising elements with rather widely differing orientations. To the historical conspirators, who had been anxious to overthrow Goulart from the day he took office, had been added important military figures alienated by the radicalization of the Goulart regime and a growing number of middle-grade officers concerned with the preservation of Brazil's democratic institutions (for all their substantial imperfections) and maintenance of the integrity of the Armed Forces in the face of the divisions resulting from a pro- and anti-Goulart polarization and sharpening left-right cleavage. If not a mirror image of the civilian middle sectors, these officers were essentially middle-class in origins and outlook and shared many the concerns with their brothers in other professions.

The historical conspirators consisted primarily of those individuals who had striven to block Goulart's accession to office in 1961. Marshal Denys, Admiral Heck, Brigadier Grun Moss, and General Cordeiro de Farias (the Military High Command of the Quadros period) backed up by a fairly significant number of retired generals and admirals, but supported by only a small proportion of active duty officers, never really accepted Goulart as President. During 1962, they were able to organize a movement embracing a few generals with secondary commands, most notably Olympio Mourão Filho, José Pinheiro de Ulhoa Cintra, Ernesto and Orlando Geisel, Antônio Carlos Muricy, Carlos Luís Guedes, and João Punaro Bley, as well as Air Force Brigadiers Márcio de Souza e Melo and Clovis Travassos. While the government may have somewhat underestimated this group, particularly in writing off the activities of retired officers as unimportant, the historical conspirators did not in fact constitute a real threat to the stability of the regime.

As of early 1964, Goulart could still count on the support of the legalists who occupied the top echelon of ministry and field commands, and was building up a *dispositivo* or security scheme of strongly nationalist and reform-minded generals adequate to balance off the known conspirators. Taking intelligent advantage of retirements and promotions, he could look forward to gradually strengthening his position or at least neutralizing the loss of officers who could be expected to move toward the conspirators as the government began to push harder for controversial reforms. Even the alienation during the second half of 1963 of important officers such as General Nélson de Melo and Pery Bevilaqua, compounded by increasingly strained relations with key governors, had not placed the regime in a dangerous position. Only if a majority of the generally constitutionalist, albeit not unconditionally legalist, officers were to join the conspirators could a coup have significant chance of success. In the last four months of 1963, their perception of Goulart's actions did lead many of these centrist field commanders to undertake contingency planning for a "defensive" coup to protect established institutions. And, as we have already seen, by the end of the year the prestigious Army Chief of Staff had taken the lead in this respect.

As 1964 began, polarization of political positions as the UDN unleashed its "revolutionary warfare" attack on the administration and Brizola threatened Congress greatly increased the possibility of an uprising by the military. Still, the President was in no immediate danger of being overthrown until the March, 1964, naval crisis convinced the yet uncommitted that action must be taken before the capabilities of the Armed Forces to intervene decisively were undermined by the spread of indiscipline through the ranks. Reaction on this issue was so strong and united that the coup succeeded almost immediately on widely separated fronts as only a handful of troop commanders supported the government and very few fence-sitters remained. The well-conceived tactical plans of the revolting officers were effectively executed, while confusion and indecision reigned on the side of the government as its security scheme (dispositivo) collapsed in the face of the adherence to the revolutionary movement of forces upon which the regime's defensive position depended.

The undoubted highpoint of the Goulart administration came on Friday, March 13, when large contingents of the Armed Forces providing heavy security, the President addressed an estimated 150,000 persons gathered in the square opposite the War Ministry. With his military ministers, friendly politicians, and leftist leaders of mass organizations at his side, Jango announced the signature of an agrarian reform decree providing for the possible expropriation of land near federal highways, railroads, or other public works that had enhanced their value; the incorporation of private oil refineries into the state's petroleum monopoly; and an urban reform law that would establish rent controls on vacant apartments. Although all the nearly a score of speakers who preceded the President to the microphones called for basic reforms, it was Brizola's denunciation of Congress and open invitation to a popular revolution that aroused the greatest response from those present—and elicited the most negative reaction from the middle class, military, and businessmen watching on television. Brizola's call for popular manifestations of support for a "nationalist and popular government" accompanied by a plebiscite on reforms helped opponents of the government depict the event as a gathering of extremist elements inaugurating a campaign of subversion of the Brazilian way of life.

Although the President's message to the opening session of Congress on March 16 was generally considered anti-climactic, compared to the drama of the rally, it contained a number of proposals with far-reaching implications: amendment of the Constitution to provide for expropriation without immediate cash payment, extension of the franchise to illiterates, eligibility of noncommissioned officers and enlisted men to run for elective office, delegation of legislative powers to the executive, and legalization of the Communist Party. Most controversial was his proposal for a yes or no plebiscite involving the entire adult population (illiterates included) on the question of basic reforms. At first, it appeared to many that the opposition had been caught off guard, thrown on the defensive and even intimidated by the momentum of Goulart's campaign for basic reforms. Congress, unwilling either to give in to the President's demands or to appear as a reactionary obstacle to legitimate popular aspirations, decided to move ahead with its own reform program, beginning with the Christian Democratic substitute agrarian reform bill.

The government and opposition alike realized that as long as General Kruel and his São Paulo-based Second Army remained firm for legality, the regime was essentially secure from any threat from the right, since this powerful force could not only control the situation in the country's industrial heartland, but also counter a Minas Gerais-based revolt. Yet even as Brizolistas and radical labor leaders mapped increasingly ambitious reform programs and Goulart's advisors planned a series of mass rallies in major cities, the tide was turning against them. On March 18, while Goulart called for reform of the Constitution at a rally in Rio de Janeiro State, ex-President Dutra broke his long silence on political matters to issue a moderately phrased call to unity in defense of democracy and the Constitution which gave heart to the opposition and was considered a challenge and provocation by the regime. Although the regime shrugged Dutra off as a voice from the past, within two short weeks events were to demonstrate that it was the euphoric and immature Brazilian left rather than the old soldiers who were detached from Brazilian reality. The ability to mobilize a large turnout for their rallies and a series of uncoordinated land seizures, combined with a flood of revolutionary rhetoric, was confused with the capacity to bring about an "irreversible" popular movement for structural reforms. The need for effective organization and institutionalization of these newly unleashed forces was lost sight of in the heavy emotions of the moment. For in the view of the young radicals, agitation was a joy, but organization a bore.

Symbolic of the radical left's growing separation from a realistic view of the situation was the fact that on March 19, just as the leftist-nationalist faction in Congress was demanding the replacement of centrist cabinet members by "representatives of the people," a mass demonstration in São Paulo of nearly one-half million men and women dramatically expressed their feeling that the country had already moved too far to the left. The "Family March with God for Liberty," sponsored by the Feminine Civic Union under the patronage of São Paulo Governor Adhemar de Barros, Senate president Auro de Moura Andrade, and Deputy Cunha Bueno, marked the commencement of a major counter-attack by opponents of the regime. The sponsoring women's group was an offshoot of IPES and drew heavily on the parent organization's financial resources and organizational know-how for this rally and a subsequent series of similar manifestations explicitly designed to answer the left's March 13 rally.

As the Easter holidays neared, the increasing polarization still appeared to be contained within the political arena. Lacerda's March 18 call to the other governors for a united front against Goulart had apparently made no great immediate impact, and leading centrist figures were emphasizing the need for reforms as often as they were expressing mistrust of the radical left and doubts as to the President's sincerity.

As long as Goulart could keep the struggle focused on the question of reforms, his position would be strong, if not unassailable. But the issue was already threatening to escape the President's definition. For circulating among the officer corps was an official, albeit confidential, message from the Army Chief of Staff which questioned the thesis that legality necessarily meant continued support of the President. Denouncing the idea of a Constituent Assembly as a step toward dictatorship, General Castelo Branco made it clear that as far as he was concerned, the Goulart regime had reached and perhaps already crossed the permissible limits of the law, and was moving toward subversion and dictatorship. The Chief of Staff's classified note to his officers made explicit his divergences with the War Minister's posture and articulated his opposition to the Armed Forces being used by the government to pressure the legislature on behalf of the executive.

The crisis which, although catching the conspirators as well as the government by surprise, was to bring down Goulart within a week began Wednesday night, March 25. After the March 13 rally, members of the Association of Sailors and Marines decided to symbolize their support for the government's takeover of the oil refineries; officers of the association disobeyed instructions of Navy Minister Sílvio Mota and attended a political gathering at the Communist-led Bankworkers' Union on Monday. As Mota publicly denounced the association for "letting itself become involved with the subversive ideas of elements outside its ranks," its leaders replied that he was responsible for naval unrest by refusing to grant their organization official recognition and to respond to its demands for improved rights and pay. News of the Minister's arrest order for forty organizers of a ceremony commemorating the second anniversary of the association further excited the nearly 2,000 sailors and marines gathered for that event at the so-called Steel Palace, the headquarters of the Metal Workers Union, on Wednesday evening. Egged on by radical labor leaders and nationalist politicians, the mutineers resolved to remain in session until the punishments were revoked and the Navy Minister replaced by an admiral sympathetic to their movement.

At this juncture the President returned from an interrupted Easter vacation in Rio Grande do Sul and undertook the quest for a formula for containing the crisis. With the technically illegal, but government sanctioned Central Labor Command threatening a general strike in support of the mutineers, Goulart felt that he could not accommodate the naval officers' demands for vigorous application of the law. Urged by his labor collaborators to show sympathy for the mutineers, who felt they were helping the President in his struggle with the conservative forces, Goulart ordered the Army not to move against them. Unwilling to take actions clearly beyond the desire of the President, embarrassed by the defection of the marines sent to surround the mutineers and feeling undercut by Goulart's order, the Navy Minister resigned. Goulart was faced with the dilemma of whom to appoint Navy Minister, since the vast majority of ranking naval officers were openly against him or at least had no sympathy for his proposed solution to the crisis. Retired Admiral Paulo Mario da Cunha Rodrigues, a seventy-three-year-old anti-imperialist, out of touch with the main currents of thought within the Brazilian Navy, was brought in to resolve the clash between the officers' insistence for discipline and the mutineers' demands. He had no success in this delicate task. Although taken at noon to Guard Battalion barracks, the mutinous sailors and marines were almost immediately released by presidential order and reacted by marching jubilantly through the center of the city ostentatiously celebrating their presumed victory.

But what Goulart took as the end of the crisis was really the beginning of the end for his regime. While the Naval and Military Clubs gathered to protest the President's actions and prestigious newspapers in Rio de Janeiro prepared to get out extraordinary editions on Saturday as well as on Easter Sunday (the latter virtually unheard of in Catholic Brazil), Marshal Denys left for a meeting in Juiz de Fora with General Olympio Mourão Filho and Governor Magalhães Pinto, a gathering at which, unbeknown to the President, agreement was reached to prepare for the initiation of armed hostilities against the federal government within the week.

Far from being alarmed by these signs that the crisis was continuing, Goulart concerned himself with the address he was to make to the Association of Subofficials and Sergeants of the Military Police at the Automobile Club that Monday evening. Even after there were clear indications that something serious was afoot in Minas Gerais, the government, instead of mobilizing troops for a possible movement in that direction, was arranging transportation to carry even more of the First Army's noncommissioned officers away from their units to a rally that would last into the early hours of the morning.

In his nationally broadcast speech of March 30, designed to pick up the themes and momentum of the March 13 discourse, Goulart gave his enemies the further provocation they were seeking. Denouncing the groups opposed to him as tools of imperialism and seeking the sergeants' support for his actions, he did nothing to allay fears concerning the path along which he was conducting the nation. Indeed, before he was through speaking at midnight the revolt was launched in Minas Gerais, with other fronts opening during the day.

The military side of the revolution, although it lasted only two days, took on a distinct nature in each main region of the country: in the First Army sharp divisions and open confrontation as the troops from Minas Gerais marched on Rio de Janeiro; in the Second Army hesitation while civilians and troops commanders waited for General Kruel to make up his mind to lead them against the legalist forces in Rio de Janeiro; in the Third Army the divisional commanders leading their troops against that Army's commanding general; in the Fourth Army coordinated action by all units under the leadership of the Army's commander. On all fronts, success came relatively quickly and with a minimum of bloodshed. Respecting the position of their opponents, who were fighting for legality as they saw it, revolutionary forces preferred to out-maneuver and out-negotiate rather than overpower. While military action was decisive, the support of organized civilian groups—and particularly the cooperation of state administrations—was of great importance. In the civilian sector, activity on behalf of the "revolution" was much greater than the scattered efforts to mobilize in defense of the regime, a far cry from the "legality movement" of 1961.

The distinction of launching the coup fell to Minas Gerais, where long-time plotters Generals Olympio Mourão Filho and Carlos Luís Guedes were not able to hold back any longer following Goulart's address to the sergeants. That Minas Gerais would initiate the coup was agreed-upon strategy—for São Paulo pronounced alone in 1932 and paid a stiff price for its temerity, while Guanabara was the regime's military stronghold and neither Rio Grande do Sul nor Pernambuco was central enough. Moreover, a revolt in Minas Gerais would all but sever communications between Rio de Janeiro and Brasília. Even geographical factors indicated Minas Gerais—a relatively small number of troops could hold off much larger forces trying to come up the mountainous terrain from Rio de Janeiro. That the *Mineiros* would be so precipitate in their action was not in the plans of Castelo Branco or his colleagues. But Mourão had been eager to move for a long time, while Marshal Denys held that the Rio de Janeiro plotters were too hesitant. Minas Gerais rose in revolt against the Goulart regime while final plans were still being formulated in other parts of the country.

The "Tiradentes Group," under the command of General Antônio Carlos da Silva Muricy, was composed of the Tenth, Eleventh, and Twelfth Infantry Regiments along with three battalions of the Minas Gerais militia (Força Publica), several batteries of 105 mm howitzers and one of light field artillery, for a total of more than 5,000 men. The major military confrontation of the campaign occurred near the town of Areal, where loyalist General Luiz Tavares da Cunha Mello was positioned with some 2,500 troops, including the Second Infantry Regiment. However, communications with First Army headquarters convinced him that the revolution was already victorious, and by late afternoon on April 1, Cunha Mello's troops withdrew, allowing the Minas column to proceed with its triumphal march to Rio de Janeiro.

Rio de Janeiro, the scene of many of the crucial events leading up to the revolution, remained the central arena throughout most of the crisis. Governor Lacerda began the mobilization of his forces on March 29, when he received word through Deputies Costa Cavalcanti and Armando Falção that agreement had finally been reached for a revolt during the course of the coming week. Castelo Branco's Guanabara conspirators apparently did not receive confirmation of the Minas Gerais revolt until the early hours of March 31. By that evening, the police, militia, and volunteer forces gathered to protect Guanabara Palace from the expected attack by Admiral Aragão's Marines and First Army tanks were almost in sight of military police and armored detachments in defensive positions around the nearby presidential residence, Laranjeiras Palace. Given the overwhelming numerical strength of the First Army situated within Rio de Janeiro, the role of the state government was to tie down as many of the legalist units as possible, thus weakening the forces that could be sent against Minas Gerais and São Paulo. While Lacerda's forces attracted the government's attention and neutralized a significant portion of its available forces, the military conspirators moved effectively and with dispatch to sap the rest of the First Army's will and ability to resist. The Praia Vermelha sector (near famed Sugar Loaf Mountain), including neighboring Fort São João, was transformed into the revolution's military redoubt by the staff and students of the War College and the Command and General Staff School under the leadership of Generals Jurandir da Bizarria Mamede and Orlando Geisel. At first disturbed because the "premature" uprising by Minas Gerais had upset his carefully prepared timetable, Castelo Branco, assisted by Generals Emílio Maurell Filho and Aurélio de Lyra Tavares, calmly continued to plan and issue orders from his offices on the sixth story of the War Ministry, while the legalist First Army commander worked on countermeasures a few floors below.

General Arthur da Costa e Silva did not play a leading role in planning the revolution and joined in its execution only after the naval crisis was well underway. He accompanied the progress of Castelo's plans and remained in close contact with General Kruel, while at least two of his closest associates, General Sizeno Sarmento and Colonel Jaime Portella, cooperated more actively with Cordeiro de Farias. Very late on March 30, or early the next morning, Costa committed himself fully to the revolution, and from that time took an active part in coordinating activities on the Guanabara front. At the very center of legalist strength, General Oromar Osório's Vila Militar, General Augusto César Moniz de Aragão spent the night of March 31 urging fellow officers not to obey the orders of a government that had betrayed the country. Fort Copacabana, of great psychological importance because of its role as heroic symbol in the 1922 Lieutenants' revolt, joined the revolution with its garrison of 700 men and provided cover while a score of officers from the schools at Praia Vermelha captured the neighboring Coast Artillery headquarters in a daring daylight attack. The effect of this victory was to influence other units to adhere to the revolution and to convince the President and his advisors that they were losing the battle for the city. While sending General Morais Ancôra to work out a solution with the Second Army Commander, Goulart prepared secretly to leave for Brasília.

Although the insurrection appeared to unfold relatively slowly in São Paulo, there was never any real reason to doubt its success there. A general wariness, based on its experiences in the 1920's and 1932, when São Paulo raised the standard of revolt only to be left on a limb as other states failed to fulfill their commitments, combined with Amaury Kruel's reluctance to take a leading role in Goulart's ouster, explained the lag. Civilian elements, chafing at the bit to begin the revolution, agreed to wait for the Army's move. Kruel, the military "swingman" in the 1964 coup, hesitated more to give Goulart a chance to save himself by breaking with the radical left than because of an unwillingness to side with the revolution. By holding up the coup even briefly and giving Goulart repeated chances to seek a compromise, Kruel emerged as the one ranking Army officer on the side of the victorious revolution who retained considerable support in the ranks of the PTB and allied elements of the PSD. Unlike that of Mourão Filho, Kruel's manifesto never directly attacked Goulart, but justified the Second Army's role in the revolution in terms of "breaking the Communist ring which presently compromises and dissolves the authority of the Government of the Republic." [8]

As forces of the state government (which possessed a well-armed 30,000 man militia) isolated labor groups attempting to demonstrate in

[8] Alberto Dines et al., *Os Idos de Março* (Rio de Janeiro, 1964), p. 145. The full text on pp. 400–401.

favor of the regime, a powerful column was being assembled near Resende. There they faced the First Army's crack School Units Group. With the presence of the Agulhas Negras Military Academy cadets commanded by General Emílio Garrastazú Médici in the front ranks of the rebel forces inhibiting the legalists from initiating combat, a truce prevailed until the arrival of acting War Minister Morais Ancôra and Kruel. The subsequent negotiations lacked major substance, since by the afternoon of April 1 it was apparent to the legalist commander that the regime he was defending had already collapsed. What concerned the conscientious Ancôra now was to avoid useless conflict. The Second Army could turn its attention to the southern front, ready to combat legalist elements of the Third Army if necessary. But by that time (the night of April 1) the revolution was already consolidating its victory in the South.

The Ninth Military Region in Mato Grosso promptly dispatched a battalion of infantry under Colonel Carlos Meira Matos to march on Brasília. By the time this column reached the capital, although it covered the nearly 1,000 miles in less than forty-eight hours, the coup was over; the same held true for the forces sent by General Guedes from Belo Horizonte. When Goulart arrived from Rio de Janeiro on April 1, therefore, Brasília was still effectively under the control of General Nicolau Fico, Commander of the Eleventh Military Region and one of his stanch supporters. Goulart, however, decided that the situation was too exposed to be tenable and at 10:00 P.M. left for Pôrto Alegre, having remained in Brasília only seven hours.

In Rio Grande do Sul, the regime's position was far from that enjoyed during the 1961 crisis. In the first place, the state government was not controlled by a Leonel Brizola and the PTB, but by Goulart's long-time political opponents. Governor Ildo Meneghetti was one of the first governors (along with Adhemar de Barros and Lacerda) to commit himself and his administration to the overthrow of the Goulart regime. Thus the state's strong full-time militia, the Brigada Militar, was not at the disposal of the federal government and could be counted on by the revolutionaries to at least offset and neutralize much of the Third Army. Even more important as the crisis unfolded was the change in this most powerful of Brazil's field commands from a cohesive force whose top echelon could act in almost complete unity to a loose amalgamation of divisions and brigades more responsive to their own generals than to the Army Commander. Instead of a stanch legalist such as Machado Lopes at its head, the Third Army was under the orders of General Benjamin Rodrigues Galhardo, who, although not involved with the coup, had close ties with some of its key figures and deep reservations about the Goulart regime.

Whereas Machado Lopes had been backed up in 1961 by the leftist and highly nationalist General Oromar Osório and the reformist Pery Bevilaqua as commanders of the key cavalry and infantry divisions, respectively, the 1964 crisis found Generals Adalberto Pereira dos Santos, Mario Poppe de Figueiredo, and Joaquim de Mello Camarinha solidly on the side of the revolution. The first general's Sixth Infantry Division, although many of its units were led by officers loyal to the government, constituted a threat to the pro-Goulart forces in Pôrto Alegre itself, while Poppe's Third Infantry Division marched in from Santa Maria and Camarinha's Second Cavalry Division, supported by General Hugo Garrastazú's Third Cavalry Division, moved toward the capital from Uruguaiana and Passo Fundo.

Thus when Goulart arrived in Pôrto Alegre at dawn on the morning of April 2, the Third Infantry Division was only a few hours away in full march. Before noon, Jango left for his ranch in the interior. General Poppe soon arrived at the head of his cavalry division and assumed control of the Third Army. In spite of Brizola's continued efforts to mount armed resistance and the unhappiness of a significant number of sergeants over the course of events, the only casualty was Air Force Lieutenant Colonel Alfeu de Alcántara Monteiro, who, for personal as well as political motives, attacked Major General Nélson Freire Lavanère-Wanderley, newly appointed commander of the Fifth Air Zone, on the night of April 2 and was killed by the latter's aides. (Many of the key actors of the political rivalries within the Army in the 1965–1969 period served in Rio Grande do Sul soon after the coup.) General Justino Alves Bastos took command of the Third Army in September, with Isaac Nahon as his Chief of Staff and Major Generals Augusto Fragoso, Alvaro Tavares do Carmo, and Augusto César Castro Moniz de Aragão as commanders of the Third Military Region, Fifth Military Region, and Sixth Infantry Division. General Afonso Augusto de Albuquerque Lima became commander of the Second Cavalry Division.

The success of the revolution in the Northeast also exceeded the hopes of all but the most optimistic of its leaders and was carried out more swiftly and effectively than even the comparable operation in the 1930 Revolution. The key figures in the articulation of the coup in this vast region were Pernambuco Federal Deputy Colonel José Costa Cavalcanti and Fourth Army Commanding General Joaquim Justino Alves Bastos.[9] Although the ouster of Governor Miguel Arraes in Pernambuco gained a great deal of publicity, throughout the rest of the Northeast, with the exception of Sergipe, the governors played a leading role in the revolution.

From a technical viewpoint, the coup was little short of a masterpiece. Although in retrospect the weaknesses of the Goulart regime stand out, they were far from apparent at the time, and were to a considerable extent the result of very intelligent tactical exploitation of potential vulnerabilities by the leadership of the revolting forces. Such a rapid and virtually bloodless overthrow of a government that possessed significant organized and mobilizable, if not mobilized, mass support was in large part a function of painstaking and highly professional preparation. Not since the wars of independence in Hispanic America were major troop units deployed and brought into action on such widely separated fronts, and only in the civil wars of the Mexican revolutionary struggle were such large numbers involved. Instead of the relative standoff and protracted strife expected by most observers, the anti-Goulart forces enjoyed their most striking successes where the government appeared strongest.

The greatest contrast between the revolutionary and legalist *dispositivos* contributing to the victory of the former was in terms of leadership. The Army General Staff under Castelo Branco in essence was the general staff of the revolution, and it could call upon the faculty and students of the War College and the Staff and Command School as well as the Armed Forces High Command of the Quadros period. In very general terms, the *tenentes* of the 1920's, with their subsequent experience in the 1930 Revolution and World War II, proved too much for the regime's mixture of legalists and leftists. Although they did not

[9] Costa Cavalcanti, who provided the link between the Northeast and developments in the rest of the country, was Minister of Mines and Energy, and subsequently Interior Minister in the Costa e Silva government.

in the end need to be used, on the civilian side the armed and organized reserves of the revolution, bolstered by the state militias, overmatched the more visible and vocal "mass organizations" of the yet immature radical left. While the War Minister and two of the four Army Commanders remained loyal to the President, the vast majority of seasoned and able senior officers were with the revolution. In a sense, the losing slate in the 1950 Military Club election had their day in 1964, since Cordeiro de Farias, Rodrigues Ribas Júnior, Nélson de Melo, Castelo Branco, Adhemar de Queiroz, Sizeno Sarmento, and Jurandir Mamede had all been on the ticket defeated by Estillac, whose runningmates included then Major Luiz Tavares da Cunha Melo as well as Nélson Werneck Sodré.[10]

In the final crisis, the alliance of the historical conspirators, moderate legalists, and military intellectual elements worked smoothly. Among the ranks of the former, Marshal Denys and General Ulhoa Cintra went to assist on the Minas Gerais front (as had Muricy), while Cordeiro de Farias and Nélson de Melo moved to São Paulo on March 31 to help work on, and with, Kruel and subordinate Second Army commanders. They subsequently shifted to Paraná, where everything was already well in hand, and were prepared to continue to Rio Grande do Sul to aid the revolution's efforts within the Third Army if the struggle had continued longer.[11] Previously, on the 29th, Cordeiro de Farias along with Generals Ulhoa Cintra and Sizeno Sarmento had met with those First Army officers committed to the revolution, in all only a handful of majors and captains.[12] The agreed-upon strategy was that those units with a predominance of revolutionary officers would obey orders to move against rebel troops and, once contact was established, adhere rather than oppose. In commands where legalist officers held the upper hand, those sympathetic to the revolution were to delay preparations for action and promote doubt and confusion. This activity contributed to the ineffectiveness of the First Army in meeting the initial

[10] See Werneck Sodré, *Memórias . . .*, pp. 294–98.

[11] Nélson de Melo had been Second Army commander earlier in the Goulart period, while Cordeiro de Farias had once been governor of Rio Grande do Sul as well as of Pernambuco. Thus each had important contacts and potential influence in these critical areas. See José Stacchini, *Março 64: Mobilização da Audácia* (São Paulo, 1965), pp. 64–65.

[12] *Ibid.*, pp. 72–74.

moves of the coup. The fact that the two first legalist units to meet the rebels went over to them was crucial for the bloodless nature of the revolution if not for its very success. Had General Muricy been forced to fire on the loyalist troops at the Minas Gerais–Rio de Janeiro border, the opportunity for subsequent peace negotiations with the First Infantry Regiment's commander might very well have been lost. And it was the news of this elite regiment's adherence to the revolution, together with that of Fort Copacabana and the subsequent capture of the Coast Artillery headquarters, that had a profound adverse psychological effect on the government itself, as well as convincing the rest of the First Army that armed resistance would be senseless.

In contrast to the able and efficient leadership of the revolutionaries, the legalist forces acted, or rather reacted, in a confused and hesitant manner, thus facilitating the task of their opponents. Certainly they missed the presence of the ailing War Minister, not only at the time of the coup itself but throughout the evolving crisis. Although he in all probability could not have made the decisive difference that Goulart's Interior Minister hypothesizes, Jair Dantas Ribeiro was undoubtedly the most respected and able senior officer Goulart had on his side.[13] Many officers would have been reluctant to disobey his direct orders, and he might have been able to prevail upon Goulart to make sufficient concessions to hold the swing man, General Kruel, in line or to make some form of negotiated settlement possible. But it would seem that his absence was equally if not more critical during the naval crisis and on March 30. Only if he could have convinced Goulart to stay away from the Automobile Club rally or to take a conciliatory line on the question of discipline might he have averted the President's downfall. But it is probable that even so he could only have postponed the final crisis.

As it was, neither the elderly Morais Ancôra nor the War Minister's deputy, General Genaro Bomtempo, was able to fill the leadership vacuum. Indeed, they could scarcely carry out their own duties. While entrusting the defense of the regime to either Marshals Lott or Osvino Ferreira Alves might have helped with the leadership problem, the government was probably correct in estimating that such a move would drive some additional units over to the side of the revolution.

[13] See Abelardo Jurema, *Sexta-feira, 13* (Rio de Janeiro, 1964), p. 163–64.

With many of the key pieces of his paper *dispositivo* out of place when the crisis broke, General Assis Brasil was virtually useless during the coup, since the basic considerations upon which his plans rested had been invalidated by the course of events. He could only bear stunned witness to the collapse of his "impregnable" paper military power structure.[14]

Convinced that Guanabara, São Paulo, and Rio Grande do Sul were the critical strategic areas, the government had been virtually unconcerned about sending hostile commanders to Minas Gerais, which to Goulart's largely Rio Grande advisors was only the tail on the First Army dog. In addition to this underestimation of the *Mineiros,* the administration had felt that the best way to handle "unreliable" officers was to give them school and staff assignments in Rio de Janeiro.[15] Such a view overlooked the danger of creating a "critical mass" of alienated officers who, even without a significant number of troops under their command, could themselves constitute an important military factor. Combined with retired and reserve officers and some of the Guanabara state forces, this provided the conspirators with a nucleus of armed strength at the heart of Goulart's presumed area of greatest strength. For unlike the situation in 1955, the government possessed neither a majority of the officers in Rio de Janeiro nor control of the governmental machinery there. The confusion and lack of adequate communications on the government side was so great that Goulart's advisors thought Cunha Melo's troops were holding off Mourão or even pushing on into Minas Gerais when in fact the rebels were halfway to Rio de Janeiro. Similarly, they believed General Zerbini was still obstructing Kruel's march at Jundai, when in reality the latter had already reached Resende. These unrealistic expectations helped convert each reverse into a traumatic shock.[16] As viewed by one of Brazil's most perceptive commentators on political affairs:

All the consumate political ability of João Goulart, as well as the enormous force of inertia which seemed to sustain the periclitian Brazilian democracy,

---

[14] Assis Brasil's subsequent testimony to a military board of inquiry reflected significant shortcomings in his military-political knowledge and inability to adapt to the changing tactical realities of the situation.

[15] See Jurema, *Sexta-feira, 13,* p. 196.

[16] *Ibid.,* pp. 202–205 contains an account of the regime's disorganization.

was not enough to avoid the inevitable. The government, demoralized by corruption, disoriented by the contradictory policy of its chief, subject to the influence of all types of adventurers, the leadership of the communist movement, and groups of immature and inexperienced "leftists," ended up justifying and even requiring a military intervention that once again interrupted the course of the legal democratic process in Brazil.[17]

[17] Fernando Pedreira, *Março 31: Civis e Militares no Processo da Crise Brasileira* (Rio de Janeiro, 1964), pp. 9–10. Chapters Ten and Eleven of my *Modernization and the Military in Brazil* discuss the overthrow of the Goulart government in detail.

◦⟪⟫◦

CHAPTER FOUR

Castelo Branco and
"Manipulated Democracy"

THE FORCES that overthrew the Goulart regime on March 31–April 1, 1964, were united chiefly in their agreement that the situation, at least as it had developed during the preceding three weeks in the directions of radicalization and indiscipline, was intolerable. Beyond their desire to end this perceived "subversion" of political order, consensus among the victorious elements was quite limited. Although the most evident, and in many respects the most fundamental, cleavage would develop between the civilian and military components of the victorious movement, divisions within the Armed Forces were to be of even greater significance as the process of disaggregation of the "Revolution" unfolded through a series of crises and "coups within the coup" during the next five years. Indeed, the very ease and speed of the military victory against the Goulart government prevented the emergence of an "authentic" leadership of the revolutionary coalition through competition within the process of armed struggle. Instead, April 2 found the country with a plurality of leaders and factions that could claim to have played crucial roles in the ouster of the old regime. Thus, the revolution as it came to power had too many owners with incompatible aspirations and contradictory, if overlapping, visions of the new order. The heterogeneity of the anti-Goulart movement was reflected in the regime which came to power.

Even the proper term for the transfer of power and the process that ensued presents more than a semantic difficulty. In analytical rather than polemical terms, the transfer of power was a *coup d'état,* a phenomenon on which a substantial comparative literature exists. In terms of its outcome—the direction, degree, and quality of the changes that ensued—the Brazilian experience does not fit either the category of revolution, as conventionally defined, or that of counterrevolution, since no real revolution had yet taken place to be reversed. Since the label "revolutionary" has been widely used in public pronouncements and official documents, it will be used in the chapters that follow as a shorthand identification of the groups and individuals supporting the 1964 coup, rather than in its more precise analytical sense. Thus, the word is intended as a means of communication, not as a sign of approval or disapproval.

Although Brazil has had only three regular heads of state and three permanent administrations since April, 1964, in reality the revolution has gone through eight distinct stages during this period, including two transitory governments. During the first, in early April, 1964, a "Revolutionary Supreme Command" issued a sweeping "Institutional Act" that set aside significant portions of the Constitution and provided the legal basis for a purge of political figures closely associated with the old order. The inauguration of Castelo Branco as President in mid-April ushered in an eighteen-month period of coexistence of military and civilian elements behind a façade of formal democracy in an administration pledged to undertake a transition toward re-establishment of a competitive, although thoroughly reformed or renovated, political system. The crisis of October, 1965, which led to the Second Institutional Act, opened a period in which the rules of the electoral game were repeatedly changed and patently manipulated to ensure the elevation to the presidency of the general who had headed the Revolutionary Supreme Command and mediated the military's intramural conflict, Artur da Costa e Silva.

Once Costa e Silva's selection as President was ensured, Brazil went through a period of feverish modification of its institutional structure by the lame-duck Castelo Branco administration, combined with further purges of the ranks of the political class. The artificiality of an imposed two-party system resulted in the rise of a new opposition movement, a "broad front" (Frente Ampla) combining those ousted in 1964 with the most deeply disenchanted of the original civilian supporters of that movement. Resistance to the renewal of parliamentary purges led to the temporary closing of Congress. The fifth period was initiated by Costa e Silva's inauguration in March, 1967, and witnessed the progressive disillusionment of those who had felt that his pledge to "humanize" the revolution presaged a significant liberalization of social and political policies. The regime's repressive response toward increasing manifestations of opposition led instead to further polarization.

With the outlawing of the Frente Ampla and the emasculation of the parliamentary opposition, the trend during 1968 was toward a resort to violence in a situation where legal forms of opposition had been rendered ineffective by the federal government's at times arbitrary use of the vast powers it had assumed under the 1967 Constitution. In the eyes of the regime, resistance to its initiatives was increasingly equated with subversion. The unequal struggle with substantial student elements and the progressive wing of the Catholic Church provided the environment for yet another coup-within-the-coup, in December, 1968, as a contest for power between rival right-wing military elements was concealed behind a concerted blow against the regime's critics. Large-scale purges were resumed under the aegis of a Fifth Institutional Act, and Congress was again recessed. As 1969 opened, President Costa e Silva found himself in a position roughly analogous to that of Castelo Branco at the end of 1965, with his authority compromised by the power of ambitious elements within the Armed Forces looking beyond him to the struggle for the presidency in 1970. At the same time, the democratic fig leaf had been eroded to the point where the regime was all but a naked dictatorship bereft of the tattered remnants of representation to a degree unmatched in the postwar era. By September, 1969, Costa was out of power, and a *junta* exercised power until the selection of another general as the new President. Thus, when Emílio Garrastazú Médici took office in November, 1969, the revolutionary government was embarking upon its eighth discernible phase in less than six years since "temporarily" assuming power.

Although it can be seen quite readily that the post-coup regime differed sharply from that which preceded it, there were also substantial carry-overs insofar as the basic institutional structure was not radically changed, particularly during the first three years, or the political culture transformed. The changes were concentrated heavily in leadership composition, political style, and policy content, with each reflecting a significant degree of reaction against the prevailing norms. Even among the veterans of *tenentismo,* there were some who were ready in 1964 to work with the politicians, as they had in the other crises since the 1930's. Others felt they had learned a lesson and wished to purge the political class more deeply than they had ever before and to retain for themselves greater initiative and autonomy of action with regard to the conduct of national affairs. Increasingly, the younger generation of officers expressed a sentiment they were to articulate in unmistakably clear terms in December, 1968: that they were tired of holding the cow while others received the cream.

The task of over-all conceptualization of the process of political modernization since 1964 is complicated by the immediacy of the events and shortness of the perspective. These difficulties can be seen even in the most systematic Brazilian efforts to carry on into the new period with analyses designed to explain the 1964 crisis. Thus, Jaguaribe, who viewed the developments of the Goulart period as an aborted if not inherently abortive effort to transform a national capitalist political economy into a form of national laborism distinct from state capitalism and far different from developmental socialism, has attempted to depict the post-1964 model as "colonial fascism."[1] Involving a strengthened governmental apparatus to preserve stability, a high degree of integration into the United States-led Atlantic Community, and a state-supervised free market economy, this type of system took form through the Institutional Acts, which

. . . provided the most formidable reinforcement of the State ever attempted in Brazil, and equipped the government with means of coercion seldom paralleled in even the most authoritarian regimes. With socio-political stability thus assured, the Campos policies were oriented toward achieving financial stability. He had the advantage, in his attempt to control inflation, of not being encumbered by the usual difficulties. The tough military dictatorship

[1] Hélio Jaguaribe, *Political Strategies* . . ., pp. 41–43 and 45–48 and his *Economic and Political Development* . . ., pp. 176–82 and 187–93.

eliminated working-class resistance to the more than proportional abasements of their real wages. The bourgeoisie, although alarmed by the recession caused by the anti-inflationary policies, was still too frightened of the last tendencies of the Goulart government and too concerned with the imminent risk of hyperinflation to accept the sacrifice of a period of bad business. The middle class, although enjoying its recovered influence, was the least patient. Its revelant sector, the military, was, however, given a fair pay rise and compensated by many other advantages resulting from its now direct and unchecked control of the State.[2]

The existence of a strong current of right-wing nationalism among the military prevented the complete implementation of the Roberto Campos–Castelo Branco model and to a large degree caused the coup within the coup of October, 1965. Jaguaribe (writing in late 1966) predicted that within a few years the alienation of the progressive sectors of the Brazilian middle class would lead to a situation in which the military would either have to return power to civilian political forces or "change in an essential form the orientation of their regime"; he viewed the former as more likely. At the same time, he conceived of the possibility of "a 'Nasserist' conversion, leading to a reorientation of the country toward socio-economic-development and national individuality" which would substantially extend the military's stay in power.[3] With regard to the opposition, Jaguaribe posited that

keeping Brazilian society stagnant and bereft of autonomy under a regime of open or veiled political-military oppression must (but has not as yet) lead to the creation of a significant revolutionary movement of the extreme Left. The possibility of such a movement erupting into violent popular revolution is directly related to the degree of economic and social stagnation prevailing and to the amount of political-military oppression exercised.[4]

The rise in influence of the right-wing nationalists, as exemplified by General Albuquerque Lima during 1967–1968, led Jaguaribe in early 1969 to foresee the possibility of an eventual coalition of this group, largely without links to significant civilian elements, and the rightist liberals who have been leaderless since Castelo Branco's death in mid-1967.[5] While containing a degree of built-in rigidity resulting from his emphasis on class-structure categories, Jaguaribe's conceptualization

[2] *Ibid.*, p. 46.
[3] *Ibid.*, p. 48.
[4] *Brazilian Nationalism* . . ., p. 68.
[5] Seminar at Columbia University, January 9, 1969.

yields significant insights into the contemporary Brazilian political system.

For Cândido Mendes de Almeida, a leading Brazilian political scientist who served as a presidential advisor to Quadros, the Castelo Branco government can best be understood through its self-image as "a new regime resulting from the collapse of the country's spontaneous development and the necessity to relaunch it within a capitalist model, commanded by a salient 'power elite.' " [6] In this regard, the regime's "reformist vision" included an "orthodox" neocapitalist emphasis on productivity at the expense of delaying the incorporation of new groups into the money economy. According to Mendes (who although aligned with the opposition retained personal ties to such influential members of Castelo's brain trust as General Golbery do Couto e Silva), rather than a dictatorship or a return to the old system, Castelo Branco sought to establish a highly centralized technocracy which could provide the requisite institutional conditions for economic planning.

In place of the old bargaining system between the President and the Congress, with its involved counterbalances, popular participation was reduced to a minimum in favor of the disciplined measures considered imperative by a technocratic elite given cohesion and a substantial degree of coherence by the acceptance of the world view and doctrine of the National War College (Escola Superior de Guerra, ESG).[7] This group operated in a power vacuum resulting from (1) the "erosion of a national bourgeoisie capable of claiming a dominant role for itself"; (2) the weak bargaining position and consequent low political autonomy of wage earners; (3) the absorption of "the most dynamic sectors of the middle class by the government apparatus and by expansion of the state economic infrastructure enterprises"; and (4) the lack of power on the part of the old landowning sectors, undercut by the Goulart regime and dependent upon the military intervention for their survival.[8] Exploiting the concentration of power in the hands of the executive and using the threat of continuing exceptional military investigations as a deterrent, the Castelo Branco regime presided over

[6] Cândido Mendes, "Sistema político e modelos de poder no Brasil," *Dados,* No. 1 (Second Semester, 1966), p. 7.

[7] *Ibid.,* pp. 9–12.

[8] *Ibid.,* pp. 13–15.

the emergence of the Armed Forces as the determining factor in the process of modernization as well as the exercise of authority.[9]

With the technocracy invoking its "monopoly of rationality" and the radical left arguing from Marxist ideological bases that a situation so full of objective contradictions could not prove viable in any but the short run, no meaningful dialogue on basic national policies was possible. Political institutions were reshaped to fit the manipulative strategies of the War College national security specialists gathered on Castelo Branco's staff and the administrative structures modified to meet the demands for rationality of the civilian technocrats marshaled behind Planning Minister Roberto Campos.[10] But the planned reformist "second stage" of the Castelo Branco regime was sharply curtailed owing largely to the substantial lag in attaining the first priority of economic stability behind the targets upon which the regime's political tactics were predicated. With development objectives postponed or deferred, the government's presumed plans for increasing political participation to provide content for an imposed bifactionalism adapted from the Mexican example were casualties of the disrupted timetable.

In an interpretation more intricately detailed, but essentially compatible with that of Jaguaribe, Mendes forsees the possibility of a "Nasserist" shift with the military assuming the roles at the heart of the economic planning process which were firmly in civilian hands during the Castelo Branco period.[11] Since the chief tension of the civil-military technocratic alliance appears to be the latent contradiction between national security and economic performance objectives, military nationalism such as has developed during the past two years was considered a real possibility by Mendes when writing in 1966. The limiting factor was the inability of military groups other than that linked to Castelo (and in part committed through him to close cooperation with the United States in what he perceived as an essentially bipolar world) to "transform their nationalist sentiment into a program and a coherent vision of Brazilian reality and its perspectives for change." [12]

[9] *Ibid.*, pp. 16–20.
[10] *Ibid.*, pp. 20–24.
[11] *Ibid.*, pp. 27–29.
[12] *Ibid.*, p. 31. The degree to which this still holds true constitutes one of the most crucial questions concerning the course of Brazilian politics at the beginning of the critical decade of the 1970's. (See the discussion in Chapter 8.) Many of the recent "crisis" books by Brazilian economists and sociologists deal more with

Nearly four years after its departure from office, the Castelo Branco administration remains the subject of considerable controversy. In terms of fairly rigorous and systematic analysis, the most meaningful interpretation appears to be that of Mendes, who views it as characterized above all by a "high index of coherence in its actions" and a "profound strategic dimension" through which a technocratic minority accomplished "a platform of changes, for the first time, by a very rigid ideological perspective of Brazilian reality."[13] Although the regime's powers were broadened by the April, 1964, and October, 1965, Institutional Acts, and the rules of the political game were modified on repeated occasions, Castelo Branco avoided the personalist exercise of authority, exercising his more arbitrary powers only under heavy pressure from influential military elements who championed drastic measures against the remnants of the old regime.

Disdaining both compromise with the old order and the quest for legitimization or consensus through symbols and social mobilization, the Castelo Branco administration placed its full emphasis on "implantation of a coherent and rigorous economic model."[14] The regime's relatively

---

the 1930–1964 period than with subsequent developments. Thus, Luiz Carlos Bresser Pereira, *Desenvolvimento e Crise no Brasil, Entre 1930 e 1967* (Rio de Janeiro, 1968), undertakes a "historical-structural" analysis of Brazilian development, which contains relatively little systematic political interpretation and only a few pages dealing with the post-1964 situation (pp. 135–37, 169–77, and 182). Its categorization of the Castelo Branco government as traditional middle class, moralist, immobilist, anti-Communist, and anti-industrialization leaves a good deal to be desired analytically. Bresser Pereira expresses a theoretical preference for socialism, and hopes for the possible emergence of developmental nationalism in place of "technocratic-military interventionist liberalism"; Paul Singer provides a more rigorously socialist analysis in his *Desenvolvimento e Crise* (São Paulo, 1968). Largely a series of essays written between 1961 and 1965, this volume includes a final essay criticizing Castelo Branco's economic policy (pp. 159–81). Since going into exile after the fall of the Goulart regime, Celso Furtado's production includes *Subdesenvolvimento e Estagnação na América Latina* (Rio de Janeiro, 1966); *Teoria e Política do Desenvolvimento Econômico* (São Paulo, 1967); and *Um Projecto para o Brasil* (Rio de Janeiro, 1968).

[13] Cândido Mendes, "O govêrno Castelo Branco: paradigma e prognose," *Dados,* No. 2/3 (1967), pp. 64–65.

[14] *Ibid.,* pp. 67 and 72–73. Robert S. Byars, in a dissertation prepared for the Political Science Department of the University of Illinois, examines the Castelo Branco regime from the division in small-group theory between task-oriented and affect-oriented leadership roles. He finds the Castelo-Campos governmental team to have very closely approximated the ideal type of task leader on all significant pattern variables.

strict self-limitation on the duration of its powers, combined with its delay in achieving basic economic goals, resulted in a series of regressive moves following periods of evident progress toward political normalization. Thus the Second Institutional Act followed the gubernatorial elections of October, 1965; the purge of the Rio Grande do Sul legislature took place during the 1966 campaign; and the canceling of some congressional mandates occurred before the November, 1966, balloting. Institutional reforms were curtailed or foregone in the absence of the favorable conditions expected to have resulted from planned economic progress. Yet the electoral calendar was carried out, even though the elections were emptied of any real significance as a major step toward redemocratization.[15]

The difficulty of transforming, reforming, or even renovating the "system" Castelo Branco inherited in 1964 may be gathered from an expert United States observer's stress upon its internal contradictions, the deeply embedded control mechanisms of its multi-layered establishment, and intractable features of the Brazilian political culture. Thus,

the several elites which have dominated Brazilian political machinery during several successive governments and their pattern of joint action to maintain control and preserve "social peace" through heavy reliance on conciliation and paternalism . . . a wide range of attitudes, devices, strategems, concessions, and alliances extending well back into the last century which have permitted Brazil to implant substantial features of a modern Western nation —liberal constitutions, great cities, and an impressive industrial plant—onto a society that is still markedly non-competitive, paternalistic, and semi-authoritarian.[16]

Of major significance for the future was the heterogeneity of the revolutionary forces, compounded by the diversity of their motives in supporting the ouster of Goulart and the inconsistencies among their future expectations. For

The movement of April thus brought together all the possessing classes of society: the agrarian sectors for fear of reform, the industrial sectors in fear of the loss of their security mechanisms, the middle classes in panic of seeing

[15] *Ibid.*, pp. 81–82.

[16] James W. Rowe, "The 'Revolution' and the 'System': Notes on Brazilian Politics, Part I: Seeds of the 'System,' " *American Universities Field Staff Reports,* East Coast South America Series, XII, No. 3 (July, 1966), 7.

the social distance which separates them from the masses reduced, all of them jointly for the even greater fear of the emergence of a pattern of development differing from the classic patterns of *American democracy,* to which they are culturally tied.[17]

1. THE FIRST FOUR MONTHS: THE NEGATIVE PHASE

Although the military movement of March 31, 1964, was an unqualified success, it did not usher in a glorious new era, as hoped by its more radical partisans, nor did it quickly lead to a return to constitutional normalcy, as expected by many of the civilians who welcomed it as preferable to either the civil strife or protracted agitation that had seemed imminent. It was instead followed by a period of purges, austerity, and frustration which seemed to be carrying the country away from, rather than toward, a perfected democracy. For while key figures within the outside the Armed Forces stressed the military institution's democratic and constitutional proclivities, it became increasingly evident that 1964 was not to be a repetition of 1954, when competitive civilian politics had been resumed within a few weeks. The Armed Forces exercised emergency constituent powers in their own name and then installed a ranking spokesman of the victorious military as President.[18] Inclined toward a systematic, albeit flexible, application of military tactics to governing the country, Castelo Branco soon discovered that the "renovation" of the Brazilian polity was even more difficult than the rationalization of its economy.

In its early weeks, the revolution bore little resemblance to the relatively structured situation that subsequently developed under Castelo Branco. As graphically described by one of the Brazilian journalists who studied it most carefully, the developments which brought about an abrupt governmental vacuum were too sudden, and their configuration too confusing, to permit rapid definition of a new order.

[17] Luciano Martins, "Aspectos Políticos . . .," pp. 36–37.

[18] The degree to which old myths die hard can be seen in the writings of Gilberto Freyre, whose analysis of the Brazilian military in his classic *Ordem e Progresso* and *Nação e exército* (Rio de Janeiro, 1949) persisted in the face of the events of 1964. In a pamphlet published in 1965 on *Fôrças Armadas e Outras Fôrças,* subtitled "New Considerations Concerning the Relations between the Armed Forces and the Other Forces of Security and National Development in Brazilian Society," the distinguished social historian termed talk of Brazilian militarism "simply ridiculous" in light of its past role and behavior.

Between four thirty on March 28 and four thirty on April 1, an insurrection developed which will be inscribed in history as the most peculiar among all those which have ever taken place in Brazil: radical, but without blood; full of contradictions among the rebels, but without a struggle; profoundly marked by hesitations, even on the part of those who wanted it most and had most prepared for it, but even at that energetic and tenacious and determined to reach the end of its objectives. In synthesis, a rebellion so contradictory and curious as Brazil is in its economic, social, human and ethnographic configuration.[19]

According to one of the chief architects of the revolutionary movement, its leadership was caught only partially prepared by the unexpectedly rapid course of events.

We were agreed with respect to the necessity of acting promptly if Mr. João Goulart wished to stage a coup, but disposed to assure him the complete tenure of his mandate if he did not. The adventurist and suicidal precipitation of some so-called leftist sectors with the consequent breaking of the principle of discipline in the Armed Forces put in gear what was or sought to be only a preventive scheme.[20]

The rapidity and completeness of the collapse of the Goulart regime found the revolutionary leadership dispersed throughout the country prepared for an armed struggle that failed to develop. In Brasília, Senate President Auro de Moura Andrade declared the presidency vacant as a result of having been "abandoned" by Goulart and shortly before 4:00 A.M. on April 2 Raneiri Mazzili was once more sworn as Provisional President. On the same morning, Mazzilli received a cable from President Lyndon Johnson conveying the admiration of the American people for "the resolute will of the Brazilian community to resolve these [political and economic] difficulties within a framework of constitutional democracy and without civil strife."[21]

This immediate recognition of a governmental change fed suspicions that the United States had supported if not sponsored the Brazilian coup. It was criticized publicly by some Washington observers and privately by low-ranking State Department officials. The

[19] Stacchini, *Março 64,* p. 1.

[20] General Golbery do Couto e Silva, as quoted by Enio Silveira in "Primer Epístola ao Marechal: Sôbre o 'Delito de Opinião,' " *Revista Civilização Brasileira,* No. 3 (July, 1965), p. 8.

[21] Quoted in Skidmore, *Politics in Brazil, 1930–1964,* p. 327.

initiative came from the U.S. Embassy in Rio de Janeiro, where Ambassador Lincoln Gordon and his staff were concerned over the possibility of armed resistance to the new regime on the part of Brizola's supporters. Hoping also to maintain the fraying thread of constitutionality through official acknowledgement of Mazzili's succession, they sought to bolster the civilian political forces in the face of the military's presumed pretensions to power. Counselor of Embassy Robert W. Dean, on the spot in Brasília, had made a close study of the Brazilian Army's actions in earlier crises as a student at the U.S. National War College in 1962–1963. In light of the 1961 episode, such a manifestation of the Johnson administration's firm support of civilian succession could reasonably have been expected to strengthen Mazzili's hand (and his questionable resolution) while staying that of some military elements. But in 1964, in contrast with 1961, Rio de Janeiro was the center of decision-making, with activity in Brasíla having very little effect. For unlike the earlier crisis, the Armed Forces had already taken the critical step of overturning the government, and power was clearly in military hands. (The question of the United States' role in the 1963–1964 crisis is treated in my *Modernization and the Military in Brazil.)*

Within the military, hierarchy prevailed. As concurred in by Kruel and Moraes Ancôra on the afternoon of April 1, the War Ministry fell to Costa e Silva as the senior active duty general in Rio de Janeiro. (He was ranked only by Cordeiro de Farias, who was in Curitiba at the time.) Major General Octacílio Terra Ururahy was immediately named to command the First Army, a move which shut out Mourão Filho, who may well have expected this key command as he arrived in Rio de Janeiro at the head of his victorious column. Indeed, Costa and Kruel appeared determined to prevent the historical conspirators from attaining positions of power.[22] First Cordeiro de Farias and then Mourão were denied command of the Third Army, while Generals Guedes and Muricy were also given no choice assignments.

In Rio de Janeiro, Costa e Silva quickly organized a Revolutionary Supreme Command, composed of himself, Navy Admiral Augusto Rademaker Grünewald, and Air Force Chief of Staff Brigadier Francisco de Assis Correia de Melo (who had been Air Minister under Kubitschek). In a telephone call to Mazzilli, who was considered by these important military elements to have wavered unduly in the 1961

[22] Consult Stacchini, *Março 64,* pp. 103–14 and 120–26.

crisis, Costa e Silva made it clear that his Supreme Command would make the major decisions. To avoid a dangerous duality of power with Brizola still at large in the interior of Rio Grande do Sul, Mazzilli accepted the de facto situation and named Costa e Silva, Rademaker, and Correia de Melo as his service ministers. Summoned to Rio de Janeiro on April 3, Mazzilli worked out with the Supreme Command a provisional cabinet, with Costa e Silva's choice, Luís Antônio de Gama e Silva, as Minister of Justice and of Education, career diplomat Vasco Leitão da Cunha as Foreign Minister, and labor ministry functionary Arnaldo Sussekind holding the portfolios of Labor and Agriculture.[23]

No sooner had Mazzilli assumed the presidency than the process of selecting a "constitutional" president to serve out the incomplete Quadros-Goulart term was initiated. A few PSD and PTB congressional leaders considered the possibility of electing Amaral Peixoto, Tancredo Neves, or some other centrist civilian politician. But it was soon evident that the decision was really out of their hands. The aging ex-President Dutra, a revered figure whose prestige had risen as the result of his democratic pronouncement in March, was also considered by the civilian politicians as a candidate who would support normalcy as against the zealously anti-leftist "hard line" military's demands for sweeping purges. The officers of the less extremist "Sorbonne" group—composed of members of the National War College, General Staff and Command School, and the Army Chief of Staff's collaborators—worked effectively behind the scenes to articulate the candidacy of Castelo Branco. (These two politicized currents within the triumphant military would become clearly delineated within a matter of months; in the initial weeks of the new regime positions were still very unclear, particularly as many officers who had joined the coup movement at a relatively late date did not yet perceive that important differences over ends as well as means existed and would become crucial.) To undermine Dutra, military spokesmen reminded UDN congressmen of his close ties to the PSD and stressed his advanced age as a disqualification. The IPES leadership was favorably impressed by these arguments and by the orientation of the Sorbonne group. A press campaign instigated

<hr />

[23] On the first days after Goulart's fall, the most detailed English language source is J. F. W. Dulles, *Unrest in Brazil: Political-Military Crises 1955–1964* (Austin, 1970), pp. 341–54.

by these elements, whose chief point of contact was General Golbery, began to extol the virtues of the "nonpolitical" (relative to the other senior officers) Castelo Branco, emphasizing his intellectual attainments, prestige within the Armed Forces, and respect for democracy. Lacerda began to back away from his early leaning toward Dutra and stressed that the next President should be a military figure capable of maintaining unity and of "preventing Kubitschek from becoming the Frondizi of Brazil." [24]

The avowed presidential hopefuls, whose participation in the revolution had been conditioned by their hopes to advance their candidacies, were alert to defend their interests with respect to the elections scheduled for October, 1965. As the UDN presidential nominee for 1965, Lacerda quickly took the initiative and invited a large group of pro-revolution governors to meet with him in Rio de Janeiro on April 3. Magalhães Pinto, Adhemar de Barros, Ney Braga, and Mauro Borges gathered promptly with Lacerda and were joined the next day by Ildo Meneghetti and Fernando Correia da Costa.[25] Magalhães Pinto made it clear that if the new president was to be a civilian, he was the logical choice as the first governor to raise the standard of revolt. The consensus was, however, that a prestigious military figure was needed to carry out the difficult tasks ahead; certainly no civilian presidential aspirant was willing to see a rival gain an edge in the competition. So at this crucial juncture almost all leading politicians accepted the view that a military man could be expected to provide a stable interim regime and preside over elections of a constitutional successor with relative impartiality. Governors Borges and Ney Braga as Army officers sounded out opinion in the Armed Forces and found that any civilian would suffer grave pressures from the Supreme Command of the Revolution. Agreement was readily reached among the governors that owing to the weakness of the Mazzilli regime and its ties to the pre-revolutionary system, the maximum constitutional period of thirty days before election of a new president should not be used. Wishing to minimize military rivalries and

[24] *Ibid.*, p. 346. Lacerda's reference was to Argentine ex-President Arturo Frondizi, ousted by the military in early 1962 as allegedly too soft toward the Peronists.

[25] Mauro Borges, *O Golpe em Goiás* (Rio de Janeiro, 1965), pp. 109–19, provides the most detailed account of these consultations and the resulting friction with Costa e Silva prior to the agreement on Castelo Branco. See also Lacerda's view as reported in Alberto Dines et al., *Os Idos de Março,* pp. 187–90.

avoid a power struggle, the governors decided to recommend a single candidate to the military.

Lacerda put forth the name of Castelo Branco as a man above party strife and respected by the officer corps; this choice elicited a favorable response from all present except Adhemar de Barros. General Augusto César Moniz de Aragão, who had played a major role at the Vila Militar (Rio de Janeiro's most important garrison) during the coup and whose prestige among his fellow officers would soon carry him to the presidency of the Military Club, assured the governors that Castelo Branco's candidacy would find all but unanimous support among the Armed Forces.[26] After preliminary talks with Costa e Silva and Castelo, the eight governors and Colonel José Costa Cavalcanti met with Costa e Silva and Marshal Juarez Távora. The "Commander in Chief of the Revolutionary Forces" (as Costa insisted upon being termed, rather than War Minister) argued vehemently for delaying the full month to allow the necessary purges and cleaning up to take place before the installation of the definitive government. Lacerda replied that such a protracted experience of a provisional president acting as a puppet of the military was inadvisable. (Here Costa's general admiration of the Argentine way of handling such matters, reflected in the constant tutelage of civilian presidents and their frequent removal, came into conflict with Lacerda's concern that no precedent be set for military tutelage of Brazil's President.) The Armed Forces chief also slapped down Magalhães Pinto, who along with Lacerda constituted a threat to his own presidential ambitions. Costa e Silva correctly perceived that his extraordinary authority would end with the selection of a president, and wished to prolong his strong man role at least for the rest of the initial thirty days. Moreover, he desired a civilian candidate or a retired military figure—a situation under which the War Minister would continue to enjoy unusual power. Costa also appeared genuinely concerned over a possible splitting of the military behind rival leaders, as had occurred late in the Empire and during the early years of the Old Republic. Juarez Távora intervened firmly on the side of the governors. The old revolutionary counseled Costa: "I don't think that in 30 days, nor in 60, nor in 90 can the Revolutionary Supreme Command exterminate from its governmental machinery the germs of sub-

[26] Statement of Moniz de Aragão in *O Globo,* August 29, 1967.

version and corruption."[27] He went on to say: "In 1930 we exercised formality and restraint in not wishing to assume the government directly. We thought of putting the civilians up front and maneuvering them from nearby. What an illusion ours was! In a short time we were left behind, completely disarticulated, without being able to do anything we had planned."[28] Politely if emphatically, Juarez Távora stressed his belief that if the governors could agree on Castelo Branco certainly the military should be able to do so.

Outraged at Costa's hostile attitude, Lacerda drafted a violent letter calling him a usurper and threatening to resign as governor of Guanabara and withdraw from public life. Although the letter was not transmitted to the War Minister by his Chief of Staff, General Sizeno Sarmento, who believed that such a public break would be harmful to the revolution, word of the sharp clash quickly spread in political circles. A breach had developed between the most influential governor and the central government, one which was never to be healed and would develop into a major political realignment as Costa e Silva's position as a presidential contender became clearer in 1965–1966. Within the military, Marshal Denys united the key "original" revolutionaries—Cordeiro de Farias, Nélson de Mello, Márcio de Souza de Mello, and Admiral Heck—behind the Castelo candidacy.[29]

Another meeting was held on the evening of April 5, at which Lacerda was represented by Juracy Magalhães, and Magalhães Pinto by José Maria Alkmim. By this time Costa e Silva had accepted the course events were taking and after considerable discussion concurred in the choice of Castelo Branco. In accepting the indication, Castelo assured Adhemar de Barros that he would show no favoritism in the 1965 presidential elections. The São Paulo governor was still unhappy that the choice had not fallen upon Amaury Kruel. Although another effort was made by the PSD-PTB politicians together with the São Paulo government to launch Kruel's candidacy as an alternative to Castelo, the former withdrew before the balloting took place. Castelo Branco and Kruel had been companions since they were classmates in the military preparatory school in Rio Grande so Sul but had become estranged

---

[27] Quoted in Basbaum, *História Sincera da República,* Vol. IV, pp. 135–37.
[28] Quoted in Borges, *O Golpe em Goiás,* p. 114.
[29] Stacchini, *Março 64,* pp. 105 and 127–29.

during the Italian Campaign in World War II. Having been War Minister when Castelo was only an Army commander, Kruel was somewhat reluctant to take a back seat in the post-revolution power structure. In this instance, Lacerda had moved so quickly in articulating the choice of Castelo that rival movements never really got off the ground.[30]

Dutra, whose hopes for a return to the presidency had suffered a major blow with the option of Lacerda and Magalhães Pinto for Castelo Branco, soon saw even the PSD slipping away from him. Aware that the more radical rightists in the military advocated banning the PSD as well as the PTB, Francisco Negrão de Lima took advantage of his long friendship with Castelo Branco to bring him to see Kubitschek, who received assurances that the October, 1965, elections would be held as scheduled. It was tacitly agreed that the PSD, as the ranking party in Congress, would be entitled to the vice presidency, with Alkmim, as a backer of the revolution and an early champion of Castelo's candidacy, the logical aspirant. By means of a letter asking for Dutra's support, Castelo Branco provided the ex-president with a graceful exit line, and on April 9 the latter withdrew. Kubitschek then endorsed Castelo publicly, and the election was only a formality. On April 11, Castelo received 361 votes with some 72 abstentions, 3 ballots cast for Juarez Távora, and 2 for Dutra. Fifty-three PTB congressmen had voted for Castelo Branco.

By this time, however, other matters had taken precedence over the formal ratification of a decision reached nearly a week before. The Revolutionary Supreme Command was determined not to "repeat the mistake of 1954" and this time to ensure that the "subversive" and "corrupt" elements linked to the overthrown regime were effectively removed from national political life. Conservative interest groups, together with many elements within the military, called immediately after the coup for the cancellation (*cassação,* or "cassation," in Brazilian legal terminology) of the mandates of elected officials closely tied to the Goulart government and for purges of "leftist, subversive, and anti-democratic" elements from the public service. While some legislators

---

[30] Castelo, a close friend of United States Military Attaché Vernon Walters, was clearly the candidate most preferred by the United States Embassy, and Borges claims that Lacerda received at least two calls from Ambassador Gordon during the governors' meeting.

exhorted their fellow congressmen to resist any such unseating of duly elected representatives of the people, many others favored at least a selective purging, and most felt some such action was probably inevitable given the mood and objectives of the revolution. Thus, on April 8 leaders of the UDN, PSD, and PSP drafted a "Constitutional Act" by which Congress would delegate to the Revolutionary Supreme Command certain powers in this sphere.[31] This measure would be legitimized by means of a two-thirds vote such as was required by a constitutional amendment or for Congress to deprive one of its members of his seat.

Satisfied neither with the scope of this proposal nor its implication that their "Revolution" as such was without its own inherent powers and intrinsic legitimacy, the military leaders put the author of the 1937 Estado Nôvo Constitution, Francisco Campos, and his one-time assistant Carlos Medeiros da Silva (since that era Vargas' Solicitor General, Kubitschek's Attorney General, and a Minister of the Supreme Court) to work on an "Institutional Act" adequate to the imperatives of a revolutionary regime. While Campos concentrated on the prologue, Medeiros da Silva, who would later draft the 1967 Constitution, wrote most of the operative articles. A meeting of the military high command had been held on April 5 and 6 to deal with this matter and the question of presidential succession. Present at these sessions were the military ministers, the four field Army commanders, Castelo Branco, and Mourão Filho. While Admiral Rademaker and Justice Minister Gama e Silva echoed the "hard line" demands for a purge of half of congress and a number of Supreme Court justices, Costa e Silva and Castelo Branco decided in favor of a strong but less authoritarian position.[32] The "hard liners" did get the period of deprivation of political rights for those processed under the Act raised from five to ten years. (In December, 1968, and January, 1969, under the Fifth Institutional Act, Gama e Silva as Costa's Justice Minister would be able to reach those who had previously escaped his wrath.)

After this document was shown to the UDN's Bilac Pinto and PSD

[31] Consult Mário Victor, *5 Anos que Abalaram o Brasil* (Rio de Janeiro, 1965), pp. 542–53 and Edmar Morel, *O Golpe Começou em Washington* (Rio de Janeiro, 1965), pp. 128–31, as well as the daily press, particularly *Jornal do Brasil, Correio da Manhã* and *O Estado de S. Paulo.*

[32] Dulles, *Unrest in Brazil,* pp. 354–60.

Chamber leader Martins Rodrigues, it was promulgated by the Supreme Command of the Revolution.[33] Bearing only the signatures of Costa e Silva, Rademaker, and Correia de Mello, the Institutional Act made clear the military's disdain for Congress by declaring bluntly that "the Revolution does not seek to legitimize itself through Congress. It is the latter that receives its legitimacy from this Institutional Act, resulting from the exercise of the Constituent Power inherent in all revolutions." In justifying their abrupt modification of constitutional provisions and tampering with the functioning of political institutions, the military ministers maintained that their rescuing of the nation from the Goulart regime, an act in which they had assumed the role of guardian and interpreters of the nation's interests, left the Armed Forces vested with legitimate authority to decree a new institutional order.

What happened and will continue to take place in this time, not only in the spirit and behavior of the armed classes, but also in national public opinion, is an authentic revolution. A revolution is distinguished from other armed movements in that the will of the entire Nation is represented in it and not the interests and will of one group. The exercise of the constituent power resides in the victorious revolution. . . . This is the most expressive and radical form of constituent power. Thus the victorious revolution, acting as a constituent power, is legitimate by its very being. It overthrew the previous government and has the capacity to constitute the new government. . . . Victorious revolution dictates juridical norms without being limited in this right by norms existing prior to its victory. The leaders of the victorious revolution, thanks to the action of the Armed Forces and the unequivocal help of the Nation, represent the People. . . . The Institutional Act . . . is destined to assure the new Government to be installed the means indispensable for the task of the economic, financial, political and moral reconstruction of Brazil so as to face in a direct and immediate manner the grave and urgent problems on which depend the restoration of internal order and the international prestige of our Fatherland. The victorious revolution needs to be institutionalized and speeds by its institutionalization the complete powers which it effectively possesses.

The revolutionary chiefs couched their decision to maintain the Constitution of 1946 with addition of extraordinary presidential powers in terms of a concession to moderation on their part. They further ad-

[33] The text of the Institutional Act can be found in George W. Bemis, *From Crisis to Revolution* (Los Angeles, 1964), pp. 240–42; Dines et al., *Os Idos de Março*, pp. 401–403; and Victor, *5 Anos que Abalaram o Brasil*, pp. 597–600.

monished Congress that the decision to allow it to continue functioning was a self-denying action on the part of the revolution, not an obligation.

The Institutional Act had nine major substantive provisions: (1) it retained the 1946 Constitution, except as amended by the Act; (2) it ordered that Congress, by absolute majority, in public session, and by roll call, elect a president and a vice president within two days after publication of the Act, and to that end it suspended the provision that military chiefs of staff or other officials were ineligible for election to the presidency; (3) it authorized the president to initiate constitutional amendments and required Congress to act on them within thirty days and to pass them by absolute majority rather than by two-thirds vote; (4) it required Congress to act within thirty days on ordinary bills submitted by the president or to consider such bills automatically approved; (5) it granted the president exclusive authority to initiate financial bills while prohibiting Congress from appropriating more funds than the president requested; (6) it increased presidential powers to declare a state of siege; (7) it suspended for six months the constitutional and legal rights of job tenure and thus allowed the president and governors to dismiss public employees for "threatening national security, the democratic regime, or public order"; (8) it enabled the Supreme Command to suspend political rights of citizens for ten years, and to cancel the mandates of congressmen, state assemblymen and municipal counselors, with the President to enjoy the same power for sixty days after taking office; and (9) it designated October 3, 1965, as the date for the election of a president and vice president.

The Supreme Command lost no time in applying its new powers. Before such democratically oriented congressional supporters of the revolution as Adauto Cardoso (who, in 1966 would rail at the regime's humiliation of Congress) could react, they issued a lengthy list of persons whose political rights were suspended for a decade and whose government offices were forfeited. It was hoped that such actions on the part of the revolutionary military leadership would spare Castelo Branco the onus of responsibility for this controversial and unpopular move.

The first round of cassations on April 10 caught nearly the entire leadership of the generally leftist and anti-United States Nationalist Parliamentary Front (FNP) although Senator Aurélio Viana (one of the four vice presidents) was spared because of a decision not to interfere with the essentially conservative upper house. Sérgio Magalhães, Leonel Brizola, Ferro Costa, Adahil Barreto, Neiva Moreira, Fernando Santana, Paulo de Tarso, Max da Costa Santos, Rubens Paiva, and Sergeant Garcia Filho—ten of the other twelve FNP officers—lost their seats and subsequently their political rights. Bento Gonçalves and Celso Passos of Minas Gerais, the lowest ranking of the FNP officers, were spared this fate. (The former had at a much earlier date been president of the organization; young Passos had been named to the consultative council in homage to his father, the late Gabriel Passos, a devoted defender of Brazil's mineral resources.) Other prominent deputies who lost their mandates included Goulart Ministers Almino Afonso, Amaury Silva, and Abelardo Jurema together with such Communists as Marco Antônio Coelho, Henrique Cordeiro Oest, Demistóclides Batista, Rogê Ferreira, and Benedito Cerqueira. Francisco Julião, the Castroite peasant organizer, was also purged. Eloy Dutra (Guanabara Vice Governor and instigator of IBAD investigation), Roland Corbisier (director of the left-wing nationalist Institute of Advanced Brazilian Studies—ISEB—until elected a deputy), Bocayuva Cunha (a director of the leftist daily *Ultima Hora),* and Amazonas ex-governor Gilberto Mestrinho were other prominent cases. The latter shared with PSD ex-governor of Paraná Moyses Lupion the dubious distinction of being removed for corruption rather than "subversion."

Also losing their political rights at this time were ex-Presidents Goulart and Quadros, PCB chief Prestes, Governor Miguel Arraes, and pro-Communist mayors Pelopidas da Silveira and Djalma Maranhão. Other well-known figures on the list were Celso Furtado, Ambassador Josué de Castro (an internationally known expert on famine), *Ultima Hora* publisher Samuel Wainer, Marshal Osvino Alves, ex-Petrobrás head Francisco Mangabeira, ex-agrarian reform superintendent João Pinheiro Neto, and Goulart aides Darcy Ribeiro, Raul Ryff, Waldir Pires, and José Joffily. Almost the entire General Labor Confederation (CGT) leadership was also included: Clodsmith Riani, Hércules Correia, Dante Pelacani, Oswaldo Pacheco, Rafael Martinelli, and Roberto Moreno. José Anselmo (the leader of the naval mutineers), Clodomir Morais (peasant league organizer and would-be guerrilla leader), ex-Communist Deputy Salvador Romano Lossaco, and Lincoln Cordeiro Oest were among the better known of the private citizens who lost their political rights.

On April 14, a few additional politicians and a considerable number of writers were included on a new list along with two dozen military figures. Congressman Alberto Guerreiro Ramos, Guanabara State Deputies Paulo Alberto, Saldanha Coelho, and Ib Teixeira, publisher Enio Silveira, Brizola advisor Franklin de Oliveira, author Edmar Morel, and José Gomes Talarico (a minor labor leader who played a prominent part in the events of March) were added to the list of the politically proscribed. By this time all leading figures of "anti-imperialist" congressional investigations (those directed against United States investment or *entreguismo*) instituted by the nationalist left in the mid-1950's and again after 1961 had been purged. Dozens of names which had been reported in jeopardy were still untouched, although most of these, such as Pernambuco deputy Oswaldo Lima Filho, were cassated in January, 1968.

The expected purge of the armed forces took place on April 11, when seventy-seven Army officers, fourteen from the Navy, and thirty-one from the Air Force were transferred to the reserves. Leading the list of Army figures who had opposed the coup were Major Generals Ladário Pereira Teles and Oromar Osório, together with Brigadiers Euryale de Jesus Zerbini, Luiz Tavares da Cunha Melo, Argemiro de Assis Brasil, Albino da Silva, Chrisanto de Miranda Figueiredo, Anfrísio da Rocha Lima, Otomar Soares de Lima, Arnaldo Augusto da Nata, and Nairo Vilanova Madeira—all key figures in the Goulart *dispositivo*. Admiral Pedro Paulo de Araújo Suzano, Vice-Admiral Cândido da Costa Aragão, and Rear-Admirals Washington Frazão Braga, Alexandre Fausto Alves de Souza, and José de Araújo Goyano were the ranking naval officers to be so punished. Major Brigadier Francisco Teixeira and Brigadiers Richardo Nicoli and Dirceu de Paiva Guimarães were the senior Air Force officers to be prosecuted at that time, but within three days they were joined by Major Brigadier Anísio Botelho, an ex-minister. At the same time, the majority of these general officers, along with a smaller proportion of those from the lower grades, were deprived of their political rights for ten years. (Interestingly, Ladário and Osório as well as five of the nine Army brigadiers escaped this additional punishment, as did Rear Admiral Alves de Souza, although none of the Air Force generals was spared this additional condemnation.) Subsequently, General Jair Dantas Ribeiro was deprived of his political rights, while Admiral Sílvio Borges da Souza Mota was merely transferred to the reserves. Far reaching as was this purge, at least by Brazilian standards, it affected only a very small proportion of the total officer corps and in no way matched the draconian measures taken in Argentina during the months after Perón's ouster in 1955.

These developments at the national level had their counterpart in the states. On May 2 the Rio de Janeiro Legislative Assembly impeached Badger da Silveira and his vice governor, subsequently electing General Paulo Tôrres out of a plethora of military candidates. A similar move against Governor Lomanto Júnior in Bahia was undercut by the sudden arrival of General Justino Alves Bastos, who lent his support to the beleaguered governor. Additional cassations occurred on May 7, with the mayors of key Rio Grande do Sul cities and a number of that state's legislators as the central figures. On June 8 legislators of four states lost their seats and political rights along with several Communist Party leaders, ISEB chief Alvaro Viera Pinto, and Rio de Janeiro federal deputy Tenorio Cavalcanti.

Under pressure from the national government, initiated by the Supreme Command, the Governor of Pará, Aurélio do Carmo, was removed from office along with the vice governor and the mayor of Belem for corruption and involvement in the contraband trade. Colonel Jarbas Passarinho (who would soon be one of the rapidly rising new military politicians) was chosen to serve out the gubernatorial term, with Major Alacid Nunes as Belem's mayor. On June 15, the sixtieth day of Castelo Branco's administration, Amazonas Governor Plínio Coelho, General Jair Dantas Ribeiro, four federal deputies, including ex-ministers Expedito Machado and Wilson Fadul, several Goulart aides, and four diplomats were among the seventy-one persons losing their political rights in what was thought at the time to be the final wave of cassations under Article 10 of the Institutional Act.[34]

Sensing that the regime's political axe was being sharpened for his neck, Kubitschek on May 25 addressed a message to the Brazilian people declaring that they had already judged him at the polls and seemed eager to have another opportunity to demonstrate their faith in him at the ballot box. In moving to deprive him of his political rights,

[34] A full listing of those removed from office or stripped of political rights during this initial period is contained in Morel, *O Golpe* . . ., pp. 248–59. See also the *Diario Official* for April 11 and 14, May 7, and June 13, as well as the daily press.

the ex-President declared, his enemies were seeking to destroy not just one candidate but democracy itself. Costa e Silva, whose presidential ambitions were ill concealed, strongly favored the cassation of the man whose popularity was the most important single obstacle to his achieving that goal. Although Castelo Branco was extremely reluctant to take this step, he did so on the evening of June 8 under heavy pressure from the "hard line" and his War Minister.

2. ESTABLISHMENT OF A "TUTELARY" REGIME

Thus, when Castelo Branco was inaugurated president of Brazil on April 15, 1964, Brazilian democracy was already in the process of being severely restricted. In spite of the brave words and promises of his inaugural address, Castelo Branco recognized that "possibly it would not have been very hard to install a dictatorship in Brazil. But, how to maintain it without the help of the Nation? Very quickly we would be heading toward a police regime destined to trap the country in a circle of force and oppression." [35] Realization of the new president's lack of political experience led Magalhães Pinto, who strongly desired to succeed Castelo Branco, to propose serving as his political tutor, dealing with the intricacies of politics while the chief executive concentrated upon administration. But Castelo had other plans.

Humberto Castelo Branco was born in 1900 in the Northeastern state of Ceará. The son of an Army officer, he attended the Colegio Militar in Pôrto Alegre (as a classmate of Costa e Silva and the Kruel brothers). As a major in the early 1930's, he was a highly respected professor of tactics at the Military Academy, and by 1940 he was serving on the staff of War Minister Dutra. One of the outstanding heroes of the Italian campaign as Chief of Operations for the FEB, he became Director of Courses at the Command and General Staff College during the immediate postwar years. In the early 1950's, Castelo was chief of a section of the Army General Staff. At the time of the 1955 crisis, he had been advanced to the prestigious post of Commandant of the Command and General Staff College. He had previously attended the French War College and the U. S. Staff and Command School. In 1958, he was the Democratic Crusade's candidate for the Military Club presidency, but lost to Justino Alves Bastos and a nationalist slate. As Director

[35] Humberto de Alencar Castelo Branco, *Discursos 1964* (Brasília, 1965), p. 36.

General of Army Education, he occupied one of the ranking desk jobs in the War Ministry. During the Goulart administration he succeeded Costa e Silva as Fourth Army Commander before being named Army Chief of Staff.[36]

Castelo assembled a generally centrist-conservative cabinet of relatively high technical qualifications in which civilians were numerically preponderant. Costa e Silva remained as War Minister with Vice Admiral Ernesto de Mello Baptista and Major Brigadier Nélson Freire Lavanère-Wanderley assuming the Navy and Air Ministries (which were traditionally held by military men). The Gétulio Vargas Foundation's Octávio Gouvéia de Bulhões was retained as Finance Minister, and UDN Senator Milton Campos (Minas Gerais) became Justice Minister. Marshal Juarez Távora, the only military figure in the cabinet outside the service portfolios, returned to the Ministry of Transportation and Public Works, a position he had held more than thirty years before. PSD Deputy Daniel Faraco (Rio Grande do Sul) took over as Minister of Commerce and Industry, with the UDN's Flávio Suplicy de Lacerda (Paraná) in charge of Education and Raymundo de Brito (Guanabara) as Health Minister. Four other ministers—Mauro Thibau (Minas Gerais) of Mines and Energy, Oscar Thompson Filho (São Paulo) of Agriculture, Arnaldo Sussekind (Guanabara) of Labor, and career diplomat Vasco Leitão da Cunha of Foreign Relations—were essentially technicians, lacking any political experience or support. A few days later, Ambassador Roberto de Oliveira Campos was named Minister of Planning and Economic Coordination. Bahian UDN Deputy Luiz Viana Filho, a distinguished academic figure, was appointed Chief of the Presidential Office with ministerial status. A National Intelligence Service (SNI) was established under General Golbery, with broad authority to act as a watchdog on political as well as security affairs.

(Given the predominance of the military in the emerging pattern of politics, the key figures in the new regime were the senior Army generals who would hold the major military commands until with the passage of time, and their transfer to the reserves, the President would be able to promote others to take their places. In light of their crucial

[36] For insight into the type of military thinking he was to bring to bear on governing Brazil, see Colonel Francisco Ruas Santos, *Marechal Castelo Branco: Seu Pensamento Militar* (Rio de Janeiro, 1968).

roles in the events of the ensuing years, the relevant biographic sketches and examination of their career patterns are given as Appendix B, which might usefully be consulted before continuing with the chronological narrative.)

The first period of the Castelo Branco government was characterized, on the surface at least, by a continuation of the purges begun under the Revolutionary Supreme Command. Hundreds, if not several thousands, of individuals linked to the Goulart regime or suspected of "subversive" activities remained under arrest. Many were confined to prison ships anchored in Guanabara Bay, as had been the case during Vargas' crackdown following the 1935 Communist revolt.[37] Most of the more important individuals sought by the victorius revolutionary forces had been able to find asylum in foreign embassies, and the steady procession into political exile began.[38] The University of Brasília had been "cleaned out" by the military, and the arrest of a group of Chinese Communist commercial representatives and journalists was played up as the nipping of a plot to assassinate the anti-Goulart leaders. When taxed about excessive repression against their opponents, the military investigators replied that "had the other side won we would all have been shot."

Military-Police Investigations (Inqueritos Policial-Militar, IPM's) were launched throughout the country during the brief rule of the Supreme Command. Soon numbering in the thousands, they involved tens of thousands of witnesses and suspects. In most cases, these IPM's were entrusted to officers identified with the anti-Vargas and anti-Goulart movements of the past decade. In a number of cases, these in-

---

[37] The literature on the 1964 repression is substantial, with Márcio Moreira Alves' *Torturas e Torturados* (Rio de Janeiro, 1966) bringing together most of the material on this subject. For an earlier roundup of a wide variety of accusations and allegations, with relatively sparse documentation but often with the ring of authenticity, consult "O Terrorismo Cultural," *Revista Civilização Brasileira,* No. 1 (March, 1965), pp. 239–97. Alceu Amoroso Lima, *Pelo Humanismo Ameaçado* (Rio de Janeiro, 1965), pp. 201–79 *passim,* presents the lament of a noted Catholic intellectual, while Mário Lago's *1° de Abril: Estórias para a História* (Rio de Janeiro, 1964) contains an account of a journalist's life as a political prisioner during this period. Consult also Carlos Heitor Cony, *O Ato e o Fato: crônicos políticos* (Rio de Janeiro, 1964) and Saldanha Coelho, *Um deputado no exílio* (Rio de Janeiro, 1965).

[38] Morel, *O Golpe . . .,* p. 135, contains a partial listing of those who found haven in foreign diplomatic missions.

dividuals had gained experience during the investigations launched by Quadros in 1961 into the affairs of the Kubitschek administration. On April 27, a General Investigations Commission (Comissão Geral de Investigações, CGI) was set up under Marshal Estevão Taurino de Rezende, who had been an active member of the anti-Communist faction in the 1950 and 1952 Military Club elections and had served with Castelo Branco on the Army General Staff during this period.[39] The regulations Taurino issued in May, permitting the IPM's to hold an individual for fifty days to hear his testimony, were an attempt to curb even more arbitrary abuses of authority. Even then, many individuals were released, generally after obtaining a writ of habeas corpus, only to be picked up and held by another IPM.

The IPM concerning the Institute of Advanced Brazilian Studies (ISEB), dissolved by the revolutionary government by one of its first decrees, took on a somewhat distinctive character insofar as one of the primary figures involved was Brigadier General Nélson Werneck Sodré. Thus, by military protocol his questioning had to be handled by an officer of superior rank, in this case General Djalma Ribeiro Cintra and finally Marshal Taurino himself.[40] As head of the history department at ISEB, Werneck Sodré had sponsored a series of secondary school Brazilian history texts written by his assistants and published by the Ministry of Education. Considered highly subversive by the revolutionary regime, these volumes were reissued commercially by a São Paulo firm in March, 1965. Coinciding with the release of Pernambuco ex-Governor Miguel Arraes at the order of the Supreme Court (which was still uncertain as to its jurisdiction over cases stemming from the Institutional Act), and his denunciation of the Brazilian participation in the Dominican intervention, the Sodré episode exemplified how the IPM's continued to be a source of controversy throughout the first year and a half of the Castelo Branco government.[41]

[39] Werneck Sodré, *Memórias* . . ., pp. 317, 382, and 608–13, deals with Taurino.

[40] *Ibid.,* pp. 574–644 *passim;* "História de 'História Nova,' " *Revista Civilização Brasileira,* No. 3 (July, 1965), pp. 27–40 and No. 4 (September, 1965), pp. 71–84; " 'História Nova': Denúncia do Procurador-Geral," *Revista Civilização Brasileira,* No. 11–12 (December, 1966-March, 1967), pp. 208–12; and a series of documents referring to action against publisher Enio Silveira in *Revista Civilização Brasileira,* No. 3 (July, 1965), pp. 321–65.

[41] On the celebrated Arraes case, consult Edgard Costa, *Os Grandes Julgamentos do Supremo Tribunal Federal, Quinto Volume, 1963–66* (Rio de Janeiro, 1967), pp. 125–66.

The seeds of further controversy were also sown during the early months of the new administration. On May 12, the government pressed Goiás Governor Mauro Borges to dismiss several members of his cabinet as suspected subversives. Borges, who had strong ideas of where a reformist-nationalist orientation left off and "pro-Communism" began, vigorously defended his aides, while his father, Senator Pedro Ludovico, denounced a UDN-backed plot with the military to overthrow the PSD-PTB state administration even though it had supported the March coup. The crisis was eased temporarily with the resignation of the individuals involved, but Borges refused to accept this out, and Castelo Branco on May 30 put an end to the first round of the Goiás incident by canceling their political rights. (This test of the revolution's political intentions would continue through the year and into 1965.)

Along with these repressive political moves some "reform" measures went forward. The law legalizing and regulating the right to strike was issued on June 1, and ten days later Agriculture Minister Oscar Thompson Filho was dismissed for having divulged the text of the administration's contemplated agrarian reform legislation without authorization. (In reality this was a blow aimed at corruption-tinged São Paulo Governor Adhemar de Barros, who had sponsored the relative political unknown for the post, but whose influence with the new government was rapidly declining.)

Early June also saw the beginning of political moves that were to be of crucial significance for the subsequent course of events. The military proponents of a drastic "housecleaning" in the political realm pressured the government for extension of the period for deprivation of political rights and suggested that the idea of presidential elections in October, 1965, was not feasible, particularly in the light of the electoral strength of ex-President Kubitschek. A massive propaganda campaign was launched against Kubitschek accusing him of having condoned corruption during his years in office. As mentioned, the ex-President fought back with a public manifesto to the Brazilian people on May 25. Following Costa e Silva's attacks upon his administration and his un-revolutionary position during the March crisis, Kubitschek on June 4 defended his record and reputation on the Senate floor.[42] On June 8, the government satisfied the UDN and "hard-line" military while affronting

---

[42] Consult Victor, *5 Anos que Abalaram o Brasil,* pp. 582–91, for details on this episode.

wider segments of public opinion by canceling Kubitschek's senatorial mandate and suspending his political rights for a decade. In addition to charges of financial irregularities, the government claimed that the ex-President had paid for PCB electoral support in 1955 and had made a down payment for Communist support in the 1965 campaign.

Whatever satisfaction Lacerda may have taken from the removal of his most serious competitor for the 1965 presidential election could not have lasted long. The revolutionary regime had moved against Kubitschek because, if allowed to run, he was almost certain to win the election scheduled for October, 1965. The military leadership could not abide the thought of those elements defeated by their coup being rehabilitated if not returned to power through elections, as had occurred after Vargas' ouster—in short, 1965 was not to be a repeat of their 1955 frustration. Lacerda, who in 1955 had called for postponement of the elections and a thorough housecleaning under the supervision of a military chief of government, had warned against repetition of that year's "errors" and pointed out that a return to power by Kubitschek would be as crippling to the revolution as Arturo Frondizi's election in 1958, with Peronist support, had proved in Argentina. But while the regime's leaders were more than ready to cut down Kubitschek, they were not prepared as a result to hand the presidency to Lacerda, and as the only remaining national political figure in full enjoyment of his political rights, Lacerda was a very forbidding favorite. With Magalhães Pinto and Adhemar de Barros leading the way by repeated statements carried in the press, along with pronouncements by General Justino Alves Bastos, Congress prepared to add prolongation of Castelo Branco's mandate to the package of constitutional amendments submitted by the administration. Receiving word of the July 8 favorable decision of a mixed commission headed by Deputy João Agripino, Lacerda returned from an extended trip to the United States and Europe, devoted to "explaining" the 1964 revolution. Reassuming the Guanabara governorship, he stressed that only elections could legitimize and popularize the government. But the military leaders solidly backed the need to extend Castelo Branco's term, with Costa e Silva going so far as to assert on July 14 that "to speak of succession now is to want to agitate the country." Pausing only to approve liberalization of the controversial Remissions of Profits Law, the Congress prepared to enact a series of constitutional amendments strengthening the hand of the incumbent President.

With Castelo Branco publicly manifesting considerable reluctance, the sincerity of which his critics doubted, his term was extended by nearly fourteen months to March 15, 1967, through a constitutional amendment of July 22. The vote was 248 to 100 in the Chamber of Deputies, with the PSD casting 64 votes, the UDN a near unanimous 61, the PTB 32, the PSP sixteen and the PDC fourteen for the extension.[43] A companion provision, passed by a vote of 314 to 32, required an absolute majority of the popular vote for election as president, thus consecrating an old UDN thesis of 1950 and 1955 (aimed against the legality of Vargas' and Kubitschek's elections) but striking a blow against Lacerda's electoral hopes. At the same time, electoral eligibility was extended to the military, albeit in a version somewhat different from that emphasizing the candidacies of noncommissioned officers for which Brizola and Goulart had worked so hard. An amendment eliminating the cash payment requirement for land expropriations was also passed, but provisions to extend the vote to illiterates failed to gain congressional approval.[44] While Magalhães Pinto, who had been one of the instigators of the postponement of the election, welcomed this "consolidation" of the revolution, Lacerda reacted strongly against this drastic blow to his presidential aspirations.[45] Seeking to avoid an open break with Castelo Branco, Lacerda denounced the Congress for "demoralizing" not only the revolution but the President by leading to his rupture of a "compromise of honor" and transforming him into a dictator. Lacerda subsequently explained on July 31 that he would feel free to criticize the government, although he was not going into direct opposition. In the view of retired General Humberto Peregrino, one of the handful of Brazilian military figures to have earned a personal reputation as a writer and intellectual, the 1964 coup had led to a situation of increasing military authoritarianism, with the consequent alienation of most civilian groups, a regime in which

the power of the State came to be exercised, in an authoritarian nature, by a military and political elite characterized by an irresponsible as well as aggressive sentiment of self-sufficiency. In consequence this elite proceeds as the absolute interpreter of the national good, put by it in terms of rightist

[43] Morel, *O Golpe . . .*, p. 209.

[44] The text of constitutional amendments numbers 9 and 10 can be found in *Revista de Direito Público e Ciência Política*, VIII, No. 2 (May-August, 1965), 216–23.

[45] See his comments in *O Estado de S. Paulo*, July 18, 1964.

reaction in the political field and financial housecleaning in the administrative plane. From this rapidly resulted a sharp break of this directing elite with nearly all currents of opinion: workers, rural laborers, students, writers, professors, artists, the middle class, producting sectors, and religious groups.[46]

Although much of this trend toward an unpopular authoritarian government still lay in the future as the country reached the reopening of schools after the July (mid-winter) vacation, several episodes had provided a harbinger of ill winds ahead. The government's position as it attempted to shift toward positive action with the unveiling of its economic recovery and development program was complicated by the continued free wheeling of the IPM's under the direction of officers of the restless hard line faction. Marshal Taurino had cautioned that there was "much more corruption in Brazil than subversion," but had met with relatively little success in his efforts to impose a more austere and disciplined mood upon the IPM's through which a number of colonels were becoming nationally known figures by means of sensational disclosures and accusations. A good deal of corruption surrounding Adhemar de Barros was uncovered in São Paulo by the IPM of General Dalisio Mena Barreto, but owing to allegations that as a close friend of *O Estado de São Paulo* publisher Julio de Mesquita Filho, a long-time critic of the Governor, he was not impartial, the vigorous investigator was replaced by General Hugo Panasco Alvim. Marshal Taurino Resende's twenty-seven year-old son was arrested for distributing a "subversive" manifesto to his economics students in Recife. Resigning in August as the regime's "grand inquisitor," Taurino struck out at the government's tolerance of "corrupt" politicians who had climbed aboard the revolution's bandwagon.[47] Asserting that his son was "not a subversive nor corrupt, but an idealist like his father," he stepped out of the thankless role in which he had at least been able to partially soften the retaliation and repression of the more "exalted" revolutionary officers. (Admiral Paulo Bosísio headed the CGI until replaced in 1965 by Panasco Alvim.)

[46] Umberto Peregrino, "O Pensamento da Escola Superior de Guerra," *Cadernos Brasileiros,* No. 38 (November-December, 1966), p. 37.

[47] Maia Neto, *Brasil, Guerra Quente na América Latina* (Rio de Janeiro, 1965), pp. 89, 106, and 231–32; Morel, *O Golpe . . .,* pp. 178–79; and Beneval de Oliveira, *Odio destroi o Brasil: uma análise da crise política brasileira de 1961 a 1964* (Rio de Janeiro, 1965), pp. 72–82.

The problems a moderate, constitutionally inclined military government could expect with the radical rightists of the Armed Forces were foreshadowed by the case of Sergipe Governor João de Seixas Doria, a progressive centrist and moderate nationalistic politician who had won a bitterly contested election in 1962 against the candidate of an old-line entrenched conservative machine. He was arrested soon after the coup and sent to Fernando de Noronha Island. Subsequently granted a habeas corpus by the Superior Military Tribunal, he was immediately rearrested and transferred to the Sixth Military Region headquarters at Salvador to testify before the IPM functioning in the Bahian capital. Given the weakness of their case under the national security law, the emphasis in the charges against him was shifted from subversion to corruption.[48] Although there is no doubt that Seixas Doria viewed Goulart's campaign for basic reforms as "audacious, but legitimately democratic," his own political and ideological position was closer to that of Carvalho Pinto than of Brizola, and no more distant from Magalhães Pinto than from Arraes.[49] Among his Northeastern colleagues, Seixas Doria was not very far to the left of Rio Grande do Norte's Aluísio Alves or for that matter Petronio Portela of Piauí or Virgílio Távora of Ceará.

In terms of the political realities of the day, Seixas Doria was vulnerable to the attacks of his local enemies largely because of hostility at the level of national leadership, resulting from his participation at the side of Goulart in the March 13 rally. His position was also weakened by the fact that the coup found him on an extended absence from his state and unable to return until the afternoon of April 1. Had Seixas Doria chosen to jump on the bandwagon he might have survived, at least a while longer, as did Badger Silveira in Rio de Janeiro. Instead he issued a calm and dignified message to the people of Sergipe which reaffirmed his support of structural reforms and called for preserving the integrity of all elected offices.[50] As a result, before dawn on April 2

---

[48] This story is treated most fully in Seixas Doria, *Eu, Réu sem Crime* (Rio de Janeiro, 1965), *passim*. While the author certainly does not feel that he was treated fairly, his account is remarkably nonpolemical and free of bitterness.

[49] This conclusion is based on my close study of his voting record, political activities and policy statements in Congress, as well is in the 1962 gubernatorial campaign. Consult Seixas Doria, *Eu Réu sem Crime*, pp. 34, 40–42, and 71–77.

[50] *Ibid.*, pp. 51–52, for the text of this manifesto.

he was taken into custody by the Army, while the legislative assembly—many of whose members were concerned with reaching an accommodation with the new order—voted his removal from office.

Seixas Doria's testimony to the IPM headed by "hard-line" Colonel Hélio Ibiapina demonstrates the difference in the thinking of the non-Communist nationalist left and military anti-Communism. For the officer, "slogan" was a Marxist term and its use by Seixas Doria apparently convinced him that the politician was subversively inclined. The latter's argument that for him a Communist was not "an enemy to destroy but a brother to convince" did not strike a responsive chord with Colonel Ibiapina. Endorsement by Archbishop Dom Eugenio Salles meant little, since in the eyes of the IPM chief this prelate (subsequently named a Cardinal by the Pope) was "one of the most red." [51]

3. DIVISIONS WITHIN THE REGIME

Although the old divisions within the military were largely overcome for the purpose of ousting Goulart, they tended to re-emerge quickly in the aftermath of the coup, in part over the question of whether the military should really undertake a "revolution," and if so, in what direction and along which dimensions.

In the course of events following the 1960 elections, in which the leaders of the November 11 movement, Lott and Denys, chose separate paths (the former toward Goulart; the latter toward the coup), many of the Vargas period cleavages were overridden if not forgotten, and the attack by the Goulart regime on the principles of military discipline and hierarchy in March, 1964, led to a very high degree of cohesion in the Armed Forces. While this was bolstered in April with the elimination from the ranks of the officer corps of the small, but previously influential group of leftist nationalists who had provided the defunct regime with its false sense of military security, the seeds of new divergences were already apparent. At the senior level the original conspirators resented having been largely deprived of the personal fruits of victory. Several of the more liberal among them would soon protest the anti-democratic

[51] *Ibid.*, pp. 83–85. Seixas Doria had visited Communist China with a congressional delegation—as well as the United States and Nationalist China, it should be added—another fact which apparently counted against him. In this respect, his case parallels that of Mauro Borges, who had made a trip to the Soviet Union as well as to the United States.

actions of the new government, but others would continue to advocate a more drastic political housecleaning. As time passed, the frustrated political ambitions of certain ranking figures would lead them to break with the Castelo Branco regime.

Most significant, however, was the emergence of the hard liners, an influential grouping of younger officers of what appeared to be a generally radical rightist position. Originally enjoying relatively close ties with *Lacerdismo* and favorably viewing the Guanabara governor's presidential ambitions, they would largely abandon Lacerda as he shifted to open opposition and wooing of the leftist electorate. The hard-line (linha dura) enjoyed a brief period of substantial influence albeit not dominance during the early weeks of the revolution. The country was under the control of a Revolutionary Supreme Command with nearly unlimited powers, and the Institutional Act provided ample justification for harassment of those felt to be enemies of the new order. Although they were disappointed when some of their targets escaped the lists of *cassados,* the hard-line officers could hope to include them in the next wave of the purge.

When, however, the Castelo Branco government allowed its major discretionary powers to lapse on June 15 instead of extending them to November 9 or to the end of its term, as advocated by the *duros,* friction within the military increased rapidly. Although many of their leaders were kept busy, if not fully satisfied, as heads of the flourishing IPM's, they were uneasy over the government's stress on moderation and rationality, along with a sharp increase in public criticism from those who had earlier condoned their actions in the name of consolidation of the revolution. The passage of time had quickly dimmed the sense of immediacy of the "Communist" threat in the minds of all but the hard liners, who were most unhappy to see public attention focused on rectification of "abuses" committed in the heat and zeal of April and May when by their standards many "subversives" were still untouched. At the beginning of August, Castelo rejected their contention that the revolution should deal more harshly with its enemies.

When the intentions of the reclaimants are well analyzed what we frequently end up finding behind the phrases of censure is the desire to injure or prejudice the overturned or opponents. Is this the role of revolutionaries? Others call for dismissals which should be on a mass scale, many times involving humble functionaries in no way responsible for the misordering encountered in the country. . . .

None of this, however, ought to signify that the Government is less interested in purging from public positions as many as are proven to be compromised or implicated in acts of subversion or corruption. This object of the Revolution ought to be inflexible.[52]

Complicating the alignments on this issue was the fact that many of the excesses in the early period took place in areas commanded by generals who had themselves been linked to the fallen regime and were now out to prove themselves more Catholic than the pope.[53]

Viewing the period since 1930 as "a kind of dynamic equilibrium, unstable and changeable" in the competition of social and economic sectors, Fernando Pedreira saw the movement of March 31 as an instance in which a number of diverse elements cooperated to end a threat to the rules of the game.[54] During the initial six months of the Castelo Branco administration, he perceived the possibility of a course such as was later to develop under Costa e Silva: "the only grave danger which could result from March 31 and subsequent developments . . . would be the gradual installation of a military dictatorship which would give rise in the Army and in the administrative machine an impenetrability and a caste spirit which they have never had in Brazil." [55] At this time, however, he saw this "Argentine way" as unlikely in light of Brazilian traditions and countervailing powerful social factors.

By mid-1964, it was evident that the old pattern of civil-military relations, one in which the Armed Forces set the limits of the political game, but only within the context of broad currents of elite group opinion, had disappeared into the realm of historial memory. The broad middle masses of the officer corps were involved in the intervention into politics to an even greater extent than in 1889 or 1930, and, in contrast to *tenentismo,* "liberty, which threatened to transform itself into license, is being disciplined and confined in more rigid limits." [56]

When Castelo Branco refused in June to prolong his arbitrary powers and appealed to the "nonsubversive" left to join in support of a

[52] Castelo Branco, *Discursos 1964,* p. 35.
[53] Pedreira, *Março 31,* p. 66.
[54] *Ibid.,* pp. 26–28.
[55] *Ibid.,* p. 29.
[56] *Ibid.,* pp. 41–42.

reformist program, it appeared that the emerging technocratic elite, particularly on the military side, was determined to carry the country toward a new political regime differing qualitatively from the formal democracy of the 1945–1964 period. The strategy to be followed was one of "obtaining an alliance with the old political machines and power structures, which are being compelled to serve the new order instead of being simply destroyed." [57] In the eyes of the elements generally termed the moderates, or "Sorbonne" group, the regrettable necessity of military intervention in exercise of the "moderating power" arose from the faults of the nation's political institutions. Unlike many of the hard liners, they did not see the country's troubles primarily in terms of "bad" individuals who had subverted and corrupted the system, but rather looked for weaknesses in the institutional structure itself. In the absence of a vast number of "extraordinary public figures, all of good faith and capable of repelling or turning aside the temptions and injunctions which stem from the phase of maturation itself," the line of argumentation of the *duros* led to affirmation of the need for a protracted period of rule by the military, who allegedly enjoyed the virtues of disinterestedness to a much higher degree than their self-seeking civilian counterparts.[58] Significant elements of the *duros* went beyond this rationale to justify military rule on the basis of the Armed Forces' role as the "natural" representative of the nation and national interests.

"The "Sorbonne" elements, on the other hand, while generally convinced of their own abilities and understanding of national problems, had a more realistic view of the level of competence required for complex governmental tasks than the normal run of the officer corps, those whose career is largely with troop commands rather than in the schools and general staff. In this sense, the Sorbonne officers are essentially elitist, but their close contact with high-quality as well as high-level civilians disposes them toward a concept of a fused technocracy rather than rule by a representative military class or caste. In brief, for the "hard liners" subversion and corruption were the fundamental problems.

[57] *Ibid.,* p. 38.
[58] The quotation, taken slightly out of context, is from Pedreira, *Março 31,* p. 47. For an example of military thinking, see General A. C. Moniz de Aragão, "O Papel das Fôrças Armadas na Revolução de Março de 1964," *O Globo,* April 2, 1965.

The Sorbonne officers believed it was essential to go beyond the negative or punitive phase and come to grips with underlying structural problems.

Division into sharply differentiated groups of "hard liners" and the "Sorbonne," useful as it is for understanding the dialectics of the Castelo Branco period, imposes a rigidity that often did not exist in reality. To some extent, both of these groupings are more a state of mind than a structured clique. Moreover, many Brazilian officers conform to neither of these ideal types but manifest a good deal of ambivalence in their attitudes and ambiguity in their positions. While both the *duros* and Sorbonnists saw quite direct and prolonged military involvement in politics as necessary, many of the centrist, relatively apolitical officers retained legalist sentiments. Some even hoped for an expeditious return to the historical pattern, in which the military remained partially isolated from the day-to-day political turmoil while exercising the "moderating power" in moments of crisis. The key to such an arbiter function was that

The Armed Forces, in reality, function at the appeals level. The interests, opinions, points of view, and political passions which circulate in civil society and which stir up its diverse factions also penetrate the military, sensitizing the mass of officers at various grades to differing degrees. For these, therefore, to act as a military movement it is necessary for the tensions to have reached a very high level to the point of neutralizing the fatcors which normally command respect for the legal order.[59]

In this respect, the crucial variables have been legalist indoctrination, military discipline, adaptability, and, above all, the conviction that the Armed Forces can act effectively as an institution only when united.

It was therefore possible for the subsequent differences between the politically oriented hard liners and Sorbonnists to be masked by the similarity of their immediate goals:

The aspirations of the young officers probably did not go much beyond what, given the circumstances could be expected of them: they wanted the reestablishment of order and of public morality, they wanted the installation of an austere and energetic government, capable of guaranteeing discipline and hierarchy, they wanted to fight corruption and subversion, the investigation

[59] Pedreira, *Março* 31, p. 53.

of crimes committed and the exemplary punishment of the guilty, who would be expelled from public life. The "moderates" wanted the same, although it could be said they wanted more, because they went farther: their object was to institutionalize the new situation, embedding it in the national political organization, making way at the same time for a more profound renovating work . . . in accord with the necessities of the evolution of the country according to how this evolution is or was considered in the National War College and the Army Command and General Staff College.[60]

The pressure of the hard line, while forcing Castelo Branco to take actions during his first months in office that he might have preferred to avoid, helped push civilian democratic elements into the government's arms as the major bulwark against a more drastic military regime. In this context, an inflammatory manifesto issued by Goulart on August 24 provided the *linha dura* with an opportunity to renew their campaign against the left more than it rallied the left to oppose the Castelo Branco administration.

During the second half of 1964 the interplay between the military factions and the President's tactics for dealing with the pressures of the hard liners, giving ground where necessary but countering with reformist moves in other areas, became quite clearly defined. The most instructive case in this respect is the government's handling of the Goiás case, which remained very much alive after the preliminary skirmishing in May that resulted in the cassations of two of Governor Mauro Borges' state secretaries.

In spite of the role he had played in support of the revolution and in working to achieve support from his fellow governors for Castelo Branco's election, Goiás Governor Mauro Borges Teixeira soon found himself in serious trouble. The traditional rivals of Senator Pedro Ludovico Teixeira's PSD machine sought to take advantage of the sharp rise in the UDN's fortunes as a result of its leaders' close identification with the new central government to win control of the state and administer a blow to the father through the ouster from office of his son. In this they were aided by the determination of General Ernesto Geisel and other key figures around President Castelo Branco not to forget Borges' support for Goulart in the 1961 crisis. Through the general in charge of

[60] *Ibid.*, p. 67.

investigations in Goiás under the Institutional Act, they gave Borges an ultimatum to form a coalition government including his political enemies.[61]

Taking his case to the President, Borges described his government as clearly of the democratic left and not at all Communist influenced. He pointed out that he had broken with the PTB locally and with the Goulart government in mid-1963. Nonetheless, three members of his administration were deprived of their political rights under the Institutional Act. Criticism of the cancelation of Kubitschek's political rights and complaints concerning the *linha dura*–oriented IPM in Goiás, headed by a zealous UDN partisan, earned Borges the animosity of important military figures, including Costa e Silva, who appeared to back those hard liners who declared Goiás to be a hotbed of subversion. Borges' appeals to Castelo Branco against such treatment brought no result; instead General Riograndino Kruel took charge of the IPM and called the Governor as a witness in November.[62] With much of public opinion and the press sympathizing with the Goiás Governor, the national administration felt compelled to demonstrate its strength. Confessions implicating the Governor had been obtained by this time, but it was widely believed that they had been extracted by torture. The most incriminating, that of one Paval Gutko who had a reputation for being mentally unstable, bears many of the hallmarks of a police falsification.[63]

The crisis came to a head in November. Borges sought a habeas corpus from the Supreme Court, which had shown signs of seeking to reestablish rule of law, to order the political impasse there resolved under the state constitution free from outside pressures. On November 23, just an hour before the court conceded this writ by a unanimous vote, Castelo Branco reiterated that a focus of "agitation and subversion" would not be tolerated.[64] (While in this instance the higher judiciary expressed their independence, they would within a year be

[61] See Borges, *O Golpe em Goiás*, pp. 119–75, for his participant account of the nine-month political conflict.

[62] *Ibid.*, pp. 190–215, contains the text of Borges' testimony.

[63] Moreira Alves, *Torturas . . .*, pp. 107–41; David Nasser, *A Revolução que se Perdeu a si Mesma* (Rio de Janeiro, 1965), pp. 407–24; and Borges, *O Golpe em Goiás*, pp. 219–92, amply cover these controversial aspects.

[64] Borges, *O Golpe em Goiás*, pp. 167–71, and *Síntese: Política Econômica Social*, No. 24 (October-December, 1964), pp. 79–80.

curbed by another Institutional Act and subsequent court packing by the President.) Accusing the Goiás Governor of having launched an "inexplicable publicity campaign to confuse national public opinion in relation to the true situation in Goiás" involving expenditures of "huge sums of unknown origins," the government moved rapidly to decree full federal intervention, an act that took place on November 26. Castelo Branco appointed Colonel Carlos Meira Mattos, one of his key military aides (and an officer who would be entrusted with at least one very sensitive task during each of the ensuing four years) as Interventor. In spite of an adverse report by the *relator* of the Commission on Justice and Constitutional Affairs, the Chamber of Deputies approved the President's action on November 29 by a vote of 192 to 140.[65] Thus the machinery of state government came completely under federal control, with the governor stripped of all power.

The central government's handling of this episode demonstrated intelligent adaptation of military tactics to an essentially political problem. The intervention was considered an initial and temporary step by which the administration seized the initiative, with the main objective being the permanent removal of Borges and selection of a constitutional successor who would be completely loyal to the revolution. This was to be accomplished at minimal political cost in terms of loss of PSD congressional cooperation. As a first move, the cassation of Kubitschek had demonstrated to the PSD that the executive was not disposed to make major concessions to the leading party in return for its support in Congress. Thus, the national leadership of the PSD was quickly disabused of the idea that Borges could be retained in power by any negotiated arrangement and chose not to make a major issue of the affair. A high proportion of the PSD congressional representation was convinced, or coerced, into voting approval of the Goiás intervention, and PSD officials in Brasília appear to have urged the state leaders toward flexibility and compromise rather than intransigence.[66]

Meira Mattos, a highly regarded tactics professor who had been Mauro Borges' instructor at the Escola Militar undertook to resolve the

[65] Borges, *O Golpe em Goiás,* pp. 300–10 contains the text of Deputy Nélson Carneiro's relatório.

[66] The preceding interpretation draws on discussions with several key congressional figures and the chief civilian aide to the Interventor.

problem expeditiously so that the Castelo Branco regime could avoid the necessity of renewing the intervention for a second sixty-day period. Warning members of the PSD-PTB majority in the thirty-nine-member state legislature that they too could easily be implicated in the continuing IPM's, the Interventor wore down Borges' supporters, some of whom were demoralized by PSD National Chairman Amaral Peixoto's lack of encouragement.[67] Once the Goiás PSD were resigned to the inevitability of Borges' removal and turned their efforts toward securing a PSD successor, Meira Mattos caught them off guard by announcing a military veto of their choice, Benedito Vaz and putting forth his own candidate, Colonel Epitácio Cardoso de Britto. He was then in the position of being able to propose a symbolic "concession," in which the federal government in reality gave up nothing and gained a nearly ideal solution from its point of view. The Interventor withdrew his man, whose name had been introduced only for bargaining purposes, to balance the PSD's acceptance of the hard line's veto of Vaz, and the President broke the impasse by suggesting Marshal Emílio Rodrigues Ribas Júnior as a compromise candidate. The legislature voted down the charges against the Governor and sidetracked the IPM's while at the same time invoking a "state of necessity" to justify declaring the governorship vacant.

Thus at the beginning of 1965 Mauro Borges was out of the governorship, but still in possession of his political rights. He was also something of a popular hero in light of his unyielding defense of his principles and initial stance of defiance, followed by restraint in the face of overwhelming odds in order to avoid useless bloodshed. The central government had demonstrated its firmness not only to the left but also in a manner designed to allay the *duros'* fears that it was too soft and lax in its vigilance concerning internal security. Even the PSD state legislators could maintain that they had yielded only in the face of irresistible pressures from the military and to free the state from continued intervention. The UDN had the satisfaction of having participated in the political destruction of the man who had dealt them a political defeat in 1960 and would no longer have to buck an unfriendly incumbent administration in the October, 1965, balloting. Indeed, in retro-

[67] *O Estado de S. Paulo,* December 23, 1964; *Jornal do Brasil,* December 23, 1964; and Correio da Manhã, December 18, 1964.

spect experienced political figures and observers were to wonder at the neatness of the solution of what had seemed to be a very sticky problem and speculate over the degree to which the surface events might have been part of an elaborate charade in which wily old Senator Pedro Ludovico traded off the remaining year of his son's term as governor to preserve him from further political embarrassments and possible *linha dura* demands for his prosecution.[68] (In an incident indirectly related to this affair, Colonel Francisco Boaventura Cavalcanti, Jr., was removed as a presidential military aide for having sent an unauthorized and harshly critical cable to *O Globo* publisher Roberto Marinho. Stung by this rebuke for indiscipline, Boaventura worked increasingly in favor of Costa e Silva's presidential candidacy; his brother was subsequently appointed to Costa's cabinet.)

4. AUSTERITY, INSTITUTIONAL REFORMS, AND ACCENTUATED DISSENTION

While the IPM's and the Goiás crisis were the most exciting political events of the latter part of 1964, other developments entered into the interaction from which the Castelo Branco administration's policies and program were gradually emerging. Planning Minister Roberto Campos' emergency measures, first announced at the end of April, had been generally if glumly received as necessary in view of the country's financial chaos and galloping inflation. Essentially, they were firmer applications of actions advocated within the Goulart administration by San Thiago Dantas and Carvalho Pinto. Even the removal of exchange rate subsidies to wheat, petroleum, and newsprint were a return to moves taken during the Kubitschek administration by Lucas Lopes and under Quadros by Clemente Mariani. By the end of July, the coffee producers, some industrial groups, and trade unions were beginning to rail at the credit restrictions and wage ceilings, but it was not until the Program of Action (Programa de Ação Económica do Govèrno, PAEG) was unveiled in mid-August that criticism began to mount.

Feeling largely free from the considerations of political feasibility that had conditioned the earlier stabilization efforts with which they had been associated in one capacity or another from the Dutra administration on, Campos and Octávio Bulhões took an essentially "technocratic"

---

[68] Variations on this interpretation have been put forth by a number of congressmen and individuals associated with the Castelo Branco administration during subsequent conversations in 1966 and 1967.

approach to the complex problems of economic policy. Their diagnosis did not differ radically from previous planning documents, even that of the Goulart government. The sharp contrast lay in the new team's determination to follow through on their full implementation, confident that the President would extend his full backing rather than sacrifice financial stabilization measures in the face of the inevitable political protests from labor (over wage freezes) and producers (over credit restrictions). Jesuit-educated and, by self-admission, prone to the "un-Brazilian" vice of excessive rationality, Campos was determined that for once technically "sound" plans would not be diluted and compromised away in the face of public criticism. With Bulhões as Finance Minister and close professional associates rather than politicians or financiers in charge of the Bank of Brazil and the National Economic Development Bank (BNDE), the government, for once, had a homogeneous and largely harmonious team in charge of economic policy. But most important was the President's nearly unconditional support for containment of inflation as the administration's first priority.

The goals of the PAEG were not themselves highly controversial. The rate of economic growth was to be restored to a level of 7 per cent annually, with regional, sectoral, and social imbalances ameliorated. But the emphasis on disinflation, with virtual price stability targeted for 1966, and the containment of government expenditures were not palatable to important sectors of society that wished to continue receiving the benefits and subsidies to which they had become accustomed. Not only those of a nationalist and socialistic orientation were opposed to the administration's plans to rationalize the capitalist system in Brazil; many businessmen were also adverse to the major readjustments that this determination implied.[69]

Austerity measures such as those implemented by Campos and Bulhões are never politically popular. And in a country where economic nationalism had been heavily stressed for the better part of a generation, the repeal of several "nationalist" provisions of Goulart period legislation (particularly limitations on profits sent abroad and expropriation of public utilities) gave rise to protests that the Brazilian economy was again being handed over to North American imperialism. The govern-

[69] The Essay on Sources contains a full discussion of bibliographic references on the economic policy dispute of 1964–1969.

ment's hopes of sharply reducing inflation while returning to a high rate of economic growth depended heavily upon international financial assistance and a sharp increase in foreign private investment, and a series of actions were taken designed to elicit a favorable response from the Johnson administration and business circles in the United States. The latter's skepticism as to the probable duration of the Campos policies, based on the Kubitschek and Quadros experiences, contributed to a situation in which Castelo Branco committed himself to complete and continued support for his Planning Minister, with the cassation of Kubitschek and prolongation of his own presidential mandate designed in part to assuage such doubts.

By the end of 1964 a situation had developed in which the administration's program, considered by both the civilian and military technocrats as reformist and viable, was viewed in a very different light by significant political leaders and groups that had backed the March revolution. Hence much as dissension on political questions developed between the directing nucleus of the new regime and the military hard liners, economic questions gave rise to tensions with important social elements. The government made little effort to explain its program to the general public, however, relying on favorable material results to demonstrate the wisdom of its policies.

In November the purchase of the American and Foreign Power utility company for $135 million provided Carlos Lacerda, the most dissatisfied of the revolutionaries, with a convenient issue for attacking Campos' policies. Lacerda denounced the action as a "scandalous" overpayment for "scrap metal." On December 3, Castelo responded by advising Lacerda that the Campos program was that of his administration and advising the Guanabara Governor to assume a clear attitude of opposition to the government. Lacerda suffered a further setback to his political ambitions when the Supreme Court ruled against his efforts to utilize those provisions of the Institutional Act which strengthened the executive in dealing with a recalcitrant state legislature, rejecting his argument by analogy between the two levels of government. Although his status as UDN presidential nominee had been reaffirmed at a party convention in November, Lacerda felt his campaign undermined by the unpopularity of the administration's policies, hence his party formed the backbone of the government's majority in Congress. Although this ambivalent relationship would continue for some time, the foundation for Lacerda's complete break with the Castelo Branco government was already laid.[70]

The government's position appeared secure at the beginning of 1965 with its triumph in the Goiás crisis, Lacerda's effort to rebuild his fences with the President, and the achievement of immediate legislative goals including a "Land Statute," which would facilitate the first stages of agrarian reform, substantial revision of tax legislation, and creation of a central bank. Yet in spite of such positive steps, the year was to be more one of major defeats than significant accomplishments. While substantial institutional, financial, and administrative reforms would be accomplished prior to October, a negative verdict at the polls, and *linha dura* discontent were to lead to substantial abandonment of the effort to renovate the system within a semi-competitive political process.

The interservice rivalry over control of carrier-based planes, which had first arisen under Kubitschek (for whom it had proved functional), was brought to a head. Castelo's first Air Minister, Nélson Freire Lavanère-Wanderley, had previously resigned rather than approve punishment for junior officers who machine-gunned a Navy helicopter in Rio Grande do Sul. Now his successor, Márcio de Souza Melo, refused to accept a decision that the carrier *Minas Gerais* would leave for a training exercise carrying planes piloted by naval aviators. Brigadier João Adil de Oliveira, who had headed the Air Force investigation into the Lacerda assassination attempt in 1954, declined appointment as minister under the circumstances. Castelo, who personally favored unification of the services under a Ministry of Defense, prevailed upon Eduardo Gomes to come out of retirement and employ his great prestige to placate the Air Force.[71] Admiral Paulo Bosísio assumed the Navy Ministry in place of Melo Baptista.

[70] Lacerda's various pronouncements during 1962 were published as *O Poder das Idêas* (Rio de Janeiro, 1963, which was reissued in 1964. His addresses and writings of the late Goulart period and views expressed during the first nine months of the Castelo Branco administration are contained in *Palavras e Ação* (Rio de Janeiro, 1965) and *Reforma e Revolução* (Rio de Janeiro, 1964).

[71] Morel, *O Golpe . . .,* pp. 217–18, and *Jornal do Brasil,* January 8, 1965, which maintains that Castelo Branco threatened to appoint an Army general as Air Minister if Gomes would not accept.

On January 26, the President issued a decree delineating the spheres of authority of the two services; the Navy relinquished its planes to the Air Force and received the latter's anti-submarine helicopters in return. This decision alienated important segments of the Navy and left the Air Force far from satisfied, but Castelo's position with the Army was sufficiently strong to deter any thought of an organized reaction. The Military Club elections of May, 1964, had seen César Moniz de Aragão, one of the less senior Major Generals and a strong supporter of Castelo, defeat both General Justino Alves Bastos and the incumbent Marshal Augusto Magessi. Moreover, the resolution of the Goiás crisis had left the *duros* relatively satisfied with the government's handling of affairs, and Army unity was temporarily at a high point.

Moving to strengthen its legislative position before seeking enactment of a major program of institutional reforms, the executive engineered the defeat of Ranieri Mazzilli of the PSD in his bid for re-election for a seventh consecutive term as presiding officer of the Chamber of Deputies. With Castelo instructing congressional leaders as to his strong feelings on the matter, UDN national president Bilac Pinto was victorious, and promptly set to work to establish a "Renovating Parliamentary Bloc" (BPR) to support the government. Built around the UDN, it also included more than one-third of the PSD's congressional representation and nearly one-fourth of the PTB deputies.

With the country in the grips of a recession, particularly noticeable in São Paulo, criticism of the central government's economic policies increased. In March Lacerda and Magalhães Pinto, whose conflicting political ambitions would subsequently force them to choose very separate paths, joined together to attack Campos and Bulhões. The National Confederation of Industries (CNI), chafing under credit restrictions, called for a complete reformulation of the PAEG. For its part the administration commemorated the first anniversary of the revolution by issuing a series of decrees implementing the basic agrarian legislation enacted the preceding November. The Brazilian Institute of Agrarian Reform (IBRA) and the National Institute of Agricultural Development (INDA) were provided with more adequate organizational structures and the criteria established for the survey of landholdings and uses which was necessary prior to possible large-scale redistribution of underutilized properties.[72]

Although sentiment was widespread within the officer corps that 1965 should be a year "free from politics" to permit execution of the revolution's economic and social program, Castelo Branco decided to proceed with the scheduled elections. Thus, in spite of warnings not only from the *linha dura* but also in the face of cautions from War Minister Costa e Silva, the President insisted upon the holding of balloting in March for a new São Paulo Mayor as a step toward maintenance of participant-representative features of the regime. The results of this first test seemed to justify his confidence, as Brigadier Faria Lima, a one-time close associate of Jânio Quadros, but supporter of the 1964 coup, was the winner in a campaign in which national issues did not appear decisive. Castelo further determined that, instead of prolonging the mandates of incumbent governors for one year, having elections for an interim one-year term, or appointing interventors for the interim as advocated by those opposing a reopening of political competition, coincidence of state and federal elections would be postponed until 1970 and direct elections held in October in the eleven states where gubernatorial terms were expiring.

Magalhães Pinto, in an effort to strengthen his presidential possibilities for 1966, had already convinced his legislature to extend his term. Thus, the presidential decision to annul this action infuriated the Minas Gerais Governor and led to his formal break with the administration.[73] Pleased at this evidence of the executive's desire to adhere to democratic procedures, Congress overwhelmingly passed the constitutional amendment requested by the President to permit legislation further defining and amplifying ineligibilities for the October elections to assure that "corrupt and subversive" elements would not return to power. (The vote on this gesture of congressional accommodation to

[72] For an evaluation of these measures, consult James W. Rowe, "The 'Week of the Land' in the Brazilian Sertão," *American Universities Field Staff Report*, East Coast South America Series, XII, No. 1 (February, 1966) and Robert E. Price, "The Brazilian Land Reform Statute" (mimeo: Land Tenure Center, University of Wisconsin, April, 1965).

[73] See *Síntese: Política Econômica Social*, No. 25 (January-March, 1965), pp. 62–64 and No. 26 (April-June, 1965), pp. 79–81.

the military's wish for curbs on political opposition was 225 to 58 and 45 to 3 on the first reading, 249 to 54 and 44 to 1 on final passage.)

The successes of late March and early April were followed by development of a situation that contained the makings of a potentially serious crisis. On March 25, a group of guerrillas calling themselves the Armed Forces of National Liberation (FALN) and led by ex-Colonel Jefferson Cardim de Alencar Ossorio attacked a town in Rio Grande do Sul and then headed north into Paraná.[74] Although the group was captured within two days, the episode aroused fears of insurgency and lent credence to *linha dura* claims that a large-scale subversive threat and conspiracy existed. On the heels of this incident, the Supreme Court granted a habeas corpus to Pernambuco ex-Governor Miguel Arraes, who had been arrested under national security legislation for publicly refusing to submit to more IPM's after having spent more than a year in custody and being interrogated by one such inquiry after another.

Irritated at a pronounced delay in carrying out his order and wishing to reassert the position of the judiciary in the face of the erosion of its authority by IPM heads, the presiding justice of the Supreme Court, Ribeiro da Costa, sent a curt telegram to First Army Chief of Staff General Edson de Figueiredo. The latter, since deceased, was an active participant in the 1964 coup and was recognized as a senior leader of the *linha dura*. In the name of the Army he objected to the aggressive tone of the jurist's communication. While insisting on the immediate compliance with the high tribunal's decision, Castelo Branco requested Riberio da Costa to retract the offensive terms of his order to General Figueiredo. The incident was closed, but far from forgotten, as the Supreme Court head wrote a letter to the President stating that he had intended no censure or warning in chiding the general for his procrastination.

The government's decision to play a leading role in the Inter-American Peace Force in the Dominican Republic, while arousing considerable public protest, was well received by the hard liners. General Hugo Panasco Alvim was subsequently named the titular commander of the Organization of American States troops, while Colonel

---

[74] For an account of this incident see "Êste Homen Quis Incendiar o País," *Manchete,* April 10, 1965, pp. 16–29.

Meira Mattos took charge of the Brazilian contingent, which constituted the major portion of the Latin American component. But the Dominican crisis did not distract their attention for long from the domestic situation. The group of zealously anti-Communist colonels involved in directing the IPM's in Guanabara, some of whom still maintained close links to Lacerda, asked the President to reinstate the discretionary powers of the Institutional Act and to press for a severe ineligibilities law. Since in the eyes of this group such stanch government congressional leaders as Adauto Cardoso and Pedro Aleixo were suspect, Castelo Branco could hardly have gone far enough to satisfy their desires without abandoning his position of essential moderation and preservation of a significant, albeit reduced sphere for congressional action. Moreover, at the same time that they were demanding a more rigorous press law and further purges, Generals Pery Bevilaqua and Mourão Filho were advocating a political amnesty.[75]

On May 18, Lacerda took to television, giving publicity to his critique of the PAEG and proclaiming the advantages of an "alternative" program he had submitted to the President. Campos replied through the same media, and the debate rapidly deteriorated to a polemic at the popular level.[76] Following this resumption of attacks upon it from within the ranks of the 1964 revolution, the administration struck back. In mid-June, two bellwethers of the hard line, Colonels Gérson de Pina and Osnelli Martinelli, were replaced as chiefs of important IPM's as Castelo asserted his authority in the face of *linha dura* exigencies. Pina, a professor at the Colégio Militar and head of the IPM concerning the ISEB, was punished for indiscipline, as subsequently was Martinelli, the chief of the IPM investigating Brizola's "Groups of 11" and perhaps the most extreme of the *duros*. An instructor at the military preparatory school in Rio de Janeiro, he had taken the lead in establishing LIDER, the Radical Democratic League, a political movement demanding reinvigoration of the revolution.

Other prominent figures among the hard liners who were in the

---

[75] On the *linha dura* at this juncture, see Murilo Melo Filho, "Si Castelo Caísse," *Manchete,* July 17, 1965, pp. 25–27, and Carlos Lemos, "Os Coroneis dos IPMs," *Jornal do Brasil,* June 6, 1965, pp. 18–19.

[76] Carlos Lacerda, *Brasil entre a Verdade e a Mentira* (Rio de Janerio, 1965), contains the texts of his May 17 and May 25 "letters to the President."

public eye as a result of their direction of IPM's included Major Cléber Bonecker, an instructor in the Army's psychology course who had been named to preside over the IPM on the Communist press; Colonel Ferdinando de Carvalho, who as presiding officer of the IPM on the Communist Party appeared to some observers as more anxious to publish a series of volumes on the Communist threat he was compiling than to wind up the work of his inquiry and turn its findings over to the military courts for their consideration; Lieutenant Colonel Celso Meyer, who conducted a series of IPM's in the field of education, including that on the National Union of Students (UNE); and Lieutenant Colonel Luiz Gonzaga Andrada Serpa, director of the IPM on the General Labor Command (CGT) and one of three brothers who took part in the anti-Goulart movement in 1954 and 1955. Criticism of the government by such original revolutionaries as Admirals Heck and Rademaker gave further credence to the view that a military crisis existed.

Again, however, the Castelo Branco regime was able to use the agitation of the hard line to convince the political parties to approve its legislative requests. Perhaps a better tactician than strategist, Castelo at times let the force of events shape his policies, or at least modified his objectives to meet changed realities. In mid-1965, however, he used the trend of developments to achieve fundamental goals.

First on the regime's agenda for the "year of correction of political distortions" (as Castelo termed 1965 in his annual state of the nation message to Congress) was concern over the manifest weaknesses of the party system and flaws in the electoral process. As early as May, 1964, the President had called for reforms which would, *inter alia,* limit the influences of economic power and political patronage on the electoral process. Responsibility for drafting the new legislation was entrusted to the Superior Electoral Court (TSE), which in August established a working group composed of three of its members and its staff director, Dr. Geraldo da Costa Manso. This commission consulted with the presidents of the Regional Electoral Courts and students of the system. Their draft legislation was turned over to the President in December and presented to the parties and concerned public for their consideration in January, 1965.

Following ninety days of reasonably open public debate and broadly based discussions within the interest groups affected, the proposed legislation was revised by a committee that included two members of Congress, Justice Minister Milton Campos, TSE Minister Colombo de Souza, and Costa Manso. On April 22, the electoral code and political party statute that had emerged from this process were sent to Congress by the executive. A great number of amendments were offered in both committee and plenary sessions.[77]

Debate was intensified in June, when the executive submitted a sweeping Ineligibilities Law which, in addition to more generalized ends, was directed at several leading gubernatorial candidates. On July 15, the President promulgated the executive's draft of the electoral code on the grounds that Congress had not acted during the requisite thirty days for each house, as provided under the Institutional Act. On the same day the President also promulgated the Ineligibilities Act and signed into law the Party Statute passed by Congress (but with fourteen presidential vetoes which in effect returned the eighty-one-article document almost to the version the executive had originally proposed). Some provisions of this new legislation were not, however, to go into effect until after the gubernatorial balloting in October, 1965.

The basic aim of the new measures was to foster wider and more effective political participation. In keeping with analysis by academic specialists that indicated electoral confusion over the bewildering array of parties and candidates (fourteen parties with all candidates running at large), the legislation reduced the number of parties by sharply raising the minimum requirements parties had to meet if they were to achieve or maintain legal status. The measures also fostered party responsibility by prohibiting interparty alliances or coalitions in any proportional representation election. Another major objective was the ensuring of intraparty democracy by increasing the degree of supervision

[77] In addition to a large number of changes proposed in committee, including several substitute bills, 564 amendments to the code and 255 to the party statute were presented on the Chamber floor. The original project of the TSE can be found as *Anteprojecto de Código Eleitoral e de Estatuto Nacional dos Partidos Políticos* (Brasília, 1965). The final text of the Electoral Code (Law No. 4737 of July 15, 1965), Ineligibilities Law (Law No. 4738 of July 15, 1965), and the Political Parties Statute (Law No. 4740 of July 15, 1965) were printed in several different forms by the Superior Electoral Tribunal and the national Congress. A summary of the anteproject of the code and the entire anteproject of the parties statute is contained in the *Revista de Direito Público e Ciências Políticas,* VIII, No. 1 (January-April, 1965), 91–124 and 125–45; the ineligibilities law is found in *Ibid.,* VIII, No. 3 (September-December, 1965), 217–26.

and control over internal party affairs by the electoral courts, and by making local party organizations more independent of party leaders at the state level. The new regulations also eliminated the formerly common practice of politicians' running for public office in a state other than that in which they actually resided. In order to strengthen party identification and thus, it was hoped, party discipline, voters were required to choose federal and state legislators from the same party, and the running mates of successful gubernatorial and presidential candidates were to be automatically elected. (Previously Brazilian voters cast their ballots much more for the man than the party label, used by many candidates as little more than a convenience for legally qualifying.)

The political party statute prescribed the conditions for the organization and legal registration of political parties and defined the responsibility of party executive committees to rank-and-file members. The new law sought to limit "dictatorial action of party leadership" and to encourage "closer links to the creative forces of society" through increased emphasis upon grassroots democracy and civil education. Adequate mechanisms for implementation, however, were not provided.

The new legislation also closed up a number of loopholes in the existing regulations designed to prevent the use of political office to maintain an individual or his relatives in political power. It maintained the old provisions that no president, governor, or mayor may serve two consecutive terms; that the president may not run for vice president at the end of his presidential term; that the president and vice president may not become gubernatorial candidates within a year after having left office; and that close relatives of an incumbent president, vice president, or governor may not be candidates to succeed their relatives, nor be candidates for Congress unless they have previous congressional service.

Under the legislation existing prior to 1965, governors, cabinet ministers, mayors of the Federal District, officials of government banks, and holders of specified other positions who seek to become presidential candidates must resign at least six months before the election. Armed forces chiefs of staff, the attorney general, certain judges, heads of mixed government-private companies and federal autonomous agencies, and certain other officials must resign at least three months before election. Any of these individuals who wish to become candidates for Congress must step down three months before the election. Similar provisions apply to state offices. The 1965 law of political ineligibilities extended these provisions to cover a large number of additional positions, including nongovernmental posts, in which the occupant would have an unfair advantage over other candidates. Thus, with regard to running for executive office or the federal Congress, the law established a three-month period of "disincompatibilization" for officers of public service enterprises, certain private companies, many firms doing business with the government, officials of banks and other sources of credit, and representatives of foreign firms or organizations. For holders of government-granted monopolies the deadline for "disincompatibilization" was set at six months before the election for the state legislature.

The Ineligibilities Act, the Electoral Code, and the Party Statute were designed to implement the constitutional amendment of June calling for legislation to "strengthen the democratic order, defend the public patrimony, repress abuses of economic power and traffic in influence on the election process." Thus most of those who served in Goulart's cabinet after January 23, 1963, were declared ineligible during 1965, and many appointees of governors who were removed by the revolution were barred through 1966. This provision derailed the candidacy of former Minister of Transportation and Public Works, Hélio de Almeida, for the Guanabara governorship.

The most debated provision of the Ineligibilities Act, however, was that which barred "those who have compromised, for themselves or others, the adequacy and normalcy of an election through abuse of economic power, act of corruption, or improper use of the powers of public office." This particular measure was aimed at ex-Finance Minister Sebastião Paes de Almeida, gubernatorial choice of the powerful Minas Gerais PSD. A regional convention of the party formalized his nomination immediately after the passage of the law in an act of defiance of the administration's clearly expressed opposition to such a candidacy. The electoral courts subsequently ruled against the wealthy banker-industrialist, known as "Tião Medonho," after the protagonist in the popular Brazilian movie "O Trem Pagador" (The Payroll Train). (Because of his massive electoral expenditures, Paes de Almeida's 1962 congressional campaign became known as the "payroll train," in recognition of the temporary prosperity it brought to each stop.)

The administration also had under active consideration a number of fundamental modifications of the existing political institutions. A joint congressional commission in August, 1965, began hearings on a series of bills that would (1) modify the judicial power by adding to the membership of the Supreme Court (thus giving the administration a firm majority) and strengthen the hands of the military courts in matters affecting "national security" and "subversion"—both broadly defined; (2) alter the functioning of Congress by making permanent the provisions of the Institutional Act which require prompt action on presidential bills, by facilitating delegation of legislative powers, and by allowing greater latitude to the executive in the area of implementing decrees; and (3) transform the executive-legislative relationship by instituting parliamentary government or a uniquely Brazilian hybrid system which would give the President greater powers in many fields while strengthening the authority of Congress in other areas.[78] But before action on these measures could be taken, the regime would find itself whip-sawed between its declining popular support and the increasing opposition to its moderate tack within the *linha dura*-oriented wing of the Armed Forces. Stepped-up efforts toward political normalization, in the absence of observable progress in the economic sphere, were to boomerang on Castelo Branco and bring about the first coup-within-the-coup.

[78] Senator Afonso Arinos comments on his "Sugestões para a Reforma Política e os Meios de Obtê-la," in *Planalto* (Rio de Janeiro, 1968), pp. 267–68. Although viewed with suspicion by the hard liners as an exponent of an "independent" foreign policy while serving as Quadros' Foreign Minister, Arinos was invited by Minister Luiz Viana Filho to submit proposals to the President for a sweeping overhaul of political institutions. Luciano Martins, whose analysis of the breakdown of the pre-1964 system was discussed in Chapter 1, stresses the degree to which "the industrializing sectors, for their part, accommodated with relative docility to this post-1964 military-led reorientation or expressly solidarized with it." *Industrialização, Burguesia Nacional, e Desenvolvimento* (Rio de Janeiro, 1968), p. 26. In response to a questionnaire put to the heads of the fifty largest national industrial groups in Rio de Janeiro and São Paulo between August, 1966, and March, 1967, some 12 per cent considered the economic and financial policies of the Castelo Branco administration "an excellent solution" to the country's problems, while 76 per cent termed them a "good" solution for some problems and poor for others, and only 8 per cent were decidedly negative.

CHAPTER FIVE

The Castelo "Dictatorship"

BY THE END of its first fifteen months in office, the regime's brand of tutelary democracy and institutional renovation seemed to have proved viable if not positively effective. The punitive phase of the revolution appeared to have ended, and the government enjoyed a substantial, albeit at times reluctant, legislative majority. The labor movement, with many of its key unions continuing under intervention, was causing no real difficulty, and demonstrations of opposition to the regime were small and sporadic, although its popularity was not high. Surrounded by an experienced administrative team, most of whose members shared the President's business-like and disciplined approach to the agenda of national problems, Castelo Branco could reasonably have been viewed as moving the country gradually toward increased normalcy. Instead, however, the broadened political debate of the ensuing three months resulted not so much in the renewal of political leadership as in the resultant implantation of a discretionary regime armed with emergency powers.

1. THE OCTOBER 1965 ELECTIONS AND THE "REVOLUTION WITHIN THE REVOLUTION"

Although the government opted for holding direct elections, it fully realized the dangers involved in permitting such balloting at a time when the full brunt of deflationary policies was being felt by the populace.

With the revolution of 1964 itself as one of the most important political issues, the regime had such a great stake in the gubernatorial races that it was determined to use its Ineligibilities Act to bar candidates who were clearly opponents of the revolution, as distinct from critics of the administration. In a sophisticated strategy which very nearly was successful, the Castelo Branco forces looked toward the elimination of Lacerda and Magalhães Pinto through the defeat of their hand-picked choices as successors by individuals who, although nominally from the ranks of the opposition, could be counted on to seek accommodation with the regime and hence to cause fewer problems for the government than had the politically ambitious "revolutionary" governors. At the same time, the President and his advisors expected their candidates to be victors in many of the other states.

The environment in which the elections took place was not highly auspicious for the administration. Organized labor, always a crucial voting factor in the major urban centers, was quite unhappy over the continued governmental intervention in important unions and federations. Moreover, Rio de Janeiro's electorally important metalworkers, who had given substantial support to the naval mutineers in March, 1964, were painfully aware that not only their most militant leaders but also the congressmen who had appeared at their "Steel Palace" headquarters at that time, had been deprived of office and political rights. Wage earners were also very dissatisfied with the decline of their purchasing power and felt the government was essentially hostile to their interests. Then, too, there was a widespread feeling that Kubitschek, whose popularity was on the upsurge in spite of the government's efforts to discredit him, had been treated unfairly by the Castelo Branco regime. The disqualification during August of the opposition's first two nominees for the governorship of Guanabara further eroded the government's popular support and created an image of an essentially authoritarian regime talking of reforms but manipulating the rules of the political game to its own narrow advantage.

Moreover, to the Brazilian voter the orientation of his government's foreign policy had also become an important issue. During the Quadros-Goulart period, significant support had developed for a more aggressively independent foreign policy. Although the maintenance of close and comfortable relations with the United States, without sacrificing independence of action, was still a widely accepted goal, in recent years nationalistic aspirations and the need for new markets for Brazilian products have made it more difficult to maintain harmonious relations with the United States. As a result of economic crises, Brazil's aspirations for a place in world diplomatic councils, and the Communist presence in the Western Hemisphere, as represented by Castro's Cuba, foreign policy issues became increasingly involved in internal politics and foreign policy questions, previously left to the experts, became political issues.

The degree of the administration's identification with the United States led to dissatisfaction on the part of those who feared United States domination and resented the loss of trade opportunities resulting from curtailment of dealings with the Soviet bloc. The traditional arguments regarding the independent formulation of Brazilian foreign policy were raised albeit often in muted tones, by politicians who saw in a reawakening of Brazilian nationalism a possible electoral springboard for themselves. The action of Brazil in the Dominican Republic crisis developed as a source of disagreement among Brazilians, many of whom felt that their government was pulling United States chestnuts out of the fire while appearing unnecessarily subservient to North American interests. A significant number of Brazilians were sensitive to assertions that their country's image as a major emerging power had suffered as a result of its role in the Dominican affair.

For most voters, the cost of living, scarcity of foodstuffs, and shortages in public services (particularly education, public health, transportation, and housing) were the most important electoral issues. By September, the increase in consumer prices was already well over the target of 25 per cent set for the entire year. Since unemployment was at a higher rate than before the coup and business failures, part of the rationalization of the economy by eliminating the profitability of nonproductive enterprises, alarming frequent, there was a widespread feeling that the government's economic policies were failing and that only wrongheaded obstinacy could explain the unwillingness of Congress to abandon or drastically modify them. In this situation, the technocrats' pride in the drastic improvement of the country's balance of payments position (in which, paradoxically, the trade surplus was so great as to be a prime cause of inflation) and in the sharp reduction in the budget deficit (down for the year to 16 per cent, from 27 per cent in 1964) did not impress the man in the street. With tax collections rigorously improved and wage policy holding firm, but the price control mechanism apparently as faulty as ever, urban voters were ready to manifest their dissatisfaction.

Among the eleven Brazilian states in which elections were scheduled, greatest attention focused on Guanabara, where a defeat of Lacerda's choice for his successor would constitute a serious setback to his presidential aspirations. He himself won less than 40 per cent of the vote in the 1960 three-way contest, and schisms had since developed in the ranks of the UDN and its electoral allies. With both of his 1960 adversaries (Sérgio Magalhães and Tenorio Cavalcanti), plus the leading 1962 vote-getters (Leonel Brizola and Eloy Dutra), deprived of their political rights, a wide-open race seemed to be shaping up. Rafael de Almeida Magalhães, Lacerda's young, hand-picked vice governor, was vetoed by the Church. Deputy Amaral Neto, the party's leading vote-getter in 1962, but since transformed into a caustic critic of Lacerda, announced that he would run on a minor ticket if denied UDN backing and was subsequently expelled from the party. Lacerda first put forth Hélio Beltrão (subsequently Planning Minister under Costa e Silva) and then persisted in pushing the candidacy of another of his state cabinet members, Carlos Flexa Ribeiro, against the wishes of many of the UDN congressmen. Although an outstanding Secretary of Education, Flexa Ribeiro lacked electoral appeal. The PSD nominated Francisco Negrão de Lima, who had governed the city under Kubitschek when it was still the Federal District, while the PTB first indicated Hélio de Almeida (Minister of Transportation under Goulart). After Hélio de Almeida was ruled out under the Ineligibilities Act, the PTB put up Marshal Lott—only to find that he failed to meet the new residence requirements. Spurred on by that probability that the PSD-PTB candidate would win, and with the election less than a month away, the PTB finally joined in support of Negrão.[1]

In Minas Gerais, there were half a dozen UDN stalwarts in contention for the nod of incumbent Governor Magalhães Pinto, who had

[1] A splinter candidate, Alziro Zarur of the "Legion of Good Will," was also ruled ineligible. On the complexities of these cases, see *Revista de Direito Público e Ciências Políticas*, VIII, No. 3 (September-December, 1965), 131–209.

hoped for the extension of his own term for another year. Like Lacerda, Magalhães Pinto chose instead to push through the nomination of an electorally unproven aide, Roberto Resende. The PSD, well endowed with proven vote-getters, nominated Sebastião Paes de Almeida, who was denied registration under the Ineligibilities Act. Israel Pinheiro, a political collaborator with Kubitschek in the past, but a very adaptable individual, was his substitute.

In rapidly growing Paraná, Governor Ney Braga nominated his Secretary of Agriculture, Paulo Pimental, rather than support the candidacy of PDC Vice-Governor Afonso Camargo Neto. The opposition put up ex-Governor Bento Munhoz da Rocha (1951–1956). A PSD victory would not have been welcomed by hard liners in the military, who viewed the incumbent Governor, an ex-Army colonel, as one of their more important "civilian" allies, but it would not necessarily have been interpreted as a repudiation of the Castelo Branco administration.

The other eight gubernatorial elections were in states of far less importance, and their individual outcomes would have relatively little national significance (although a general wave of opposition victories might underscore the regime's lack of popular support). In Goiás, the revolution was a prime issue, since much debate centered on the 1964 federal intervention and the subsequent ouster of Governor Mauro Borges. Borges' father, Senator Pedro Ludovico, supported a candidate strongly opposed by the present military governor. (The PSD's first choice, Sebastião Arantes, was ruled out by the Ineligibilities Act.) The UDN backed Otavio Laje de Siquieros, the choice of Deputy Alfredo Nasser, former Minister of Justice. In Alagoas a recrudescence of violence presaged a bitter and bloody campaign. The roots of this lay, however, in local rivalries, not national affairs. Opposition candidates included Deputy Abrao Moura for the PTB, ex-Governor Muniz Falção (now a deputy) for the PSP, and Senator Arnon de Mello for the PDC. Incumbent UDN Governor Luiz Cavalcanti obtained PSD backing for his party's candidate, Senator Rui Palmeira. In Maranhão, the strongly entrenched PSD, if it had not split so deeply over differences between Senator Vitorino Freire, state boss for over three decades, and Governor Newton Belo, would have been favored to defeat the bid of UDN Deputy José Sarney, one of the leading congressional progressives to survive the April, 1964, post-revolution purge. Freire backed the candidacy of Deputy Renato Archer (son of Senator and ex-Governor Sebastião Archer), while Belo put up Costa Rodrigues, prefect of the state capital, on a PDC ticket.

In Pará, where Lieutenant Colonel Jarbas Passarinho had been acting as governor since the revolution, the elections provided a test between traditional machine politics and the new "revolutionary" order. With its major leaders disqualified, the long-dominant PSD invited UDN Senator (and ex-Governor) Zacarias de Assuncão, a reserve general, to be its candidate. The administration nominated Major Alicid Nunes, who until stepping down to campaign had given Belém a dynamic municipal administration. In Paraíba, the PSD sent a proven campaigner, Senator Rui Carneiro, against UDN Senator João Agripino, a nationalist who played an important part in the Quadros administration. Governor Aluisio Alves of Rio Grande do Norte succeeded in bringing the PSD and PTB wings of his coalition together behind Senator (and Monsenhor) Walfredo Gurgel for governor. The opposition slate was led by Alves' strong political rival, Senator Dinarte Mariz, with Deputy Tarciso Maia as his running mate. (Mariz served as governor during the 1956–1961 term after easily winning election to the Senate in 1954. His hold on the UDN forced Alves, himself a four-term UDN federal deputy, to run as the PSD's candidate in 1960.)

In Santa Catarina, UDN Senator and ex-Governor Irineu Bornhausen was able to dictate the nomination of his nephew, Senator Antônio Carlos Konder Reis. Governor Celso Ramos (PSD) supported State Deputy Ivo Silveira. In Mato Grosso, the PSD attempted to oust the UDN from control through the candidacy of Pedro Pedrossian, a young political protégé of Senator Felinto Müller. No elections for governor were scheduled for 1965 in such key states as São Paulo, Rio Grande do Sul, Rio de Janeiro, Pernambuco, and Bahia along with Ceará, Espírito Santo, Sergipe, Piauí, Amazonas, and Acre.

Nearly 7 million voters participated in the election of eleven new state chief executives on October 3, 1965. In Guanabara, a large turnout gave Negrão de Lima, the PSD-PTB candidate, 582,000 votes, enough for an absolute majority of the total votes cast (roughly 52 per cent) and a sizable plurality of nearly 140,000 ballots over the UDN's Flexa Ribeiro. The defeat caused Lacerda to resign his UDN presidential nomination and gave considerable added substance to ex-

President Kubitschek's role as Brazil's "great elector." In Kubitschek's home state of Minas Gerais, his long-time political associate Israel Pinheiro rolled up an impressive vote count of 855,000 to 690,000 over UDN candidate Roberto Resende and severely undercut incumbent Governor Magalhães Pinto's position as a national leader.

In Paraná, Paulo Pimentel, supported by Governor Braga's PDC-UDN administration, handily turned back Munhoz da Rocha (PSD-PTB). The victor's close to 550,000 ballots gave him an absolute majority of nearly 52 per cent of the total and a plurality of more than 40,000 votes. In neighboring Santa Catarina, the incumbent PSD's Ivo Silveira beat out UDN Senator Antônio Carlos Konder by a slim margin. Goiás produced one of the closest races with the administration-backed Otavio Laje de Siqueiros edging out the PSD nominee, José Peixoto da Silveira. The PSD won in Mato Grosso, where Pedro Pedrossian, a young businessmen representing the party's "new look" in that state, gained 53.5 per cent of the vote to UDN candidate Ludio Coelho's 46.5 per cent.

The five contests in the northern half of the country saw the UDN victorious in three states and the PSD in one, with the PSP the apparent winner in Alagoas, which remained in dispute long after the ballots were counted. In Pará, Major Alacid Nunes, backed by a coalition put together by Governor Passarinho, crushed the old-line PSD machine's candidate. Monsenhor Walfredo Gurgel won over Dinarte Mariz in Rio Grande do Norte. In the tournament of senators in Paraíba, the UDN's João Agripino emerged on top by 178,000 to 165,000 for PSD Senator Rui Carneiro. In Maranhão, where thousands of "phantom electors" were cleared off the rolls by vigorous action of the electoral courts during August and September, UDN progressive José Sarney got 54 per cent of the vote, trailed by Costa Rodrigues with 28 per cent and Renato Archer with 18 per cent of the votes. The results ended more than thirty years of machine domination by PSD boss Vitorino Freire while also setting back the plans of Governor Newton Belo (Costa Rodrigues' sponsor) to wrest control of the state PSD from the aging Senator. In Alagoas, the PSP's Muniz Falção received a plurality of nearly 15,000 ballots over Senator Rui Palmeira, but fell short of an absolute majority as the third candidate, Senator Arnon de Mello, was the choice of nearly 25,000 voters. Federal intervention was required to re-establish peace in this "frontier" state.

Although regime strategists could make a case that, taking all factors into account, the elections had not gone badly, the general feeling of the public was that the government had received a major setback. For although the inner circle around Castelo knew that the isolation and undermining of Lacerda and Magalhães Pinto were perhaps the regime's priority electoral goal, those not privy to such confidential matters saw only that the UDN candidates in two key states (Guanabara and Minas Gerais) had been trounced by at least nominal opponents of the government, elected on the strength of PTB as well as PSD voters. Most important, the *linha dura* officers, who had been convinced from the outset that the elections were an unwise and unnecessary risk, viewed the results as too similar to those of 1954 which had served as a precursor to the return of the "corrupt and surversive" Vargas crowd behind the Kubitschek-Goulart ticket the following year. (In point of fact, Negrão de Lima and Israel Pinheiro came to cooperate quite closely with the Castelo Branco government during the period in which their tenure in office overlapped.)

Thus a military crisis, albeit relatively quiet and largely concealed from the general public, developed as soon as the trend was clear from the early Guanabara returns. For in the eyes of the hard liners, both Negrão de Lima and Israel Pinheiro were Kubitschek men. The ex-President had dramatically returned from sixteen months of exile in Paris the very morning of the election. (By returning to Brazil before any election results were available, Kubitschek hoped to avoid the charge either that he was returning to stir up a crisis or that he had dared to come back only after his way had been made safe by the victory of his allies.) As the defeat of his candidate became apparent, Lacerda—whose appeals to public opinion in crisis situations had helped topple governments in 1954, 1961, and 1964—called for annulment of the results in the name of preserving the revolution and incited his still numerous contacts within the military, chiefly within the *linha dura* faction, to take matters into their own hands.

On the night of October 5, the "white coup" that was to alter significantly the course of the revolution took place. At the Vila Militar, General Afonso Albuquerque Lima and colonels of the *linha dura* began to mount a movement to remove Castelo Branco from office, Naval officers up to the level of admirals considered similar action at the headquarters of the First Naval District. Colonel Osnelli Martinelli mobilized LIDER (the Radical Democratic League, the most ideological right-wing Army grouping) while less extreme elements met at various commands to debate the crisis. Costa e Silva went personally to the Vila Militar and during hours of heated discussion worked out the basic outlines of a compromise, which included his guarantee that the government would move strongly to reinvigorate the revolution and issue a Second Institutional Act if required by the situation. Demands for abolishing the PSD were accepted for future action. Implicit in the *duristas'* acceptance of Costa e Silva's call for discipline was the assumption that he would not only ensure that the government behave in a manner responsive to the wishes of the officer corps, but that he would be Castelo's successor in March, 1967. If in Planning Minister Roberto Campos Brazil had a virtual prime minister within the functioning of the Castelo Branco government, it now also had an heir apparent in the person of the War Minister.

Although the general lines of the Second Institutional Act took shape immediately after the threat of an overt coup was eliminated, Castelo Branco and his advisers worked diligently to find a solution short of such an open admission that their effort at reform within relative institutional normalcy had failed. Aware of the possible downward spiral away from any substance of democracy that reassumption of discretionary powers might initiate, the government sought to convince both the Lacerdist wing of the UDN and the pro-Kubitschek elements of the PSD, some of whom suddenly entertained unrealistic ideas of exploiting their electoral gains to seek restoration of their leader's political rights, to accept constitutional amendments and legislative changes that would sufficiently strengthen the executive to negate the necessity of recourse to more drastic actions.

On October 7, Milton Campos stepped down as Justice Minister, in part over his distaste for the prospect of possible unconstitutional moves by the regime. His replacement was Juracy Magalhães, long-time advocate of "realism" within the UDN and an individual with a closer relationship with both Lacerda and Kubitschek than the *Mineiro* jurist he replaced. Politically astute and experienced in comparison with the civilian technocrats and military tacticians of Castelo Branco's cabinet and staff, Juracy had the advantage both of being an old *tenente* and of having kept clear of the disputes, infighting, and maneuvering of the past year and a half while absent from the country as Ambassador to the United States. Although Lacerda heated the atmosphere in mid-October through an intemperate television tirade in which he went so far as to declare that the President, "ugly outside and horrible inside," made him vomit, his subsequent resignation of the UDN nomination opened the possibility of a resolution of that party's contradictory position.

Standing by its view that PSD victories and UDN defeats at the state level should not be equated with voter repudiation of the national administration, and stressing the fact that pro-revolution candidates had won in a majority of states, the executive pressed for congressional approval of its previously proposed modifications of the existing structure of political-governmental institutions. Already under legislative consideration were measures aimed at: (1) transforming the executive-legislative relationship either through institution of a true parliamentary system or by adoption of one of a number of alternative hybrid arrangements; (2) permanently altering the working of Congress by incorporating into the Constitution those provisions of the Institutional Act that required prompt action on the President's legislative proposals as well as by allowing greater delegation of legislative powers and permitting wider latitude to the executive in the issuance of decree-laws; and (3) amplifying the jurisdiction of the military courts in matters concerning subversion (broadly defined) and national security while also giving the regime a reliable majority on the Supreme Court by increasing its total membership. While reiterating that the results of the elections must be respected, the government sought a more sweeping ban on the political activity of those individuals who had been deprived of their political rights and proposed a constitutional amendment giving the federal government veto power over appointments of state secretaries of security and commanders of the state police and paramilitary forces.

On Sunday, October 24, Juracy asked the leaders of all parties in Congress to go along with such "apparently undemocratic measures to save democracy." The next day, the Senate was ready to vote on the requested security amendment, but only 165 of the requisite 205 votes were available in the Chamber. On Tuesday night, with some 360 deputies present, the government could muster just 190 votes, as the pro-Lacerda elements of the UDN withheld their customary support. A vote was put off until the following day, but on the morning of the 27th Congress awoke to the announcement of the Second Institutional Act. As it was to occur late each spring (October or November) from 1965 through 1968, the Congress demonstrated its independence, and the result was a further move toward direct military rule.

Drafted by Vargas-era jurists Vicente Rao and Francisco Campos together with Nehemias Gueiros, one of Castelo's legal aides, the act granted the President the power to suspend Congress and govern by decree, provided for the issuance of complementary acts as deemed necessary by him, and broadened his power to decree a state of seige. It also reinstated the provisions of the original act that allowed the President to dismiss government employees, "cassate mandates" (remove elected officials), and suspend an individual's political rights for ten years, and it greatly increased the executive's control over government expenditures. The new act also eased the procedure for amending the Constitution. It increased the membership of the Supreme Court to sixteen and that of the Federal Appeals Court to thirteen—in order to allow Castelo Branco to appoint enough new judges to offset the existing majority on each court, which consisted of judges appointed by Kubitschek and Goulart. The act also extended the authority of the military courts to try civilians in cases involving national security. Most important, the Second Institutional Act provided for the indirect election of the President by Congress and dissolved the existing political parties. Although the act bore the signatures of all the military ministers, Air Marshal Gomes had acquiesced with greatest reluctance in putting an end to the UDN, a party which had twice honored him with its presidential nomination.[2] Although the issuance of such an act was forced upon Castelo by the hard liners, he had retained substantial control over its specific content, and would determine its applications.

The October crisis has been almost universally interpreted as a major defeat for Castelo Branco and evidence of the failure of his essentially technocratic approach. Certainly the pressures from the *linha*

---

[2] Castelo's October 27 speech on the Second Institutional Act and Complementary Act No. 1 is contained in his *Discursos 1965*, pp. 33–44 and *Revista de Direito Público e Ciências Políticas*, IX, No. 2 (April-June, 1966), 168–79; Institutional Act No. 3 and Complementary Acts through 9 appear on pp. 180–99 of the latter.

dura, combined with the failure of the economic recovery policies to take hold in time to have a favorable effect on public opinion, led to the paradox of a revolutionary government which had placed self-limitations upon its powers appearing unable to attain its objectives within these restraints. Thus, in the eyes of one well-trained and qualified observer, the failure of the Castelo Branco administration's blueprint for rehabilitating the economy and reforming society within a framework of tutelary democracy stemmed from an underestimation of Brazil's political realities, as reflected in

the assumption that a technocracy (especially one guided almost solely by economic technicians) which airily ignores the basic stuff of politics can make even technically correct policies work when they are over-laid on a society as underorganized and nonparticipative as the Brazilian . . . the entire notion of "inputs" into a political system—the human supports, demands, and mobilization stemming from authentic political parties, interest groups, ideologies, and even myths—is virtually ignored in an exclusive concentration on "correct" policies, "rational" decisions, and a "good image" abroad.[3]

Yet in spite of the sacrifice of important features of democratic formalism, the Castelo Branco government was far from finished by the "coup within a coup," which forced it to abandon a strategy of reforming the political infrastructure while permitting its components to function with some degree of autonomy. Tutelage moved toward control in Castelo's dealing with the legislature and political groups, but in regard to pursuit of other fundamental goals it remained far from a lame-duck administration. Indeed, in the sixteen and a half months left of his mandate, the President, largely freed from the necessity of sparing congressional sensitivities, accomplished considerably more in the legislative sphere than he had during the year and a half in office preceding the October crisis and the Second Institutional Act.

2. THE "NEW MODEL" ELECTIONS

Castelo moved quickly to recapture the initiative. Instead of using his broad discretionary powers under the new Institutional Act to undertake the purge of civilian political ranks (including the Guanabara and

---

[3] James W. Rowe, "The 'Revolution' and the 'System': Notes on Brazilian Politics, Part III: The 'Revolution'—Generals and Technocrats," *American Universities Field Staff Reports,* East Coast South America Series, XII, No. 5 (August, 1966), 3.

Minas Gerais governors-elect) desired by the hard liners, the President closed LIDER, reassigned many of the officers who had been active in the movement to force his hand, and guaranteed the inauguration of Negrão de Lima. The latter, for his part realized that his tenure in office depended upon Castelo, at whose wedding back in 1921 he had offered the first toast to the newlywed couple (as his brother stood in for Amaury Kruel as best man). Hence he cooperated more closely with the federal government in most ways than had his predecessor.

Castelo almost completely remade his cabinet during November, December, and January. Ney Braga (an ex-Army officer and ex-president of the PDC) assumed the Ministry of Agriculture; Deputy Peracchi Barcelos (former commander of the Rio Grande do Sul Militia) became Minister of Labor; and Admiral Zelman Campos de Araripe Macedo was made the new Navy Minister. Juracy Magalhães took over the Foreign Ministry, with Senator Mem de Sá replacing him as Justice Minister. Pedro Aleixo became Minister of Education, and young Paulo Egídio Martins assumed the Ministry of Commerce and Industry.[4]

On November 23, in a speech at Alagoinhas, Bahia, Castelo directly challenged the *linha dura,* declaring that "as to these people who proclaim an insurrection, the government prefers to face it rather than to skirt it because we do not recognize any autonomous force within military circles. If such exists, it should take a hard look at its dimensions and shift from harmful conspiracy to open action." [5] Having met with considerable success in reestablishing control over the military situation, the regime moved confidently toward a fundamental restructuring of its political base. Complementary Act No. 2 of October 30 laid down the norms for an interim functioning of political parties during the establishment of a bipartite system. The party situation was further modified by Complementary Act No. 4 of November 20, which provided for the provisional registration of political organizations sponsored by at least 120 federal deputies and 20 senators. Since, for reasons of conviction or convenience, nearly 250 deputies and more than 40 sena-

[4] Very interesting sidelights on the policy questions involved at this juncture can be gleaned from the President's comments at the swearing in of each new Minister contained in Humberto Castelo Branco, *Discursos 1965,* pp. 279–80 and 325–30 and *Discursos 1966* (Rio de Janeiro, 1967), pp. 307–18.

[5] Quoted in "Panorama em dois anos de Revolução," *Jornal do Brasil,* April 4, 1966.

tors joined the government-sponsored National Renovating Alliance (ARENA), opposition elements had no choice but to band together in a single organization, the Brazilian Democratic Movement (MDB). Indeed, formation of the MDB was delayed by the quest for additional senators willing to affiliate with the opposition so that it could be legally recognized.[6]

The MDB program stressed the defense of the legal order and human rights along with economic development and a foreign policy of "national affirmation." The emphasis of ARENA was on refinement of representative democracy, the elimination of undue economic power in elections, promotion of development without inflation, and maintenance of Brazil primarily within the Western value system and international order. All but a handful of the UDN, most of the PSD, and a majority of the minor party legislators joined ARENA; the backbone of the MDB was the ex-PTB.

In early January, Costa e Silva formally launched his presidential candidacy amidst rumors that Castelo and the Sorbonne officers were still looking for an alternative, or a means of undercutting the War Minister. On February 1, however, the President agreed to support his War Minister's bid for the ARENA nomination in return for a commitment to continue his program, particularly in the economic-financial sphere, and the nomination of a War Minister sufficiently strong to guarantee military unity and security in the 1967–1970 period. Warning of the dangers of military dictatorship, Castelo Branco justified the Institutional Acts as "vigorous instruments of democracy" that preserved the two main expressions of a democratic regime, a functioning Congress and freedom of the press. Costa e Silva affirmed that, if elected, he would govern the country within a "strictly democratic" regime.

Institutional Act No. 3, promulgated on February 5, 1966, replaced direct election of governors with selection by state legislatures, scheduled legislative elections for November 15, and eliminated the election of mayors of capital cities. Requirements for electoral residence were reduced to two years. President Castelo Branco thus yielded in part to the hard line pressures he had resisted prior to the 1965 elections and established a system (subsequently perfected by other complemen-

[6] See the Caderno Especial of *Jornal do Brasil,* June 18, 1967. This has been confirmed to the author by several MDB leaders.

tary acts) under which the "revolutionary" candidates for president and governors could not lose, thus avoiding the possibility of another crisis such as that of October. By the same token, the "opposition" governors elected in October, 1965, in Guanabara and Minas Gerais, thankful for having been allowed to take office, were integrated into the national administration's scheme of power.

The next three months of 1966 were a period of relative political calm, broken only by the outburst of General Justino Alves Bastos in mid-May, when Castelo Branco refused to set aside the residence requirements of the 1965 electoral code and allow him to run for governor of Rio Grande do Sul. General Alves Bastos was promptly replaced as commander of the Third Army by General Orlando Geisel, a dependable ally of the President. Generals Amaury Kruel (who aspired to the governorship of São Paulo), Carlos Luís Guedes (who apparently had hoped to become mayor of Belo Horizonte), and Antônio Carlos Muricy (whose eye was on the Pernambuco governorship) heeded the lesson and swallowed their disappointment.

Castelo Branco's attempts to delay the ARENA convention were not successful. In late May, Costa e Silva was formally nominated for the presidency, to the chagrin of many of the President's advisors, both military and civilian. Rumors of plans for *continuismo* abounded, and the removal of Adhemar de Barros as governor of São Paulo in early June was interpreted by some observers as another step in an administration plan to prepare the way for Castelo Branco to cancel the elections and hold on to power, as Vargas had done in 1937.[7]

In reality, the ouster of Adhemar was the final step in the executive's strategy of eliminating the civilian governors who demanded an excessive voice in national affairs as a result of their leadership in the 1964 revolution. Thus, with Lacerda and Magalhães Pinto already out of office, the notoriously corrupt Adhemar was overdue for political elimination. The final straw which brought about his ouster was the São Paulo state government's insistence on issuing short-terms bonds, popularly termed *"ademaretas,"* which undercut federal efforts to curb inflation.

---

[7] The group around the President had at an earlier time seen General Mamede as a possible candidate, but he was reportedly unwilling to play a role which might split the Army as had been the case in 1955.

The President had broken with the São Paulo governor in mid-March over the governor's continued attacks on Campos' policies and encouragement of General Kruel's possible presidential candidacy for the MDB. Moreover, Adhemar had been talking with the followers of Jânio Quadros (who had nearly defeated him for the governorship in 1962) concerning the formation of a majority in the state legislature to block the ARENA candidacy of Roberto de Abreu Sodré for re-election as its presiding officer. On the economic side, the vast number of patronage appointments by Adhemar and his issuance of public debt certificates (*títulos da dívida pública*) threatened to compromise severely the central government's financial program. Hence the regime moved to eliminate São Paulo as a base for politicking and agitation for direct presidential elections. In this context, the June 5 ouster of Adhemar was a significant move toward centralization of power and restriction of political competition.

Thus, even before the elections were to be held, the handwriting on the wall was more than plain. One of the closest Paulista analysts of the Brazilian political process, in an essay "The End of Civil Power," forecast that the day of party or even interest group determination of national policy had already passed.

It matters little if those who govern us tomorrow are civilian or military in their professional condition; the fact is that it will be the bureaucratic and military mentality that will command the Brazilian process from now on. . . .

It is not old style fascism which we have ahead. Not even Nazism–Nazism at least had political imagination and could create along side the monstrosity of crematory ovens and concentration camps a diabolical ideal which mobilized an entire Nation for disaster. What awaits us is the domination of Military Power allied to Technocracy.[8]

He went on to conclude that "preoccupied in consolidating its power and perhaps in giving the Technocracy the aid necessary for rebuilding the finances, the Sorbonne confused politics and politicking and, seeking to suppress the second, killed the first." [9] After an abortive effort by ex-PSD elements to obtain backing for Marshal Cordeiro de Farias as MDB presidential nominee, the opposition decided in early June not to participate in the indirect election for the presidency.

[8] Oliveiros S. Ferreira, *O Fim do Poder Civil* (São Paulo, 1966), p. 8.
[9] *Ibid.*, p. 54.

During July, politics increasingly took on an atmosphere of crisis. One complementary act followed another, beginning with No. 11 which provided for federal intervention in *municípios* where mayors were cassated or had resigned, and leading up to No. 18, which limited still further congressional authority to amend bills proposed by the President.

Castelo was again compelled to reconstitute his cabinet as a number of ministers stepped down to be eligible to run for election to other offices. In a politically more important move, Cordeiro de Farias had been replaced by technocrat João Gonçalves de Souza on June 16 after expressing extreme dissatisfaction over administration acceptance of Costa e Silva as the revolution's presidential candidate. Justice Minister Mem de Sá, like Cordeiro opposed to the candidacy of Costa e Silva, resigned rather than assume any responsibility for canceling the mandates of deputies in his home state of Rio Grande do Sul. His successor was the President's chief executive assistant, Luiz Viana Filho. Pedro Aleixo, nominated by ARENA as Costa e Silva's runningmate, left the Education Ministry to a technocrat, University of Rio de Janeiro Rector Raimundo Moniz de Aragão—brother of the general who had recently been re-elected to the presidency of the Military Club and was soon to be appointed Director General of Military Education.

Until July 1, Costa e Silva did not leave the War Ministry. He was replaced by Marshal Adhemar de Queiroz, a close associate of the President and a major organizer of the 1964 revolt. Seeking to be elected governor of Bahia, Viana Filho departed from the Justice Ministry in mid-July; he was replaced by Carlos Medeiros da Silva, who stepped down from the Supreme Court to take over the engineering of a sweeping institutional reform. Soon after Peracchi Barcelos, also bitten by the gubernatorial bug, gave way to Luíz Gonzaga de Nascimento e Silva in the Labor Ministry, and Ney Braga relinquished the post of Agriculture Minister to Severo Fagundes Gomes. Thus, Castelo Branco entered the final eight months of his administration with a cabinet of technicians devoid of political support but fully disposed to carry out his proposals for restructuring the governmental institutions.[10]

The administration's heavy-handed intervention in the succession problem at the state level was evident in the worst possible light when

[10] The presidential comments on the transfer of these ministries are contained in *Discursos 1966*, pp. 319–44.

it was faced by strong opposition to its chosen candidate in Rio Grande do Sul. There, significant elements of ARENA who were unwilling to accept Peracchi Barcellos as the next governor joined with the MDB to launch the candidacy of Rui Cirne Lima, a respected jurist whom the Castelo Branco regime was itself considering for appointment to the Supreme Court. Instead of accepting the competition, the national government responded on July 14 by canceling the mandates of four state deputies supporting Cirne Lima. The fact that this highly partisan action was accompanied by a wave of cassations, involving more than a score of legislators in a dozen other states, only strengthened adverse popular reaction. Moreover, this move had been preceded by the issuance of Complementary Act No. 14, which severely restricted the convocation of alternates, thus further limiting the MDB's possibilities of finding a means to elect its gubernatorial candidate in any state.[11]

The departure of Costa e Silva from the War Ministry and uncertainty about the government's plans concerning a new Constitution added to the tension that had begun in June with the ouster of Adhemar de Barros and the resignation of Marshal Cordeiro de Farias.[12] Rumors of new lists for cassations led the MDB to call for a special session of Congress to interpellate the new Justice Minister. At the same time, the student problem arose once again as security forces strove to prevent the National Union of Students (UNE) from holding a congress in Belo Horizonte. Complementary Act No. 16 of July 18, which made it impossible for an ARENA legislator to switch to or vote for the MDB candidate in either the presidential or gubernatorial elections, and the cancellation of the mandates of four more Rio Grande do Sul legislators, led the MDB to adopt a position of abstention in these indirect races. It also began to consider self-dissolution, or collective resignation, as a sign of protest against further arbitrary actions. The executive's immediate response was Complementary Act No. 17 of July 22, which provided for the automatic suspension of political rights for ten years of any legislator who might resign for such motives. Meanwhile, a manifesto of bishops of the Northeast in support of the rural workers precipitated a clash with military authorities, and a terrorist attempt against

[11] "Para gaúcho o homen é Ruy," *Visão,* July 8, 1966, p. 14.
[12] See "Falhas da Constituição refletem crise" and "Candidatos traça os seus rumos," *Visão,* July 8, 1966, pp. 11–13 and 46–47.

Costa e Silva's life in Recife on July 25 focused attention on the tense situation in that region.[13]

At the same time that the Justice Minister was assuring a rather skeptical Congress that elections would be held as scheduled on November 15, a statement designed to aid many ARENA candidates, the government issued Complementary Act No. 20. This decree reinstituted the individual ballot distributed by the candidates for most areas of the country. On August 9, in the midst of widespread criticism of the new act, General Amaury Kruel suddenly resigned command of the Second Army and issued a manifesto accusing the Castelo Branco government of having betrayed the revolution of 1964.[14]

In the face of administration threats to limit Congress' role in shaping the new Constitution, or even to promulgate it by decree, the MDB legislators adopted obstructionist tactics. At this juncture, Carlos Lacerda returned to the political wars with a demagogic appearance before a congressional investigating committee. Lacerda's subsequent open letters the *Jornal do Brasil* and *Tribuna da Imprensa* received wide attention, as did the report of a masterly interview criticizing the government as negative and repressive in the widely read *Visão*, which was reprinted in most of Brazil's newspapers. Also in the second half of August, ex-President Joao Goulart expressed support for the formation of a "broad front" (Frente Ampla) of opposition elements, including both Lacerda and Kubitschek. The latter added fuel to the fire by issuing a letter saying that approval by Congress of the Castelo Branco regime's proposed new Constitution would be "an international humiliation." [15]

Selected in most cases by Castelo Branco, without special regard for their electoral appeal, the twelve new governors chosen on September 3 were relatively young and came chiefly from incumbent administrations. Their average age was forty-seven; two were still in their thirties. Six came from the Chamber of Deputies and five from state

[13] The flavor of the period's "byzantine" maneuverings is reflected in "CB quer Costa no linha da Sorbonne," *Visão,* July 29, 1966, pp. 11–13.

[14] "Em busca das intenções ocultas," *Visão,* August 19, 1966, pp. 13–16.

[15] Lacerda's several key articles and addresses of this period are collected in *Crítica e autocritica* (Rio de Janeiro, 1966). His earlier call for a "revolution against the revolution" is carried in the Sunday supplement of *Jornal do Brasil,* April 4, 1966. *Visão* and, to a lesser extent, *Manchete* carry several relevant articles in each edition during this period.

legislatures; one was a state finance secretary. Few would have run strongly in direct elections, and as a whole the group could be considered as closer to federal interventors than freely chosen governors.

In São Paulo, the electoral picture prior to the Third Institutional Act had favored former Governor Carvalho Pinto (ex-PDC). Herbert Levy (ex-UDN), Brigadier Faria Lima (*Janista*), and a candidate supported by Governor Adhemar de Barros appeared to be his chief competitors. When direct election for governor was eliminated, Carvalho Pinto turned instead to the Senate race and the ARENA leaders chose State Deputy Roberto de Abreu Sodré over Vice Governor Laudo Natel. (Shortly thereafter, Natel succeeded to the governorship as a result of the cassation of Adhemar de Barros.) Removal of de Barros in June eliminated the possibility of an alliance of his supporters with those of Jânio Quadros and the MDB and assured the victory of Abreu Sodré. The MDB's General Dalysio Mena Barreto, an active figure in the 1964 coup, withdrew late in the race.

In Rio Grande do Sul, Colonel Walter Peracchi Barcellos (ex-PSD) gained the ARENA nomination over Deputy Tarso Dutra (ex-PSD), but two sets of cassations and a complementary act were necessary to undermine the opposition candidacy and ensure Peracchi's election. In the September 3 elections, Peracchi received only 23 votes and thus earned the dubious distinction of becoming the least legitimate governor in Brazil—in reality, little more than interventor.

In Rio de Janeiro, Marshal Paulo Tôrres, elevated to the governorship by the 1964 revolution, sought to impose the candidacy of his nephew, but was forced by the ARENA directorate to shift his support to State Deputy Paulo Mendes. Because of Tôrres' conflict with Raimundo Padilha, the ambitious majority leader in the Federal Chamber of Deputies, Castelo Branco picked the state president of ARENA, thirty-seven-year-old first-term Federal Deputy Jeremias Fontes, as a compromise candidate.

In Bahia, Castelo Branco and Foreign Minister Juracy Magalhães imposed on ARENA the candidacy of Luíz Viana Filho, the former's cabinet chief and Justice Minister. (Magalhães' son was duly named as Viana's running mate, while the Viana's son assumed his father's place on the congressional ticket.) Castelo Branco's intervention was felt also in Pernambuco, where Deputy Nilo Coelho (ex-PSD) emerged as the preference of the greater number of ARENA leaders, and João Cleofas received the senatorial nomination. Ex-governor Cid Sampaio, who probably would have been the strongest candidate in a direct election, was left aside. In Ceará the President passed over the most logical candidate, Deputy Paulo Sarazate, in favor of Plácido Castelo, a state deputy with a long career of service in various administrative posts. In Sergipe, an impasse between three ARENA candidates was broken by the President's choice of Deputy Lourival Baptista for the nomination.

Acre witnessed a minor league repetition of the Rio Grande do Sul crisis, when Federal Deputy Jorge Kalume was assured election by means of the cassation of opposition deputies. Christiano Dias Lopes (ex-PSD), in Espírito Santo, and Helvídio Nunes de Barros (ex-UDN), in Piauí, were peacefully selected by ARENA conventions, as were Antônio Lamenha Filho, seven times the president of the state assembly, in Alagoas, and Daniel Aerosa in Amazonas.

The election of Costa e Silva was never in doubt, since, given the rules established for the balloting, the badly out-numbered MDB decided not to run a candidate. The government standard-bearer, however, "campaigned" for nearly three months in a series of trips that took him into all regions of the country. In addition to maintaining some semblance of a normal presidential succession, these travels enabled the prospective President to meet with governors and state political figures, as well as to listen to local interest-group leaders present their views on economic and social problems. Although the campaign had no discernible effect on the outcome of the indirect balloting, it provided the candidate with an opportunity to learn a great deal about the country and people he would soon be governing. It also put Costa e Silva on display for the first time in other than a military context. Heavy press coverage helped create a more satisfactory image of the new national leader, who proved more capable in such an environment than his critics had predicted. Indeed, compared to Marshal Lott in 1960, Costa e Silva performed like a political professional.

The candidate's many speeches, however, did not provide a clear picture of the course his future government would follow, beyond reaffirming the continuance of the revolution in a more democratic manner, with repeated promises to "humanize" in an unspecified manner it's economic policies. Every major group was promised greater attention to its needs and problems. However, questions on specific policies were generally met by the answer that a broadly representative advisory task force was presently studying the subject and would welcome all suggestions of the questioners. "Re-democratization" was stressed sufficiently well to convince significant opposition elements that a fruitful dialogue with Costa e Silva would be more probable than with Castelo Branco. Although they were unwilling to vote for the ARENA candidate, most MDB elements considered that his inauguration would be a definite step forward. And even the "broad front" organized by Lacerda to oppose Castelo Branco was being tentatively offered to Costa e Silva as an alternative to ARENA backing, if he was to opt for a liberal program.[16]

In the actual balloting on October 3, Costa e Silva received the vote of 252 ARENA deputies and 40 ARENA Senators, as well as those of MDB Deputy Anísio Rocha of Goiás (subsequently deprived of his political rights), unaffiliated Oscar Correia (Minas Gerais, ex-UDN), and Rubens Berardo, who as vice governor of Guanabara was not standing for re-election. The 255 deputies who voted for him had received just over 4.6 million votes in 1962, and the abstaining MDB deputies had received nearly 2.8 million votes when elected. The opposition congressmen whose mandates had been canceled by the revolution, however, represented another 1.5 million 1962 electors. ARENA Senators Arinos de Mello Franco and Mem de Sá abstained from voting for their party's candidate, and the relatively few MDB congressmen present walked out before the voting began.

Drama was added to this generally anticlimatic event by MDB Vice Leader João Herculino (Minas Gerais, ex-PTB), who denounced the election while dressed from head to foot in black, mourning what he said was the "death of democracy," and by Senator João Abraão (Goiás, ex-PSD), who called the preceedings a shameful farce and invoked the name of Juscelino Kubitschek as the true choice of the people. This speech caused such an uproar that the presiding officer suspended the session for a few minutes. In these circumstances, on his sixty-fourth birthday, Marshal Arthur da Costa e Silva became Brazil's President elect. (Both Herculino and Abraão would lose their political rights after the December, 1968, crisis.)

The leadership of Congress, under Adauto Cardoso (who had re-

[16] See "Revolucão: linha dura pode ser caminho," *Visão*, September 23, 1966, pp. 15–19.

placed Bilac Pinto as presiding officer of the Chamber when the *Mineiro* congressman had accepted appointment as Ambassador in Paris), tried to convince the President to revoke the provisions of the Second Institutional Act permitting cancellation of legislative mandates before undertaking consideration of the proposed new Constitution. Instead, Castelo on October 12 ordered the cassation of six federal deputies, including MDB co-Vice Leader Doutel de Andrade and Sebastião Paes de Almeida, thus serving notice that the government would not permit "corrupt or subversive" politicians to stand for re-election in the November 15 congressional balloting. For eight days, these individuals remained in the capital under the protection of the Chamber president, who refused to recognize the legality of the executive's action. Thus Brazil was once again treated to the spectacle of a major spring crisis. As had been the case the preceding October, the federal legislature had been pushed to a point at which even some important pro-administration leaders felt compelled to stand up against further undemocratic actions by the President.

Castelo Branco responded by issuing Complementary Act No. 23 of October 20, which placed Congress in recess until a week after the November 15 congressional elections. At dawn, Colonel Carlos Meira Mattos, who had returned from the Dominican Republic to command the military police of the Federal District, led a contingent of combat ready troops into the Congress building. The ensuing dialogue between Meira Mattos and Cardoso dramatically underscored the gap between the military and political-juridical thought processes.

"Colonel, I am the President of the Chamber. It is lamentable that in order to enforce the recess decree Congress has been subjected to a military occupation."

"I regret, Mr. President, that you, a revolutionary leader, are now in the service of the counter revolution."

"It is your mistake, Colonel. I am at the service of civil power."

"And I am at the service of military power." [17]

Following the October crisis, which brought in its wake Adauto Cardoso's resignation as Chamber president—although he was subse-

[17] Castelo Branco's October 20 radio address explaining the congressional recess is contained in his *Discursos 1966*, pp. 279–81. Consult also "As causas da surprêsa de da crise." and "A previsão do tempo de espera," *Visão,* October 21, 1966, pp. 11–14 and 29–33.

quently named to the Supreme Court by Castelo—attention finally turned to the congressional campaigns.

A substantial number of procedural details of the electoral code had been modified by Law 4961 of May 4, 1966, Institutional Act No. 3, and the subsequent series of complementary acts. Candidates were required to file a statement of their financial situation and present a clean bill from the police. A few days before the registration deadline of October 16, a majority of candidates were not yet formally registered, and both the MDB and ARENA in many states rushed into the electoral tribunals at the last minute to complete their lists of candidates. Moreover, much more stringent and detailed regulations concerning campaign propaganda and finances were put into effect. Electoral propaganda could begin only after a candidate had been duly nominated and was the responsibility of the political organizations rather than being left largely to individual candidates, as in the past. Special campaign finance committees in each constituency were made responsible for the receipt and disbursement of all funds, and candidates who undertook expenditures on their own were subject to cancellation of their registration. Political organizations were forbidden to receive foreign assistance, public funds, and contributions from companies doing business with the government. The electoral courts were granted ample authority to enforce these new rules, so alien to past Brazilian practice, both directly and through interparty inspection commissions.

Propaganda could not be designed to "inflame public opinion," "exploit racial or class prejudices," "instigate violent action to subvert public order," "defame individuals or government authority," "appeal to avarice," or "adversely affect urban cleanliness." In this last respect, election officials and police in major cities barred the traditional jungle of huge cloth banners hung across the streets, the posters plastered on buildings, and the slogans painted on walls.

The system of proportional election had been modified slightly by the provisions of several complementary acts. The official ballot was to be used in São Paulo and Guanabara, in all state capitals, and in twenty-five other cities of more than 100,000 population (eight of which are found in the state of Rio de Janeiro, five in Minas Gerais, and three each in Rio Grande do Sul, Paraná, and Maranhão). In the rest of the country, the individual ballots distributed by the candidates were used as in the past. Official ballots were employed in urban centers, which contained roughly 10 million voters out of an electorate of 23 million. (This included 6.5 million in the states of São Paulo and Guanabara; 2.6 million in twenty state capitals and Brasília; 1.1 million in the additional twenty-five cities of over 100,000 population, with 440,000 of these in the state of Rio de Janeiro alone. Given the expected higher turnout in urban areas, the actual vote cast was divided nearly evenly between the two methods of voting.)

Registration figures reflected not only population growth but also two other factors: the significantly higher literacy rate of those who had turned eighteen since 1962, and the requirement of the 1965 electoral code that eligible women register and vote even if not gainfully employed. Out of an estimated total population of 84.7 million, there were nearly 23 million registered voters. Thus, the electorate had risen to roughly 27 per cent of the country's inhabitants from the 24.6 per cent recorded in 1962. In Guanabara, the figure was nearly 39 per cent, whereas in São Paulo, Rio de Janeiro, and Rio Grande do Sul the proportion was over 30 per cent. The largest numbers of voters continued to be found in São Paulo (nearly 5 million), Minas Gerais (approximately 3 million), Rio Grande do Sul (1.9 million), Guanabara (more than 1.5 million), Paraná (nearly 1.5 million), Bahia (1.4 million), and Rio de Janeiro (1.4 million). Pernambuco and Ceará nearly reached the level of one million registered voters.

Many candidates encountered widespread apathy toward the elections among the people and a lack of interest in the issues that were being so hotly debated in the halls of Congress and on the editorial pages of major newspapers. Almost everywhere, ARENA candidates found strong indications of discontent with government policies; they responded by stressing their independence and playing down their ties to the national regime. Thus, ARENA senatorial candidate Carvalho Pinto in São Paulo got his biggest cheers when he criticized the Castelo Branco regime and spoke in favor of direct election of the President. In Minas Gerais, many ARENA nominees sought a way to conceal their affiliation, even on the ballot itself. One of the main themes of the MDB campaign was denunciation of the incumbent regime as an arbitrary dictatorship, although very substantial freedom of press and speech was permitted. "On November 15 it is the people who will cassate" became the opposition's most popular slogan.

The Castelo Branco government—perhaps more than the 1964 revolution itself—became the major focus of political debate. The many key actors in the events of March–April, 1964, who had broken with Castelo Branco—Carlos Lacerda and Amaury Kruel leading the way—kept hammering at the theme that the President and his associates had betrayed the aims of the revolution. Certainly, the fact that a majority of the most important figures of the March revolution (Lacerda, Adhemar de Barros, Magalhães Pinto, Kruel, Alves Bastos, Mourão Filho) had gone into opposition reinforced the critics' image of the President as one who willfully and arrogantly insisted that his way was the only road for the revolution.

Communism as such did not develop into a very significant issue, except in those states, most notably Guanabara, where the registration of certain candidates was challenged or denied on the grounds that they had "Communist" ties or backgrounds. Indeed, the report of the Military-Police Investigation (IPM) on the Communist Party, released in October, implicated Guanabara Governor Negrão de Lima and a large number of MDB politicians. Much controversy arose because many respected individuals were included among the nearly 1,000 persons "accused" by the IPM report. The registration of twelve MDB candidates in Guanabara was denied on the grounds of their alleged close "Communist" ties, in spite of the fact that their names did not appear in the 157 volumes of this IPM report.[18] This and the impugnation of Federal Deputy Roberto Saturnino in Rio de Janeiro as a "Communist," resting as it did more on assertion than on evidence, helped activate the issue of Communism during the last month of the campaign.

Corruption emerged late as an important issue. Certain candidates had had their registration delayed or denied on these grounds, creating lively controversy in the areas of their political support. In Guanabara, for example, efforts were made, allegedly at the instigation of the federal government, to discredit Carlos Lacerda and his associates with charges of large-scale misappropriations of funds during his administration as governor. Accusations of corruption were also brought by the federal government against Kubitschek, when he refused to oppose Lacerda's proposals for an opposition alliance.

The many changes in the electoral rules, particularly the return to

[18] The major findings were published in a four volume series *Inquérito Policial Militar No. 709, O Comunismo no Brasil* (Rio de Janeiro, 1966–1967).

the individual ballot in most of the country, combined with efforts by military and intelligence authorities to deny registration to some opposition nominees, brought the question of freedom of elections to the fore. The question of ineligibilities was most acute in the state of Rio de Janeiro, already heavily hit by the cassations of 1964 and mid-1966. There, shortly before the deadline, the registration of no fewer than six MDB congressional candidates and thirteen nominees for the state legislature was challenged by federal officials. In a series of turbulent sessions, the Regional Electoral Tribunal allowed the registration of five of these candidates but upheld the ban on the rest. An even larger number of government candidates was disqualified, which is partly explained by the fact that many politicians considered corrupt or subversive had joined ARENA hoping to avoid cassation, only to find themselves vetoed by military and security officials. To avoid public embarrassment, ARENA leaders substituted other candidates for some of the challenged politicians before submitting their list of nominees for registration by the electoral tribunal.

In Guanabara, security officials also raised objections to a significant proportion of MDB federal deputy candidates and nearly a score of legislative assembly nominees. The MDB leadership agreed to replace twelve of these candidates, but on the eve of the election the matter was still unresolved, being hotly contested in the electoral courts. On November 11, the government suspended the political rights of eighteen individuals, including congressional candidates. Here too, ARENA chose to clear its nominees with security officials before submitting them for registration.

This procedure of impugning candidates was repeated on a smaller scale in many other states, and the electoral tribunals varied widely in their tendency to rebuff or accept such pressures from the military or federal security agencies. Many observers expected that in those states where the indirect gubernatorial elections were most affected by central-government pressures—such as Rio Grande do Sul—the voters would manifest a greater tendency to strike back at the polls on November 15. Certainly MDB politicians worked assiduously in this direction. Many ARENA candidates responded by adopting a "me-too' position in favor of direct elections, denying that they personally had any responsibility for Castelo Branco's institutional or complementary acts.

Similarly, the ARENA senatorial candidate in Guanabara, in the face of popular sentiment for a political amnesty embracing most, if not all, the "Cassados," came out publicly in favor of "selective revision" of whatever injustices might have been committed in the early stages of the revolution. Many MDB candidates found rather ingenious ways to bring into their campaigns the image of figures deprived of their political rights, and the heavy continuing press attention given to efforts to form a broad opposition front kept Kubitschek, Goulart, and Quadros in the public eye.[19]

Academic freedom emerged as a major issue, as a result of the student unrest that began in late July and resulted in strikes and mass demonstrations in mid-September. The protests against the indirect election of Costa e Silva and clashes between liberal spokesmen of the Church and conservative military elements also raised the issue of possible infringements upon—or, in the government's view, abuses of— freedom of expression. On balance, these exchanges increased the number of Brazilians who perceived the regime as reactionary and dictatorial. These two issues became the major theme of a number of candidates, chiefly young opposition newspapermen seeking votes in Guanabara and São Paulo, where the electorate included many students and middle class intellectuals.[20]

The leading constitutional issue was the intense controversy over the regime's determination to promulgate a new basic charter for the nation before leaving office. The situation was complicated by the shortness of time available, by the fact that the present Congress had already been purged of more than one-fifth of the members elected by the people in 1962, and by the probability that after November 15 a significant proportion of those remaining would be lame ducks repudiated by the electorate. The administration, convinced of the necessity of permanently incorporating major provisions of its institutional acts into the country's basic charter and remembering its failure in October, 1965, to gain congressional approval of proposed amendments, refused

[19] The most comprehensive source yet available on the 1966 elections is a special issue of the *Revista Brasileira de Estudos Políticos,* No. 23/24 (July, 1967–January, 1968) coordinated by Orlando M. Carvalho and including studies of varying quality on eleven states, as well as three detailed community studies.

[20] Consult "aí está o fato nôvo que faltava," *Visão,* November 25, 1966, pp. 11–15.

to renounce any of its levers over the national legislature. It specifically retained the power to cassate members of Congress. Moreover, as borne out by subsequent developments, it was actively considering a new institutional act that would give Congress little chance to modify the executive's constitutional projects. It even considered issuance of a Constitution by fiat. The prospect of such a by-passing of Congress sparked widespread controversy and caused even the administration's congressional leaders to object to the emasculation of the legislature's role. Moreover, jurists and opposition leaders encountered a generally favorable public response to their thesis that revision of the Constitution should be left to a newly elected legislature, which would not be subject to intimidation by the executive.

When the voting was over on November 15, the government had held onto and even strengthened its position in Congress. ARENA senatorial candidates were successful in eighteen states, and the party elected roughly two-thirds of the new Chamber. On the eve of the elections, the cassated and realigned lower house was composed of 254 ARENA deputies, 149 from the MDB, 4 unwilling to affiliate with either, and 2 vacancies. In the Senate, the proportion was 43 to 23. Since all the governors chosen in September, 1966, came from its ranks and all the governors elected in 1965 had either formally joined or made clear their preference for it, ARENA appeared to be in a commanding position.

A closer look at the results, however, shows both that the governing party was weakest in the modernizing urban centers (where the opposition rolled up impressive victories) and that ARENA's vote-getters, even in some of the more traditional areas, were major political figures who had stressed a semi-independent stance and criticized the administration's economic policies. Moreover, under the Brazilian system of proportional representation, the large proportion of blank or null protest votes cast by the most militant elements of the opposition indirectly contributed to the ARENA candidates by weakening their MDB challengers. (Null votes totaled nearly 7 per cent of the 17,285,556 ballots cast, blank votes more than 14 per cent. Concerted campaigns led by students in Guanabara, São Paulo, and Rio de Janeiro helped raise the proportion of blank and null votes in these states to 25.4, 35.4, and 25.9 per cent, respectively.)

With 8,731,635 votes, ARENA elected 277 federal deputies compared to the MDB's 132 on 4,195,470 votes. But in Guanabara, Rio de Janeiro, and Rio Grande do Sul the opposition held decisive edges, while in São Paulo the MDB candidates ran nearly even with those of the government party (1.22 million and 1.41 million, respectively). The big ARENA margins came in Minas Gerais, Bahia, Ceará, Pernambuco, Paraná, Santa Catarina, and the small states. Even in these states, the MDB did quite well in the cities. Thus, the government was victorious in the traditional rural areas, while the opposition had the backing of the voters in the modern urban sector. Moreover, ARENA benefited from having well-known vote-getters, while the MDB's most popular leaders had lost their political rights or were otherwise barred from running.[21] (The breakdown of cassations under the First Institutional Act was twenty-four PTB deputies compared with only seven from the PSD and two from the UDN. The fifteen minor party congressmen who lost their seats ranged from progressive to radical, and would almost certainly have joined the MDB had they retained their political rights.)

At the state level, ARENA won 731 legislative seats (with a total of just over 9 million votes), while the MDB gained 345 posts (with a vote of over 5 million). Guanabara (40 to 15), Rio de Janeiro (34 to 28), and Rio Grande do Sul (28 to 27) were the only states in which the opposition controlled the new legislatures. Yet nationwide this represented a net gain of 48 seats for the MDB. In São Paulo, for example, the MDB picked up 20 seats for a total of 53), and in Minas Gerais gained 15 deputies (from 4 to 19 in an 82-seat Assembly).

The senatorial contests became by default the most important direct elections and drew a strong field of contenders from both ARENA and the MDB. In São Paulo, ex-Governor Carvalho Pinto accepted the ARENA nomination, thus pushing Senator Padre Calazans into the MDB, which decided also to launch Araripe Serpa and Dagoberto Salles on *sub-legendas* in the expectation that they would draw *Janista* and *Adhemarista* voters to the MDB cause. Carvalho Pinto won handily with nearly 2 million votes to 681,111 for Araripe Serpa and only 230,000 for the incumbent.

In Guanabara, ARENA put up Danilo Nunes, former president of

[21] All figures are from the final official returns of the Superior Electoral Tribunal by courtesy of Dr. Geraldo Costa Manso and Minister Victor Nunes Leal.

the legislative assembly and UDN candidate for vice governor in 1965, against MDB candidates Benjamin Farah, Danton Jobim, and Mário Martins. (Incumbent Afonso Arinos de Mello Franco decided against seeking re-election.) Realizing how heavy the odds were against him without Carlos Lacerda's backing and with insufficient promise of administration resources for his campaign, Nunes withdrew and was replaced by a fellow judge of the tribunal of accounts, Venâncio Igrejas. The victory went to Martins, who received Lacerda's endorsement, by a margin of 363,000 votes to 272,000 for Benjamin Farah of the old PTB machine. The ARENA candidate polled only 174,000 votes or a mere 16 per cent of the total. On the congressional side, journalist Márcio Moreira Alves, subsequently the trigger of the 1968 crisis, won election, while Marshal Amaury Kruel could muster only 13,470 votes to end up as the MDB's first alternate. For ARENA, candidates long associated with Lacerda ran strongest, while Colonel Martinelli, the founder of LIDER, fell short of 6,000 votes to end up as third alternate for his party.[22]

In Rio Grande do Sul, ARENA incumbent Guido Mondim won re-election over the MDB's Siegfried Heuser by a very narrow margin of 34,000 votes out of 1.6 million ballots cast. Key to his victory was the government party's decision to use the maximum three "sublegends," as the MDB's sole candidate received twice the vote of the "victor."

In Minas Gerais, the situation remained undefined until the end of September, because ARENA Senator Milton Campos was undecided whether to run for re-election if the MDB put up a candidate against him. Campos finally accepted the ARENA nomination. The MDB convinced Professor Darcy Bessone to make the Senate race. (The MDB had seriously considered nominating Federal Deputy Carlos Murilo Felício dos Santos—nephew of Juscelino Kubitschek and married to a niece of Governor Israel Pinheiro—who might have attracted many PSD votes from Milton Campos, but he too decided to play safe and settled for re-election.) The two-time Vice-presidential nominee and ex-governor won easily.

[22] Maria Terezinha V. Moreira has published two useful analyses of the degree of renovation of the Guanabara legislature and congressional delegations: "A Renovação dos Quadros Políticos na Guanabara," *Revista de Ciência Política*, I, No. 1 (March, 1967), 127–48, and "Composição do Poder Legislativo da Guanabara," *Ibid.*, I, No. 3 (September, 1967), 47–74.

Rio de Janeiro was another of the few states where the incumbent withdrew from the competition; Senator Miguel Couto Filho ran instead for the Chamber so that Ex-Governor Marshal Paulo Tôrres could be the ARENA standard-bearer. Deputy Augusto de Gregório, the MDB candidate, lost a close race to the ex-Military Club president.

In Pernambuco, the MDB incumbent, Senator Barros de Carvalho, died in early September and was replaced on the ticket by Armando Monteiro Filho (ex-PSD). João Cleofas, unsuccessful UDN gubernatorial candidate in 1962, ran successfully for ARENA. Bahia's ARENA Senator Aluízio de Carvalho faced a strong challenge from the MDB's Tarcílio Vieira de Melo (minority leader in Congress) with the margin one of fewer than 14,000 votes (or well under 2 per cent). Indeed, Vieira de Melo was a victim of the unusually high number of null votes.

One of the most bitterly contested races took place in Paraná, where ex-Governor Ney Braga, the ARENA candidate, faced incumbent MDB Senator Nelson Maculan (ex-PTB) and former Vice-Governor Affonso Camargo Neto (ex-PDC). The latter had the backing of Bento Munhoz da Rocha (ex-PSD), a man who polled over 500,000 votes in the 1965 gubernatorial election. Reserve General Braga, who had been Agriculture Minister until three months earlier, was a moderately comfortable winner.

In Ceará, where two seats were at stake, owing to the deaths of a senator elected in 1962 and his alternate, ARENA put up Deputy Paulo Sarazate and Menezes Pimentel. The former won an eight-year term fairly easily; the latter edged out his MDB opponent for the incomplete term. MDB candidate Matos Carvalho in Maranhão was beaten by ARENA Deputy Clodomir Millet, who was supported by Governor Sarney.

In Paraíba, MDB Senator Rui Carneiro's bid for re-election seemed a difficult struggle against ARENA Deputy Ernani Sátiro (ex-UDN national president), until the latter was forced out of the race by Governor João Agripino, who alleged that Sátiro did not have adequate financial resources to continue the campaign. The subsequent nomination of millionaire Aluízio Campos, consistently a loser in his bids for electoral office, led the highly respected Sátiro to announce his retirement from politics, but Castelo Branco intervened to convince him to run for re-election to the Chamber. Carneiro coasted home as one of the four MDB Senate victors. In Sergipe, aging UDN boss Leandro

Maciel displaced incumbent Senator Heribaldo Vieira as the ARENA nominee. The weak MDB nominated Oviedo Teixeira as its sacrificial candidate.

In Goiás, MDB Senator João Abraão, elected in 1965 to replace the cassated Juscelino Kubitschek, defeated ARENA's José Fleury. The Mato Grosso political strong man, ex-Governor Fernando Correa da Costa successfully replaced Senator Lopes da Costa as ARENA standard-bearer against MDB Deputy Wilson Martins (ex-UDN).

In Espírito Santo, ARENA Senator (and ex-Governor) Carlos Lindemberg was hardpressed by Solon Borges from the MDB, with Senator Jefferson de Aguiar (ex-PSD) also in the race on an ARENA *sub-legenda*. ARENA in Alagoas nominated Teotônio Vilela to seek the seat of MDB Senator Silvestre Péricles Góis Monteiro, and his victory ended the sway of that political family.

In Pará, the nomination of ex-Governor Jarbas Passarinho by ARENA left incumbent Senator Zacarias de Assunção (defeated by Passarinho's candidate for the governorship the preceding year) out in the cold. Moura Palha was the MDB nominee to take a drubbing from the revolutionary Colonel, whose victory was to set him on a path toward a cabinet post and perhaps, eventually the presidency. Piauí's ex-Governor Petrônio Portela, running for ARENA, was to have been challenged by his predecessor in the state house, MDB Deputy Chagas Rodrigues; the latter encountered difficulty in having his registration accepted because of old charges of corruption, and Portela won going away.

In Amazonas, both sides resorted to *sub-legendas* ("sub-legends"), or multiple slates of candidates. ARENA put up Senator Vivaldo Lima (ex-PTB) and ex-Senator Alvaro Maia against MDB Deputy João Veiga and Senate Alternate Desirée Guarany. The aging incumbent was reelected. MDB Senator Adalberto Sena in Acre beat back a challenge by the revolutionary governor, Captain Edgar Cerqueira Filho.

The battle in Rio Grande do Norte and Santa Catarina lay largely within ARENA. In the former, Senator Dinarte Mariz and Governor Walfredo Gurgel (who was a senator until winning the governorship over Mariz in 1965) disagreed over granting ex-Governor Aluízio Alves, an ARENA *sub-legenda,* to run alongside Francisco Duarte Filho, a compromise candidate selected by Castelo Branco. Duarte Filho won easily, while Alves polled a record vote for the Chamber.

In Santa Catarina, ARENA Senator Irineu Bornhausen (ex-UDN) and former Governor Celso Ramos (ex-PSD) fought over the nomination, which was tantamount to election. In return for his withdrawal, the former was able to name ex-UDN Deputy Alvaro Catão as the nominee for Senate Alternate and received a guarantee that the new vice-governor would also be from the ranks of the UDN.

3. THE CASTELO CONSTITUTION AND THE INSTITUTIONALIZED REVOLUTION

Even before the elections, the regime had started the machinery in motion for drafting and adopting a new Constitution. Indeed, congressional desire for a significant role in shaping the new charter had been at the root of the October crisis. Thus, while Costa e Silva was beginning to organize his future administration, mixing old allies of the April, 1964, interim government (many of whom were hard liners) with some of the other revolutionary elements subsequently alienated from the Castelo-Campos administration, the President and his "Sorbonne" advisors undertook to institutionalize as much of their earlier blueprint for a "reformed and renovated" political-governmental structure as time would allow. For although this was a lame duck regime, it was one with extraordinary powers—including those to cancel mandates, suspend political rights, and close Congress. The President-elect cooperated by departing for an extended foreign trip, thus freeing Castelo Branco of the embarrassment of his presence and sparing himself the potentially compromising problem of having to take a position on any of the administration's more controversial actions.

The opposition temporarily gained the initiative through the dramatic "pact of Lisbon," in which Lacerda and Kubitschek personally came together in support of the Frente Ampla as a step toward restructuring and reorienting the opposition toward the former's presidential candidacy in 1970.[23] Castelo responded swiftly, however, issuing a series of nearly 40 decree laws on the eve of the reopening of Congress and announcing an integrated series of decisive moves to complete the consolidation of the revolution. First and foremost of these was the

[23] In addition to the newspapers of the period, consult Murilo Melo Filho, "O Encontro JK-Lacerda," *Manchete,* December 3, 1966, pp. 6–9; "Manifesto esqueceu questão basica," *Visão,* November 4, 1966, pp. 11–14; and "O Pacto e o futuro dos partidos," *Visão,* December 9, 1966, pp. 11–15.

enactment of a new Constitution, combined with a sweeping administrative reform, a stringent press law, national security legislation with broad ramifications, and important changes in the field of intra-governmental financial arrangements.

As early as April, 1966, Castelo Branco had appointed a commission of four distinguished jurists to prepare a draft document that would incorporate into a modernized version of the 1946 Constitution the basic features of the institutional acts, together with provisions of the many complementary acts that merited permanent application. Although Miguel Seabra Fagundes resigned from the commission on August 5, principally over his support for direct election of the President, the project of Levy Carneiro, Temistocles Cavalcanti, and Orozimbo Nonato was made public two weeks later.[24] Dissatisfied by the work of this commission, which had been selected by the liberal Mem de Sá while he was still Justice Minister, the President authorized Medeiros Silva to undertake a thorough revision more in keeping with the spirit of the institutional acts and objectives of the revolution. The resulting project, as unveiled on December 6, appeared likely to encounter heavy resistance in Congress, not only from the MDB but also from the liberal constitutionalists within the ranks of ARENA itself.[25]

On December 7, the government issued Institutional Act No. 4, summoning Congress to meet in special session from December 12 to January 24 for "discussion, voting and promulgation of the draft Constitution presented by the President of the Republic." [26] A mixed commission of 11 senators and an equal number of deputies was given just four days to consider the project, which after approval by an absolute

[24] Published as "Caderno da Constituição" supplement to *Correio da Manhã,* August 25, 1966.

[25] Basic for a consideration of the 1967 Constitution in the context of Brazilian experience and exceptional acts and decrees of the Castelo Branco administration are the two volumes by Osny Duarte Pereira, *A Constituição do Brasil 1967* (Rio de Janeiro, 1967) and *A Constituição Federal e Suas Modificações Incorporadas ao Texto* (Rio de Janeiro, 1966). The version of the latter work reissued with the 1967 study includes a supplement containing Complementary Acts Nos. 9–34, issued from May, 1966, to January 31, 1967. Duarte Pereira is very critical of the Constitution, but his studies provide much of the material necessary for a less passionate consideration of the issues and problems involved. See also "Diálogo, o caminho para Carta," *Visão,* December 16, 1966, pp. 11–15.

[26] Text in Duarte Pereira, *A Constituição do Brasil 1967,* pp. 353–55.

majority at a joint session of Congress within another four-day period, could be returned to the commission for such amendments as Congress might propose within five days. Twelve days were allowed for the commission's work at this stage, and an equal period for debate in plenary session of the Chamber. The voting on amendments was to end by the 21st, with promulgation required by the 24th. During this special session, the executive retained the right to issue decree laws on matters of national security and finances; and during the subsequent recess before inauguration of the new government would have the power to legislate by decree on administrative affairs as well.

In an effective tactical gambit, the President on the one hand promised not to exercise his powers to cassate during the period of congressional consideration of the new Constitution, an act which helped undercut the Frente Ampla's attacks, while on December 21 submitting a very controversial press law extending government supervision and potential censorship, an act that took considerable attention away from the limited congressional role in the adoption of the basic charter.[27] Castelo also kept up a steady stream of complementary acts, chiefly in the financial realm, as the "disciplining" of federalism advocated by Roberto Campos to give the federal government sufficient power to ensure the success of its policies was put into effect even while the relevant constitutional provisions were being considered by Congress. (Complementary Act No. 24 had been issued on November 18 with two others following before the end of the month; Nos. 27–31 were decreed during December, and three more were promulgated in January.)

The members of Congress were well aware of the circumstances under which Brazil's five previous constitutions had been adopted. The Constitution of 1824 had been issued by imperial proclamation after the Constituent Assembly was dissolved by force. The Constitution of 1891 was drafted by a commission of five, revised by Ruy Barbosa, and amended by the legislature. The Constitution of 1934 was drafted by an executive commission and debated, modified, and approved by a constituent assembly. The Constitution of 1937 was simply decreed by the President. The 1946 Constitution was the work of an elected represen-

---

[27] See "Oposição segue as previsões" and "Castello pretende estimular debate," *Visão*, December 23, 1966, pp. 12–14.

tative constituent congress. The many Congressmen who had participated in the prolonged democratic process of framing the 1946 Constitution were particularly frustrated by the essentially rubber-stamp
role imposed upon them in 1966. Their major objections concerned the
dropping of the "United States" from the name of the country which
they feared would legitimize further centralization of power, the indirect
election of the President, the very broad character of the national security provisions, and the centralizing nature of the provisions concerning public finances and taxation. Within the ranks of ARENA, scholar-
statesman Afonso Arinos, convinced equally of the merits of his proposal and the virtual impossibility of its acceptance, again pleaded with
the Senate from which he would soon take his final leave, for adoption
of a parliamentary system as the best suited to bridge the gap between
military and civil power.[28]

Although over 1,500 amendments were introduced by Congress,
very few were approved by the mixed commission presided over by
Deputy Pedro Aleixo, the Vice President-elect. Even the man entrusted
with responsibility for the Commission's report, Senator Antônio Carlos
Konder Reis, was lukewarm concerning the final product, terming it at
least a substantial improvement over a regime of institutional acts.[29]
With only one night to put together the final report from those of the
subcommittee, Konder saw the product approved by a vote of 223 to
110 in the Chamber, and 37 to 17 with 7 abstentions in the Senate. Yet
the clock had to be stopped before midnight on January 24 to allow
time for the final touches and balloting. A sign of future difficulties
could be seen in the decision of 107 ARENA deputies to vote favorably
with extreme reluctance under party discipline, reserving the right to
seek fundamental amendments after March 15 with a new President in
office and the discretionary powers of the institutional acts having
lapsed.

The Constitution's explicit provisions with regard to the military
were less significant than the very broad basis provided for future na-

[28] Afonso Arinos, *A Reforma Constitucional de 1966* (Brasília, 1966), Part v,
pp. 16–18.

[29] *Visão,* January 13, 1967, contains a series of very useful articles concerning
political reactions to the debate on the Constitution and Press Law. See, in particular, "O testamento da Revolução," pp. 20–23 and "Carto aberta as discussões,"
pp. 24–26.

tional security legislation and its linkage with the Press Law. In the original administration draft, the Armed Forces were considered "permanent national institutions, organized on the basis of hierarchy and discipline within the limits of the law, under the supreme authority of the President of the Republic." Their role was defined as one "to defend the Country and guarantee the free exercise of constitutional powers, and to maintain order within the Constitution and the laws." The government draft as submitted to Congress added the adjective "regular" after the word "permanent" and deleted the phrase "within the limits of the law." The military's mission was simplified to "defend the country and guarantee the constituted powers, law, and order." The final version as promulgated only added to Article 92 a qualifying "and within the limits of the law." [30]

Passage of the Press Law (somewhat weakened, but still a formidable lever over the communications media) and enactment of the Constitution, which was to go into effect on March 15, were not the last of the unpopular tasks Castelo had assumed in large part to make things easier for his successor. On February 8, the President decreed a currency reform combining a substantial devaluation with introduction of the "new cruzeiro" worth 1,000 of the old. Within the week, he resumed suspension of political rights, following this initial list of 18 with another of 44 on February 27 and a final list of 28 on his last day in office— along with two or more complementary acts. Thus, the major purges under the original institutional act during 1964—with 116 elected mandates canceled; 378 cases of political rights being suspended; 544 compulsory retirements for political reasons; 1,528 firings; 555 forced military retirements; 165 involuntary transfers to the reserves; and various other punitive acts, for a grand total of more than 3,500 in the federal sphere (plus at least an equal number by state and municipal authorities) —had occurred under the original impetus of the Supreme Command.

[30] The Constitution of 1967 is reprinted in *Revista de Ciência Política,* I, No. 1 (March, 1967), 195–238. An analytic article which places it in a meaningful political setting is "Breve crônica de um Constituiçáo," *Visão,* January 27, 1967. pp. 11–15, supplemented by "Carta aprovada, revisão pleiteada," *Ibid.,* February 3, 1967. pp. 13–14. Innovations with respect to political rights and the party system are given a detailed discussion in Paulo Bonavides, *A Crise Política Brasileira* (Rio de Janeiro, 1969), pp. 45–67. The most penetrating critical study of the Castelo Constitution is Oscar Dias Correia, *A Constituição de 1967* (Rio de Janeiro, 1968).

But close to 250 individuals were "cassated" by Castelo's government between late October, 1965, and March 15, 1967, during the life of the Second Institutional Act.

In a feverish burst of administrative energy, 151 decree laws were issued on February 26, 27, and 28, bringing the total in a little over a year to 312. Among the most important was the fundamental administrative reform, the draft of which had been public for months, but which was not submitted to Congress owing to its complexity and the number of entrenched interests affected.[31]

As the "First Government of the Revolution" drew to a close, the Armed Forces were deeply entrenched in the direct as well as indirect exercise of power. Their influence, if not necessarily its legitimacy, was fully recognized by the traditional power contenders.

Indeed, at the very end of the Castelo Branco period large-scale Brazilian industrialists considered the military to possess as much "real power" in the polity as the industrialists, high-level government bureaucrats and bankers combined, and nearly four times as much as that of the politicians. This was in very sharp contrast with their perception of the Kubitschek regime, where the politicians were considered to have been half again as influential as the industrialists, with the bankers third and the military a poor fourth (the latter having only one-third the power of the politicians, half that of the industrialists, and two-thirds that of the bankers). When the question was put to them by Brazilian sociologists in terms of institutions, over half the representatives of large industry viewed the Armed Forces as the most powerful organization under the Castelo Branco regime while one-third saw them as second in influence. For most of the rest (38 per cent), the state was considered the most powerful. By contrast, almost half perceived the state as having been dominant under Kubitschek, with 26 per cent singling out political parties.[32] With regard to economic policy, however, the same industrialists held at the time of transition from Castelo to Costa that bureaucrats

---

[31] See the "Caderno da Reforma Administrativa" issued on September 16, 1966, as a supplement to *Correio da Manhã*. "A consumação a toque de caixa," *Visão*, February 17, 1967, pp. 11–13, gives a sense of the political atmosphere at this juncture. *Jornal do Brasil*, March 12, 1967, contains a useful summary of all the decree laws, the major flood of which began on November 16, 1966.

[32] Luciano Martins, *Industrialização, Burguesia Nacional, e Desenvolvimento*, pp. 133 and 141.

were more influential than the military and bankers as important as the Armed Forces (two-fifths and one-fifth for these two civilian sectors compared with slightly less than one-fifth for the military). The same respondents felt that the politicians and bankers had overshadowed all other groups in the old system as it flourished during the Kubitschek administration (with just under one-half and less than one-fourth respectively).[33]

One of the final acts of the Castelo Branco regime, and a move destined even more than the administrative reform to leave its stamp on the political system, was the promulgation by executive fiat of a comprehensive National Security Law implementing the new Constitution's provision that the security of the nation was the responsibility of all. In inspiration and basic outlines a product of the War College, but with the final formulation by the Justice Minister (who had taught there for three years), this controversial measure incorporated major portions of the "Sorbonne" doctrine into the juridical structure of the nation. Two days later, at the inaugural session of the ESG's new term, Castelo reminded the institution of its responsibility to help orient national policy.

In spite of the limitations on political competition, Castelo turned over to his old classmate a Brazil in substantially better condition than it was in when he received it from Costa in April, 1964. For all the polemic concerning economic policies, inflation was coming under control and the process of accelerating growth had begun. In addition to the significant institutional modifications implemented in January and February, Castelo also left to Costa e Silva a reorganized Congress (with 170 new members taking office in February) and strengthened government party.[34] The greatest shortcoming lay in the Sorbonnist disdain for public opinion and popular organization, making the regime dependent on Castelo's leadership and discipline. And while Castelo had cleaned up the situation for the new President, he had also to a degree tied Costa's hands. The key to the nature of the Castelo Branco regime appears to have been the symbiotic relationship between the Armed Forces and the civilian "technocracy," as exemplified by Roberto Campos, with the former valuing the economic rationality and adminis-

[33] *Ibid.,* p. 142. Martins also engages in some interesting sectional disaggregation and comparison of differential political behavior.

[34] Consult "As angústias da transição de poder," *Visão,* March 3, 1967, pp. 11–16.

trative order the latter promised to provide and the technocrats seeking a guarantee of social tranquillity from the military so that their programs could be followed through and fully implemented. Together they left Brazil, three years after the revolution of 1964, with reformed institutions, a ten-year economic plan, and a dissatisfied population.

CHAPTER SIX

⁓ᗯᗯ⁓

Costa e Silva:
The Failure of "Humanization"

IN TAKING OFFICE ON MARCH 15, 1967, Costa e Silva enjoyed the advantage that almost all important segments of public opinion expected his administration to be a relief from the increasingly authoritarian trend of the first revolutionary regime. The opposition was disposed to cooperate with his efforts to "humanize" the revolution, and important figures of the movement of March, 1964, who had become alienated from the Castelo Branco administration were prepared to join in the new government. Moreover, few really expected dramatic improvements or sweeping changes in the new order imposed by Castelo Branco—incremental improvements and changes in degree would do.[1] Thus, although an overwhelming majority (some 80 per cent in the polls) favored direct elections, and a clear majority expressed preference for substantial modifications of the new Constitution, return to a multiparty system, a largely civilian cabinet (more of technicians than politicians), and a diminuition of the influence of the *linha dura,* not many appeared very

[1] "O que o Brasil espera de Costa e Silva," *Manchete,* March 11, 1967, pp. 8–15, contains the results of a public opinion poll in the country's five major urban centers. Although more than half believed that Costa would give them a "better" government than Castelo had, and only 3 per cent felt it would be worse, their expectations for major changes were relatively limited.

optimistic that moves in these directions would be forthcoming. And those whose expectations were highest would soon be the most bitterly disappointed, for the departure of the Sorbonne generals from power opened the way for the resurgence of the *linha dura*.

By late 1967, Brazil would experience unrest greater than that at any point of the Castelo Branco regime, and further deterioration would lead to a crisis situation during the latter half of 1968 that would result in another "coup within a coup," issuance of a stringent Fifth Institutional Act, dissolution of Congress, and cassation of many individuals whose actions during 1964–1967 marked them as moderates and liberal constitutionalists. Rather than a more "humane" tutelary democracy, Brazil under Costa e Silva was to slide into the type of unrestricted military dictatorship Castelo Branco had largely been able to avoid even after October, 1965.[2]

1. THE SECOND GOVERNMENT OF THE REVOLUTION: CONTINUITY WITH CHANGE

The administrative personnel appointed by Costa e Silva, while including individuals who had become critics of the Castelo Branco government, were drawn entirely from among the backers of the 1964 coup. The President himself, a line officer in contrast to Castelo's long experience in school and general staff positions, was relatively adept at military politics but inadequately prepared for other areas of national policy making.[3]

By contrast, his Vice President, Pedro Aleixo, was one of the country's most experienced parliamentary politicians. Born in 1901, he had been a *Mineiro* classmate of Negrão de Lima and Milton Campos. Elected to the Constitutional Assembly in 1933 and to Congress in 1934, Aleixo was elevated by Vargas to government leader in place of

---

[2] A perceptive interpretation of the transition from Castelo to Costa as an "end of an epoch" is contained in James W. Rowe, "Brazil Stops the Clock, Part I: 'Democratic Formalism' before 1964 and in the Elections of 1966," and "Brazil Stops the Clock, Part II: The New Constitution and the New Model," *American Universities Field Staff Reports,* East Coast South America Series, XIII, Nos. 1 and 2 (March, 1967).

[3] For a biographical sketch consult "Costa e Silva: A História de um Presidente" in *Manchete,* March 25, 1967, pp. 4–7.

Raul Fernandes in 1935. Two years later, he ousted the prestigious Antônio Carlos from the Chamber presidency. As president of the Minas Gerais section of the UDN, he did not run for the first post-Vargas congresses, serving instead as Secretary of Interior in the state administration of Milton Campos. Returning to the Chamber in the 1958 elections, he became government leader under Quadros and opposition leader during the Goulart period before becoming majority leader during the Castelo Branco government and finally accepting the Education Ministry in January, 1966. Yet little of his wide-ranging experience was to be utilized by Costa e Silva, who appeared to have reservations concerning Aleixo's ties to the Castelo forces, and in September, 1969, the military were to ignore his existence when the President became incapacitated.

The executive staff organized by Costa e Silva clearly lacked the intellectual qualities of the advisors of the departing President. As head of the presidential staff, Minas Gerais Congressman Rondon Pacheco, although an experienced politician, was certainly not one of the outstanding figures of his party or his state, and lacked the cultural and literary polish of Luíz Viana Filho, a renowned historian and member of the Brazilian Academy of Letters. Similarly, Brigadier General Jaime Portela as Chief Military Aide did not have the administrative and governmental experience of the outgoing General Ernesto Geisel, who moved to the Superior Military Tribunal. As head of the SNI, General Emílio Garrastazú Médici (whom few expected to emerge as Costa's successor), was much more limited in intelligence experience than General Golbery, the architect of that agency. In addition to being a *Gaúcho* (from Rio Grande do Sul) and having served as Costa's chief of staff in the Third Military Region, Garrastazú's role in the 1964 revolution recommended him to the President. As Commandant of the Military Academy at Agulhas Negras he had cooperated closely with Costa e Silva. After sitting out much of the Castelo period as military attaché in Washington, the future president was promoted to major general and given command of the Third Military Region. (Golbery had been named to the *Tribunal das Contas* by Castelo on the eve of leaving office.)

The Costa e Silva cabinet, which was to survive intact even through the implantation of the dictatorship in December, 1968, included a very heavy military representation. In addition to the three service ministries, five other cabinet posts were entrusted to military men, while eight went to civilians. Thus, the civilian and military ministers were evenly balanced in numbers, with the latter holding an edge in terms of the political importance of their positions.

For the crucial post of Army Minister (so renamed by Castelo's administrative reform law), Costa e Silva chose General Aurélio de Lyra Tavares, Commandant of the Escola Superior de Guerra. A military intellectual who was not deeply involved with the Sorbonne group in its clash with the *linha dura,* Lyra Tavares appeared to be the ideal officer to be entrusted with the task of maintaining unity and discipline within an Army whose senior officers had largely been promoted and appointed to their present positions by Castelo Branco. As Navy Minister, Costa selected Admiral Augusto Hamann Rademaker Grünewald, an anti-Castelo officer who had been his collaborator in April, 1964, on the Revolutionary Supreme Command. The sixty-one-year-old Rademaker was joined in Costa's cabinet by Air Minister Brigadier Márcio de Sousa e Melo, one year his junior in age, who had served in Castelo Branco's cabinet for less than a month at the end of 1964, leaving in protest in the dispute over carrier-based aircraft. (However, Rademacker's essentially anti-Air Force sentiments were softened by the fact that Melo was the son of an Admiral, and the two "minority" service ministers got along well together.) The new Air Minister's anti-Goulart sentiments had been so strong that he sat out 1963 and early 1964 on leave without a command. Thus the generally legalist and moderate Lyra Tavares was teamed with two relatively hard liners with close personal links to the President.

The strategic Interior Ministry, with its control over the regional development agencies, went to Major General Afonso Augusto de Albuquerque Lima, who at fifty-seven was one of the senior officers most admired by the colonels of the *linha dura* and a strong contender for the presidency after Costa e Silva's term.[4] Also linked to the *duristas* was Minister of Mines and Energy, Colonel José Costa Cavalcanti. Only forty-nine years old at the time, he had served as a military attaché in Washington in 1955–1957 and subsequently as secretary of the United States-Brazilian Mixed Military Commission. Chosen by Cid

---

[4] For a statement of the Minister's outlook, see Murilo Melo Filho, "A Frente Ampla do Grande Interior," in *Manchete,* June 10, 1967, pp. 128–29.

Sampaio to be Pernambuco's Secretary of Security in 1959, Costa Cavalcanti was elected to the Chamber in 1962 and took an active part in articulating the 1964 revolution. As presiding officer of the National Security Committee, he often acted as a spokesman for the *linha dura,* among whom his brother, Colonel Francisco Boaventura Cavalcanti, was a leading figure.

Transportation Minister Mário David Andreazza was a rising Army Colonel who had been one of Costa e Silva's chief aides in the War Ministry and during his presidential campaign. Only forty-eight years old and with substantial experience in intelligence work, he was universally considered to be a possible future presidential aspirant.[5] A friend of Costa Cavalcanti since their days together in 1950–1952 as instructors at the General Staff and Command College, Andreazza was less identified with the hard liners than the former or Albuquerque Lima. The forty-seven-year-old Colonel Jarbas Passarinho, who relinquished his seat as Senator from Pará to head the sensitive Labor Ministry, was even more the prototype of the modern military technician. Closely linked to Petrobrás and journalism before the revolution of 1964 catapulted him into the governorship and political prominence, Passarinho was more oriented toward the Sorbonne than the hard-line way of viewing matters (a fact which would prove important in impelling him toward a key role in the government which succeeded that of Costa in October, 1969).

The senior military man in the cabinet, albeit long removed from active duty, was General Edmundo de Macedo Soares e Silva. One of the veterans of *tenentismo,* who spent two years in jail after the 1922 revolt, the sixty-five-year-old Macedo Soares was best known for his work as builder of the Volta Redonda steel mill and long-time head of the National Steel Company.[6] A turn as governor of Rio de Janeiro State, the presidency of the National Confederation of Industries, and the leadership of the Latin American iron and steel producers' association provided him with ample credentials for the Ministry of Commerce and Industry. Of all the cabinet, his association with Costa e Silva had

[5] A statement of his views is found in Murilo Melo Filho, "Estratégia Global para os Transportes," in *Manchete,* July 22, 1967, pp. 118–21.
[6] Murilo Melo Filho, "O Que Interessa e Produzir," in *Manchete,* June 24, 1967, pp. 46–48, contains a statement of Macedo Soares' views on major policy matters.

the longest gestation if not the deepest roots, going back to their times as cadets.

Two of the civilian ministers were also friends of the President. Dr. Leonel Miranda, the sixty-three-year-old Health Minister, had known Costa e Silva for at least a decade, while Justice Minister Luís Antônio da Gama e Silva had held the Justice and Education Ministries under the Revolutionary Supreme Command in April, 1964. A hard liner who had advocated wider purges and a longer period for deprivation of political rights, the fifty-three-year-old Gama e Silva had been Rector of the University of São Paulo. By way of contrast, Education Minister Tarso Dutra held his post in the cabinet for purely political reasons. The strongest ARENA congressional vote-getter in Rio Grande do Sul, his ambitions for the governorship had been thwarted by Castelo's decision to back Peracchi Barcelos for that post in 1966. Thus, by appointing the fifty-one-year-old Deputy, Costa e Silva conciliated the major wing of the Rio Grande ARENA, which supported Dutra in his power rivalry with the new Governor. Although he had been a member of the Education Committee in the Chamber, Tarso Dutra demonstrated little aptitude for his new post, but he was retained by Costa in the face of repeated campaigns for his replacement.[7]

By far the most politically powerful member of Costa e Silva's cabinet was Minas Gerais ex-Governor José de Magalhães Pinto, named Foreign Minister. One of the country's leading bankers, with fifteen years in Congress preceding his five-year term as chief executive of Brazil's second most populous state, Magalhães Pinto was one of the few civilian politicians considered to have prospects of achieving the presidency. Still a full year on the near side of sixty when he assumed the prestige-laden position at the helm of Itamaraty, the "authentic" 1964 revolutionary pledged a dynamic and flexible policy of national affirmation, in contrast to the strongly pro-United States orientation of Brazil's diplomacy under his predecessor, Juracy Magalhães.[8] An "op-

[7] For a detailed interview with the Education Minister, see Arnaldo Niskier, "Tarso Dutra: O Desafio da Educação," in *Manchete,* April 8, 1967, pp. 76–77.

[8] The major themes of the new administration's somewhat more nationalist foreign policy can be found in Ministério das Relações Exteriores, Secretaria Geral Adjunta para o Planejamento Político, *Documentos de Política Externa de 15 de março a 15 de outubro de 1967* (Rio de Janeiro, 1968). For a journalistic assessment of the man, see Murilo Melo Filho, "Magalhães Pinto: Soberania e prosperidade," in *Manchete,* May 13, 1967, pp. 34–36.

erational" nationalist, the pragmatic and politically ambitious Magalhães Pinto stressed the economic dimension of foreign policy. His "diplomacy of prosperity" appeared in many respects to resemble a less dramatic version of the "independent" foreign policy articulated by his *Mineiro* colleague Afonso Arinos during the Quadros period.

The critical post of Finance Minister was entrusted to Antônio Delfim Neto, a young (thirty-eight years of age) *Paulista* economist who had served on the planning staff of Carvalho Pinto and as Finance Secretary for Governor Laudo Natel following the ouster of Adhemar de Barros from the São Paulo governorship. Costa e Silva's primary economics tutor during the pre-inauguration period, the rotund bachelor would play a larger role in policy-making than had his predecessor.[9] With the relatively close cooperation of Central Bank president Ruy Leme, the Bank of Brazil's Nestor Jost, and Jaime Magressi de Sá of the National Economic Development Bank, Delfim was in a stronger position to implement his program than any finance minister before 1964.[10] One of the chief reasons for the increased influence of the Finance Minister was the character of the new Planning Minister, Hélio Beltrão. In sharp contrast with the wide-ranging scope of Roberto Campos' authority as the dominant member of the cabinet throughout the Castelo Branco administration, this experienced public administration technician was destined to play a less salient role in the new cabinet. A key figure in the constructive works of the Lacerda government in Guanabara, the fifty-year-old Beltrão had accepted the reduced scope of the Planning Ministry in Costa e Silva's administrative scheme, and he was viewed as chiefly responsible for consolidating much of the institutional restructuring inherited from the frenetic activity of the last months of the Castelo Branco regime.[11]

Rounding out the cabinet were Agriculture Minister Ivo Arzua Pereira, forty-two-year-old former Curitiba mayor, but a technician rather than an expressive politician, and the forgotten man of the Costa

---

[9] On his economic policy views, consult Antônio Delfim Netto, *Planejamento para o Desenvolvimento Econômico* (São Paulo, 1966). On the man, see Murilo Melo Filho, "O Jovem Delfim do Tesouro," in *Manchete,* April 29, 1967, pp. 122–23.

[10] Consult a series of interviews with these officials in *Manchete,* September 30, 1967, pp. 134–45.

[11] See Murilo Melo Filho, "Beltrão: Liberdade e Otimismo," in *Manchete,* May 6, 1967, pp. 20–22.

government, Minister of Communications Carlos Furtado Simas, named to afford Bahia at least token representation in the administration.[12] The cabinet status of "civil household" chief Rondon Pacheco, a forty-seven-year-old *Mineiro* congressman and original secretary general of ARENA, overshadowed these two regular ministers as did that of the head of Costa's "military household," General Jaime Portela. The latter, a fifty-five-year-old career officer who was one of Costa e Silva's chief aides in the 1964 coup, would gain in influence as well as become a center of controversy as the Costa e Silva administration progressed. Having sided with Carlos Luz against Lott in 1955, Portela was in the bad graces of the government until 1964, with the exception of the brief Quadros period. Subsequent experience on the Army General Staff and as chief aide to the War Minister prepared him for the significantly expanded role attributed to his new position by Castelo Branco's National Security Law. (His promotion to three-star rank in mid-1969 led to widespread speculation concerning his military future, but the subsequent replacement of Costa e Silva by Garrastazú Médici would undercut his aspirations.)

Costa e Silva inherited a military situation which would bear the stamp of Castelo Branco for some time to come. Legislation sponsored by Castelo ending most of the extraordinary promotions and benefits connected to retirement had led to a rush of transfers to the reserve during mid-1966 to take advantage of the last opportunities for such advantages before the October 10 deadline. The unusually large number of vacancies in the upper ranks of the officer corps were filled at the end of the year by a major series of promotions. No fewer than seven new full generals were named, headed by Jurandir Mamede, Alvaro da Silva Braga, Rafael de Souza Aguiar, Augusto Fragoso, Alberto Ribeiro Paz, Antônio Carlos Muricy, and Ernesto Geisel. The last two officers were promoted by Castelo over several others widely considered to have been higher on the list of eligibles put forth by the Army High Command. Sizeno Sarmento, a close collaborator of Costa e Silva's who had previously served as Lacerda's Secretary of Security, and Carlos Luís Guedes, a hard liner who had helped launch the 1964 revolt, were

[12] Murilo Melo Filho, "Ivo Arzua: A Batalha da Fartura," in *Manchete,* May 20, 1967, pp. 34–35. Simas was the only civilian minister ignored by this series of interview articles.

passed over for advancement to four-star rank, as were Alvaro Tavares do Carmo and Alfredo Souto Malan, who were lower in seniority. In the extensive promotions continuing down through the military hierarchy, Lacerdistas and hard liners fared poorly. (The nine promotions to major general held significant implications for the future, since many of these individuals would be hard-pressed to obtain advancement to the higher rank until pushing retirement age, owing to the fact that the newly promoted full generals would stay on active duty until the end of 1970 in most cases and then would be succeeded by major generals of greater seniority. Among these "junior" three-star generals, João Dutra de Castilho, João Bina Machado, Newton Fontoura de Oliveira Reis, Nogueira Paes, and Itiberê Gouvêa do Amaral would bear watching in the events of late 1968 and 1969.) Although Costa e Silva promoted Sizeno Sarmento to full general in late March, and at the same time advanced three officers from brigadier to major general, the opportunity for promotions on a large scale was denied him by the recent nature of advancement to the top grades within the Army. Thus individuals closely linked to Castelo Branco, albeit in most cases maintaining good relations with the President, remained in most important command positions down through 1969.

The Costa e Silva government was very slow to define its policies and programs. For several months after the inauguration, the adjectives most used in the newspapers and political commentary to describe the new administration were indecision, perplexity, expectation, indefinition, and timidity. This very lack of political activity bought time for the new administration while in a deeper sense wasting it, as political discussions among the opposition and within Congress centered on whether the failure to define policy positions was a conscious tactic or a result of a lack of preparation and political intelligence on the part of the regime. (In part, the "inactivity" of the Costa e Silva government was essentially relative, i.e., perceived in contrast to the almost frenetic energy of Castelo's regime in its final weeks in office.) Although the new administration appeared to show signs of willingness to consider possible revision, if not repeal, of some of the Castelo Branco regime's decree legislation, this turned out to be but a means of keeping the opposition off balance as well as offering some hope to economic interests and bureaucratic cliques who felt injured. Similarly, its original vacillation concerning the continued effects of the provisions of the Institutional Acts, which themselves lapsed with the change of regime and the coming into force of the new Constitution, was only a temporary tactic.

The opposition and much of the urban public hoped that "humanization" implied selective review of punitive acts if not amnesty, relaxation of wage constraints, amendment of the National Security and Press Laws, limited constitutional revision, return to direct elections, and restraint in the use of decree laws.[13] There was further expectation concerning whether the government's financial policies would involve substantial modifications, albeit within the theme of "revolutionary continuity" or would see only palliative measures to soften the impact of some of the harshest provisions of the Campos program.

The Frente Ampla, which had posed as an alternative base of support for Costa e Silva should he wish to break out of the political straitjacket of ARENA bequeathed him by Castelo Branco, moved quickly to probe the government's intentions. The issuance of its long-awaited manifesto was again postponed, in large part because the Minas Gerais elements of the old PSD preferred to follow Magalhães Pinto's suggestion that they work to strengthen the "civilist" tendencies within the regime and for redemocratization on the bases of nationalism and free enterprise. Instead, the front's leaders decided to explore how far Costa e Silva was willing to go with concessions in his efforts to prevent center-left elements within the MDB from radicalizing and merging with the Frente Ampla to form a third party. At the instigation of Carlos Lacerda, Hélio Fernandes began to publish signed political articles in his *Tribuna da Imprensa* in violation of the prohibitions on such activities by *cassados* (a term appended to those whose political rights had been suspended). This move was to test the opposition thesis that the punitive measures of the institutional acts had lost their effect with the lapsing of the acts and the return to a constitutional regime. When the government failed to react decisively with respect to this "provocation" (as it was termed by the *linha dura*), additional moves were planned to

---

[13] The attitude of the more militant congressional opposition is reflected in "Discurso Pronunciado Pelo Deputado Mata Machado e Publico no DCN de 30–3–67," in *Paz e Terra*, No. 4 (August, 1967), pp. 229–42, which includes the comments of several other MDB leaders. See also "O primero desafio está lancado," in *Visão*, March 31, 1967, pp. 11–14.

place the government in the position of having to choose between its campaign commitments of normalization or pacification on the one hand and revolutionary continuity on the other.

At this juncture, in view of the executive's ambivalence, Congress enjoyed its greatest opportunity to play a significant role in affecting the course of events. It chose instead to become bogged down on a narrow issue of institutional self-interest: the question of whether, in light of an apparent inconsistency in the new Constitution, the function of presiding over joint sessions of Congress was a prerogative of Vice President Pedro Aleixo or fell within the domain of Senate president Auro de Moura Andrade. Although the opposition viewed this as a possible opportunity to force the government to open the door to the question of amending the Constitution, the resulting sterile struggle severely injured the legislative branch in the eyes of the public—and of the hard-line elements of the military. At the same time, the significant groups within ARENA sympathetic to modification of the Constitution and National Security Law were restrained from playing the opposition's game by the pettiness of the issue.

2. EMERGENCE AND DECLINE OF THE "FRENTE AMPLA"

In many respects, the key figure at this juncture was Carlos Lacerda, whose alienation from the government under Castelo Branco was not viewed by many as an irrevocable break with the revolution itself. Planning Minister Hélio Beltrão, Magalhães Pinto, and Lacerda's remaining friends within the military strove to bring about a rapprochement with the new government; this very possibility all but paralyzed the organizational work of the Frente Ampla. The breakdown of the negotiations, the subsequent rapid articulation of a broadened opposition front, and the ensuing polarization and "hardening" of the government's line were within a relatively short time to set Brazil on the road toward dictatorship rather than the promised re-establishment of democracy.

Perhaps the most controversial figure in Brazilian public life, Lacerda had in the course of his career assumed positions from near one end of the political spectrum to the other. Often taxed for his political inconsistency, Lacerda in reality manifested the ambivalences inherent in his position as the brilliant son of an aristocratic, radical father, a paternalistically populist intellectual whose political successes were more oratorical and parliamentary than organizational. Active as a young Communist when Mauricio de Lacerda was at his peak as a tribune of the people, Carlos made his mark first in journalism. In 1938, while still in his early twenties, he became a reporter for the *Observador Econômica e Financiera* under Olympio Guilherme and Valentim F. Bouças. In 1941, he joined the *Agencia Meridional* of press lord Assis Chateaubriand's *Diarios Associados* chain and soon began to write for *O Jornal,* its flagship paper. By 1946, Lacerda had shifted to *Correio da Manhã,* where his "Tribuna da Imprensa" column became the most widely discussed feature of political journalism in Brazil. When *Correio da Manhã* publisher Paulo Bittencourt failed to publish his attack upon a refining concession granted by the Dutra regime to a powerful economic group, Lacerda left the daily and in 1947 founded his own newspaper under the popular title of his column.

Lacerda's career in elective politics began in 1947 with his election to the municipal council in the then Federal District. Swept into the Chamber of Deputies in 1950, he emerged as the most severe critic of the Vargas regime. Polling a record 160,000 votes in 1954, he spent ten months in exile after the November, 1955, "preventive coup," returning in October, 1956, to defend successfully his mandate against government demands for his expulsion from Congress. In 1958 he was overwhelmingly re-elected and in 1960 he became Guanabara's first elected governor. Impressed in 1962 with leftist arch-foe Leonel Brizola's electoral triumph as a political carpetbagger in Guanabara, Lacerda worked for the overthrow of the Goulart regime while determining subsequently to broaden his own political base from the urban middle class to embrace the workers and marginal groups orphaned by the 1964 purge of leftist politicians. Thus the often-heard accusation that Lacerda was a man who could only destroy revealed only one facet of this complex individual with a true political genius, albeit talents not always used with moderation. Far from a centrist, in the usual use of the term to connote a tendency toward conciliation, Lacerda was equally distant from being either a reactionary (as often painted by the radical left) or a revolutionary. The requirements of being a successful urban populist in a changing system more than "opportunism" help explain his political inconsistencies. Although his tactics changed, his objectives remained fundamentally unaltered.

Lacerda's strategy, like that of most other opposition groups, was largely neutralized during the early months of the Costa administration by the latter's amorphous profile and absence of major initiatives. The maneuvering on the part of the government and opposition, much of it shadowboxing, but with serious implications, continued through April and May. At the same time, substantive as well as tactical differences within the opposition slowed the progress of the Frente Ampla. Goulart and the radical wing of the MDB preferred to await the possibility of the PTB's re-emergence rather than be swallowed up in a movement in which Lacerda would be the "owner of the game." Returning from a prolonged absence in Europe and the United States, Kubitschek wished time to sense the possibilities of the new situation. The exchange of visits between Kubitschek and Lacerda, as well as the constant consultations of their representatives, provided the regime with a challenge it could not easily ignore, or rather one which the *linha dura* would not let it ignore.[14] Proposals to offer Lacerda the U.N. ambassadorship, or even the Ministry of Education, while sowing dissension in the ranks of the opposition, also raised divisions between the "democrats" and the *duristas* in the cabinet. (The nucleus of the hard line within the Costa e Silva cabinet was composed of Albuquerque Lima, Costa Cavalcanti, and Gama e Silva along with the Air and Navy Ministers. Generals Garrastazú Médici and Jaime Portela, who held cabinet rank, were also associated with this tendency, which preferred at the time to be termed the *linha justa* or *linha de conciência Revolucionária*.)

In the absence of a unified program of action, each minister announced isolated measures to cope with major dissatisfactions in his area of responsibility. Thus, Delfim Neto reduced the interest rate and raised the exemption from income tax, the Labor Minister promised an end to the drop in the purchasing power of the workers, and the Minister of Agriculture, seconded by the President, pledged more adequate credit for agricultural producers. Costa Cavalcanti spoke of harnessing atomic energy to Brazil's developmental needs, and Albuquerque Lima

[14] See "No país das contradições e desafios" and "Exilados: perto dos olhos, longe do coração," in *Manchete*, April 21, 1967, pp. 11–14 and 24–25.

committed the government to do more for the Northeast while at the same time incorporating the Amazon region into the life of the nation. The Minister of Education agreed to admit to the universities all the "excess" students who had passed the entrance examinations even though space and professors were lacking and the resulting overcrowding fed student unrest. As a result of these diverse beginnings, a number of contradictions came to light; for example, when the Minister of Transportation declared the government's determination to build the long-discussed bridge from Rio de Janeiro to Niteroi and pave the Belém-Brasília highway, the Finance Minister termed these "still projects, the execution of which depends upon obtaining external financing."

More serious was the incoherent labor policy. Minister Jarbas Passarinho declared the administration's intention to return the monopoly of job accident insurance to the National Social Security Institute (thus undoing Castelo's Decree Law No. 293), but the Minister of Commerce and Industry vigorously defended the retention of this function by private enterprise. Costa e Silva supported Passarinho's position in his May Day address, but subsequently yielded to Macedo Soares' importuning to the degree of announcing that the matter would be subjected to long and careful study. The unions, whose hopes had been raised by Passarinho's early declarations, were now perplexed by his silence on the issue and departure to Geneva for an International Labor Organization meeting. Having received more warnings than promises from Castelo's succession of Labor Ministers (Arnaldo Sussekind, Walter Peracchi Barcelos, and Nascimento Silva), organized labor was pleased to have a minister who offered them some concrete possibilities of a better deal rather than a bitter pill. They were dismayed that Colonel-Senator-Minister Passarinho appeared to have been overruled and undercut by his colleagues in the cabinet as well as in the Armed Forces.[15] They remained doubtful about what the Labor Minister's newly announced doctrine of "Christian solidarity" would mean in concrete terms.

A certain degree of tension existed during this period between the

[15] In addition to the daily press, the flavor of this period is captured in "Front interno, a preocupacão Comun," *Visão*, April 28, 1967, pp. 11–15. A detailed analysis of the accident insurance question is found in "Um seguro que ameaça provocar acidentes," *Visão*, July 14, 1967, pp. 14–15.

personnel of the new government and their predecessors. The latter constituted a shadow cabinet of the "Republic of Ipanema" (so-called from the location of Castelo's apartment and the constant coming and going of his advisers and ex-ministers) and kept a careful watch on revolutionary orthodoxy. Thus, Roberto Campos, at a gathering of notables celebrating his fiftieth birthday, strongly cautioned the Costa e Silva administration on the dangers inherent in modifications of economic and foreign policy. This continued coaching from the sidelines led Delfim Neto to retort: "The exercise of an economic policy requires a good deal of luck, much skill, and hard effort, but above all humility. When hypothetical solutions are applied, the existence of margins of error should be borne in mind. One cannot help viewing with a certain preoccupation those who imagine themselves as the owners of the road to salvation."[16] Marshal Cordeiro de Farias criticized the new President's actions, although he refuted retired Admiral Silvio Heck's allegation that there existed a conspiracy against Costa on the part of economic interests favoring the preceding regime. To ease the tension, Castelo decided to leave on a lengthy European trip.

During the second half of April, while rumors spread that the government might agree to a selective review of cassations, the Army Minister advised the officer corps to remain cohesive remembering that "the Government already had the opportunity to reiterate several times its decision not to review such acts, considering this to be inopportune and incoherent with the objectives of the Revolution." General Mamede, as a representative of the officers most closely linked to Castelo, strove to put stories of divisions within the military to rest with a public pronouncement that "the Army is a monolith"; but his replacement as commander in São Paulo at the end of April by the newly promoted Sizeno Sarmento did little to quiet such speculation. The new Second Army Commander's words on the occasion of the President's visit to São Paulo in late May did, however, help put to rest fears (or hopes) that the military was seriously divided.

The period of governmental indefinition drew to an end at this juncture. Finally, on May 24, Costa e Silva defined his government's position: "The revolutionary process will continue until the complete elimination of past distortions, mistakes, and incomprehensions, with

[16] *O Estado de S. Paulo,* April 21, 1967.

the real implantation of new methods of administration and new patterns of national politics." [17] On the foreign policy front, there appeared to be a gap between Costa's endorsement of Magalhães Pinto's emphasis upon "sovereignty" and the playing down of Brazil's security commitments (particularly in terms of opposition to an Inter-American Peace Force) and the preceding administration's close alignment with the United States. None-the-less, Costa e Silva demonstrated concern with the problems of subversion in his exchange of visits with Argentine President Juan Carlos Onganía. On the informal level of gentlemen's agreements, the government backed the Army Minister's view that the threat by a common enemy and "new processes of aggression" called for a larger role by the Armed Forces.[18]

The administration's shakedown period was not without at least a mini-crisis within the military. Curbed by Castelo after pushing him to the brink in October, 1965, and feeling in part responsible for Costa's installation in power, the colonels of the *linha dura* began to assert themselves, showing little consideration for military hierarchy and discipline. (In this regard it may be helpful to consider the *hard line* as much as a state of spirit which could be accentuated by the course of events as a relatively small hard-core faction which under certain circumstances strikes a responsive chord in a broader spectrum of the military.) In early June, Colonel Boaventura Cavalcanti articulated the views of this group in his address on assuming command of Fort São João in the heart of Rio de Janeiro. On June 23, these officers grilled Delfim Neto concerning his policies at an "informal" evening session in a private residence. Considering this a breach of the military's hierarchical discipline, Costa relieved several participants of their commands, including Boaventura, Ruy de Castro, and Colonel Amerino Rapôso, who was transferred out of his sensitive post within the SNI as head of its Guanabara operations. Retired Generals Nemo Canabarra Lucas and Dalisio Mena Barreto selected this juncture to announce formation of a self-styled Brazilian Nationalist Party (PNB) as part of a propaganda campaign against the "denationalization of industry" through foreign investment and in favor of a nationalistic atomic energy policy.

[17] *Jornal do Brasil*, May 25, 1967.
[18] See "O raio oculto das relações externas," *Visão*, June 2, 1967, pp. 11–12.

In mid-year, an issue also arose over the case of Sergeant Manuel Raimundo Soares, whose mysterious death in Rio Grande do Sul had led to a local scandal in September, 1966. An investigating committee of the state legislature was highly critical of Major Luis Carlos Mena Barreto's handling of the IPM on subversive networks in Rio Grande do Sul and in July accused Colonels Washington Bermudez and Lauro Rieth of being responsible for the death of the leftist noncommissioned officer. The hard liners brought heavy pressure against the Assembly to withdraw or modify this finding.[19] (Although the *linha dura* would have to bide its time as Costa e Silva sought to follow a conciliatory political course, they would have their day in December, 1968.)

On June 27, Planning Minister Hélio Beltrão finally announced the government's long-awaited development plan which, *inter alia,* called for implementation of the Castelo regime's administrative reform and priority action in the fields of housing, health, and education, along with emphasis on transportation, communications, and basic industry.[20]

Congress, to this point, had done little more than mark time and begin consideration of the eighteen "complementary laws" required to fully implement a number of provisions of the new Constitution. However, the heterogeneity underlying the inauthenticity of ARENA was almost as obvious in Brasília as it was on the state level during the modifications of state charters to conform to the new national fundamental law. The party's "Red Guard," led by Rafael de Almeida Magalhães, the personable young politician who had been Lacerda's vice governor, represented reformist attitudes and the desire to escape from presidential-military tutelage while giving ARENA some degree of programatic consistency and coherence. At cross-purposes to this movement for "democratic normalization" was the *Guarda Costa,* which expressed within Congress many of the sentiments of the *linha dura* and contained such figures as Brigadier (Ret.) Haroldo Veloso, the architect of the pocket Air Force revolts of 1956 and 1959. Assimi-

[19] *Revista Civilização Brasiliera,* No. 9–10 (September-November, 1966), pp. 298–305, discusses this case.

[20] For a detailed analysis of the economic-financial situation at mid-year, see "Um Saldo Positivo," *Visão,* June 30, 1967, pp. 22–34. More critical views on the first quarter at least are expressed in "Debate Sobre a Política Econômica do Govêrno CB," in *Revista Civilização Brasiliera,* No. 15 (September, 1967), pp. 147–89.

lating into its ranks the "Black Guard," which had been checking the growth of UDN control over the party and, under the leadership of Clóvis Stenzel renaming itself ARPA (Revolutionary Parliamentary Action), this clique—like its rival—undermined the efforts of such established leaders as Senator Daniel Krieger (ARENA president) and Chamber leader Ernani Sátiro to implant a minimum degree of party discipline.[21]

The political balance within the revolution was upset abruptly on July 18, with the death of Castelo Branco in a mid-air collision just outside the Ceará capital of Fortaleza. Ironically, the T-33 jet trainer which, without injury to itself, hit the light plane in which the ex-President was returning from a trip to the interior of the state was piloted by the son of one of Castelo's close comrades in arms, General Alfredo Souto Malan (and grandson of Malan d'Angrogne, a key military figure in 1930).[22] Tired by his train trip to the fazenda of renowned writer Raquel de Queirós, Castelo (who had only recently returned from his European trip) changed his plans at the last moment in favor of flying back. His death resolved the struggle for the loyalty of ARENA leaders in favor of Costa e Silva. It also brought temporary consternation to the ranks of the Frente Ampla, who had that very day decided upon a strategy of exploiting the cleavage between Castelo's followers and the Costa e Silva administration.

Hélio Fernandes, who had recently won a favorable Supreme Court ruling on his right to exercise his profession as a journalist in spite of having been deprived of his political rights, became the center of a political furor by heaping abuse upon the generally respected albeit not widely popular ex-President. In lieu of an obituary, he ran a front-page editorial declaring:

With the death of Castelo Branco . . . , humanity lost little, or better yet, it lost nothing. With the ex-President a cold, unfeeling, vengeful, implacable, inhuman, calculating, cruel, frustrated man disappeared without grandeur, without nobility; dried up within and without, with a heart like a true Sahara Desert. . . .

[21] See, for example, "Só tiros e retórica quebram o vazio," *Visão,* July 7, 1967, pp. 12–13.

[22] A detailed coverage of the accident can be found in *Jornal do Brasil,* July 19, 1967. Its political ramifications are discussed in "A solução é somar não dividir" and "Uma herança e muitas interrogações," *Visão,* August 4, 1967, pp. 9 and 12–16.

Castelo Branco, in the course of his long life neither loved nor was loved. How can one cry over such a man, whose death can only arouse indifference, whose life was a spiteful act of mistrust and detachment—without any gesture of courage, without an emotional content, without a moment of grandeur, an instant of piety, contemplation, or humility? [23]

Such a scurrilous attack on the hero of Monte Castelo and mentor of the Brazilian officer corps could go neither unnoticed nor unpunished. With Army hotheads speaking of physical violence against the inflammatory journalist, Costa e Silva ordered Fernandes' arrest and confinement on Fernando de Noronha Island, from which he was subsequently transferred to a small town in São Paulo. But he had achieved his goal of contributing to the growth of tensions between the Armed Forces and the opposition.[24] In the wake of this incident, the government barred Lacerda, widely viewed as Fernandes' political patron, from television. The Frente Ampla leader continued, however, to attack the government in the press. General Augusto César Moniz de Aragão, President of the Military Club and Army Director of Training, launched a series of articles in the conservative daily *O Globo* that, after the Hélio Fernandes episode, reached the level of a personal polemic with Lacerda. On August 30, he was instructed by Army Chief of Staff General Orlando Geisel to desist as this was drawing too much attention to the Frente Ampla. The government's action in muzzling Aragão, well within military regulations, may also have been prompted by fear of a physical clash between the hot-tempered officer and Lacerda that could lead to untoward developments. (The proud general seems to have nursed his resentment over this episode, and subsequently catalyzed a military crisis in mid-1969.)

Less than six months after taking office, the Costa e Silva administration found itself beset by problems on every side. The embarrassing

[23] *Tribuna da Imprensa,* July 19, 1967.

[24] Fernandes, who may well have hoped to utilize this "martyrdom" as the foundation stone for a future political career, deeply resented the fact that Castelo had suspended his political rights on the very eve of the 1966 congressional balloting, in which his election as federal deputy appeared assured, perhaps with an impressive vote total. His rapidly written and instantly published book, *Recordações de um Desterrado em Fernando de Noronha* (Rio de Janeiro, 1967) not only contains a defense of his actions but is replete with behind-the-scenes political revelations of the kind that make his *Tribuna da Imprensa* a valuable source of political facts as well as fictions. Lacerda's articles of August 25, 26, 28, 29, and 31 are reprinted in *Recordações* . . ., pp. 175–216.

struggle between Pedro Aleixo and Moura Andrade over the presidency of Congress, the dispute concerning the government takeover of the accident insurance business, an impeachment effort against Governor Pedro Pedrossian in Matto Grosso, the controversy over the role of the military in the deposition of mayors throughout the Baixada Fluminense surrounding Rio de Janeiro, and the increasing pressures from the Armed Forces for a hardening of the government's attitudes toward student and Church opposition as well as toward the Frente Ampla contributed to a growing sense of malaise. Congressmen returned from the July recess with a renewed awareness of how low they had fallen in public esteem.[25] A tendency among the legislators in favor of demonstrating some degree of initiative and independence could be discerned (and would bear fruit within three months). On the other hand, discovery of a small guerrilla movement in Minas Gerais and a conspiracy allegedly involving one of the regular congressional correspondents in Brasília, when taken in conjunction with widespread student revolts and the beginning of a critical and even hostile attitude on the part of the Church, which had enjoyed fairly good relations with Castelo's government, disposed the administration to show firmness rather than a flexibility that might be mistaken for weakness or insecurity.

The Independence Day parade on September 7 saw a small and unenthusiastic crowd in Rio de Janeiro view a parade of more than 25,000 troops. Pressed by the authorities, Kubitschek left the country once again. But in late September, when the government was striving for maximum peace and normalcy for the massive influx of financiers and businessmen expected for the annual meeting of the Governors of the International Monetary Fund in Rio de Janeiro, Lacerda dropped his political bombshell. An atmosphere of tension and expectation was created by his trip to Uruguay to establish a political alliance with Goulart as a step toward strengthening the Frente Ampla.[26] While renouncing any intention to seek vengeance or a return to the past, Lacerda, from Uruguay and on his return, refused to accept the legitimacy

[25] Murilo Melo Filho, "O Regime Está em Férias?," *Manchete,* August 19, 1967, pp. 19–20.

[26] On this encounter, see "Lacerda e Jango no Uruguai: A Frente Mais Ampla," in *Manchete,* October 7, 1967, pp. 13–15. A broader statement on the Front's objectives can be found in Carlos Lacerda, "Frente Ampla: O que é, o que não é para que serve," in *Manchete,* September 30, 1967, pp. 19–26. Consult also "As perspectivas para a Frente," *Visão,* October 19, 1967, pp. 9–13.

of the government's policies, reiterating that the Frente's objective was "popular union for direct elections" rather than the elevation of any particular candidate, himself included, to the presidency.

Yet the Frente Ampla remained only an alliance at the top, unable to overcome the mutual distrust of Juscelinistas, Lacerdistas, Janguistas, and Janistas. Never, apparently, did the Costa e Silva government view it as a potential vehicle for escaping from the path toward increasing military tutelage; instead they considered it a potentially dangerous foe to be neutralized if not destroyed. The young radicals of the MDB were favorably disposed toward the Frente. Older PTB figures, however, were still very reluctant to follow Lacerda's leadership, and those linked to the Vargas family and backers of Brizola actively opposed this "unholy allience," as did establishment types such as MDB president Oscar Passos. Jânio Quadros, who in July had met with Kubitschek, still remained aloof from the Frente, in part in the hope that the government might restore his political rights in return for his neutrality. Thus, although Lacerda was finally willing to break with his remaining *linha dura* friends to gamble on the coalition with Kubitschek and Goulart, there was no great rush to get on the bandwagon of this "non-legal" movement. The government, for its part, strove to tighten ARENA "fidelity" to prevent defections to the potential third party.

Conflicts within ARENA, generally between the traditionally rival ex-PSD and ex-UDN elements, caused the congressional majority to place heavy emphasis upon a bill reinstituting the system of "sub-legends" resorted to by the Castelo Branco regime for the November, 1966, elections.[27] The main demand for the sublegends arose from the many ex-governors within ARENA's congressional ranks who wished to return to the statehouses or at least move up to the Senate in 1970. Paradoxically, the more "Castelist" line within the administration became increasingly influential in the months after the ex-President's death. The anti-inflationary policies of Delfim Neto and Beltrão withstood the pressures for relaxation of salary disputes and increased investments by Passarinho and Albuquerque Lima.[28] Similarly, Magalhães Pinto's nationalist campaign to force the doors of the "nuclear

[27] The issues of this period are amply discussed in the pages of the daily press and newsmagazines.
[28] Compare Antônio Delfim Netto, "Sálarios e mágicos," *Visão*, November 2, 1967, p. 19, with "O sálario das divergências," *Visão*, October 12, 1967, pp. 12–13.

club," against the wishes of the United States, was curbed by military opposition, and nuclear policy became the preserve of the Ministry of Mines and Energy rather than the Foreign Ministry. Costa e Silva's announcement on October 5 to ARENA leaders that he was determined not to modify either the Constitution or wage policies squelched those leaders of the government party who had hoped to meet the challenge of the Frente by means of wage concessions, a return to direct elections, and gradual reduction of military influence within the regime.

Indeed, by the final months of 1967, a majority of ARENA congressmen disagreed with basic elements of the government's program. Thus the administration parliamentarians personally favored greater autonomy for the states, direct election of the President, and a multiparty system, while opposing delegation of powers, major military expenditures, and the existing national security law.[29] The executive found itself faced with a significant end-of-the-session parliamentary revolt, such as Castelo had experienced in October, 1965, and October, 1966. Against the express wishes of the President, the Chamber—many of whose members felt that they had even less access to the presidency than under the preceding regime—voted to convoke a special session during the January-February summer recess period. It also rejected for the first time a presidential decree law unfavorable to the municipalities, and attempted to circumvent the constitutional provisions that had stripped Congress of the right to initiate legislation involving additional government expenditures.[30] Moreover, twenty-nine ARENA deputies voted for an MDB-sponsored constitutional amendment restoring direct elections. Ex-PSD national chairman Ernani do Amaral Peixoto expressed a view that would become quite generalized within a year when he opined that it was "better to have Congress closed than to have it open, marginalized, and humiliated."

The end of 1967 also witnessed a minor military crisis that demon-

[29] Carlos Castello Branco, "Como Pensa o Congresso (e como votaría se pudesse)," *Realidade,* December, 1967, pp. 30–42. See also "O jeito de acomodar," *Visão,* October 26, 1967, pp. 12–13.

[30] *Jornal do Brasil,* December 10, 1967, contains a review of the August-December legislative session. See also "Como vai a política," *Visão,* November 16, 1967, pp. 9–16. "Ernani Explica a Crise Congressional," *O Cruzeiro,* December 9, 1967, pp. 104–105 is useful, along with "De como o Congresso andou 180 Km, tomou 500 mil cafés, e falou 12 mil vezes," *Visão,* December 21, 1967, pp. 12–14.

strated that the potential for discord still existed within the Armed Forces. In April, Admiral José Santos Saldanha da Gama, a minister of the Superior Military Tribunal and president of the Foundation for Sea Studies, had granted an interview to the student magazine of the Navy School, *Galera*. The ex-Secretary General of the Navy Ministry and two-time president of the Naval Club (elected in 1965 and re-elected in 1967), the Admiral was a prestigious figure. When the very frank interview was published, it caused a scandal. In what could only be interpreted by the government as an affront, the respected naval leader, whose very name evoked memories of the crises of an earlier era and the notable role of his Grand Uncle declared that the Army had turned upon the Brazilian people and betrayed its traditions by staying in power after the 1964 intervention:

I think that the revolution carried out a duty, which was to overthrow a frankly subversive government, which was carrying Brazil down very dangerous ways, but I also think that it largely failed because it did not put the country back on its normal path. The military continue to interfere violently in the nation's destinies; it is everywhere, defending something that it calls national security but that I call internal security. The military does not live its basic purpose which is preparation for the external defense of the country. The enemy of the military is the civilian population; it exists to occupy the country; it is everywhere except in the barracks where it ought to be, carrying out its purpose. . . . The Brazilian military preoccupies itself only with what happens within its frontiers, it wishes to have its prestige assured by the greater or lesser interference it can have in the internal life of the nation. It is capable of even permitting an occupation of the country, as long as it continues to have assured to it the right to direct and internally police the nation.

In early December, Saldanha da Gama was quoted in an article in a widely read magazine as saying that Argentine President Juan Carlos Onganía was a "nondescript little Latin American dictator" and that the Army was so concerned with students painting walls that it failed to defend national interests.[31]

In a second *Galera* interview, on December 15, the Admiral asserted:

We struggle today between a conception of civil government and the preoccupation of the military in tutelage of the country. The military says that if it

[31] *O Cruzeiro*, December 9, 1967, pp. 38–39.

does not take charge of the nation the civilians are not capable of governing it. I remember, nonetheless, that originally the blame for this is with the military itself which in 1889 interfered without being called. . . . The only way to end this situation is to strengthen civil power and see that the military is obliged to take care of its own affairs.[32]

He further accused the Army of undermining Brazilian federalism through its newly established control of state paramilitary forces. In the ensuing controversy, which included a sharp censure by Foreign Minister Magalhães Pinto, Saldanha resigned as head of the Naval Club, and Naval School Commandant Admiral Alexandrino de Paula Freitas Serpa was relieved of his post.

The end of the year also witnessed a renewed polemic between Lacerda and the military. Speaking in Pôrto Alêgre on December 16, Lacerda declared that militarism had become the nation's curse and the Armed Forces the usurpers of authority that should reside with the people.

No matter how patriotic he may be, no military [man] has a monopoly of patriotism; neither does the fact of being military confer on anyone competence to substitute his for the decision of the people. The patriotism of the military consists always in acting at moments of crisis. But the same patriotism orders them not to remain in power, dislocating the people to put themselves in its place. No one is against the military. But everyone ought to be against militarism, beginning with the military themselves who would be in the end also the victims of this sickness which ignites ambitions in some and generates divisions among all. Military corruption, or that protected by the military, is the worst of all, because it is armed.[33]

Lacerda spoke again in Rio de Janeiro on December 26 and in São Paulo on the following day. His words brought an angry reply from Albuquerque Lima, who termed the Frente Ampla a focus of agitation and called upon the government to act against it. Denying that the regime was militarist, he termed Brazil in transition toward an "authoritarian democratic regime" as a result of the failure of classic forms of liberal democracy rather than the will of the Armed Forces.[34]

[32] Reprinted in *Ultima Hora,* December 20, 1967.

[33] *Jornal do Brasil,* December 17, 1967.

[34] Both Albuquerque Lima's remarks and the December 26 speech of Lacerda can be found in *Jornal do Brasil,* December 27, 1967.

Replying to an open letter from Albuquerque Lima in the early days of the new year, Lacerda waved aside the Interior Minister's profession of a lack of political ambitions by recalling similar disclaimers on the part of Costa e Silva, as well as Castelo's protestations that he would not permit extension of his term past its original January, 1966, expiration date.[35] The military, he said, "are not exclusive proprietors of the truth, nor owners of Brazil." While ex-PSD elements withdrew from the Frente in fear of the military reactions he was provoking, Lacerda began to intensify his attacks upon the government, which retaliated by barring him from radio. To compensate for this loss of media exposure, Lacerda shrewdly utilized many invitations to deliver commencement addresses to criticize the military regime, which, he said, was standing with its boots on the prostrated body of the Brazilian people. Although the newspapers were warned not to give any publicity to the opposition leader's activities and pronouncements, Moniz de Aragão and ten other generals protested forcefully to the regime over "the infamies asserted against the Armed Forces." General Sizeno Sarmento assumed a moderating stance between the outraged *duristas* and the President, a move with important implications for the major crises that would shake the regime before the end of 1968.

On January 27, Lacerda delivered his most devastating speech, at the Economics Faculty in São Paulo, in which he accused the military of "marrying itself to the decadent oligarchy." The First, Second, and Third Armies were called to alert status in a move designed as much to establish control over some of the more "exalted" spirits within the *linha dura,* who spoke of drastic action against Lacerda, as to intimidate the opposition. In Congress, MDB leaders Artur Virgílio and Martins Rodrígues strongly criticized government "hysteria." (A year later, they would be deprived of their mandates and have their political rights suspended for a decade as a consequence of performing their legal role as parliamentary spokesmen for the opposition.) Albuquerque Lima reportedly took advantage of the opportunity to advise the President of the need for a restructuring of the cabinet and drastic alterations in the government's economic and financial policies. (A year later, he would himself leave the cabinet over this issue.) The hard liners advocated

[35] Murilo Melo Filho, "As Cartas da Sucessão," in *Manchete,* January 20, 1968, pp. 20–21.

firm action against both Lacerda and the *cassados,* combined with effective moves in the fields of public health and education (where Leonel Miranda and Tarso Dutra were considered remiss in their ministerial responsibilities). Since the increase in the cost of living in 1967 had been held to 25 per cent, they called for a shift of priorities to development rather than further containment of inflation. At the same time, they hammered away on the threat of "subversion" to justify a hardening of the regime's policies in the political sphere.[36]

The renewed stress on subversion had begun on November 27, when General Moniz de Aragão's strongly anti-Communist speech was published in *O Globo,* on the anniversary of the 1935 revolt. His criticism of the Church for aiding "subversive" groups was echoed by Colonel Ferdinando de Carvalho, who denounced the existence of a Communist plot with such overtones in Curitiba (where he had been reassigned after completion of the IPM on the Communist Party). At this point, the Communist movement, severely disrupted by the 1954 revolution and the ensuing period of investigations and political purges, pulled itself together. In December, the Sixth Congress of the PCB finally took place. The congress passed a political resolution which acknowledged that economic growth had indeed begun to stagnate under Goulart, but stopped short of accepting that as a justification of the coup, noted a drop in the militance of the working class as a result of its incorporation of thousands of recent migrants to the cities; singled out the struggle against the government's salary policy as critical for allying the proletariat and urban petty bourgeoisie; recognized the value of the progressive sectors of the Church in the "anti-dictatorial front"; and viewed nationalism as perhaps the most effective catalyst for a broadened opposition.[37] A mixture of legal and violent tactics was sanctioned, varying with the "objective conditions" in each region. At the same time, the meeting ratified the expulsion of "leftist adventurists" who would embark upon a path of guerrilla warfare, to the neglect of organizational work among the masses. (The chief advocates of this

[36] For the flavor of the period, see "1967–1968," *Visão,* December 28, 1967, p. 21, and "A obsessão de anticipar catástrofes," *Visão,* January 19, 1968, pp. 20–21.

[37] Major excerpts from the Political Resolution of the PCB Congress are contained in *Jornal do Brasil,* December 31, 1967, p. 16.

militant line within the PCB, Mário Alves de Souza Vieira and Manoel Jover Teles, were dropped from the Executive Commission in May, 1965, but continued to constitute an isolated minority within the Central Committee, along with party theoretician Jacob Gorender, until September, 1967, when Teles and Carlos Marighella were expelled from the Party and Gorender was "suspended.") The theses of the Chinese Communist Party were strongly condemned and the hostile attitude of the Cuban Communists criticized.

With most of the PCB's top leaders in exile or underground, avoiding jail sentences, the work of implementing the congress's tactical line progressed slowly. Indeed, the most noted activities during 1968 were the series of bank robberies and bombings masterminded in São Paulo by Carlos Marighella, who had become a convert to violent revolution and resigned from the PCB Executive Commission in December, 1966. In mid-1968 the group expelled from the PCB at the end of 1967 combined with POLOP, a small splinter group that had existed since 1960, to establish the Communist Workers Party (POC). Later called the PCB Revolucionário, it carried out a policy of urban terrorism and rural violence.

3. THE NEW OPPOSITION AND GENERATIONAL CONFLICT

While the Frente Ampla involved a very great proportion of the political opposition's energies during 1967, developments of greater significance and with even broader ramifications had been taking place, particularly within the student movement and the Church. To an even more marked extent than in 1963–1964, the students and the Church would be critical elements in the radicalization and polarization of positions that would result in the establishment of an openly dictatorial regime.

Friction between the government and the students had begun immediately after the 1964 coup, with the arrest of radical student leaders and subsequent passage of legislation dissolving the existing student organizations. Named after Castelo Branco's Minister of Education, the so-called Suplicy Law authorized a structure of student organizations under substantial government control and free of ideological or partisan political content. The resort to strikes by students was expressly prohibited.[38] The rationale of the law was that, with troublemakers removed and autonomy severely restricted, student organizations could be used to channel interests toward academic matters. This proved quickly to be an illusive vision, if not a complete illusion.[39]

The Suplicy Law quickly became a negative symbol for large sectors of the university students. Castelo Branco himself was hissed at the Architecture Faculty of the Federal University of Rio de Janeiro in March, 1965. A student-organized plebiscite on the new law was announced by the UNE as an overwhelming repudiation of the government's measure, but complete figures were never released. A partial UNE Congress was held in São Paulo in July, but its plans to boycott the elections for directorates under the new law were thwarted by the compulsory nature of the vote (on pain of nonadmission to examinations). Nevertheless, a variety of tactics, including antigovernment slates pledged to resign immediately, blank votes, and purposeful nullification of ballots, were employed to demonstrate repudiation of the Suplicy Law. In general, the vote showed continued strong support for the now technically illegal UNE and a relatively low index of acceptance of the new "controlled" organizations as legitimate or meaningful.

This same period witnessed what was to be the first in a series of severe crises at the model University of Brasilia.[40] Invaded by troops in April, 1964, when its rector and vice rector, the noted educators Anísio

[38] Law 4,464 of November 9, 1964, approved by a vote of 126 to 117 with 5 abstentions. The National Student Directorate established by this law was to meet in Brasília rather than Rio de Janeiro, and to function only during the school holidays.

[39] In addition to the previously cited dissertation of Dr. Robert Myhr, the most detailed study of the Brazilian student movement is Arthur José Poerner, *O Poder Jovem: História da participação política dos estudantes brasileiros* (Rio de Janeiro, 1968). Materials on the post-1964 period are still rather scarce. Sulamita de Britto, "A Juventude Universitária e a Política," *Cadernos Brasileiros,* No. 48 (July-August, 1968), pp. 5–19 is a useful analysis of the 1964–1966 experience and can be supplemented by a collection of newspaper articles selected by her in "A Crise entre Estudantes e Govêrno no Brasil," *Paz e Terra,* No. 3 (1967), pp. 191–240, and "O Radicalismo Estudantil," *Cadernos Brasileiros,* No. 35 (May-June, 1966), pp. 71–77. Something more of the student environment is presented in José Maria Mayrink, " A Inquietude Universitária," *Cadernos Brasileiros,* No. 39 (January-February, 1967), pp. 44–54.

[40] A. L. Machado Neto, "A Ex-Universidade de Brasília: Significação e Crise," *Revista Civilização Brasileira,* III, No. 14 (July, 1967), 139–58.

Teixeira and Almir de Castro, were purged, the University was largely rebuilt under Zeferino Vaz. During the second quarter of 1965, the university was torn apart by a crisis over the contracting of a Rio Grande do Sul philosopher dismissed from his previous post under the Institutional Act; Vaz was immediately succeeded as rector by Laerte Ramos de Carvalho from the University of São Paulo. The dismissal of a young sociologist who refused to return to his civil service post at the Ministry of Education led to a strike by faculty and students on October 9. A prolonged military occupation of the campus was followed by the dismissal of fifteen professors and the resignation of 210 others in protest. The university did not reopen until well into the next academic year.

In December, 1965, the government formally ordered the elimination of UNE as a "frankly subversive" entity. Following conflict over the payment of newly instigated tuition fees, a concerted wave of student protests and demonstrations against the government took place in mid-March, 1966. The demonstration in Belo Horizonte ended in a violent clash with the police and a request for sanctuary within a Church, events that presaged the larger crisis to come. The "illegal" 28th UNE Congress in Belo Horizonte during July, 1966, involved the Church more deeply in the student-government conflict, since the meeting was held in the cellar of a Franciscan church. At the beginning of September, a dispute over the introduction of tuition payments flared into a general strike of university students throughout the country. Arrests of a large number of São Paulo students led to sympathy strikes and finally a "National Day of Struggle against the Dictatorship," on September 22. The government's response was to launch a University Movement for Economic and Social Development (MUDES) to enlist student support for its policies, but this organization quickly slipped into oblivion in spite of substantial government subsidies.

Although as President-elect Costa e Silva had spoken bravely of a meaningful dialogue with the students, his government soon experienced intensified friction with them. The new administration did not substantially modify the detested Suplicy Law, nor was it able to transform the students' strong desire for university reform into support for its moves in this direction. Indeed, misunderstanding and conflict quickly developed over the government's efforts to modernize the educational system along the lines recommended by North American advisors, formalized in a series of agreements with the United States. In April and May, 1967, students attacked the agreements as an "imperialist" plot to control Brazil's educational system. When the Education Minister approved them, the students launched a major series of demonstrations and clashes with the military in all major population centers.[41]

July and August saw the outbreak of a serious student crisis. On July 3, the police invaded a dormitory of the University of São Paulo and arrested a large number of students who resisted the forcible expulsion, including a priest. Cardinal-Archbishop Rossi added his voice to the protest by professors against unnecessary brutality. The Governor as well as federal authorities affirmed their intention to thwart the holding of UNE's annual congress.[42] However, the students once again outmaneuvered the authorities, holding their congress at a Benedictine monastery near Campinas. Its progressive Prior, Father Francisco de Araújo (known as Frei Chico), and a number of North American monks were subsequently arrested. Given the presence of nearly 400 students for a period of more than three days, the explanation that the hosts were unaware of the purpose of the meetings did not convince the military, particularly Second Army Commander Sizeno Sarmento, soon to take over the Rio de Janeiro-based First Army.[43]

As the student scene calmed down after August, attention was focused on the escalating friction between the regime and the Catholic Church, as well as on the dissension within that institution. Accustomed in the past to view the Church as a bulwark of stability, many in the military confused its newly found social conscience with giving aid and

[41] A relatively comprehensive and reasoned statement of moderate Brazilian nationalist views on the MEC-USAID agreements is contained in Sérgio Guerra Duarte, " A Presença Americana na Educação Nacional," *Cadernos Brasileiros,* No. 46 (March-April, 1968), pp. 35–59. See also his "Uma Frustração Nacional: A Educação," *Cadernos Brasileiros,* No. 42 (July-August, 1967), pp. 27–35. A more critical assessment by a United States scholar is Ted Goertzel, "MEC-USAID: Ideologia de Desenvolvimento Americano Aplicado a Educação Superior Brasileira," *Revista Civilização* Brasileira, III, No. 14 (July, 1967), 123–37.

[42] "Congresso da UNE Aguça a Crise Igreja-Govêrno," *Paz e Terra,* No. 6 (April, 1968), pp. 181–97 provides a relatively complete account of the Church side of the episode.

[43] Frei Chico's ideological position that the only justifiable violence is that of the oppressed against the oppressor can be examined in his "O Cristão e a Violência," *Paz e Terra,* No. 7 (1968), pp. 99–112.

comfort to subversive agitators. This was accentuated as militant elements of the Church came to champion the causes of the students and to march by their side—or at their head—in anti-regime demonstrations. Conservative clerics and anti-Communist laymen offered support to the military's contention that the Church had shifted dangerously to the left.[44]

Whereas Castelo had managed to avoid significant clashes with the Church (although the hard line took verbal pot shots at the progressive clergy), the Costa e Silva regime quickly found itself embroiled in a series of conflicts with reform-minded sectors of the clergy who leaped to the defense of the radical students in their clashes with the authorities. The Catholic hierarchy, which had endorsed moderate structural reforms in 1963, had become alarmed at the subsequent radicalization of the Goulart regime and welcomed the 1964 revolution as averting a threat of "the implantation of a bolshevik regime in our Land." [45] Yet, except for a few virulently anti-Communist priests and laymen, the Church was not particularly pleased with the abusive treatment handed out to representatives of the Catholic left. (Father Francisco Lage of Belo Horizonte, for example, was sentenced to twenty-two years before being allowed to escape to exile in Mexico; Padre Alípio de Freitas was given a twenty year-term.) Many were sympathetic to the plight of those students who had been active in literacy campaigns, popular culture movements, and organizational work among the rural populace. Some missed the intellectual stimulation of Dominican Brother Carlos Josaphat's short-lived publication, *Brasil Urgente*. The exception was the group associated with the Tradition, Family, and Property

---

[44] The most comprehensive and analytical study of the Church's historical role in politics is a draft doctoral dissertation by Margaret Todaro for the Department of History, Columbia University on "Pastors, Prophets and Politicians: A Study of the Political Development of the Brazilian Church, 1916–1945." On its contemporary social and political action a dissertation by Thomas Bruneau, "Conflict and Change in the Brazilian Catholic Church" (University of California, Berkeley, Department of Political Science, 1970) is the most thorough work. The Essay on Sources of this book contains a discussion of the expanding literature on this topic.

[45] "Declaração Sôbre os Acontecimentos de April e Maio de 1964," issued by the National Conference of Bishops of Brazil and reprinted in *Paz e Terra*, No. 6 (April, 1968), pp. 160–62. The same issue of the progressive Catholic review, pp. 149–279, contains a valuable collection of documents tracing the Brazilian Church's position from 1963 to the end of 1967.

movement, who since before 1960 had championed private property as an absolute moral value.[46] However, under the leadership of the conservative but not intransigently reactionary Cardinal Archbishop of Rio de Janeiro, Dom Jaime de Barros Câmara, the Church generally accepted the course of events from April, 1964, to the end of 1965 as an unavoidable if lamentable stage in national recuperation.

With the passage of time and the dissemination of the results of the Second Vatican Council, the balance of influence within the hierarchy shifted in the direction of the more enlightened moderates, such as Dom Eugenio de Araujo Salles (attacked by an IPM in 1964 but named Cardinal in March, 1969), who replaced the aged Augusto Alvaro Cardinal da Silva in Bahia soon after the 1964 revolution, and Dom Agnello Rossi, who succeeded to the position of Cardinal-Archbishop of São Paulo when the politically erratic Cardinal Vasconcellos Motta was eased into semi-retirement in 1964. Dom Vincente Scherer in Pôrto Alegre (who was also named a Cardinal in March, 1969) represented the elements of the hierarchy between the centrists and conservatives, while the dynamic Dom Helder Pessoa Câmara, appointed just before the 1964 coup as Archbishop of Olinda and Recife, emerged as the leading spokesman for the reformist clergy of the Northeast and other Catholic elements who felt that the Church should actively champion the interests of the underdogs in Brazilian society.[47] Dom Helder was born in Ceará in 1909, held important posts in the education sphere from the mid-1930's to 1952, and then for a dozen years was deeply involved in the problems of urban slum dwellers as auxiliary bishop of Rio de Janeiro. He was one of Pope John XXIII's most effective agents of modernization, which earned him many bitter enemies as well as loyal supporters. Dom Helder has been less hostile to the government

[46] Their first major publication was Antônio de Castro Mayer, Geraldo de Proença Sigaud, Plínio Corrêa de Oliveira, and Luiz Mendonça de Freitas, *Reforma Agraria: Questão de Consciência* (São Paulo, 1960).

[47] The best analysis of this influential hemispheric Church leader is an Institute of Current World Affairs newsletter by Frances M. Folland, written in early 1968. On the evolution of Dom Helder's thought during this period, compare "Evangelização e Humanização num Mundo em Desenvolvimento" (delivered in Recife on May 2, 1965), reprinted in *Paz e Terra*, No. 1 (July, 1966), pp. 235–42; "Imposições da Solidaridade Universal" (delivered on June 19, 1967), reprinted in *Paz e Terra*, No. 5 (October, 1967), pp. 159–68; and "A Violência—Única Opção" (delivered April 25, 1968), reprinted in Paz e Terra, No. 7 (1968), pp. 89–97.

than are many of his young protégés, who feel more strongly that the existing order in Brazil is one of stratified violence, featured by a permanent system of oppression and dehumanization directed against the masses, whose feeble attempts to resist are denounced as subversive.

While the numerically predominant moderate current of the hierarchy was not inclined to mount a struggle against the government, or even to condemn it for injustices that had not been corrected, it was not ready to relinquish its right to speak out against such injustices. Many Catholic leaders felt that the very tutelary nature of the regime accentuated the Church's duty to interpret popular sentiments, which were in danger of not being heard in the clamor of polarizing politics. Then, too, much like the Army itself, they demonstrated a tendency to come to the defense of their fellow churchmen when the latter were under attack, even when they did not entirely approve of their actions.

The first major clash between the Church and the military took place in the Northeast during the latter part of 1966. In March, the Workers' Catholic Action (ACO), Rural Catholic Action (ACR), and Catholic Agrarian Youth (JAC) had issued a manifesto declaiming against the injustice of the laborer's lot. At a gathering of the region's bishops in mid-July, Dom Helder pushed through a strong endorsement of this pro-labor position. General Itiberê Gouvêa do Amaral, Commander of the Tenth Military Region, with headquarters in Fortaleza, denounced Dom Helder as an "agitator" who took pleasure in "histrionic excesses and show-off attitudes on TV" and had carried the disorganization of the Church in Pernambuco to a point where it was ripe for Communist infiltration.[48] In sending circulars to this effect to all priests in the area, the General offended moderates in the Church elsewhere in the country, who sprang to Dom Helder's defense.

Following an unsuccessful effort to have the Vatican call Dom Helder to an assignment in Rome, Castelo Branco put an end to the immediate crisis by making General Rafael Souza Aguiar commander of the Fourth Army, based in Recife but with authority over the Tenth

[48] "Igreja militante está em campanha," *Visão,* August 26, 1966, pp. 22–25. A number of important documents concerning the conflict between the Bishops and the military in the Northeast during the second and third quarters of 1966 are collected in *Paz e Terra,* No. 2 (September, 1966), pp. 240–87, under the title "Nôva questão religiosa?"

Military Region as well. Aguiar was an old friend of the prelate from the period in the 1950's when they were both working with the populace in Rio de Janeiro. But the controversy had filled the newspapers and airwaves for more than two months, and the same basic issue would arise repeatedly in other areas as hardline soldiers and militant priests viewed each other with mistrust. Indeed, Dom Jorge Marcos, the Bishop of Santo André in São Paulo, and Dom Antonio Fragoso, the Bishop of Crateús in Ceará, among others, were already embroiled in disputes with the local military representatives.

In early May, 1967, the National Conference of Bishops of Brazil took a further step toward identifying the Church with the aspirations of the masses by calling for redistribution of landholdings. At the same time, Catholic Workers' Action (ACO) in the Northeast issued a manifesto, "Development without Justice," which criticized established institutions in terms stronger than those that had touched off the Church-Army crisis in the preceding year. In mid-August, a Mineiro Laymen's Manifesto, signed by many conservative catholics, bitterly attacked the hierarchy for its leftward swing. In October, a meeting in Salvador of prominent "Christian Politicians" of the Northeast supported a reformist line for the Church, countering the position of the conservative laity. Catholic Workers Action and Catholic University Youth in São Paulo both issued "radical" manifestoes shortly thereafter. On November 5, the arrest of four youths accused of distributing a "subversive" pamphlet from a Church-owned vehicle led to a prolonged conflict between the Bishop of Volta Redonda, Dom Waldir Calheiros, and military authorities who at that time were engaged in a political "clean up" operation in the suburban communities surrounding Rio de Janeiro, where the *linha dura,* who had enjoyed a free hand when Marshal Paulo Tôrres was the State's Interventor, were in the process of engineering the ouster of mayors considered unsympathetic to their goals.

In this climate—and with the tension provoked by Lacerda's 1967 polemic with the Army nearing its peak—the Central Commission of the National Conference of Bishops released a joint declaration in which they reiterated their faith in the country's youth: "We adults cannot have the same rhythm as the young, but we need to accept the contribution of their dynamism. We do not commit the madness of provoking hopelessness among Youth through the hardening of positions. . . . If it is the hour of the young, we will not delay the encounter marked with history." [49] In Congress, a militant Catholic layman delivered an incisive defense of the Church's position against its conservative critics.[50] Although not fully conscious of it at the time, he was guaranteeing that his political rights would be suspended when Brazil returned to a regime of Institutional Acts a year later.

As the summer holiday drew to a close and the Costa e Silva administration faced the end of its first year in power (and the fourth anniversary of the revolution), a serious breakdown of meaningful communication with the Church and students aggravated its manifold problems in the overtly political arena. Gone completely were the feeling of relief and expressions of hope that had predominated less than a year before. Lacerda was actively seeking support from those disillusioned with the government, emphasizing the themes of militarism and "the revolution that wasn't made." At the same time, he was cultivating elements that had never favored the 1964 revolution by stressing his newly established ties to Goulart. Congress, including its ARENA majority, which had proved rebellious during the last part of the 1967 session, showed an inclination to continue the struggle for a meaningful degree of autonomy and participation in decision-making rather than return to a role of near automatic subservience.

The year which was to prove to be the last chance for avoidance of deeply rooted military dictatorship began inauspiciously with the government's issuance on January 4, 1968, of Decree Law 348 reorganizing the National Security Council (CSN) and elevating its Secretary General to cabinet status. Since this post was held by the Chief Presidential Military Aide, critics claimed that its effect was to elevate the *Casa Militar* to a de facto superministry. Although the executive maintained that the decree consolidated only existing legislation and gave the Council no important new attributes, substantial opposition developed within Congress as it was realized that under present circumstances only ten of the twenty-five CSN members would be civilians—the Vice President,

[49] See "A Igreja na Vanguarda," *Manchete,* December 16, 1967, pp. 25–29; *Síntese: Política Econômica Social,* No. 36 (October-December, 1967), pp. 60–64; and "A ponte oferecida" and "A crise do diálogo," *Visão,* December 14, 1967, pp. 9 and 58.

[50] Edgar G. de Mata Machado, "A Igreja Voltada para o Futuro, o Govêrno Apegado ao que Passou, *Paz e Terra,* No. 7 (1968), pp. 301–15.

Chief of the Civil Household, and the eight civilian cabinet members.[51] Since under the Constitution Congress had sixty days to act on this decree, it promised to remain a bone of contention during the crucial opening months of the new session.

Early in February, Bahia Governor Luiz Viana Filho took the initiative in suggesting a political pacification including a *modus vivendi* with the MDB. São Paulo Governor Abreu Sodré, who had close ties with Lacerda, made a similar, albeit independent, proposal for a "Governors' Front" to strengthen civil power. Spokesmen for the hard line strongly indicated their intransigent opposition to any government consultations with Kubitschek, Quadros, or Goulart on this matter. When Frente leaders accused General Portela of exercising undue influence over the presidency and interfering in the areas of responsibility of the civilian ministers, *durista* Colonels Hélio Lemos, Caracas Linhares, and Boaventura Cavalcanti attacked the front as a vehicle for Lacerda's political ambitions and asked for its suppression. Although the Guanabara ex-governor was still in full possession of his political rights, the regime objected to United States Ambassador John Tuthill's two meetings with him. Albuquerque Lima was particularly vociferous in this regard. Having for some months stressed the need for effective Brazilian "occupation" of the Amazon region, he now denounced the proposal of Herman Kahn's Hudson Institute for the creation of a series of great lakes in that area. His subsequent statements, including testimony before Congress on March 15, lent support to nationalist fears of imperialist designs against Brazil's sovereignty, a theme that had been second only to petroleum in the nationalist campaigns within the Armed Forces in the late 1940's and 1950's.[52] (The youngest in a distinguished military family, his *tenente* brother had risen as far as command of the Second Army and a stint as Chief of Staff before retirement in the early 1960's. A second brother, retired General José Varonil de Albuquerque Lima, was serving as director of Petrobrás, the state petroleum entity.)

[51] This decree is discussed at length in *Jornal do Brasil* and *Correio da Manhã* of January 11, 1968, as well as in "Todo o poder a segurança," *Visão*, February 2, 1968, pp. 18–19.

[52] See General Tácito Lívio Reis de Freitas, "A Amazônia em Foco: O Caso do Instituto da Hiléia," *Revista Civilização Brasileira*, No. 17 (January-February, 1968), pp. 36–48. See also Arthur Cezar Ferreira Reis, *A Amazônia e a Cobiça Internacional* (Rio de Janeiro, 1968).

On February 21, the Supreme Court, which had been relatively circumspect during the period of the Second Institutional Act and Costa's first month in office, declared Article 48 of the National Security Law of 1967 unconstitutional, a ruling which displeased many in the military. In a parallel move Congress succeeded in getting the executive's list of 235 strategically located *municípios* that were to lose their autonomy as "security areas" reduced to seventy, with insurgent ARENA elements playing a key role.[53] The same day, within the ARENA caucus, José Bonifacio of Minas Gerais bested incumbent Batista Ramos for the Chamber presidency by a vote of 142 to 108, thus consolidating UDN dominance of the party. A month earlier, Rafael de Almeida Magalhâes had resigned as ARENA vice leader and criticized the government for turning its back on a moderate and modernizing approach to the country's problems.[54] Together with a number of the younger deputies first elected in 1966, he formed an "independent bloc" to act within ARENA. The appointment of Colonel Carlos Meira Matos, the officer who had closed Congress by force of arms in October, 1966, to head a special commission to study the educational crisis did not seem a positive response to this group's call for meaningful dialogue and a fresh approach to the students. It also brought home to some observers the extent of military involvement in the universities: the Rector of the University of Guanabara was the brother of the Army Minister, and the Rector of the University of Rio de Janeiro was the brother of the politically aggressive Military Club president.

The situation became more tense when in Minas Gerais, on March 15, Lacerda accused the Armed Forces of having become the effective ruler of the country with General Portela rather than Costa operating as the real chief executive. (Shortly before, Kubitschek had received a prolonged and apparently spontaneous standing ovation at the Carnival Ball in Rio de Janeiro's *Teatro Municipal,* an occurrence without precedent in Brazil.) The President's state of the union address, also on March 15, did not offer the opening desired by the advocates of national union and pacification, although he avoided the use of the term "revolu-

[53] See the discussion of the political implications of this issue in "Segurança, paz e pacificação," *Visão,* March 1, 1967, pp. 12–13.
[54] His lengthy letter analyzing the situation is printed in *Jornal do Brasil,* January 17, 1968.

tion" in describing his regime and promised that the municipal elections scheduled for November would be held in a climate of liberty. Speaking as the presiding officer of Congress (Moura Andrade had been sent off to Spain as Ambassador), the Vice President indicated that amendments to the Constitution might subsequently be considered—if they conformed to the basic precepts of the revolution and provided that Congress first voted the measures the government considered necessary to strengthen the system. Wholesale amendments or a Constituent Congress would not, however, be acceptable to the regime.[55]

The extent of political disagreement within the military became apparent in the aftermath of this incident when hard-line Colonel Ruy de Castro was given five days of punishment for supporting the idea of a civilian successor to Costa e Silva. On March 23, Marshal Poppe de Figueiredo called for the restoration of direct elections in 1970, to be followed by a broad political amnesty in 1971. Concern was heightened by rumors that ex-President Dutra had fully approved this initiative of his former aide.[56] General Orlando Geisel responded to these challenges at his swearing in as Chief of the Armed Forces General Staff on March 29, as the regime continued to seek means of silencing the political criticisms of reserve officers. The blurring of the old distinctions between hard line and Sorbonne had already been underscored by the break of some elements of the former group with General Portela for having "abandoned historic Costismo" to adopt the *Castelista* line of the War College.[57] (But, as will be demonstrated in the succeeding section, the ESG could with almost equal justice be said to have modified if not abandoned its traditional line after mid-1967.) If Costa e Silva and his advisors felt that after a year in office they were getting a surer grasp on the reins of power, the remainder of 1968 would bring far more difficult challenges than they had yet encountered.

[55] Consult "Pessimismo, questão de ótica," *Visão*, March 15, 1968, pp. 17–18.
[56] *Jornal do Brasil*, March 24, 1968, covers this episode.
[57] See *Correio da Manhã*, January 11, 1968.

◠◠◠

CHAPTER SEVEN

The Descent into Dictatorship

BY THE END of their fourth year in power, the Brazilian Armed Forces were substantially more enmeshed in running the country than most of the officer corps had expected, or for that matter wished. Rewarding as many found the exercise of power after the frustrations of the early 1960's, the military was discovering some of the drawbacks of their new role as the nation's directors and managers rather than guardians and moderators. Indeed, some were encountering the same doubts concerning the advisability of the Army's exercising a ruling function (although not necessarily its ability to do so) as had plagued their predecessors in the early 1890's before they relinquished governmental authority to a civilian elite. Their growing concern that the path along which they had rushed headlong might turn out to be a cul-de-sac was accentuated by a spreading realization that some of the difficulties they had attributed to possible tactical errors on the part of the Castelo Branco government were proving to be equally intractable for the Costa e Silva administration. A new team and a revised game plan were not getting them any nearer to the elusive goal line of a stable political regime accepted as legitimate by the Brazilian people.

Marshal Poppe de Figueiredo, who had chosen premature retirement at the end of 1965 when passed over for four-star rank by Castelo Branco, acknowledged that the indirect choice of Costa e Silva for the presidency and failure to consult the people on the new Constitution had undermined the regime's claim to legitimacy. Many younger officers came to share his doubt that the country could be prepared for democracy without meaningful popular participation. In light of the developments of December, 1968, and September, 1969, there was substance to Poppe's warning that yet another military president would "reinforce the accusation, already made at present, that the country is prisoner of a military minority, which intends to perpetuate itself in power, or that militarism has implanted itself in Brazil." [1]

In early 1968, however, there was still a relatively widespread confidence on the part of the intellectual elite of Brazil's Army concerning their ability to run the nation, with even greater certainty regarding the Armed Forces' capacity to function over a prolonged period of time as a very close watch dog on civilian administrations, feelings that stemmed in large part from the high proportion of their careers spent linked to the several levels of the military's system of higher education.[2] Questions of intellectual formation and political socialization as well as of institutional interests are involved in the military's major contribution to, if not full responsibility for, the emergence of a dictatorship by the end of 1968 and the deep split within the Army evident by mid-1969. Hence consideration of the military educational system and the content of Brazil's broad and relatively coherent national security doctrine must precede resumption of the chronological analysis of the demise of the regime of restricted representation and its replacement by an outright dictatorship.

1. MILITARY EDUCATION AND NATIONAL SECURITY

By the second quarter of 1968, nearly a year after Castelo Branco's death, the complex pattern of military politics—both on the level of factions and cliques and in terms of doctrinal differences—had undergone significant change. Although observers generally held that the National Security Council (CSN) was a stronghold of the *linha dura*

[1] Marshal Mario Poppe de Figueiredo, "Civilismo e Segurança Nacional," *Jornal do Brasil,* Caderno Especial, July 1, 1968.

[2] Carlos Maul, *O Exército e a Nacionalidade* (Rio de Janeiro, 1950), particularly in its opening essay "Notas sôbre o Exército Brasileiro," reflects the officer corps' self-image of their "patriotic" and integrating role in the national scene. See also Samuel Guimarães da Costa, *Formação democrática do exército Brasileiro* (Rio de Janeiro, 1957) and Hermes de Araújo Oliveira, *Guerra Revolucionária* (Rio de Janeiro, 1965) for contrasting approaches to the question of the Armed Forces' qualifications to speak for and defend the national interest.

and the War College (ESG) of the Sorbonne group, this was both an exaggeration and an oversimplification. Moreover, as would soon be evident, such a classification was meaningful only for the officers above the grade of lieutenant colonel—those who had already attended the Army General Staff and Command School (ECEME). Among the captains and majors, only about one-third of whom would eventually be selected for courses that opened the door to the higher career ranks, national life and problems were viewed in a less elitist manner. Moreover, for these younger officers, student discontent and popular dissatisfaction were more immediate concerns than they were for their superiors, who had been more thoroughly initiated into the mysteries of the Brazilian national security doctrine. Hence divisions within the Armed Forces as well as cleavages and misunderstandings between the military and the civilian populace would be important in the emergence of the crisis that climaxed the final quarter of the year.

The educational system had been instrumental in determining the political orientation of the Armed Forces since the positivism of the military academy in the 1870's gave rise to republicanism. In the 1960's under the influence of the concepts of national security and "revolutionary war," a neo-Florianism was resurgent, much as had been the case during the 1920's with *tenentismo*.[3] The *tenentes,* in part as a result of their indoctrination with liberal democratic ideals while still cadets, reinforced by the teachings of the French military mission, were still attached to the formal trappings of representative processes and institutions. Thus Castelo Branco had striven to maintain as much as possible of the formal institutions of representative government even while centralizing and strengthening political authority. But Castelo and Costa e Silva represented the end of the generation whose political socialization had been completed in this manner.

The active duty generals of 1968 were a transitional group. But most of the major generals and brigadiers had been students in the War College in the postwar era, while the colonels had gone through the Command and General Staff School during this period of "cold war" atmosphere. For the younger of these, even the mid-career course

---

[3] Although the choice of terminology and the historical parallelism are the author's, much of the stimulus for considering the present generational differences within the Army in terms of "as teses sorbonianas" comes from Fernando Pedreira's essay, "O nosso Exército antes e depois," *Correio da Manhã,* February 11, 1968.

(EAO) was an experience of the Korean War period (together with the anti-leftist reaction of the 1950's within the Clube Militar), while many of the majors and almost all of the captains had passed through the academy when the instructors were already of this new generation and orientation. The effect of these new military precepts was, in Pedeira's words, to

give militarism, that is the occupation of political power and public administration by the military, the technical, moral, and even political "justification" which it was lacking. Even more: displacing and supplanting the old liberal principles, these theses eclipsed, among the officers of the three services, that which would constitute the most effective and legitimate brake against militarist temptations.[4]

The workings of this process can be comprehended only through an examination of the War College as an institution and of the doctrines produced, revised, and disseminated therein. Rarely if ever has one educational institution, in less than two decades of existence, had so profound an impact upon the course of a nation's development. The War College (Escola Superior de Guerra or ESG) was founded in 1949. By 1955, nearly half the new general officers had already been through it, and by 1962 the proportion had risen to nearly 80 per cent. At the time of the 1964 coup nearly two-thirds of the active-duty generals were ESG graduates, and by 1969, the active-duty general who had not attended ESG was about as rare as a one-legged soccer player.

The importance of the ESG can be seen in the relationship of today's senior generals to that institution. Not only was Lyra Tavares its Commandant in 1966–1967, but General Candal da Fonseca (appointed Fourth Army Commander in late 1969) was his deputy and interim head until Augusto Fragoso took over. Generals Humberto da Souza Mello and Idálio Sardenberg have served recently as Chiefs of the Department of Studies (a position occupied by Castelo Branco in 1957–1958), while Air Minister Márcio de Souza e Mello was Director of the Armed Forces General Staff and Command Course in 1959–1960.[5]

The War College was established in the aftermath of World War II for the study of basic problems involved in the development of foreign

---

[4] *Ibid.*

[5] A complete rundown on who attended the ESG and when is available both through the class lists of the school and the individual entries for each officer in the *Almanaque do Exército,* an annual register containing basic career data on all active-duty officers.

policy and its coordination with the necessities of national security.[6] The original selection process and nomination of candidates to the ESG lies in the hands of the Armed Forces General Staff; but since presidential approval is required, additions and deletions may occur before courses begin in March. The Superior War Course, the most intensive and prestigious, contains a ratio of more than one civilian to each officer drawn from the Armed Forces. The Information Course is similarly mixed in its composition. Only the smaller Armed Forces General Staff and Command Course is comprised entirely of members of the military. Mixing within its student body a high proportion of civilians with officers of the colonel-brigadier level, the ESG provides for a broader understanding of the relationships between the military, the civilian side of government, and private sector groups.

Over the years, a systematic doctrine of national security (segurança nacional) has been worked out, and it is applied to actual problems as well as to future trends.[7] Development policy, in an interdisciplinary context, receives nearly as much emphasis as security policy. Mixed working groups grapple with theoretical and practical problems in these two fields. With "national security" defined as embracing every-

[6] Law No. 785 of August 20, 1949, provided for transforming the school being organized by a commission under General Oswaldo Cordeiro de Farias into an "institute of higher studies, destined to develop and consolidate the knowledge necessary to the direction and planning of national security." The most convenient source on the history and development of the ESG is General Augusto Fragoso, "A Escola Superior de Guerra: Origen—Finalidade—Evolução," *Segurança & Desenvolvimento,* XVIII, No. 132 (1969), 7–40. (This article was the opening address of the ESG commandant to the 1968 class.) The review, formerly the *Revista da Associação dos Diplomados da Escola Superior de Guerra,* was renamed in 1968 in a move designed to increase its circulation among the decision-making and public opinion-forming elites of the country; it publishes selected conferences from the regular series of the ESG. Thus, No. 130 of 1968 contained eight such lectures, while No. 131 included contributions by Vice President Pedro Aleixo, ex-Planning Minister Roberto Campos, economist Mário Henrique Simonsen, and technocrat José Garrido Torres.

[7] Consult Umberto Peregrino, "O Pensamento da Escola Superior de Guerra," *Cadernos Brasileiros,* No. 38 (November-December, 1966), pp. 29–38. The author is a retired officer who for many years directed the Biblioteca do Exército. In the same issue see also Tarcísio Holanda, "Era Tarde para o General . . .," pp. 65–73. A special issue of the *Revista Brasileira de Estudos Políticos,* No. 21 (July, 1966), is devoted to a collection of essays on "Segurança Nacional," written by faculty and graduates of the ESG. Many of these articles draw heavily on conferences, documents, and studies of the War College.

thing—external and internal—affecting national life, the range of topics considered in the year-long course is very wide. Thus, proposals for the modernization of the country's political institutions, and electoral reform in particular, could and did emerge from the ESG. The several books of Generals Golbery do Couto e Silva and Aurélio de Lyra Tavares (discussed in the Essay on Sources) provide a good starting point with regard to the thought of the War College-influenced Brazilian military on these matters. Long associated with the ESG, the former was of great influence in the Castelo Branco administration, while the latter was Costa e Silva's Army Minister.[8]

The War College doctrine is founded upon a definition of national security as "the relative degree of guarantee which the State, through political, economic, military and psychosocial actions can provide, at a given epoch, to the Nation over which it has jurisdiction for the pursuit and safeguarding of national objectives in spite of existing antagonisms." [9] A significant distinction is made between the Nation as a "social phenomenon resulting from a particular stage of evolution of a human society" or "historical-cultural structure formed by a particular parcel of humanity" and the State as the "organism of a political nature which promotes the conquest and maintenance of national objectives." The Nation's essential attributes are man, land, and institutions; those of the State are population, territory, government, and sovereignty or the crucial element of self-determination.[10]

[8] See particularly the 1967 edition of Golbery's *Geopolítica do Brasil* and Lyra Tavares' *Segurança Nacional: Problemas Atuais* (Rio de Janeiro, 1965). The importance of Golbery's book for an understanding of not only the Castelo Branco regime but also the Costa e Silva government is emphasized by Oliveiros S. Ferreira, " La geopolítica y el Ejército brasileño," *Aportes,* No. 12 (April, 1969), pp. 111–32.

[9] Professor João Batista Viana, quoted in Peregrino, "O Pensamento da Escola Superior de Guerra," p. 33.

[10] These concepts are defined in great detail and set in a matrix of geopolitical jargon in Antônio Saturnino Braga, "Introdução ao estudo da Segurança Nacional; Primeira parte: Sociedade, Nação, Estado, Poder e Política. Política Nacional," and Eduardo Domingues de Oliveira, "Segurança Nacional: Conceitos Fundamentais," *Revista Brasileira de Estudos Políticos,* No. 21, pp. 7–31 and 71–99. In the same issue "national power" is analyzed in depth in Eduardo Domingues de Oliveira, Ismael da Motta Paes, and Paulo Emílio Souto, "O Poder Nacional: Considerações Gerais," pp. 101–34, as well as a series of special essays on its political, psycho-social, economic, and military components, pp. 135–234.

The basic functions of the State are seen as a political-institutional organ or as an instrument of collective well-being. It has responsibility for furthering the all but immutable Permanent National Objectives (ONP's) and the more situational Current National Objectives (ONA's). The possibilities of attaining these objectives depend upon National Power, and National Policy, or the intelligent application of power in all its forms from violent coercion to moral authority in pursuit of objectives. As such, National Power is the integration of political, economic, psycho-social, and military power brought to bear through National Strategy and its derivative, the National Strategic Concept (CEN), defined as the "synthetic enunciation of the Current National Objectives within the reach of National Power, for the progressive satisfaction of the permanent interests of the Nation." [11] By means of a Strategic Examination of the Situation carried out through Complimentary Studies, the CEN is translated into the operational terms of General Guidelines of Planning (DGP's).

National Security Policy is to be complemented by a Development Policy which should be determined as rationally as the former. This implies insulation if not isolation from the distortions imposed by politics, and leads to the adoption of a highly technocratic position on economic planning.[12] With the "well-being of the collectivity" the supreme objective of national policy, the orientation of the ESG contains a liberal and even moderately reformist element involving "increasingly ample bases for the conscious and effective participation of the people" and "growing social integration founded upon our principles of social justice and Christian ethics." Within the somewhat rigid framework of ESG doctrine, national objectives are reassessed and national policy readjusted each year by a fairly numerous group, including many of the ablest military minds and experienced civilians from diverse sectors of national life.

The doctrine of national security was given its basic structure and

[11] General Golbery explains the methodology for the formulation of a "Concept of National Strategy" as the fundamental directive of National Security Policy in the appendices to his *Geopolítica do Brasil,* pp. 259–75. See also Herick Marques Caminha, Ismael da Motta Paes, and Paulo Emílio Souto, "Estrategia Nacional," *Revista Brasileira de Estudos Políticos,* No. 21, pp. 235–55.

[12] See, in the same review, Omar Gonçalves da Motta, "Introdução ao estudo da Segurança Nacional; Segunda parte: Política de Desenvolvimento," pp. 33–69.

elaborated chiefly during the 1952–1955 period of turmoil and instability. It largely reflected the Juarez Távora position with regard to the political-military conflicts of the time. With the establishment of the Institute of Advanced Brazilian Studies (ISEB) under the Kubitschek government as a civilian-led, nationalist-oriented counterbalance to the ESG, the latter tended to harden its basically neo-capitalist, pro-United States, and anti-Communist positions. At this juncture, the distinction between "national policy" and "government policy" was instituted: the former term applied to optimum policies resulting from application of ESG precepts to the needs and priorities of the moment, the latter described those policies actually followed by the administration. This gap between the War College's formulation of national policy, and the government's actual policies widened during Goulart's tenure as President.

The academic year at the ESG runs from March through December, with the first eight weeks devoted to study of basic national security doctrine and ESG "methodology" followed by twenty-two weeks during which the participants attend lectures on national and international affairs and debate their relevance to problems of security and development. During this time, all the members of the cabinet and most agency heads and second echêlon officials of key ministries usually address the course, with a few selected foreign diplomats and academic specialists also invited to present conferences. In the final ten weeks, attention is focused on efforts at practical application and elaboration of adequate structures for planning.

The content of ESG instruction and debate reflects a particularly narrow and conservative strain of social science, even relative to the U.S. National War College. At sessions of the 1969 course, discussion concerning "Contemporary Political Structures" demonstrated little awareness of recent North American or European scholarship in this field, particularly the Huntington-Rustow-Wriggins type of operationalized comparative analysis. Participation and authority were, however, frequently viewed as antithetical, with some means for their reconciliation needed for development of a viable representative regime. The faculty tended to stress the concept, widely held by those associated with the ESG in the past as well, that "democracy is a way of life rather than any particular institutional structures, and flexibility in forms may well be necessary to preserve the essential values of this way of life." [13]

Some division was apparent between those viewing civic education as indoctrination and those who stressed the need for it to be firmly rooted in experience. With regard to the question of stability, emphasis upon efficiency and security seemed to predominate, but a significant current stressed legitimacy and participation as necessary to long-run viability. The crisis of contemporary democracy was frequently phrased in terms of its underdeveloped capacity for self-defense against the emergence of a dynamic, determined, and ruthless Communist rival. The USSR was viewed as checkmated by the fascist threat of the inter-war period, but was a formidable challenger after the Second World War. A high proportion of the participants expressed reservations concerning the tendency of outside speakers to stress constitutional formalism rather than to analyze the reality of institutions and attitudes. Several officers displayed an implicit realization of the conflicting bases of claims to representation—numbers, force and influence, and expertise —parallel to David Apter's theoretical formulations (discussed in Appendix A), while others articulated concern with quality and authenticity of representation as more important than the mechanics of electoral systems.

The debate provoked by a Catholic sociologist's incisive conference on "Contemporary Social Structures" revealed a lively questioning of the stereotype "capitalist" and "socialist" models, focusing on the use of technocrats as a common developmental feature in all modern systems. The position of Brazilian youth emerged as the area of greatest immediate concern, with the participants putting forth several variations on the theme that student alienation could be ended only by providing concrete programs to meet the challenges of development, and not by slogans. Very little familiarity was demonstrated with the works of Brazilian social scientists on industrialization, urbanization, and social change. There was no mention, even veiled or indirect, of the interpretation of the influential "São Paulo" school of sociological analysis led by Florestan Fernandes, Fernando Henrique Cardoso, and Octavio

[13] This section is based on the author's observation of several sessions and conversations with students and faculty during July–August, 1969.

Ianni—whose books still dominated the social science shelves of Rio de Janeiro's bookstores.

The importance of the War College in shaping the views of a major portion of Brazil's postwar political elite, both military and civilian, can further be seen in the fact that during the twenty years of its functioning it has produced some 2,000 graduates of the year-long courses ministered there. Through 1966, its nearly 1,600 alumni included 800 senior officers of the Armed Forces; 424 government officials (including 39 congressmen, 23 judges, 200 higher echêlon bureaucrats from the ministries, 97 leading administrators of autonomous agencies, and 45 state officials); and 328 individuals from the private sector, chiefly businessmen and industrial managers.[14] The 1,116 officers graduated through 1967 included 620 from the Army, 272 from the Navy, and 224 from the Air Force. All civilian graduates are incorporated into plans for mobilization in case of national emergency, in posts accorded rank of colonel or above.

Attending lectures given by the regular staff, ranking government officials, and distinguished foreign visitors is only one aspect of participation in ESG activities. Small group "teams" work jointly on solutions to selected problems in the economic, social, and political spheres, and trips to various corners of the country ensure some familiarity with all the regions of the Brazilian subcontinent. The year is climaxed with a twenty-day visit to the United States to inspect military and industrial installations as guests of the United States government. This traveling and living together create a cohesion and personal ties that mere classroom attendance does not. As a result, it greatly reinforces the function of the ESG as a vehicle for the cooptation of groups from all social sectors of the elite into the ideological and programatic outlook of the military technocrats. Thus, the alumni of the ESG, civilians perhaps even more than military, tend to retain close ties to members of their class and to feel a strong fraternal bond with the larger community of War College graduates. The ADESG, as the alumni association is known, carries with its membership participation in a continuing communications network, including special conferences and "inside" information on military thinking. In a decade and a half its magazine has

[14] Glauco Carneiro, "A Guerra da 'Sorbonne,' " *O Cruzeiro,* June 24, 1967, pp. 16–21.

published 133 issues and serves to inform members in other cities of what is occurring at the center of the group's activity, Rio de Janeiro, where a majority of the War College graduates still live and work. In other cities, the local ADESG branch carries on "educational" activities such as annual series of lectures on national security.[15] During the 1967–1969 period, more than 200 extension courses were conducted throughout the country, and this activity has since increased.

During the Castelo Branco administration, there still existed a substantial number of officers never systematically exposed to the Sorbonnist doctrine as elaborated at the ESG. With the passage of time, however, this "gap" is being reduced. In addition to the fact that many of the colonels of 1964–1967 have since reached sufficient rank and seniority to attend the War College, the National Security Doctrine is also being taught at lower levels in the Armed Forces hierarchy.

The system of military education that has the ESG as its capstone extends down through several additional levels, two of which are basic to the political socialization and intellectual formation of the officers. As a result of the close Brazilian–United States cooperation after 1943, the Army Command and General Staff School (ECEME) in the postwar period moved sharply away from the French style of instruction toward the United States model. (Colonel Orlando Geisel, now Army Minister in the Garrastazú Médici government, played a major role in this transition.) This modernization was completed in the 1955–1958 period, with Castelo Branco directing the school's full integration with ESG philosophy and doctrine before returning to the senior institution. The next few years saw the school concentrate upon consideration of the relative priorities for nuclear, conventional, and subversive warfare, and establishment of a division of studies and research. Commandants Hugo Panasco Alvim, Jurandir Mamede, and João Bina Machado all encouraged greater originality and participation on the part of the officer students in updating doctrine to fit the era of "revolutionary warfare." Under General Reinaldo de Almeida, who commanded the ECEME during 1967 and 1968, intensive attention was paid not only to professional matters but also to the new problems arising from the Armed Forces' exercise of governmental authority. The lieutenant colonels

[15] See, for example, *IV Ciclo de Conferencias Sôbre Segurança Nacional* (Belo Horizonte, 1968).

assigned to the school for three years of study (with about 65 students per class) were exposed to many of the same themes as their senior colleagues at the ESG, although the outside speakers were often under secretaries instead of ministers.[16]

If in the past the *"Doctrina da Segurança Nacional"* has been inculcated at the higher ranks through the ESG and ECEME, recent innovations guarantee that the Brazilian Army officers will be introduced to these views while still cadets. The Military Academy of Agulhas Negras (AMAN), under the influence of General Carlos de Meira Matos as its Commandant during 1969, has also begun a basic revision of its curriculum in keeping with the view that "the enemy is now within, not a threat of direct attack across our borders." The social sciences, heretofore buried in the fourth year of a course of studies stressing engineering and the physical sciences combined with a smattering of positivist philosophy and public administration, have been elevated to a prominent, if not predominant, position in the last three years of the cadets' work.

This modification of the formal educational component of the military's socialization process coincides with changes in the recruitment process. By 1966, the Brazilian Army was becoming so inbred—more than 40 per cent of the incoming cadets were the sons of military men—that a law was passed to allow the top three male students at any recognized civilian high school to enter the Academy without taking the formal examination. As a result of this law, and a concentrated effort by the regime to drum up interest in the military career, the proportion of entrants from civilian secondary schools rose from less than 10 per cent for the 1962–1966 period to nearly half for the 1967, 1968, and 1969 plebe classes.

---

[16] These paragraphs are based on discussions with several ex-commandants of the ECEME, as well as perusal of a number of unpublished documents pertaining to its evolution and operation. That Castelo Branco was not alone in being repeatedly assigned to the ECEME at varying stages of his career is evidenced by the fact that one of his predecessors as Commandant, General Tristão de Alencar Araripe (1946–1949), had been its subdirector of instruction (1939–1940), chief of the tactics department (1934–1935), and instructor (1930) after having studied there in 1927–1929. Sérgio Marinho, *Aspectos de Sociología* (Rio de Janeiro, 1958), contains an introductory sociology course given at the ECEME in 1956 by a professor of the military academy. Complete with examination and answers, it reflects the anti-Marxist brand of social science that the officer corps was being taught, at a time when a pronounced leftist and nationalist orientation was predominating in the sociological outpouring of the Brazilian intellectual community.

In 1969, the senior class at AMAN was small (170), more as a result of recruitment difficulties during 1965–1966 than of the 20–25 per cent dropout rate between entrance and graduation. With regard to geographic origin, some 336 of the 1,215 cadets were from Guanabara, followed by São Paulo (185), Rio Grande do Sul (159), Minas Gerais (135), and Rio de Janeiro (68). The drop in the *Carioca* proportion and the increase in the number of *Paulistas* were the most significant changes in traditional recruitment patterns.[17]

It is too early to assess what the long-range ramifications of the shift in the regional and social bases of recruitment to the officer corps may be. There is, however, another politically significant career trend. In recent years, the links between elements of the private sector and the military have been further strengthened by the marked tendency of officers to leave the relatively low-paying service career for more financially rewarding positions in commerce and industry. Already observable in the immediate postwar years, the trend became more pronounced during the rapid industrialization and economic expansion of the Kubitschek years. With the accession of Goulart to power a new factor in military-civilian relations was added, as some anti-Communist officers were unwilling to serve under the left-leaning President and others perceived that their prospects for advancement were limited. Furthermore, the soaring rate of inflation rapidly undercut military pay scales and increased the economic pressures upon officers to transfer to the reserve and assume employment which, added to their retirement pay, would enable them to deal more adequately with the monetary and educational needs of their families.[18]

---

[17] The proportion from Guanabara entering in the 1964–1966 period had been nearly 42 per cent, which had dropped to less than 28 per cent with only a partial renovation of the student body, while the São Paulo contingent had risen from just over 8 per cent to more than 15 per cent. The data on the 1964–1966 period comes from Alfred Stepan's unpublished doctoral dissertation (scheduled to be issued by Princeton University Press during 1971), while that on the 1969 composition of the student body was obtained by the author on a visit to AMAN in August, 1969. In terms of proportion of cadets to total population, Guanabara was overrepresented in 1964–1966 by a ratio of 9 to 1, and Rio Grande do Sul by nearly 2 to 1. São Paulo (1 to 2) and Minas Gerais (7 to 10) were underrepresented, as were most of the other states.

[18] For a somewhat differently focused discussion of this phenomenon, see Ivan Pedro de Martins, "Notas Sôbre o Militar Brasileiro," *Cadernos Brasileiros*, No. 38, pp. 75–83, particularly pp. 81–82.

2. DOCTRINAL DIFFERENCES AND CONFRONTATION POLITICS

Prior to the 1964 revolution, the "Sorbonne" group had on several occasions come very close to having political power and even control of the government in their hands. Vargas' victory over Brigadier Gomes in 1950 was a major disappointment in this regard, although the ESG was still in its infancy at the time. During the Café Filho interregnum in 1954–1955, the Sorbonnists enjoyed substantial influence, since Juarez Távora was one of the President's closest advisors. However, this was a caretaker regime, not one able or disposed to undertake major policy revisions or institutional reorganization. The 1955 elections offered greater promise in this respect, but instead of electing Juarez Távora to the presidency, the War College group was forced to swallow his defeat by Kubitschek, a bitter pill indeed for its more politically oriented members. The subsequent course of events widened the gap between the Sorbonne group and the President, as the latter adopted a nationalistic tack in 1959.

The Quadros period was again one of frustration of high hopes. With Cordeiro de Farias as Chief of the Armed Forces General Staff and its representatives installed on the presidential staff (including the National Security Council) the Sorbonne's influence appeared to be on the rise—only to be dashed down by the abrupt turn of events in August, 1961, and Goulart's subsequent coming to power. Under "Jango," the War College increasingly became a place where the government could assign officers whom for political reasons it preferred not to have in troop commands ("incompatibilizados"). As pointed out previously, it was at this juncture that the Sorbonne group entered into close cooperation with the businessmen and industrialists through General Golbery's crucial participation in IPES. With the triumph of the 1964 revolution, this group suddenly came to play a predominant role in policy-making.

The Sorbonne faction then had as its center a group of officers who, by long association with the War College, had been in close contact with the politicians, bureaucrats, industrialists, journalists, and businessmen who attend its courses.[19] Including such outstanding figures as

[19] For a critical view of the Sorbonne outlook, see Stacchini, *Março 64*, pp. 115–18.

Golbery, Ernesto Geisel, Mamede, and Souto Malan, the Sorbonnists were strongly anti-Communist. But, unlike many of the *linha dura,* they were able to distinguish between "subversives" and nationalist reformers. Indeed, through this broadening experience and detailed study of national problems and foreign affairs, they had come to have much more sophisticated views on development and national security matters than the often stereotyped perceptions and black-and-white interpretations common to many of their military brethren. Viewing General Golbery as the embodiment of Sorbonne views and values, Oliveiros S. Ferreira analyzes him as "a military man formed in the school of liberalism, although a liberalism without social vigor . . . who waged war against the Axis and who believes in Democracy—if he does not define it well— as the specific form of political organization for the western world." [20] For the Sorbonne group, significantly, liberty and property are instrumental, not absolute values. Hence, during 1964–1969 they progressed from champions of free enterprise to hostility toward excessive profits, to criticism of the profit motive, and, finally, to a substantial abandonment of the sanctity of property.

Most Sorbonne officers tended to look down on the "historical plotters" of the 1962–1964 period as lacking in political sense. After the coup, they favored retaining as much as possible of the normal order, reforming and renovating the system rather than implanting a military regime. In the eyes of their critics, the politically attuned Sorbonne elements were trying to seize control of a movement they had joined at a rather late stage, compromising with a corrupt political class and preserving discredited institutions. From the *linha dura* viewpoint: "When the revolutionaries, unpreoccupied with politics, overthrew Goulart and had nothing to put forward in exchange, almost naturally the 'Sorbonne' took over. Imperceptibly." [21]

Although the ESG or Sorbonne orientation has been heavily felt in the Armed Forces General Staff (EMFA), and the establishment of the SNI under Golbery fulfilled another of their aspirations, the creation of a unified Ministry of Defense (i.e., of the Armed Forces) remained a major objective. The Navy, and Admiral José Santos Saldanha da Gama in particular, intransigently opposed such unification. The Navy-Air

[20] "La Geopolítica . . .," p. 120.
[21] Stacchini, *Março 64,* p. 117.

Force dispute over carrier-based aviation was one facet of interservice rivalry aired in public. But a fundamental tension also existed between the Army and the Navy over the question of whether to emphasize internal security and anti-guerrilla warfare measures, or defense from extra-continental attack. The Navy, which saw its role and influence diminished by the growing stress in the 1960's on military problems remote from its capabilities, attempted to refocus interest on defense from external enemies. Memories of the days in which Brazil had been a major naval power stayed alive in the minds of the admirals, long after the generals had come to view new warships as prohibitively expensive, in comparison not only with trucks and guns but also with planes, whose utility in internal warfare was apparent. The chief incident in which this military linen was washed in public was the late 1967 episode featuring Admiral Saldanha da Gama's angry and impassioned outbursts in the press.

The leaders of the Sorbonne group were from among the Army generation formed in *tenentismo,* but the officers who lately have replaced the ESG's founders as the staff and faculty of the institution are of a subsequent generation. Their attachment to the formal trappings of democracy may well be less than that of the *tenentes,* who manifested a deep ambivalence in this respect as they

exerted themselves to preserve, with the collaboration of respected jurists, the appearances of legality and of constitutional order. From Positivism little remained except its implicit conservatism and the cult of technocracy. Deep down they continued opposed to "politicking," that is to partisan life, and unyielding enemies of politicians whom they despise. They prefer the technician and the planner who reach out to them with national salvation through formula and organization chart.[22]

The perceived shortcomings of the programs of the Sorbonnist Castelo Branco regime logically resulted in a re-evaluation of some of the content of the doctrines of development and national security within the ESG, but not of the basic approach or "methodology" (as the *Sorbonnistas* are wont to say in preference to ideology). During the second half of 1967 the ESG, under General Augusto Fragoso, began to shift its doctrine in the direction of nationalism grafted onto, albeit not inseparably bonded together with, technocracy. The *idée fixe* of the

[22] José Arthur Rios, "Atualidade do Tenentismo," *Cadernos Brasileiros,* No. 38 (November-December, 1966), p. 16.

inevitability of a Third World War was substantially softened if not abandoned. In its place there began to emerge a concept of Brazil's shared interests with the other developing nations, particularly in the area of trade and atomic energy. As mentioned previously, this corresponded closely with Foreign Minister Magalhães Pinto's striving for emphasis on sovereignty if not "independence" in the sense of the 1961–1964 period.[23]

The 1967–1968 rethinking of national policy was in its basic outlines not dissimilar to that which had begun under Quadros only to be plowed under during the subsequent protracted crisis. Nationalism in particular was on the upswing among the military. Thus, even General Orlando Geisel, in his November 27 speech on the anniversary of the 1935 Communist revolts, had struck a more nationalist note than was his wont. As early as June, 1966, Oliveiros S. Ferreira had identified this tendency, observing that

Really in spite of the fact that many of the members of the "linha dura" were against the economic policy of the government for which it had or was supposed to have of anti-nationalism, identifying itself in this opposition, tactically with large sectors of agriculture, they are not basically what could be termed followers of economic liberalism. On the contrary, it can be said that many of those who participated in the near revolt of October 6 and 7, 1965 are more nationalist (read "nasserist"), less civilist, and less liberal than what could be thought of by their contacts and by the political leadership which they still judge to reside in Carlos Lacerda. For one or another reason they have, more than the Sorbonne, adversion to the so-called Economic Power.[24]

By mid-1968, the distinction between hard line and Sorbonne was becoming blurred, with the former containing a significant wing that tended to place nationalism above anti-Communism, although by no means becoming tolerant of "subversives."[25]

---

[23] For a study of Brazilian foreign policy stressing the themes of interdependence with the West even in a changing international environment, see J. O. de Meira Penna, *Política Externa Segurança e Desenvolvimento* (Rio de Janeiro, 1967). The author, a career diplomat of ambassadorial rank, was a War College graduate. The modification of ESG doctrine is discussed in Murilo Melo Filho, "O Que há com os Generais," *Manchete,* August 5, 1967, pp. 16–17.

[24] *O Fim . . .,* pp. 28–29.

[25] An inquiry into military opinion by means of interviews was carried out by a team of Brazilian researchers in 1965–1966. The results of this limited study are embodied in Mário Afonso Carneiro, "Opinião Militar," *Cadernos Brasileiros,* No.

Although most of the colonels who had made their mark during the IPM's of 1964–1966 were no longer in active service (with the exception of Ferdinando de Carvalho, who would soon be transferred from Curitiba to an assignment in Washington, D.C.), the ranks of the *duros* included a number of individuals widely held to be general officer material on the strength of their professional qualifications: Boaventura Cavalcanti, Hélio Lemos, Hélio Mendes, Amerino Rapôso, Caracas Linhares (sent off to Rome as attaché), Ruy de Castro, Luiz Alencar Araripe, Walter Baere, Tarcisio Nunes, Sebastião Chaves, Gustavo Cordeiro de Farias, Anselmo Lira, Antônio Morais, Marcelino Rufino, Igrejas Lopes, and José Carlos Amazonas. With the break between this group (and its fanatically anti-Communist Air Force counterpart, headed by Brigadier João Paulo Burnier) and Lacerda virtually complete, the politically ambitious Interior Minister sought to consolidate the leadership he had asserted during the October, 1965, crisis.

In mid-July, Albuquerque Lima called for "the real participation of the people of all socio-economic levels in the modern processes of economic development." [26] Shortly thereafter, at the ARENA convention, an informal private poll found sixty delegates favoring Magalhães Pinto for president in 1970, with thirty-six for Andreazza, thirty-five for Jarbas Passarinho, thirty-one for Carvalho Pinto, twenty-six for Abreu Sodré, and twenty-three for Daniel Kreiger, a result that did not please the Interior Minister (who had received seven votes, ranking him thirteenth, behind even General Sizeno Sarmento). Aware of the need to step down and return to active military service before March 15,

---

38 (November-December, 1966), pp. 17–28. The smallness of the sample and the arbitrary basis of its stratified composition—twenty-one Army, ten Navy, and nine Air Force; one-half mid-grade officers, one-fifth junior officers, and one-tenth sergeants, etc.—limit its usefulness. Yet it provides some tentative insights into the thought processes of the average (as distinct from the exceptional) officer. More systematic attitudinal work has been inhibited by the strong negative reaction to a poorly handled effort by a United States doctoral candidate in history, who on May 10, 1964, mailed detailed questionnaires to general officers. Nationalist elements picked this up as highly suspicious, concentrating their fire on the most sensitive questions, such as "What is the greatest deficiency of Brazil today?" and others dealing with party affiliation and ideological preferences. See Morel, *O Golpe . . .*, pp. 189–92. The judgments above are based on press coverage, conversations with military leaders, discussions with expert Brazilian observers, and, to a lesser degree, inference from actions and events.

[26] *Jornal do Brasil,* July 16, 1968.

1969, Albuquerque Lima began emphasizing the need to create a Fifth Army with jurisdiction over the vast Amazon regime.

The Democratic Crusade had begun its campaign for the 1968–1970 term of office in the Military Club the preceding December. Headed by hard-line General Joaquim Francisco de Castro, Jr., Chief of the Secret Service of the Justice Ministry, and containing hard liners Tarcisio Nunes and Gustavo de Farias on its directorate, along with Colonel Arnizant de Melo, the Crusade decided to back General Carvalho Lisboa only after its "nationalist" wing discarded the idea of running Colonel Boaventura Cavalcanti. General Leontino Nunes de Andrade was nominated for first vice president, with the board of directors slate (deliberative council) including Generals Muricy and Newton Fontoura de Oliveira Reis along with hard-line Colonel Andrade Serpa. The candidates for the financial council featured such notables as Generals Manoel Mendes Pereira, Lauro Alves Pinto, and Brigadier César Montagna (the hero of the April 1, 1964, attack on the Coast Artillery headquarters). When incumbent president Moniz de Aragão wrote articles calling Justino Alves Bastos "unfit" for the position, that two-time ex-president withdrew from the race, leaving Carvalho Lisboa the victor by default.

Following the March promotions, a major shuffling of Army commands had taken place. Orlando Geisel went from Army Chief of Staff to Chief of the Armed Forces General Staff, replacing Air Force Lieutenant Brigadier Nélson Freire Lavenère-Wanderley. Adalberto Pereira dos Santos moved up to the position vacated by Geisel, with Sizeno Sarmento taking over the First Army. Newly promoted General Manuel Rodrigues de Carvalho Lisboa became Second Army Commander (succeeding Sarmento), Alfredo Souto Malan received command of the Fourth Army, and Souza Aguiar came back to Rio de Janeiro to head the Department of General Provisions (substituting for the retiring Alberto Ribeiro Paz). The discreet, cautious, and efficient Alvaro da Silva Braga continued to head the Third Army, and Mamede and Muricy remained in the Department of Production and Works and the Directorate of Personnel. Recently advanced to Brigadier, Meira Matos replaced General Lauro Alves Pinto as Inspector General of Military Police—a post that gave him authority over some 200,000 men of the twenty-two state military organizations. In a move that would have a significant effect on the course of events in the December crisis, João Dutra de

Castilhos, commander of the garrisons on the Bolivian border (ninth military region), took over the Vila Militar's First Infantry Division.

In the July 25 Army promotions, Edson de Figueiredo was one of two raised to major general, and eight new brigadiers were created. A recent law had substantially increased the number of positions at each rank above those which had prevailed since 1955. While the quota of full generals on active duty remained at eight, there were now to be 25 major generals (an increase of 2), 51 brigadiers (up by 3), 353 colonels (13 more than before), 700 lieutenant colonels (a rise of 35), 1,423 majors (increased by 78), 2,481 captains (up 136), and 1,688 first lieutenants (225 new vacancies at this level). The ensuing wave of advancements did not, however, significantly offset discontent among the younger officers over material shortages and political issues.

Army Minister Lyra Tavares persisted in portraying the military as continuing in its traditional "democratic" role, insisting that "no one is more civilian than the Brazilian soldier invested with a civilian function." In answer to charges of militarism, he replied that the "civic conscience of the soldier" was the greatest barrier to a military dictatorship. In addition, however, to the frequent laments of Generals Mourão Filho and Pery Bevilaqua (which reached the point of joining with Amaury Kruel in the MDB's mid-year call for redemocratization), several other recently retired generals counseled a return to the barracks.[27]

If in theory, or rather at the level of doctrine, the ESG succeeded in integrating development and national security as "the two complementary, although distinct sides of the exercise of National Power," in practice the two were not so easily harmonized.[28] On August 23, the

[27] Lyra Tavares, O Exército . . ., pp. 20, 95–99. and 125–43, and his press conference reported in Jornal do Brasil, August 23, 1968, as well as Mário Poppe de Figueiredo, "Civilismo e surgança nacional," Caderno Especial of Jornal do Brasil, June 30–July 1, 1968.

[28] The formulation is from Wanderly Guilherme dos Santos, "Uma Revisão da Crise Brasileira," Cadernos Brasileiros, No. 38 (November-December, 1966), p. 56. The government's Plano Trienal is discussed in "Um plano para que o País recomence a crescer," Visão, July 5, 1968, pp. 38–50, and Carlos Lessa, "Programa Estratégico de Desenvolvimento: Diagnóstico da Contradição," Correio da Manhã, August 25, 1968. The full text of the plan is available as Programa Estratégico de Desenvolvimento: 1968–1970 (Rio de Janeiro, June, 1968). Consult also "Homen é a meta de IV Plano de Sudene," Visão, June 7, 1968, pp. 63–69.

CSN met to discuss a draft paper on the "National Strategic Concept." At this gathering, the existence of two rival if not antagonistic groups within the cabinet was confirmed, as Albuquerque Lima was quite clearly at odds with the Finance and Planning Ministers. For while it was easy to agree upon the Permanent National Objectives in principle, differences over degree and priorities soon emerged during the process of operationalizing them into "Essential Elements of Government Policy" and basic planning guidelines.[29]

This potentially serious military cleavage had been pushed aside at the end of March by the violent student crisis that suddenly erupted. Relatively quiet since the preceding August, the university students were preparing major demonstrations against the regime for the anniversary of the 1964 revolution. General Portela banned these symbolic acts, and the police were mobilized for countermeasures. A relatively small protest outside the student restaurant in downtown Rio de Janeiro resulted in the fatal shooting of eighteen-year-old Edson Luís Lima Souto and gave the student movement a martyr and symbol it had heretofore lacked. The body was taken to the MDB-controlled Legislative Assembly and large-scale parades were mounted. Over two hundred students were arrested on March 31. Although the huge crowd attending his funeral was relatively orderly and self-disciplined, major clashes with the police ensued, and the Army moved in to take control of the center of the city.[30]

[29] *Jornal do Brasil,* August 24, 1968, provides a fairly adequate summary of the debate over "development and security" in the Security Council. Mário Henrique Simonsen, *Brasil 2001* (Rio de Janeiro, 1969), undertakes to refute the pessimistic outlook for Brazil's long-range economic growth put forth by Herman Kahn's Hudson Institute. Putting aside the technical aspects of this brilliant young Brazilian economist's argument, I find substantially persuasive his conclusion that, with due application of rationality and effort, extrapolations of past performance trends need not be determinant limiting factors. Rejecting both the statist and distributive thrust of the structuralists such as Celso Furtado and the idea that the import-substitution model for development is adequate for the future, he calls for a new model of accelerated development that stresses savings, education, and economic-administrative rationality, together with expansion of exports and family planning to contain the demographic explosion. For an essentially pessimistic survey of Brazil's future in light of the magnitude of its present problems, see José Itamar de Freitas, *Brasil Ano 2000: O Futuro sem Fantasia* (Rio de Janeiro, 1969).

[30] March 31 special editions of *Jornal do Brasil, O Jornal,* and *Correio da Manhã* contain graphic coverage of these incidents. See also "Abril, Documentário Extra,"

As sympathy manifestations spread to other cities, the government chose to treat them as part of a subversive plot. A large number of priests and nuns joined in the celebration of the seventh day mass for Edson Luís Lima Souto on April 4. Leaving Candelaria Church in downtown Rio de Janeiro at the evening rush hour, they were attacked by large contingents of security forces backed by armored vehicles. The violence and arrests led to further solidarity demonstrations in other cities during the ensuing days, with increasing Church defense of the student protesters.[31] Under growing pressure from the *linha dura,* Costa authorized Justice Minister Gama e Silva to ban the Frente Ampla. The government decided to close off the channels for normal political disagreement, but at the same time resisted hard-line demands for a new Institutional Act, at least for the time being. Far from the liberalization that had seemed possible even a month before, the regime closed up more tightly; instead of encountering a formula for compromise or accommodation, it embarked on a blueprint for hardening.[32] Much as in 1963–1964, but with the roles of the government and opposition reversed, little opportunity was afforded the moderates to find ways to avoid polarization and ultimate violent confrontation.

However, the government appeared prepared to give a little where "security" did not appear to be involved. Thus a metal workers strike in Belo Horizonte was tolerated and May Day demonstrations by workers were met with the promise of an immediate bonus—a term all but outlawed since 1964. Following the massive report of the Meira Mattos' commission, the bureau chiefs in the Education Ministry were all fired, although Tarso Dutra was retained as Minister. Priority attention was promised to educational problems, and the President apparently took under advisement Meira Mattos' conclusion that "excessive repression leads to a growing radicalization." Boding ill for the future, however, was the government's resort to absenteeism in Congress to avert a key vote on modification of the party system that it might well otherwise

---

Paz e Terra, No. 6 (April, 1968), pp. 281–97 for a detailed reportage of the crisis. Its political ramifications are analyzed in "Violência, despreparo, endurecimento," *Visão,* April 12, 1968, pp. 21–22.

[31] Three leading figures of the progressive wing of Brazilian Catholicism express their views upon the Church's contemporary socio-political role in *Cadernos Brasileiros,* No. 48 (July-August, 1968), pp. 81–94.

[32] See "CS retomaria o diálogo político," *Visão,* April 26, 1968, pp. 18–21.

have lost (the bill becoming law through expiration of the sixty-day period for consideration allowed by the 1967 Constitution).[33] When only 180 of 220 ARENA deputies present voted, Daniel Krieger resigned as party president (he was subsequently re-elected at the national convention). Over 150 deputies signed petitions calling for the return to a parliamentary system.

With the resumption of student strikes and demonstrations, the political situation resumed its deterioration. In late May, 150 students were arrested at the Medical School in Belo Horizonte. Nearly 4,000 troops in Rio de Janeiro repressed university manifestations against the Education Minister on June 19, and the following day police surrounded students as they left a meeting, arresting some 400. On the 21st, a violent clash left one policeman and two civilians dead and scores injured. A massive parade took place on June 26 in Rio de Janeiro, and on the same day 480 kilos of dynamite were stolen in São Paulo. The theft of a quarter ton of explosives six months earlier had been followed by a series of terrorist bombings, including a massive explosion at the *O Estado de São Paulo* on April 20; the new robbery was accompanied by a large blast at Second Army headquarters in which a soldier was killed. Convinced that these and a wave of bank robberies were not isolated acts, the authorities denounced a widespread terrorist network, including but not limited to students.[34] The interview in the July issue

[33] *Jornal do Brasil,* June 1, 1968. Meira Mattos' report is reprinted in *Paz e Terra,* IV, No. 9 (October, 1969), 199–241. Consult also "Brasil: empiezan a fallar las instituciones," *The Economist para América Latina,* May 29, 1968, p. 12, and "Sublegendas esfacelam a oposição," *Visão,* May 24, 1968, pp. 23–24. The text of the sublegends law as well as that depriving 68 municipalities of their autonomy as "areas of national security" can be found in *Revista de Ciência Política,* II, No. 3 (July-September, 1968), 114–25.

[34] *Jornal do Brasil,* July 21–22, 1968, contains a statement to this effect by General Bretas Cupertino, Director of the Department of Federal Police. See also "Brasil: la protesta gana adeptos," *The Economist para América Latina,* July 24, 1968, pp. 10–11; *Jornal do Brasil,* June 16–17, 1968, special section on "para onde vai a universidade brasileira?"; and "Dom Helder: a tentado anda por perto," *Visão,* May 10, 1968, pp. 23–24. Excerpts from Rio de Janeiro student leader Vladimir Palmeira's speeches during the June-July period can be found in *Cadernos Brasileiros,* No. 48 (July-August, 1968), pp. 52–54. The entire January-June, 1968, issue of *Síntese: Política Econômica Social* (Nos. 37–38) was devoted to the problem of the Brazilian universities. See particularly "A Crise da Juventude," pp. 84–96.

of *Realidade* with UNE president Luís Travassos, entitled "They Want to Overthrow the Government," promised little respite for the regime.

In fact, the July winter vacation did not bring any substantial relaxation of tensions. Jânio Quadros, back from an extended stay in Europe, publicly accused other political leaders of accommodation and denounced the government as resting on force alone. Mid-July witnessed a weekend of terrorist activity in São Paulo, one that led to emergency National Security Council meetings and a statement that the government would "attain the goals of the revolution through the decisive action of the Armed Forces."[35] Student demonstrations resumed, and the annual meeting of the National Conference of Bishops issued a manifesto in favor of structural reforms (in spite of behind-the-scenes government requests to soften its language). Dom Helder announced the creation of a "nonviolent" movement of "Moral Liberating Pressure." A week-long strike in a São Paulo industrial center was climaxed by the seizure of the factories and supervisory personnel by the workers, followed by massive police intervention. In Rio de Janeiro, some 500 actors and actresses demonstrated against the regime's censorship of the theater.

Ex-President Quadros, continuing his move into the partial vacuum left by Lacerda's silencing, initiated a flurry of political consultations that placed the government in a dilemma. To punish him would contribute greatly to his rehabilitation as a national leader, a goal he had been seeking without success since 1962; but to ignore his violation of the ban on political pronouncements by *cassados* would set a precedent that could be exploited by those seeking to launch a replacement for the Frente Ampla. While experienced politicians counseled ignoring Quadros' statements, the *linha dura* insisted upon action against a *cassado* who had asserted in a message to the MDB president that the government was leading the country to a "collective tragedy." But the order to report to police headquarters for questioning, instead of intimidating Jânio, spurred him to take a stronger and more explicit stand in opposition to the government. Refusing to seek exile in a foreign embassy, Quadros on the one side and the hard liners on the other forced the government's hand. On July 30, Quadros was sentenced to 120

[35] "Constituição continua por enquanto," *Visão*, August 2, 1968, pp. 21–25. *Jornal do Brasil*, July 20, 1968, includes a special section on terrorism.

days of confinement in Corumbá (on the Bolivian border), exactly the measure best designed to let him play the martyr.[36]

The opening in August of the second half of the legislative year found Congress in much the same insubordinate mood it had been in the preceding August. Amnesty for students and strikers was actively debated, as the President called for "understanding and tranquillity." Although the amnesty bill was finally defeated by a vote of 198 to 145, no fewer than 35 ARENA deputies crossed the aisle to vote in favor of this anti-government measure.[37] (Those most active in this initiative, as well as those pushing a congressional investigation into the sale of land to foreigners, were among the first to be deprived of their mandates following the December "coup with a coup.") August 19 brought a triple bombing of political police headquarters in São Paulo. The radicalization of the political situation was also reflected in General Moniz de Aragão's charges of "rebellion" against the MDB, the invitation of the country's most strongly anti-reform churchman, Bishop of Diamantina Dom Geraldo Sigaud, to address the officers of the mid-career course at the Vila Militar, and *linha dura* opposition to any political bargaining by the administration to gain Congressional support.[38]

On August 28 a number of students were arrested as part of an alleged terrorist ring in São Paulo. The next day, the University of Brasília once again became the focus of the crisis as 300 security agents and military police moved in to arrest a group of student activists. Congressional leaders, including many within ARENA, were angry over this ill-timed move; they concentrated their fire on the Justice Minister, who was accused by some of cultivating the *linha dura* to further his own political ambitions. Indeed, no fewer than seventy ARENA deputies signed a manifesto expressing dissatisfaction with the regime's handling

---

[36] See Murilo Melo Filho, "O Desafio de Jânio," *Manchete*, July, 1968, pp. 17–19 and "Brasil: por primera vez Lacerda calla," *The Economist para América Latina*, August 21, 1968, pp. 16–17.

[37] "Congresso não arrancara anistia," *Visão*, August 30, 1968, pp. 37–39.

[38] Dom Geraldo had recently led a dozen conservative bishops (of the more than 240 men holding such rank in the Brazilian Church) in condemning the Conference of Bishops' document and, through the Brazilian Society for Defense of Tradition, Family and Property, had directed a letter to the Pope denouncing Communist infiltration of the Brazilian clergy. See *Jornal do Brasil*, July 23 and 26, 1968. Consult also "A Igreja em Agonía," *Visão*, April 12, 1968, pp. 66–75 and "Dom Helder: humanismo ou rebelião?", *Visão*, May 24, 1968, pp. 47–57.

of the incident. This episode triggered another wave of student demonstrations in Rio de Janeiro and other major population centers.

3. THE DECEMBER CRISIS AND THE FIFTH INSTITUTIONAL ACT

By the beginning of September, there were abundant signs that Brazil was headed for another political crisis. But the course of events during the ensuing three months proved to have more serious consequences than even the cassandras had foreseen.

August had witnessed congressional restlessness, increased resort to violence, and student strikes, as well as the beginning of a major division within the regime. Terrorist bombings, which had peaked in May before dropping to four incidents in June and only three in July, had risen to nine in August.

Responsibility for the renewed terrorism is difficult to apportion between the leftist revolutionaries and right-wing extremists. By mid-1968, it was already apparent that the revived Anti-Communist Movement (MAC) and the Communist-Hunting Command (CCC) were seeking to provoke a witch hunt by carrying out acts of terrorism for which the leftist opposition would be held responsible. These organizations and other intransigent right-wing militants were by August coordinating their actions through a self-styled Anti-Communist Armed Front (FAAC).[39]

The question of right-wing military involvement in terrorism emerged into the open in late September, when Air Force Major Brigadier Itamar Rocha denounced the participation of a key ministry official and the crack air-sea rescue service (PARA-SAR) in strong-arm tactics against opponents of the regime. The Brigadier declared that, during the April crisis, PARA-SAR personnel in civilian clothes had taken part in repression of demonstrators. He had brought this to the attention of the head of the Air Minister's staff, Brigadier João Paulo Burnier, but received no satisfaction as Burnier was the leader of the militant anti-Communist faction. Deputy Haroldo Veloso, along with Burnier a leader of the 1956 and 1959 "vest pocket" rebellions, criticized Brigadier Rocha, while Lacerda came to his defense.[40]

[39] *Correio da Manhã,* August 27, 1968. See also the round-up on bank robberies in *Visão,* July 19, 1968, pp. 48–53, and an article in *Jornal do Brasil,* November 3–4, 1968.

[40] *Jornal do Brasil,* October 8, 1968.

Lack of firm presidential leadership was another major contributing factor to the growing sense of malaise. By early 1968, there were assertions that Costa e Silva, resting at the old winter palace in Petrópolis (largely unused since Vargas), was not only tired but in poor health, and that effective power was being exercised by General Portela and Justice Minister Gama e Silva. While much of this was political hyperbole, by September the President was being criticized as lazy and indolent. The situation described by the regime as "normalcy" was viewed by many observers as more in the nature of a vacuum or an "interval in the expression of public discontent." [41]

The political situation was further complicated by the maneuvering that was already going on for the 1970 governorship and senatorial races and efforts by contending state leaders to exploit if not manipulate the November 15 municipal elections to further their candidacies.[42] The question of presidential succession aroused civilist attitudes in some ARENA leaders, while feeding ambitions and rivalries within the military. Early in October, in a lecture at the ESG, Albuquerque Lima made clear his disagreement with the monetarist orientation of Delfim Netto and Beltrão. Calling for creation of an equivalent of the National Security Council in the development field, he manifested a desire to see the military have a greater say on economic policy and fiscal priorities.[43] From this point on, he began to make public pronouncements that looked suspiciously like campaign speeches several times a week. Integration of the Amazon and housing were among his socio-economic planks, and he also denounced Church progressives for demoralizing the country's youth.[44] He defined the regime as "hard because of its very nature"; and on November 18 he called for "ten more years of revolution." Costa e Silva was widely believed to have been unhappy over his Interior Minister's "premature" campaigning, but took no action.

Although in launching his candidacy independent of the chief executive's will, Albuquerque Lima was following a strategy similar to

[41] "Brasil: un vacio para Costa e Silva," *The Economist para América Latina,* September 18, 1968, pp. 10–13. See also "CS é 76% simpático. Isso basta?", *Visão,* June 7, 1968, pp. 21–22.

[42] There is an adequate rundown of this situation state-by-state in "Em alguns Estados e de foice," *Visão,* July 5, 1968, pp. 23–25.

[43] "A corrente inconformada do Govêrno," *Visão,* October 11, 1968, pp. 21–23.

[44] *Jornal do Brasil,* October 16 and 19, 1968.

that employed successfully by Costa e Silva himself, he was not working from nearly as strong a position. Far from being the Army's ranking officer and holder of the pivotal service ministry, he faced serious competition both from officers senior to him and from several below his rank but closer to the President. Among the latter were General Portela and Transportation Minister Andreazza, who requested transfer to the reserves in October. But the most serious challenge to Albuquerque Lima's premature campaigning was to come from the man who by the end of 1970 would be the second ranking general, Sizeno Sarmento. (With the retirement of all but one of Castelo's generals by November, 1970, Sarmento would have seniority over the others promoted by Costa e Silva. However, General Fragoso, who was only 60, could continue to 1972.)

After his promotion to full general and assignment to São Paulo as Second Army Commander at the end of March, 1967, Sarmento was frequently spoken of as a potential Army Minister. With his transfer to the First Army a year later, speculation began to focus upon him as a presidential possibility. Born in Manaus in June, 1907, a battalion commander during the Italian campaign, he had performed in a discreet and effective manner as Interventor in Amazonas under Dutra. In 1960, he had accepted an invitation to serve as Lacerda's police chief, but circulatory ailments forced him to spend most of the period until the 1964 coup on disability leave. Considered a "civilian in uniform," although not a Sorbonnist and quite estranged from Castelo Branco, he generally appeared equally distant from the *linha dura*.[45]

Upon assuming command in São Paulo, Sarmento had declared that "the Armed Forces do not accept insinuations from those who want to divide them and will not deal with the corrupt and subversive." Although he had not yet assumed his new post in Rio de Janeiro at the time of the student crisis of late March and early April, he took a firm line in June and July. By repeated declarations against subversion, corruption, Communism, and a return to the pre-1964 order, Sarmento solidified his influence over the Rio de Janeiro garrisons.

On October 12, Brazil experienced another major student crisis when military and state authorities broke up the thirtieth UNE Con-

[45] Rumo a Brasília via Campo de Sant 'Ana?", *Visão*, July 19, 1968, pp. 23–24.

gress, meeting in a small town some forty miles west of São Paulo. Unlike the convention of the preceding year, attended by only seventy student leaders, the 1968 gathering had over 1,000 participants from all parts of the country.[46] Rio de Janeiro students reacted by seizing the old UNE headquarters in Flamengo and holding it for half a day. A clash with the police on October 22 left a medical student dead, and two workers were killed the next day during a protest rally. Concurrently with the student crisis, urban terrorism took a dramatic turn for the worse. On October 12, U.S. Army Captain Charles Chandler, who had been studying at a São Paulo university for two years and was about to return to the United States, was machine-gunned to death in the presence of his family. A note left at the scene claimed this act was in retribution for the United States special forces' involvement in the death of Che Guevara in Bolivia. Right-wing extremists were clearly responsible for the bombing two days later of Editôra Civilização Brasileira, which had published many books (as well as a review) highly critical of the regime. On the 28th, the Sears Roebuck department store in São Paulo was bombed. On November 8, the targets of the escalating violence were the *Jornal do Brasil* and the Soviet Consulate in Rio de Janeiro.

In this context, the November 15 elections in nearly 1,500 municipalities were all but anti-climactic. While ARENA candidates won in most areas, the campaigning and balloting served to underscore popular disenchantment with the artificially restricted party system. Of greater interest to most observers was the drama taking place in Brasília, as the executive became caught in a confrontation between Congress and the military, whose rigidly self-righteous attitude left no room for compromise. (Although Senate president Gilberto Marinho was a reserve general, as was the MDB president, Senator Oscar Passos, the issue was in the less promising arena of the Chamber of Deputies.) The crisis of early April, which in retrospect was the beginning of the end for the semi-representative regime, had demonstrated the dilemma of a military partially but not completely in power. An insecure government of men thoroughly imbued with a rather rigid doctrine of national secur-

[46] The press first reported 1,240 arrests, although official figures on those actually booked totaled only 712. See *O Estado de S. Paulo and Jornal do Brasil,* October 13–17, 1968.

ity was prone to exaggerate the subversive threat and to meet demonstrations of opposition—channeled into the streets because other effective means of protest had been foreclosed—by excessive repression. A vicious circle was set up. Now a dominant part of the government and at the heart of the crisis itself, the Armed Forces were not in a position to exercise the function of moderating power as they had historically.

As early as May, MDB Chamber Leader Mario Covas had accused the government of complicity in a plot to destroy the opposition. At about this time, Labor Minister Jarbas Passarinho (who may be considered the most "civilian" of the military ministers, as Gama e Silva was the most "militarist" of the civilian cabinet members) lashed out at a neo-fascist movement seeking to spread fear and discredit as Communists sincere democrats who favored improving the position of the workers. Subsequently, MDB deputy Simão de Cunha denounced a "nazi-fascist" plan to implant an authoritarian dictatorship. Then, on September 6, *Correio da Manhã* claimed to have uncovered a conspiracy for a rightist *golpe* by military elements associated with the regime.

Differences over strategy and divisions on policy issues within the regime were not readily exploitable by the opposition. Indeed, the greater the attacks upon the regime, the more the military pulled themselves together in its defense. They also became increasingly defensive as they perceived their actions as "misinterpreted" and lamented "lack of understanding" on the part of the population.[47]

On November 1, the newspapers published a recently circulated manifesto of some 385 Army captains attending the mid-career course at the Officer Specialization School, or EAO. While carefully stating that it was directed only at military problems that could be resolved within the Armed Forces, this unusual "class" document expressed discontent with the state of national affairs, at least insofar as they affected the Army. Complaining first of "outdated organization" and "nonexistence of a basic doctrine of training and instruction coherent with Brazilian reality," the young officers lamented that the Brazilian Army "is today considered a usurper and special-seeker in the national

[47] See "Los militares quieren acción," *The Economist para América Latina,* October 30, 1968, pp. 13–16.

life." [48] They called for more vigorous repression of corruption and denounced subversives trying to discredit and divide the military. In sum, according to the captains, it was "time for a change." The seriousness of their discontent was underscored by reports of a stronger version drafted by the infantry officers which had included criticism of several ministers by name.[49]

At this juncture, the Church strove to exert a moderating influence, but with scant success. The National Commission of Bishops at the end of October established a special subgroup for dialogue with the government "every time the Church feels the need of an encounter to relax the tensions." [50] Cardinal Rossi of São Paulo established a " Movement of Collective Action for Justice" (MACPJ) to offset the conservative Tradition, Family, Property movement of lay Catholics.

The incident that would result in the implantation of dictatorship had its roots in the August 30 invasion of the University of Brasília by the Army. On September 3, Deputy Márcio Moreira Alves, one of the young radicals of the MDB and author of two books and many articles considered subversive by military authorities, in an impassioned speech called for a "boycott of militarism" and recommended to parents that they keep their children out of the September 7 Independence Day parade as a gesture of protest. He also suggested that freedom-loving girls refuse to date officers. Already convinced of a "subversive" conspiracy to discredit the Armed Forces in the eyes of the public and highly indignant over what they viewed as an unpatriotic as well as insulting attitude, the military demanded that the young journalist-politician not go unpunished because of his congressional office.

By mid-October, rumors were rife of an imminent power play by hard-line military elements. The visit of the Queen of England during the first week of November served to cool down the crisis, but subse-

---

[48] *Jornal do Brasil,* November 7, 1968, contains most of the text. Its implications are analyzed in "Críticas sérias de jovens oficiais," *Visão,* November 28, 1968, pp. 25–26 and "Capitães começam vida política com Manifesto da EsAO," *Jornal do Brasil,* December 8, 1968.

[49] *Jornal do Brasil,* November 2, 1969.

[50] "Brasil: la Revolución diluida" and "Brasil: diálogo con los infieles," *The Economist para América Latina,* November 27, 1968, pp. 7–8 and 15–16. See also "Agora a violência vem da direita," *Visão,* October 25, 1968, pp. 21–24.

quently pressure was placed on the Chamber of Deputies to strip Moreira Alves of his parliamentary immunity so that he could be prosecuted under the National Security Law. Such a "servile" attitude had been taken by Congress in 1935 on Vargas' demand, but had been denied in the case of Lacerda two decades later. The military was sure that Congress would yield, and Costa e Silva gave assurances that the sovereign decision of the legislature would be accepted by the Armed Forces. Such was not to be the case. Once again, as during the preceding three years, the deputies chose to demonstrate their independence at the end of the legislative session.[51]

On November 21 wholesale changes were made in the justice committee of the Chamber so that the vote would be favorable to the government rather than running as high as a predicted 21 to 10 against. (Several of the ARENA congressmen dropped at this time would be stripped of their mandates after the coup.) The administration had expected cooperation from the committee chairman, Djalma Marinho, but instead he stepped down. The weakness of ARENA as a vehicle for the executive's will, evidenced with the declaration of 107 deputies against the new Constitution early in 1967, was now disconcertingly clear (as had been the case with the Revolutionary Parliamentary Bloc in the October, 1965, crisis). While General Sarmento released documents purporting to show involvement of priests in Minas Gerais with subversion—the Army commander there was the general who more than two years previously had attacked Dom Helder Câmara in Fortaleza as a Communist—the opposition newspaper *Correio da Manhã* and the student government office of the Guanabara State University's medical school were bombed on December 7. Three days later, as the reconstituted Chamber justice committee approved the punishment of Moreira Alves by a 19 to 12 vote, the Supreme Court granted freedom to forty-six of the student leaders held since the UNE Congress—a move that greatly upset many in the military.

On Wednesday, December 11, the Supreme Court issued writs of *habeas corpus* for thirty-three more students and the next day ordered

[51] For the atmosphere of the pre-coup period, see "Como fica difícil Govêrno forte errar," *Visão,* September 27, 1968, pp. 21–23; "Crise já no eixo Executivo-Supremo?", *Visão,* November 8, 1968, pp. 21–24; and "General e candidato é caso político," *Visão,* December 8, 1968, pp. 29–30.

the release of Vladimir Palmeira and Luís Travassos. With 372 members present (249 ARENA and 123 MDB), the Chamber proceeded to vote down action against Márcio Moreira Alves by a vote of 216 to 141, with fifteen abstentions. No fewer than ninety-four government party congressmen balked against a measure considered vital by the executive, convincing the military that Congress could not be allowed to function. Furthermore, the officers tended to carry over into the sphere of party politics a military concept of discipline. Thus "abandonment" of the government by centrist ARENA elements on a critical issue was viewed as partaking somewhat of desertion in the face of the enemy. In the minds of hard-line military, punitive action was required.

The military crisis of December, 1968, while broadly comparable to that of October, 1965, had a unique character of its own. Although continuing press censorship has clouded many of its details, the major outlines show a quite unified action on the part of the First Army under General Sizeno Sarmento. Pressed toward action by several of his "faceless" subordinates—Dutra de Castilho of the Vila Militar, Ramiro Gonçalves of the Armored Division, and Câmara Sena of the Coast Artillery (whose greatest previous visibility had been as assistant chief of Quadros' Casa Militar) in particular—the stocky commander of the Rio de Janeiro and Minas Gerais garrisons played much the broker role Costa e Silva had in the 1965 "coup within a coup." While accepting the need for a new Institutional Act, he moved to head off any powerplay that would have left Albuquerque Lima and associated *linha dura* elements in a dominant position. As opposition leaders and militant critics of the regime were arrested by the hundreds, the stringent Fifth Institutional Act appeared out of the portfolio of hard-line Justice Minister Gama e Silva, whose intransigence had contributed substantially to the polarization during the preceding weeks.[52]

---

[52] "A crise de expectiva." *Visão,* December 6, 1968, pp. 102–106, pulls together many of the dimensions of the developing crisis before the final denouement. Army Minister Lyra Tavares, who in July had stressed the need to keep out subversive ideas, expressed support for the regime's action in a secret circular on "The Army and the 5th Institutional Act" cited by James N. Goodsell in *The Christian Science Monitor,* February 19, 1969. At least one senior general heading a department of the Army Ministry strove with effect to convince junior generals to give Costa e Silva time to find an adequate solution (according to confidential conversations with several participants in these events).

The justifying paragraphs of the Act read very much like those of April, 1964, and October, 1965, with emphasis on "guaranteeing the authentic democratic order, based on liberty, respect for human dignity, combating subversion . . . and the fight against corruption." Draconian as its provisions were, the populace was reassured that they would be employed only to "confront directly and immediately the problems of restoring internal order and the international prestige of our country." [53] The Act granted the President authority to recess legislative bodies, to intervene in the states without limit, to cancel elective mandates and suspend political rights, to suspend constitutional guarantees with regard to civil service tenure, etc., to confiscate property acquired by illicit means, issue complementary acts, and to set aside the right of habeas corpus. All such actions were to be beyond judicial review. Complementary Act No. 38, issued at the same time, closed Congress indefinitely. Thus the "humanization" of the revolution promised by Costa e Silva two years earlier ended with the imposition of censorship stronger even than that known during the Estado Nôvo. As the hard line had exploited a political crisis to radicalize military opinion and force Castelo to the right in 1965, now it maneuvered Costa into a position in which he had to yield to their demands.

In the eyes of the administration, ARENA rather than increasing in coherence and discipline, had deteriorated as an effective parliamentary majority for the government, beginning with its mutterings of discontent over the Constitution in early 1967, through the congressional "rebellion" of late 1967, and finally to the "desertion" of one-third of its members in the December, 1968, crisis vote. When his majority bloc had failed him in October, 1965, Castelo had dissolved the existing parties and created ARENA; in December, 1968, the Costa e Silva regime responded by purging Congress and closing it indefinitely. For not only had the Chamber of Deputies balked, but a group of ARENA's most prestigious leaders in the Senate—including party president Daniel Krieger, Carvalho Pinto, Milton Campos, Mem de Sá, Ney Braga, and Arnon de Melo—criticized the new Institutional Act.

[53] The text can be found in *Visão*, December 20, 1968, pp. 21–23, as well as in the daily newspapers of December 14. English-language materials on this crisis are still very scarce, but include a perceptive essay by Frances M. Folland, "The Prospects for Brazil," *The New Leader*, January 20, 1969, pp. 5–8, and several articles by James Nelson Goodsell in *The Christian Science Monitor*, February 11 and 19, and March 3 and 14, 1969.

The first cassations under the Costa e Silva regime followed on December 30. Márcio Moreira Alves, Hermano Alves, and Renato Archer (who had been a key articulator of the Frente Ampla) were the most prominent of the eleven deputies turned into political nonpersons. The suspension of Lacerda's political rights was of even greater significance. January 16 witnessed the most extensive purge of the national legislature to that date. Senators Aarão Steinbruch and João Abraão were ousted, as were thirty-five deputies including such notables as Oswaldo Lima Filho, Martins Rodrigues, Ivette Vargas, Mário Covas, Raul Brunini, João Herculino, and Antônio Cunha Bueno (the latter two among seven who retained their political rights). More surprising was the forced retirement of Supreme Court Justices Hermes Lima, Evandro Lins e Silva, and Victor Nunes Leal, as well as General Pery Bevilaqua from the Superior Military Tribunal.

The salient Brazilian precedent for this judicial purge action was the decree of the Visconde de Sinimbu at the end of 1863 retiring four ministers of the Supreme Court whose rulings had offended the Emperor.[54] As in that case, the newly elected presiding justice resigned in protest. In addition to Gonçalves de Oliveira, Lafayette de Andrada also joined the three "expelled" ministers in retirement. In 1931, the revolutionary government had forced the retirement of six ministers, while reducing the court's size from fifteen to eleven, and Costa e Silva followed suit, issuing Institutional Act No. 6 on January 31, eliminating five seats on the high court (thus returning it to the size prevailing before Castelo "packed" it in October, 1965, under the Second Institutional Act).

February 7 saw yet another major list of cancellations of mandates with suspension of political rights. Among the thirty-three congressmen affected—eleven from ARENA and twenty-two from the MDB—were Senators Mário Martins and Artur Virgílio, together with such important deputies as Aluísio Alves, Pedro Gondim, Cid Carvalho, and Ney Maranhão. Thus, with no assurance that the cassations had ended, a total of seventy-seven of the 409 members of the lower house had been purged, including eighteen from São Paulo alone and seven of Guanabara's twenty-one representatives. The MDB had lost nearly 40 per cent of its strength in the Chamber and was all but bereft of leadership.

---

[54] See "Dois Juízes, Duas Interpretações," *Veja,* January 29, 1969, pp. 12–13.

A number of the cassations were clearly directed at the potential gubernatorial successors. Aluísio Alves, Pedro Gondim, Aarão Steinbruch, Martins Rodrigues, Oswaldo Lima Filho, and João Herculino were unacceptable to the regime as prospective governors. Very heavily hit within ARENA were the members of the "center bloc" or "nonaligned group." Although Rafael de Almeida Magalhães was spared, the axe fell on the political heads of Marcos Kertzman, Jorge Curi, Flores Soares, Israel Novais, and Murilo Badaró. In general, those who had proven "insubordinate" on the amnesty bill, or who had strongly defended Márcio Moreira Alves, were eliminated from political life, as were the legislative spokesmen for Lacerda, Quadros, and Kubitschek.

Concurrently with the February punishments, the regime also decreed the indefinite recess of state legislatures in Guanabara, Rio de Janeiro, São Paulo, Pernambuco, and Sergipe, alleging corrupt practices (such as an excessive number of special sessions) that had enabled the legislators to receive payments and advantages above those to which they were morally entitled. As in 1964, a General Investigations Commission (CGI) was established to supervise the new wave of Police-Military Inquiries, and subordinate bodies were created at the state level. On February 26, Institutional Act No. 7 canceled all elections scheduled to be held before the November, 1970, balloting for Congress and governors. It also severely limited pay to legislators, placed curbs on special sessions, eliminated any compensation to municipal councilmen in cities of under 300,000 population, and placed in recess the legislatures of Goiás and Pará. To demonstrate a reformist as well as a repressive force, Institutional Act No. 8, issued the following day, provided for cutting through bureaucratic procedures and red tape that had held up the agrarian reform, (yet little more would be done in this field until after the next change of administration).

Shaken by the recent crisis, which demonstrated graphically how far control of events had slipped from his hands, Costa began almost immediately to recover the initiative and to restore his eroded authority within the inner circles of the regime. In a December 16 address to the Army Command and General Staff School, he reaffirmed that "whenever necessary, as now, we will make new revolutions within the revolution." But he also spoke of the inevitability of normalization and enjoined the Army to "fix, construct, unite, pull together to carry the country forward," putting aside animosities and thinking in terms of "the nation predominant over the interests of groups." [55]

The departure of Albuquerque Lima from the cabinet in late January was perhaps the most significant development strengthening the President's authority. Feeling their interests prejudiced by austerity measures and particularly by modification of the tax laws, a number of politicians from the Northeast sought out the Interior Minister as their champion. Rather than heeding Albuquerque Lima's requests for increased financial assistance for the area and budgetary support for its state administrations, Costa e Silva reaffirmed his option for a strong anti-inflationary program. At the end of the month, Albuquerque Lima submitted his resignation, which was promptly accepted. Choosing to keep cabinet changes to a minimum, the President moved Costa Cavalcanti into the Interior Ministry and promoted Antônio Dias Leite from head of the government iron-ore exporting company to replace the reserve brigadier as Minister of Mines and Energy. Since the latter was the brother of Colonel Boaventura Cavalcanti and well respected by the other hard-line officers, this shrewd shift minimized military response to Albuquerque Lima's declaration calling for public works, reforms, and energetic moralization and expressing his disagreement with a policy "prejudicial to regional development, the housing program, sanitation, industrialization, and agrarian development." [56]

The administration further undercut the impact of Albuquerque Lima's dissidence by stepping up the all but moribund agrarian reform, dismissing "excess" federal employees, and taking action against businessmen believed to have been lax in paying their income taxes or complying with other government regulations. At the same time, it affirmed that a return to constitutional normalcy was still in the indefi-

[55] See "As novas perspectivas," *Visão*, January 17, 1969, pp. 19–20, as well as "Por distintos derroteros," *The Economist para América Latina*, December 25, 1968, pp. 7–8, and "La hora sombría," *The Economist para América Latina*, January 8, 1969, pp. 11–12.

[56] On this episode consult *Jornal do Brasil*, January 15 and 28, 1969; "Se agudiza el conflicto de opiniones," *The Economist para América Latina*, February 5, 1969, p. 8; and "Para resguardar la democracia," *The Economist para América Latina*, January 22, 1969, pp. 11–12. Since this publication's correspondent in Brazil seems to rely quite heavily upon Albuquerque Lima as a source, these articles present the story essentially from his point of view. See also Odylo Costa, Filho, "A Saída de Ministro," *Veja*, January 29, 1969, p. 14.

nite future. Keynoting a private sector "First Seminar on Internal Security," the Justice Minister articulated his theory of the "permanent revolution," declaring that "the revolutionary power retook the process to prevent, in the political and psycho-social field, ideological warfare and subversive war from again taking control of the country." He defined democracy as "a magic word, a concept that varies in time and space, principally in an instant, like that through which we are passing, that is the moment of Revolution." [57] The Church, professing to offer its "loyal collaboration," but in a manner that might better be interpreted as an assurance of its loyal opposition, reaffirmed the need for urgent basic reforms and reminded the President of the pervasive desire for redemocratization.[58]

[57] "Palavra mágica no tempo e no espaço," *Visão,* February 28, 1969, pp. 21–22. For the ambient of the moment, see also "Brasil: elecciones con disciplina castrense," *The Economist para América Latina,* February 19, 1969, pp. 13–16.

[58] "Pronunciamento dos bispos," *Visão,* March 14, 1969, pp. 17–18. Compare this with their position eight months earlier, as reported in *Correio da Manhã,* July 21, 1968.

CHAPTER EIGHT

The Sixth Year of the "Revolution"

As Brazil entered the third year of Costa e Silva's government and the sixth year of the "revolution," only the dimmest shadows of representative processes remained operational. In taking stock of the preceding five years of military tutelage, the President stressed in his state of the union message the significant economic progress of his administration: a 6.5 per cent growth in the GNP during 1968, following a 5 per cent growth in 1967; exports at the level of $1.9 billion. Moreover, the rise in the cost of living had been kept under 25 per cent for two consecutive years. He also pledged that the new year would witness "completion of the Revolution's reforms" and "compatibilization of the legislative power with the highest mission reserved for it by the Brazilian people." But the collective resignation of ARENA's leadership underlined that retrogression in the political field had accompanied economic development. On March 21, the National Security Law was modified to provide stiff penalties for terrorism, bank robberies, and interruption of essential services. Moreover, incitation to sedition, even in private, was made punishable by military courts, as was "fostering of animosity toward the Armed Forces." Statements by regime spokesmen made it clear that counter-revolution (a political judgment) was now a crime, on a par with judicially proven subversion.[1]

[1] An assessment of government intentions is contained in "Firmemente en el poder," *The Economist para América Latina,"* April 2, 1969, pp. pp. 9–10. See

As the military entered into their sixth year in power, civilian and moderate military elements within the regime were advocating a reconvening of the Congress at least by August, after the winter vacations. But before any relatively "normal" functioning of the political system would be allowed, it was apparent that changes going much deeper than the proposed modification of the government party's name from ARENA to Party of the Brazilian Revolution would be instituted. Reduction in the length of congressional terms, elections by districts, abolition of the alternate system, prohibition of re-election of legislative officers, tying of pay to actual attendance, severe restrictions on the number of special sessions, limitation of parliamentary immunity, and strict party fidelity (including delegation of votes to the party leaders on "political" questions) were among the modifications of legislative authority and procedures considered necessary by the regime.[2] While most politicians viewed the events of the preceding months as temporary measures arising from a crisis in which they had underestimated the military's hypersensitivity, astute observers questioned whether the course of events since 1964 did not indicate that "normalcy" might be long delayed. Luiz Alberto Bahia, on the way out as chief assistant to Guanabara Governor Negrão de Lima as the result of heavy military pressure, perceptively analyzed the Fifth Institutional Act as the final break between the elected politicians and the elite of the military bureaucracy after a series of crises and accommodations going back over two decades.

The history of Brazil, in the postwar period, is the history of these compromises between representation and the upper civil and military bureaucracy. . . .

But it was during this period of Kubitschek's mandate that the three seeds of the negation of the hegemonic cycle of the class of representative politicians were sown. . . .

The move of the capital to Brasília released a slow, but inexorable coup against the reign of representative power in the exact proportion to which the absence of efficient communications between the microphone of the rostrum and the ear of the man in the street made it remote from public opinion. . . .

---

also "Normalização e oposição," *Visão*, April 11, 1969, pp. 23–24. Costa's address on the fifth anniversary of the revolution is discussed in *Jornal do Brasil*, March 31, and April 1, 1969. The President's marathon press conference, televised in four parts on successive evenings, is covered in *Jornal do Brasil*, April 1–4, 1969.

[2] "Os dez mandamentos dos políticos," *Veja*, March 5, 1969, pp. 15–16, and *Jornal do Brasil*, March 30 and 31, 1969.

The First Institutional Act didn't yet condemn the representative political class. . . . Act No. 2 maintained the political class, but ended the parties. . . . The two parties created by the Revolution were not accepted by the representative class. . . .

The Fifth Institutional Act, not prescribing the time of its duration, generates an expectancy of continued and indeterminant exceptionality, in contrast to the preceding ones, which, self-limiting in time, always produced an expectation of normalcy. . . . Whatever normalizing solution will have to confront the question of the role and functions of the representative political class in the face of the other political class. . . . The techno-bureaucratic political class will have imposed the power of the State over the power of the independent organizations of society.[3]

The course of events during the second and third quarters of the year were to demonstrate that the crisis was every bit as deep as Bahia forsaw. More than three years had intervened between the first and second major crisis within the ruling military. But less than nine months after the December, 1968, *golpe,* the Costa e Silva government was overthrown from within through a pre-emptive coup by the senior military, in the face of a growing challenge by less senior officers that threatened their positions as well as that of the President. For the first time in Brazilian history, a military *junta* governed for weeks (instead of a few days, as in April 1964), while the search for a new government bogged down in virtual stalemate before a least common denominator of the military factions was found in a heterogeneous cabinet under the little-known Emílio Garrastazú Médici.

1. AN AUTHORITARIAN REGIME WITHOUT AUTHORITY

The sensational kidnaping of U.S. Ambassador C. Burke Elbrick in front of his residence in Rio de Janeiro on September 4 was not a sudden or isolated gesture of opposition to the military regime, as depicted in much of the world's press. It was rather a dramatic act in a long and escalating series of clashes between an essentially dictatorial government and the several elements in the body politic dedicated to its downfall. The kidnaping, as well as the events preceding it and the renewed wave of repression that ensued, underscored the political dilemmas of this potential world power: the Armed Forces in control of the country but deeply divided over how to exercise such responsibility;

[3] "O futuro da Classe política," *Visão,* March 28, 1969, pp. 19–23.

the virtual nonexistence of political parties; stringent curbs on protests and press censorship in a country long accustomed to substantial liberty and tolerance of a vigorous opposition; universities crippled by purges and chronic ineptness on the part of a long succession of Education Ministers; and a Church whose hierarchy is torn between fear of "subversion" and distaste for the military's repressive measures as well as plagued by deep generational conflicts within the lower clergy and its lay ranks. The authorship of the kidnaping and the reaction on the part of the field-grade officers revealed the societal complexities of the present situation—professional-class cosmopolitan radicals resorting to uncharacteristic violence when all channels of "normal" opposition activity had been closed off by force arrayed against colonels and majors of essentially lower middle-class origin demanding vigorous repression against this threat to the established order. But at the end of March, 1969, the regime appeared more to be recovering from the crisis of the preceding December than to be heading into an even more serious one.

With Albuquerque Lima at least temporarily put in his place, General Portela singled out by Costa e Silva for praise as one of the unsung heroes of the 1964 coup, Andreazza strongly commended for his effective work, and Magalhães Pinto also basking in the sunshine of kind presidential words, the question of presidential succession was largely in abeyance as the second half of Costa's term got underway. But since it could not be held back for long, the wave of Army promotions announced on March 25 took on added significance. Ex-Military Club president Augusto César Castro Moniz de Aragão, SNI chief Emílio Garrastazú Medíci, and José Canavarro Pereira were elevated to full generals. The six new major generals were Ramiro Tavares Gonçalves, Lauro Alves Pinto, Reinaldo Melo Almeida (son of José Américo de Almeida), Ednardo Davila Melo, Henrique Carlos Assunção Cardoso, and Sílvio Couto Coelho Frota (in command of the First Military Region). Among those raised to brigadier were hard-liner Antônio Carlos Andrade Serpa, João Batista Figueiredo, and Walter Pires Albuquerque. The ensuing reassignments saw General Garrastazú take over the Third Army, vacated by Alvaro da Silva Braga, who replaced Antônio Carlos Muricy as Director General of Personnel as the latter moved up to become Army Chief of Staff. Adalberto Pereira dos Santos relinquished this key post to become a member of the Superior Military

Tribunal. Moniz de Aragão took charge of the Directorate of General Provisions as Souza Aguiar departed for New York and the Brazilian U.N. Mission as substitute for the retiring Lieutenant Brigadier Nélson Lavanère-Wanderley. José Cannavaro Pereira was named the new Second Army Commander, with Souto Malan remaining in charge of the Fourth Army and Sizeno Sarmento continuing in command of the First Army. Orlando Geisel as Chairman of the Joint Chiefs of Staff and Jurandir Mamede as Director General of Ordinance and Production also stayed fixed. Carlos Alberto Fontoura, until November, 1966, sub-chief of the War Minister's Staff, was entrusted with control of the SNI. For his part, Albuquerque Lima was assigned as chief of the Directorate of War Material within the Army Ministry in Rio de Janeiro—where he could be watched carefully, but also where he could remain in close contact with his hard-line admirers.

Other significant command assignments saw Breno Borges Fortes become Army Vice Chief of Staff, Dióscoro Gonçalves Vale assume command of the garrison of Brasília and the 11th Military Region, Henrique de Assunção Cardoso taking over the 3rd Military Region, Tarso Vilar de Aquino as the new commander of the Armored Division, Walter Pires de Albuquerque named to the 2nd Cavalry Division, Francisco Bastos de Aguiar given the 6th Infantry Division, and Ernani Airosa da Silva becoming Second Army Chief of Staff, with Carlos Alberto Cabral Ribeiro as the new First Army Chief of Staff. Within the Army Ministry, Gustão Guimarães de Almeida was appointed cabinet chief for the General Staff, João Bina Machado was named Director of Instruction and Training, Isaac Nahon assigned as the new Director of Active Duty Personnel, and José Codeceira Lopes indicated as Director of Remounts. Nogueira Paes assumed the post of Director General of Personnel on an interim basis as General Silva Braga moved temporarily to the Superior Military Tribunal as Mourão Filho took extended leave from his position there. Reinaldo Melo Almeida became the Army's Second Vice Chief of Staff, being replaced as Commandant of the Command and General Staff School by Brigadier Adolfo João de Paulo Couto, who in turn was succeeded as Commandant of the Military Academy by the rapidly moving Carlos Meira Matos. The latter's vacated post as Inspector General of Military Police went to ex-Army Second Sub-Chief of Staff Augusto de Oliveira Pereira.

Albuquerque Lima's close colleague Brigadier Euler Bentes Monteiro, who had headed SUDENE until resigning when his mentor left the cabinet, was given a temporary desk assignment as chief of the Superior Commission of Economy and Finances.[4]

Although Congress remained in recess, the administration undertook during April a flurry of legislation by decree reminiscent of the latter stages of the Castelo government. Institutional Act No. 8 of April 2, providing for administrative reform in the states and municipalities of over 200,000 inhabitants, reflected how commonplace recourse to this exceptional juridical instrument had become. São Paulo political theorist Miguel Reale was entrusted with the task of drafting new electoral, party, and ineligibilities laws. The job of revising the basic legal codes, a challenge that had thwarted three presidents and fourteen justice ministers since undertaken by Quadros in 1961, was also pushed to completion by commissions of jurists hand-picked by Gama e Silva.

In Rio de Janeiro, political speculation, if at a low level by normal Brazilian standards, was again on the upswing with Carnival well past and the soccer World Cup competition not until 1970. Opinion polls taken in mid-April found over 60 per cent of the *Cariocas* willing to express a preference for one or another of the candidates for the ARENA presidency (with Andreazza and Jarbas Passarinho leading the way), while some 85 per cent volunteered views on the most active and effective minister (once again, Andreazza led with 22 per cent, followed by Beltrão with 14 per cent, and then by Delfim Neto, Passarinho, Tarso Dutra, Magalhães Pinto and Gama e Silva, bunched between 6 and 9 per cent).[5] As the most positive achievement of the revolution after five years in power, the residents of Guanabara stressed the attack on cor-

---

[4] The military reassignments are reported with a minimum of interpretation or speculation in the newspapers of late March and early April. For an interesting pamphlet by perhaps the most influential of the Brigadiers, see General Carlos de Meira Mattos, *Ensaio Sôbre a Doutrina Política da Revolução* (Brasília, March, 1969). Within the framework of National Security Doctrine, this disciple of Castelo Branco disinguishes between those "national objectives" requiring preservation and perfection, those needing to be actively defended, and those remaining to be conquered. He indicates priority goals to be attained within the span of a single generation so that by the end of the century Brazil will be "a politically respected, economically developed, and socially stable country." For the evolution of his thought consult *Projeção Mundial do Brasil* (São Paulo, 1961) in which quite elemental geopolitical categories are employed.

[5] Pesquisa JB/Marplan published in *Jornal do Brasil*, April 13–14, 1969.

ruption (28 per cent), resumption of economic development (12 per cent), the repression of subversion (also 12 per cent), the relative containment of inflation (7 per cent), university reform (5 per cent), and tax reform (4 per cent). Only one person in twelve interviewed took the position that there were no significant accomplishments, although nearly one in four professed to have no opinion.[6]

Instead of moves toward normalization as predicted by optimistic observers, a massive purge was initiated the last week of April. An initial list of 44 individuals was followed by one of 175 names approved at the April 29 meeting of the National Security Council, acting under the very broad powers of the 5th Institutional Act. The first of these lists included such internationally known scholars as sociologist Florestan Fernandes, physicist José Leite Lopes, and historians Eulália Lamayer Lobo and María Leda Leite Linhares. The more sweeping follow-up previewed by this decree caught nearly all of the social scientists of the University of São Paulo—Fernando Henrique Cardoso, Octavio Ianni, Paulo Duarte, Emílio Viotti da Costa, Paulo Singer, Luís Pereira, and Paula Beiguelman—along with physicist Mario Schemberg, newly inaugurated Rector Hélio Lourenço de Oliveira, and prominent intellectual Caio Prado Júnior.[7] Compulsory retirement was also decreed for forty-three diplomats and Foreign Ministry officials, headed by Sérgio Correia do Lago and Vinicius de Morais (better known as a popular composer and poet than as a diplomat). Antônio Callado, one of the nation's leading journalists and author of a best-selling political novel, was deprived of his political rights and barred from the exercise of his profession (although this provision was subsequently rescinded following international protests). Fifteen federal deputies—among them Estácio Souto Maior (ARENA, Pernambuco), Francisco Chagas Rodrigues (MDB, Piauí), and Florencio Paixão (MDB, Rio Grande do Sul)—had their mandates cassated and lost their political rights. No fewer than fifty-eight state legislators, fifteen from São Paulo alone, suffered the same fate.

With Commissions of Investigation busily at work in each state,

[6] For an enlightening comparison with public opinion in the 1966 period consult *Jornal do Brasil*, November 15, 1966. The mood of mid-April is also caught in "Especulações e incertezes," *Visão*, April 25, 1969, pp. 21–22.

[7] Consult *O Estado de S. Paulo, Jornal do Brasil,* or *Correio da Manhã,* April 30, 1969, for a complete list.

rumors of additional such lists were rife in Belo Horizonte, Salvador, and Recife. Yet at this same juncture the government made a further move to redeem its reform promises, issuing Institutional Act No. 9 of April 25, providing for payment in twenty-year bonds for lands expropriated for agrarian reform—with income tax statements as the basis for valuation.[8] A nearly 25 per cent rise in the minimum wage announced on May 1 brought this in Rio and São Paulo up to the level of NCr 156 (about U.S. $40) per month and to NCr 100 (roughly $25) in the Northeast. While talk of normalization, particularly reopening of Congress, continued, the new government leader for the Chamber followed the prudent example of his predecessor, who had accepted appointment to the Superior Military Tribunal, and took a post on the Tribunal of Accounts. Although Vice President Aleixo was announced as entrusted with studying the problem of "compatibilizing the Revolution with political institutions," more significant as an omen of times ahead was the President's decision to purge the *linha dura*'s Colonel Francisco Boaventura Cavalcanti, whose outspoken criticisms of the regime's course included support for direct elections in 1970.

The chain of events that reached its climax in September began with Boaventura's compulsory transfer to the reserves on May 19 for an alleged "lack of the duty of loyalty to his hierarchical superiors, articulating the organization of a government of exception headed by a person incompatible with the principles of the Revolution. . . . [he] divorced himself from the fundamental rights of a military [man], taking a position incompatible with his condition of a superior officer in active service." [9] After study of his actions during the preceding months, a commission had found that in the November-December crisis Boaventura had "entered into a understanding with congressmen, including some from the opposition, manifesting his solidarity with those who were against the giving of permission to process a deputy for his infamous and villainous defamation of the Armed Forces, and incited them to vote against the aforementioned measure." Military dissention was now

---

[8] These matters had been dealt with in an Institutional Act No. 8 of February 27 which was so poorly designed that it was abruptly withdrawn for redrafting. Thus an Institutional Act concerning administrative reform issued on April 2 was reassigned the number 8.

[9] Decree reprinted in *Jornal do Brasil,* May 20, 1969.

out in the open for all to see as a brother of one of Costa e Silva's ministers was cashiered for encouraging Congress to thwart the executive's will.

The precarious state of political renovation was underscored at this juncture by the postponement of municipal conventions designed to restructure ARENA and MDB. Complementary Act No. 54 of May 19 set these back from the first Sunday in July to August 10, with regional and national conventions rescheduled for September 14 and October 12, respectively. This effort to reorganize the parties from the bottom up and give them more "authentic" leadership subsequently fell victim to the political crisis that removed Costa e Silva from office.[10] Announcement that with off-shore drilling petroleum self-sufficiency might be reached by 1971 was met with more skepticism than enthusiasm by a public surfeited with promises of great accomplishments just around the corner. A public opinion poll in late May revealed that 59 per cent of those questioned favored reopening Congress, with 21 per cent opposed and 20 per cent not interested. Only 26 per cent, however, felt that it should be reopened immediately, while 67 per cent called for reforms first. Asked if the country was ready for a return to constitutional normalcy, some 49 per cent responded affirmatively, with 30 per cent saying no.[11]

When Costa e Silva spoke at the Vila Militar on May 24 concerning the possible need for further "revolutions within the revolution," he did not know that the next one would involve his premature retirement as president. "Revolutionary normalcy," a concept put forth by the Justice Minister to justify continuance of the regime's arbitrary powers, was to prove a controversial subject within the military no matter how much semantic and forensic skill Gama e Silva might devote to the subject. As anti-revolutionary extremism and revolutionary extremism appeared to be once again on a collision course, the military was divided over whether to get even more deeply into the business of running the country—in order, in their view to do it right—or to avoid burning any

[10] For the contemporary perspective, however, see "modêlo da segurança em busca da legitimação, "*Visão,* May 9, 1969, pp. 22–23.

[11] Pesquisa JB/Marplan reported in *Jornal do Brasil,* May 25, 1969. The backing and filling on "normalization" is treated in "A Caminho do partido dominante," *Visão,* June 6, 1969, pp. 21–22.

more political bridges that might be needed for an orderly withdrawal in the future to a less central and commanding position in the political arena.[12]

In the eyes of the Armed Forces high command in mid-1969, the fundamental dilemma was one of developing a "democratic system which can defend itself against a permanent enemy." The old clientilistic system and the traditional "political class" were perceived as a faulty foundation for such a political edifice, while the modernizing elements of the early 1960's were viewed as ideologically disloyal "subversives" who needed to be barred from further leadership roles. Thus the necessity of "stopping in order to go forward." To the more perceptive military figures, the existence of a dilemma, if not a fundamental contradiction, in this line of thinking was apparent. A moratorium on competitive political activity until basic problems were resolved and new leadership emerged might seem a viable strategy at first glance, but begged the critical question of how and from where the "renovation" of political cadres might take place. Essentially, the senior Army leadership in July and August, 1969, placed their bets on the ability to imbue entrepreneural groups with a sense of "national security and development doctrine" through the ESG and its extension courses, while depending on public sector–linked technocrats to counterbalance any excessively free enterprise orientation on the part of the "new breed" of businessmen and industrialists.

Thus the Army General Staff appeared to welcome the call of Commercial Association President Ruy Gomes de Almeida to his fellow businessmen to take an active part in the "renovation" of the parties, and looked favorably on indications that the entrepreneural strata as well as military men would compete with the established politicians in the ARENA municipal conventions.[13]

---

[12] The contradictions in the regime's thinking and the division between the more authoritarian and traditionally liberal wings of its civilian side are perceptively explored in "Democracia partidária-modêlo brasileiro," *Visão*, June 20, 1969, pp. 23–26.

[13] These impressions are based on conversations with a number of general officers and businessmen in Rio de Janeiro during July and August, 1969. Gomes de Almeida's addresses of June 3 and 4 are reprinted in *Empresariado e Renovação Nacional* (Rio de Janeiro, 1969), as well as *Revista dos Classes Productoras*, XXXII, No. 1020 (June, 1969), 6–21. See also "Uma presença adequada de empresarios na política," *Jornal do Brasil*, July 17, 1969. A speech by Gomes de

Other important currents of thought, not yet represented at the level of the Armed Forces high command, but already finding expression among a minority of the lower-ranking generals, were also considering the conflict between the security aims of the revolution and the pragmatic long-run necessity (if not more immediate desirability) of a return to a civilian regime. While varying in the degree of urgency felt (along with differences on priorities and timing), these elements generally agreed upon agrarian reform, development of the interior, and appeal to nationalist sentiment as prerequisites for the establishment of a viable relationship between a military-civilian government and the civilian body politic. Many combined authoritarian leanings with deep-seated reformist tendencies, a factor that helped blur ideological distinctions. Interacting with widespread feeling among the less authoritarian officers that the military had to stay in power for some time to come, in spite of its increasing unpopularity, to ensure that the "subversives" and "corrupt" politicians who had been purged were not allowed to return; these orientations contributed to an often sincere, albeit at times cynical, position that "we would like to turn the government back to civilians, if we could find any leaders with an adequate concept of national security."

The Army faction supporting Albuquerque Lima sought not only to consolidate leadership over the *linha dura,* but also to form an alliance if possible with remaining Castelista elements in support of an "authentic" revolution. The Castelistas, for their part, were still intensely loyal to the late ex-President's memory and principles; they felt that Costa e Silva had capitalized on the frustration of the middle mass of the military and the dissatisfaction of the hard liners to curtail, if not positively hamstring, Castelo's efforts after October, 1965. In their view, the fundamental shortcomings of the revolution stemmed from Costa's

---

Almeida's São Paulo counterpart on "O Papel das Forças Armadas no Apoio a Iniciativa Privada," is reprinted in the same issue of *Jornal do Brasil.* Brazilian business and industrial interest groups publish a large number and wide variety of magazines, bulletins, and newsletters. Among the more useful for following their perceptions of national developments are the *Revista das Classes Productoras,* monthly organ of the Confederação dos Associações Comercias do Brasil and the Associação Comercial do Rio de Janeiro; *Problemas Brasileiros,* monthly publication of the Conselho Tecnico de Econômia, Sociologiá e Política da Federação do Comércio do Estado de São Paulo; and the *Boletim Informativo,* weekly review of the Federação e Centro das Industrias do Estado de São Paulo.

undercutting of what had been a rational and comprehensive program for national recovery and institutional reform. While recognizing the weaknesses of their own administration in the fields of agriculture and education, the Castelistas perceived this situation as worsening rather than being rectified under the successor government. Like the supporters of Albuquerque Lima, for whom they generally demonstrated little respect and less affection, the Castelistas were by mid-1969 convinced that the Costa e Silva administration was a failure and that the revolution could not afford two more years of "misgovernment, drift, and political decay." But they were not yet prepared to act.

2. THE COLLAPSE OF THE COSTA E SILVA GOVERNMENT

The purge of Colonel Boaventura, rather than serving as a warning to the dissatisfied officers, was only the curtain raiser for a more serious military crisis. Shortly thereafter, four-star General Augusto César Castro Moniz de Aragão, who from 1964 to 1968 had presided over the prestigious and influential Clube Militar, took issue with the Army Minister over his handling of the Boaventura affair. When Lyra Tavares replied to the effect that this was not his business, Moniz de Aragão, in mid-June, denounced alleged acts of favoritism involving the President's brother, son, father-in-law, and brother-in-law. He also charged that excessive expenditures of government funds on glamorous highway and bridge projects were designed to build up Transport Minister Andreazza, a long-time close associate of Costa e Silva, as his prospective successor. Moniz de Aragão's call for a "pure, austere, and efficient" government before the dissatisfied younger officers should "unleash a storm which would carry us all to chaos and the unforeseeable" led to his suspension from the Army high command, but won him new-found popularity among the field-grade officers.[14]

---

[14] The heated letters exchanged between Moniz de Aragão and Lyra Tavares did not appear in the heavily censured press, but circulated in xeroxed and thermo-faxed copies to key political figures and opinion leaders. The one with the greatest impact, that of June 17 from Moniz de Aragão to the Army Minister, speaks *inter alia* of a personality cult; "public scandal" over the naming of the President's brother to the Rio Grande do Sul Tribunal of Accounts; the unjustified return to active service of retired General Severo Barbosa, father of Dona Yolanda; Colonel Alcio Costa e Silva's questionable business dealings; and the "huge funds chan-

Although for a brief period in mid-July the moon landing eclipsed politics almost as completely as a soccer championship or carnival, the stepped-up activities of terrorist bands and vigorous government countermeasures soon contributed to a sense of growing crisis, and the possibility of a "colonels' coup" to replace Costa e Silva with a younger and more energetic general became a favorite topic of discussion among political analysts.[15]

Urban violence and terrorism—still a relatively strange and disturbing phenomenon to the Brazilian military, much less the civilian population—assumed dramatic proportions in mid-year, just in time to undercut moves toward reconstitutionalization by strengthening the hands of the most security-minded regime elements. On July 16, extremists destroyed a São Paulo television transmitter located a few short blocks from the statehouse, bringing to three the total of such dramatic destructions of mass communications facilities in a period of a week.[16]

---

neled to the Minister of Transportation for the realization of a dubious policy, while the Armed Forces, particularly the Army, are resenting the lack of means essential to the defense of the regime." Giving further substance to Moniz de Aragão's allegations was the appearance of a lavish special supplement to popular newsmagazine *Visão* for July 18 on "A Política dos Transportes no Brasil," with a cover picture of a tanned, trim, and pearly-toothed Andreazza standing before a map of Brazil showing proposed development of inland waterways. The contents of this elaborate 156-page public relations work carries home the Transportation Minister's slogan of "Integrate the Country for the Future." A massive special edition of photo-magazine *Manchete* on "Progresso do Brasil," also gave greatest emphasis to the highway system, railroad network, shipping and ports—all parts of Andreazza's bureaucratic realm.

[15] A thoughtful, if in light of censorship, restrained look at the country's situation less than a month before the September "white coup" is Luiz Alberto Bahia's unsigned lead article in *Visão,* August 15, 1969. The regime's political-constitutional dilemma is defined as "either adapt the revolution to representative democracy, with all the risks which this entails for national security in the form conceptualized by the regime, or adapt representative democracy to the revolution, in a species of authoritarian state of law of the Franco, Salazar, or Integralist type." Bahia also notes the point, observed clearly in my own conversations with Army leaders, that the military are tired of encountering the same old political faces while their own institution provides for continuous renovation of leadership cadres through compulsory retirement. Indeed, no one remains more than a decade in the "Senate of the Generals" nor more than four years on its steering committee.

[16] While the Rio de Janeiro upper class viewed this development as political terrorism (64 per cent to 8 per cent for "coincidences"), the middle class was less certain (50 per cent to 32 per cent), and the lower class quite skeptical (32 per

This brought to a head the confrontation between São Paulo Governor Abreu Sodré and the more security-oriented elements within the military, who demanded that the state's top officials entrusted with the maintenance of public order be replaced by high-ranking Army officers. After several generals expressed a lack of interest in the post, the Governor assumed personal charge of the public security department.[17]

On July 26, naval intelligence announced the arrest of twenty-seven members of "Revolutionary Movement 8." The MR8 was founded in 1968 by Niteroi University students and originally active in Paraná, but it returned to the Rio de Janeiro area at the beginning of 1969 to acquire funds through a series of bank robberies. The naval investigation revealed that a branch manager of the Bank of Brazil had embezzled NCr 3 million, part of which he gave to the MR8 and part to the Popular Revolutionary Communist Party (PCPR), while depositing the rest to his own account in a Swiss bank. Not to be overshadowed by the Navy, the First Army announced solution of a major robbery that had occurred in May, while General Sarmento pledged that troops of his command would "meet violence with violence." The wave of arrests of suspected "subversives" included that in São Paulo of Ricardo Zaratini, author of the 1966 bomb attempt in Recife against Costa e Silva's life. A bombing of Cardinal Agnello Rossi's residence on August 5 was linked to the left-wing revolutionaries under Carlos Marighela, while an unsuccessful hold-up attempt in Rio de Janeiro on August 7 led to the

---

cent to 34 per cent). These figures come from the Pesquisa JB/Marplan reported in *Jornal do Brasil,* July 27, 1969. One out of six respondents who viewed these acts as political terrorism approved of terrorist tactics, 79 per cent expressed disapproval. "São Paulo Contra o Terrorismo, *Manchete,* August 2, 1969, pp. 38–41, covers the destruction of the three television stations. The author, in São Paulo during the first week of August, personally observed an incident of politically motivated automobile theft.

[17] *Correio da Manhã,* July 30, 1969; *Folha de S. Paulo,* August 5, 1969; and *Jornal do Brasil,* August 5, 1969, analyze this episode. For a midyear roundup on terrorist activity, see "Qual Será o Próximo Passo de Terror?" *Veja,* July 30, 1969, pp. 16–18. The new outburst of terrorism in São Paulo coincided with the report of an IPM looking into the June, 1968, bombing of Second Army headquarters authored by the Popular Revolutionary Vanguard (VPR) headed by ex-Captain Carlos Lamarca and Communist Party ex-congressman Carlos Marighela. For details consult *O Globo,* August 5, 1969.

imprisonment of José Duarte dos Santos, a sailor court-martialed in 1964 for mutiny.[18]

Paradoxically, the very success of the crackdown on the violence-inclined leftists was a decisive factor in their decision to kidnap the U.S. Ambassador, and this embarrassing episode contributed to sentiment among the military that a more effective executive was needed in place of Costa e Silva. Thus, while the rest of August appeared a period of relative calm and attention turned again to moves toward normalization and the reopening of Congress, it was but the lull before the storm. Andreazza's declaration that consideration of the succession question be left for the second half of 1970 so that the government could concentrate its undivided attention on the tasks at hand would shortly seem almost grotesquely distant from the reality of impending crisis.

As Brazil approached its September 7 Independence Day celebration, its continuing institutional crisis and leadership vacuum remained unresolved. Instead of the long-awaited normalization, including the reopening of Congress—closed since the December "coup within the coup"—they had been led to expect, Brazil's 93 million inhabitants were informed on Sunday, August 31, that President Artur da Costa e Silva had suffered a "circulatory impediment" and that responsibility for governing the country had been assumed temporarily by a junta composed of the three Armed Forces Ministers. Since this move meant that Vice President Pedro Aleixo, the top ranking civilian within the regime, was being barred from assuming power even temporarily and given the notoriously right-wing identification of two members of the junta, Brazilians were quickly alerted to the fact that for the fourth time since the military came to power in 1964, apparent progress toward political normalcy had been superseded by an even more arbitrary regime of

[18] The MR8 story is detailed in the daily papers of the period, particularly *Jornal do Brasil,* July 26, 29, 30, August 2 and 5, 1969, as well as Murilo Melo Filho, "MR-8 As Armas da Subversão," *Manchete,* August 9, 1969, pp. 28–29. The First Army investigation is reported in *O Globo,* August 4, 1969; *Ultima Hora,* August 6, 1969; and *Jornal do Brasil,* August 6, 1969, which also has an article on the São Paulo bombing, as does *Correio da Manhã* of that date and of August 8, 1969. General Sarmento's declaration is carried in *O Globo* and *Jornal do Brasil,* August 8, 1969, and the news of Zaratini's arrest in *Correio da Manhã,* August 1, 1969.

exceptional powers. Once again, the Armed Forces' perception of the imperatives of the "revolution of 1964" overrode the already frequently modified constitutional norms. For the fourth time since the March 31, 1964, coup (under the Revolutionary Supreme Command in early April, 1964; in the October, 1965, crisis; in December, 1968; and now under the junta), the hard liners were able to convince much of the middle mass of the officer corps that a tougher attitude was necessary to preserve the revolution.

The Moniz de Aragão incident had left the Army Minister substantially demoralized. The undermining of the President's position became apparent when First Army Commander Sizeno Sarmento first reportedly cautioned against further punishment of General Moniz de Aragão and then vetoed Costa e Silva's attempt to name General Emílio Garrastazú Médici as Army Minister. By late August, power within the Army was shifting toward Chief of Staff Antônio Carlos Muricy, and rumors of an eventual "colonels' coup" were rife. To head off such a rupture of hierarchy, some senior officers advocated a preemptive *golpe*. Their opportunity came with Costa e Silva's physical incapacitation.

Thus, in spite of its quick resort to force and its outward show of vigorous action, the caretaker junta was in a weak position. The major threat to it came not from the yet relatively disorganized civilian opposition, but rather from within the Armed Forces themselves. The kidnaping of U.S. Ambassador C. Burke Elbrick on September 4 served to accentuate and aggravate the already deep cleavage within the Brazilian officer corps. The senior member of the junta, Admiral Augusto Hamman Rademaker Grünwald, who had played a secondary role in the short-lived Supreme Revolutionary Command of April 1–9, 1964, over which Costa e Silva presided as War Minister, was poorly regarded by many of the Army's field grade officers. His prominence if not predominance within the junta was all but intolerable to the several contenders for political leadership among the Army's senior generals. Indeed, his influence within the junta was largely a function of the weakness of Army Minister Lyra Tavares' position as a result of the internal Army crisis.

In this context, the kidnaping of the U.S. Ambassador was a well-conceived gesture to demonstrate the existence of a vigorous underground opposition and to attain maximum international publicity for its objectives while at the same time demonstrating the regime's lack of authority. It placed the junta in an extremely delicate position, for in satisfying the desire of the United States to safeguard Ambassador El-brick's life, the military ministers further aliented important elements within the three services already disenchanted with the regime.

The kidnaping of the United States Ambassador was apparently planned by a group of newspapermen and ex-student leaders, heretofore associated with the so-called "festive left" (*esquerda festiva*), a group of intellectuals roughly comparable to the "parlor pinks" of the 1930's and 1940's in the United States. Frustrated by the degree to which the regime's disruption of the clandestine apparatus in Rio de Janeiro during July and clamp-down on the opposition in São Paulo were enabling it to project a strong and efficient image abroad, they at last decided to put into operation one of the symbolic gestures they had discussed at their frequent informal social gatherings which served as a means of letting off steam. Terrorist activities had received relatively little atten-tion abroad, and Brazilian political journalists, forbidden since Decem-ber from publishing critical articles, while at the same time witnessing developments viewed by them as disastrous to the country's interests, eventually required an outlet for their pent-up resentments. This they found in the Ambassador's kidnaping.

By demanding publicity for an opposition manifesto as a prime condition for Elbrick's release, they served notice that such revolution-ary groups as the MR-8, VPR, and National Liberating Action (ALN) were still functioning. The requirement for the freeing of fifteen political prisoners underscored the repressive nature of the regime, while the careful selection of the individuals involved guaranteed internal dissen-sion within the military. In particular, long-time Communist Party leader in Recife Gregorio Bezerra, Ricardo Zaratini (recently arrested after escaping punishment for the 1966 bomb attempt against Costa e Silva), student leader Vladimir Palmeira, José Duarte dos Santos (newly cap-tured after a long manhunt), newspaperman Flávio Tavares (held re-sponsible for a guerrilla movement in Goiás) and ex-Sergeant Onofre Pinto, leader of the assassination of U.S. Army Captain Charles Chand-ler, were individuals the right-wing military radicals were very unhappy to see set at liberty.[19] Both paratroops and naval officers engaged in acts of indiscipline attempting to thwart the release of the prisoners, while leaders of the hard-line colonels had advocated an ultimatum to the kidnapers to free the Ambassador or see their fifteen friends summarily executed. Only partially mollified by the regime's round-up of hundreds of suspected oppositionists and decreeing of the death penalty in cases of terrorism, a punishment alien to Brazil since independence, the *linha dura* elements were not reconciled to the permanence of the junta, preferring a stronger new government headed by an Army general more closely tied to their way of thinking.

Thus Brazil entered a month-long search to find a new government, with disagreement within the Armed Forces not only over who would be the new chief executive, but also over the length of his mandate: whether he should serve out Costa's remaining period, be granted a full term, or (in the name of maximum continuity in the future) be given both. The solution reached, far from giving promise of future stability, was a compromise designed to avert an open power struggle. The deep divisions evident within the Armed Forces and the continued dissatisfaction of important younger elements with the outcome of the succession contest all but assured that future "revolutions within the revolution" would come, perhaps long before the scheduled end of the longterm lease on the presidential palace presented to General Garrastazú Médici by his fellow "Cardinals and Archbishops" of the Brazilian military.[20]

[19] The Brazilian newspapers and newsmagazines of the first half of September contain very heavy coverage of these events, albeit with a careful eye to the regime's censors, particularly owing to the arrests of many journalists during the investigations. The most comprehensive journalistic coverage in the United States was that of *The New York Times* which in August ran articles by Joseph Novitski on Albuquerque Lima and the impending military crisis, as well as a roundup on terrorism on August 15; Novitski's articles on the kidnapping appeared daily from September 5 through 12. A run-down on the released prisoners is contained in an article by Juan de Onis in *The New York Times,* September 9, 1969. "A Doença de Presidente," *O Cruzeiro,* September 11, 1969, pp. 4–5, and "O Primeiro Dia," *Manchete,* September 13, 1969, pp. 4–10, are useful articles on the installation of the *junta. Jornal do Brasil,* September 8, 1969, contains the results of a public opinion poll indicating little interest in the party convention and leadership elections scheduled for the following week.

[20] Referring to the succession question in July and August, senior generals repeatedly maintained that "we are the Cardinals of the military institution, and like those of the Church we will not permit a bishop or deacon to be the new pope."

3. DISUNITY, SUCCESSION, AND THE QUEST FOR VIABILITY

Even while the junta was grappling with the complications introduced by the Elbrick affair, a growing number of voices within the military were calling for a more permanent solution to the succession crisis. These were opposed by elements closely linked to Costa e Silva, who hoped that their political sponsor would eventually be able to reassume the functions of his office. Indeed, at first considerable speculation existed over the degree of Costa e Silva's incapacitation and even whether his illness was more political than physical. (As a popular play on words had it, the President had been "impeded from circulating" rather than suffering an impediment in his circulatory system.) The politically well informed knew that there had been considerable military opposition to the President's recently announced decision to hold partial municipal elections on November 30, and that the same groups were even more adamantly opposed to the planned reopening of Congress. Although in the week preceding his collapse Costa e Silva had given in on the questions of direct election of governors and choice of his successor in 1971 by the new rather than the lame duck Congress, he had insisted on the modifications of the Constitution being issued as an amendment (a means less offensive to the civilian politicians) rather than proclaimed through an Institutional Act.[21]

On August 27, the military ministers had informed the President of the extensive unrest within each of the services over his proposed normalization of political life and reiterated their reservations concerning the constitutional revisions in the form finally worked out between Costa and Vice President Pedro Aleixo the preceding day. On August 28, it was announced that the President was suffering from a bad case of influenza, and the next day he arrived in Rio de Janeiro already manifesting signs of partial paralysis. Not until late on the afternoon of Sunday, August 31, however, was the public informed that Costa had

[21] Costa's position on these matters is discussed by his press secretary, Carlos Chagas, in the initial installment of a series of articles in *O Estado de S. Paulo* and *O Globo* beginning on January 7, 1970. Scheduled for subsequent publication as a book, "Os 113 Dias de Angústia" covers the period from August 26 through Costa's death on December 17, 1969. "O Homen que Féz a Constituição," *Veja,* August 27, 1969, pp. 16–17, analyzes Vice President Pedro Aleixo's role in working for the reopening of Congress and influencing Costa in favor of normalization.

suffered a "circulatory crisis with neurological manifestations." Even then, the full extent of the presidential illness remained a matter of doubt and speculation, heightened by the arrival on September 12 of a renowned French specialist, Dr. François L'hermite, who within a week expressed the opinion that Costa e Silva would recover full control of his speech and right-side muscular functions only after prolonged rest and therapy.[22]

During the early stages of its existence, the junta made extensive use of punitive powers, cassating the mandates of Bahia Federal Deputy Oliveira Brito and Rio de Janeiro Congresswoman Julia Steinbruch on September 12. The next day, fourteen professors of the University of Minas Gerais, an institution which had been spared in the April, 1969, academic purge, were compulsorily retired. On September 30, Senator Pedro Ludovico (the father of cassated Goiás Governor Mauro Borges Teixeira) and seven federal deputies—including PSP leader Arnaldo Cedeira and three wives elected in 1966 to replace their purged husbands —lost their mandates and political rights. Institutional Acts (seven of which had already been issued between December, 1969, and August, 1969) became commonplace during the junta's tenure in office. Institutional Act No. 12 of August 31 established the provisional regime; No. 13 of September 5 provided for banishment of subversives (to legitimize the release of the fifteen prisoners); and No. 14 of the same date established the death penalty (overruling Article 150 of the 1967 Constitution).[23]

In spite of an emotional protest by Transportation Minister Andreazza that to discuss selection of a new president without consulting Costa bordered on treason, by mid-September the rough outline of succession procedures had been worked out among the highest ranks of the military and selection mechanisms were taking shape. The 118

[22] Quoted in "Discute-se Sucessão," *Veja,* September 17, 1969, pp. 18–21. The story of developments during the rule of the *junta* has been pieced together from the Carlos Chagas articles and daily coverage in *Jornal do Brasil,* as well as a number of contemporary articles in *Veja, Visão, Manchete,* and *Fatos e Fotos.*

[23] For the text of AI 12, see *O Estado de S. Paulo,* September 2, 1969, or *Veja* September 3, 1969; for that of AI 13, consult *O Estado de S. Paulo,* September 9, 1969; AI 14 is reprinted in *ibid.,* September 10, 1969, and analyzed in "O Pena de Morte," *Veja,* September 17, 1969, pp. 26–29; with AI 15 (postponing municipal elections where mayors had been cassated) in *O Estado de S. Paulo,* September 11, 1969.

Army generals on active duty (as well as the sixty admirals and sixty-one Air Force general officers) were each to discuss the problems, goals, and priorities of the revolution with their subordinates and sound out sentiments on the succession question. On the basis of the top choices of each senior officer, generals of four-star rank were to compile a list of the three preferred candidates of their commands. These were subsequently consolidated into a list for each service and finally narrowed down to a single choice for the Armed Forces. Thus, while the process of consultation would reach down to the level of colonels, the great electors would be the seven members of the High Command of the Armed Forces, a body which had never formally met since its creation several years before. In this system, suggested by the Navy, the military ministers (who comprised the junta), the three service chiefs of staff, and the Chief of the Armed Forces General Staff constituted the final electoral college. With just over two-thirds of the Army's generals based in the Rio de Janeiro area, the ex-capital was to be the most important arena of the intramural maneuvering which preceded the final choice.

The Brazilian Army's command structure, which in September, 1969, came to be the country's major political party, includes twelve military regions (RM's), each under a three-star general, which are grouped into four armies headed by full generals. The First Army comprises the Rio de Janeiro-based 1st Military Region and the Minas Gerais-centered 4th RM. The Second Army, which in 1969 contained ten generals, is made up of São Paulo's 2nd RM and the 9th RM in Matto Grosso. The Third Army, with a total of fifteen generals, combines the 3rd RM of Rio Grande do Sul and the 5th RM (Paraná and Santa Catarina). The Fourth Army, which included only seven generals, is made up of the 6th RM (Bahia and Sergipe), the 7th RM (Alagoas, Pernambuco, Paraíba, and Rio Grande do Norte) and the 10th RM (Piauí, Maranhão, and Ceará). The 8th RM based in Pará and adjoining territories, the 11th RM (Goiás and the Brasília Military Command), and the 12th RM (Amazon Military Command) are independent of the four armies.

These field commands occupy fewer than half the Army's senior generals. Other posts of four-star rank whose occupants took part in the 1969 "election" include that of Army Minister, Army Chief of Staff, and the heads of the three major departments of the Army Ministry:

General Provisions (DPG), Personnel (DGP), and Production and Works (DPO). (The most important major components of each of these are in turn commanded by three-star generals; the others by two-star officers.) The Commandant of the National War College (ESG) is by custom also a four-star general. The Superior Military Tribunal (TSM) provides a prestigious place for deserving senior generals facing retirement, or for side-lined active-duty generals with inconvenient political orientations. Fully half the generals participating in the selection of Brazil's new President occupied these desk jobs and, in varying degrees, were out of touch with the sentiment of the middle-grade officers exercising troop commands.

Among the four-star generals, Garrastazú Médici, Orlando Geisel, and Antônio Muricy soon emerged as the leading candidates for the presidency. Jurandir Mamede and Sizeno Sarmento took an active part in the deliberations (the latter ruled out of contention by his history of heart trouble). Souza Aguiar was excluded from consideration (owing to his absence from the country at the United Nations), as was Moniz de Aragão, who was still suspended from the Army High Command for his earlier clashes with Lyra Tavares. Second Army Commander José Canavarro Pereira was junior to the other four-star generals, while Souto Malan's influence was undermined by his abrupt transfer from the Fourth Army to the desk job of Quartermaster General (Department of General Provisions). During the early stages of the succession crisis, the name of Labor Minister Jarbas Passarinho, himself a retired General, was put forth as a possible contender, but it soon became apparent that the only real rival to the four-star generals' choice would be Albuquerque Lima, who was actively campaigning and who in mid-September released a position paper designed to calm fears among influential business circles that he was a radical nationalist.[24]

The Castelistas, who had been taken aback on September 4 by the sudden death of Brigadier Faria Lima (the popular ex-Mayor of São Paulo, whom they had been considering as a presidential hopeful for

[24] *The New York Times,* September 18 and 28, 1969. The statement of the Central Commission of the National Conference of Brazilian Bishops calling for normalization is contained in *O Estado de S. Paulo,* September 21, 1969, and analyzed in *The New York Times* of that date. Useful interviews with Andreazza and General Meira Mattos were carried in *Veja,* September 24, 1969, pp. 3–6, and October 1, 1969, pp. 3–6.

the scheduled 1971 elections), saw General Orlando Geisel as their best hope, but he did not strike many of his fellow generals as prime presidential material. The consultations reportedly showed Garrastazú Médici as the strongest candidate among the field commands (the leader in his own Third Army as well as in the Second Army, runner up to Sizeno Sarmento among the First Army's generals, and trailing Albuquerque Lima and Geisel in the Fourth Army). While Albuquerque Lima finished in the show position in the First, Second, and Third Armies, as only a three-star general he was weaker within the Army Ministry than Armed Forces Chief of Staff Geisel, who ranked second to Guarrastazú Médici on the final Army list.

In the face of discontent among the younger officers, the senior generals agreed upon a coalescing of Castelista and Costista elements behind General Emílio Garrastazú Médici. While the presidential choice thus fell to a man who had been quite close to Costa e Silva, the War Ministry was to be given to General Orlando Geisel (whose brother had been one of Castelo's intimate associates), with General Muricy remaining as Army Chief of Staff. The Navy and right-wing militants in the Army and Air Force were granted the satisfaction of seeing Admiral Rademaker selected as Vice President. Air Force stability was ensured by retaining that service's representative on the junta as Air Minister in the new government.[25]

Finally given the formal endorsement of the High Command of the Armed Forces on October 7, Garrastazú Médici addressed the Brazilian public on radio and television. Admitting that "Brazil is still far from being a developed nation, living under a regime which we cannot consider fully democratic," he set the "installation of democracy" and the "bases of our social and economic development" as the goals of his administration. Calling for the collaboration of all classes and regions, he excoriated the pre-1964 system, while promising a "profound transformation" of existing institutions. Liberty was pledged to those groups which freed themselves from "subversive and corrupting" influences,

[25] Joseph Novitski, in *The New York Times,* October 6, 1969, recounts Albuquerque Lima's dissatisfaction and the dissent to the selection procedure entered by ex-Navy Minister Ernesto de Mello Batista. Other evidence of military opposition to the choice of Garrastazú Médici is contained in the series of articles by Carlos Chagas cited above.

with the people to be protagonists rather than spectators in the "march for development." Violence would be met with violence, but all Brazilians were invited to "use all the stones available to build the future" rather than to look back or throw rocks.[26]

On October 17, the wide-ranging Amendment No. 1 to the 1967 Constitution was finally promulgated. It significantly broadened the authority of the federal government to intervene in the states "to end disturbance of order, threat of its irruption, or corruption of the public power." [27] Limitations were placed upon the number and pay of state legislators, and municipal elections were to be held simultaneously throughout the country. Parliamentary immunity was severely limited, with provisions of the National Security Law overriding the rights of federal legislators (Article 32).

Conflict of interest (incompatability) provisions were greatly strengthened, while the grounds for expulsion were substantially broadened to include, *inter alia,* acts of "infidelity to party" (spelled out in detail in Article 152). Time limits for congressional consideration of presidential legislative initiatives were made more stringent (Article 51), while the executive's decree-law powers were amplified. The Superior Military Tribunal, whose jurisdiction had been broadened by the National Security Law, had its essentially military composition reaffirmed and strengthened; not only were ten of its fifteen members to be active duty flag officers, but two of the civilians were to be selected from its career service of prosecutors (Article 128). The death penalty, along with banishment and confiscation of property, was introduced for "external, psychological, subversive, or revolutionary war" (Article 153). Combined with the provision in the 1967 Constitution for decade-long deprivation of political rights for "intention of subversion of the democratic regime or corruption," this article gave the government a more

[26] *O Estado de S. Paulo,* October 8, 1969. There is a discussion of the speech and a biographic sketch of Garrastazú Médici in *The New York Times,* October 8, 1969. Consult also "Garrastazú Médici, presidente disconocido," *Visión,* December 19, 1969, pp. 22–30. A public opinion poll published in *Jornal do Brasil,* October 19–20, 1969, indicated that only 24 per cent of the Rio de Janeiro public had heard or read their new ruler's speech. Of the minority who were informed on this matter, nearly four-fifths rated the address as excellent or good, terming it in most cases "firm" and "sincere."

[27] Article 10, paragraph III of *Constituição da República Federativa do Brasil, Emenda No. 1* (Brasília, 1969), p. 13.

substantial legal basis for curbing opponents of the regime. The duration of a "state of siege" decree was extended from 60 to 180 days. All actions of the junta, as well as those of preceding regimes under Institutional and Complementary Acts, were expressly excluded from any form of judicial review (Article 182), and the Institutional Acts promulgated since December 13, 1968, were to remain in full effect for as long as the President wished. The presidential term of Garrastazú Médici would run until March 15, 1974 (Article 183). Explicit provisions were made for Costa e Silva's income and expenses (Article 184), and special benefits for veterans of World War II were written into the Constitution (Article 197). Thus, the junta presented the new President with a substantially modified Constitution to go into effect with his taking office on October 30. It also decreed a further strengthening of the National Security Law and a more stringent ineligibilities law.[28]

On October 14, the presidency was formally declared vacant by Institutional Act No. 16. Complementary Acts No. 72 and 73 summoned Congress to meet on October 22, with the presidential election to take place on October 25. Thus, Congress, after more than ten months of a military-imposed recess, was summoned back to Brasília to ratify the military's choice for president and vice-president. On the appointed day, by a vote of 293 in favor and 76 abstentions, Garrastazú Médici and Rademaker were duly declared occupants of the presidency and vice presidency. The MDB, its representation reduced from 127 to 66 in the Chamber of Deputies by the purges of the December, 1968–September, 1969, period of dictatorial rule, decided to assume a very prudent stance to avoid the possibility of another closing of Congress or cancellation of the congressional and state elections scheduled for November, 1970. The government party, chastized by the cassation of twenty-eight of its representatives who had stood up against the military in the 1968 crisis, pledged to cooperate fully with the new President.[29]

[28] *O Estado de S. Paulo,* September 28 and October 24, 1969.

[29] On the reopening of Congress and constitution of the new government see "Os Novos Limites do Congresso," *Veja,* October 22, 1969, pp. 16–22; "Médici e o Govêrno de participação," *Visão,* October 24, 1969, pp. 21–26; Murilo Melo Filho, "Médici, Que é o Nôvo Presidente," *Manchete,* October 25, 1969, pp. 4–11; "As primeiras opções do Presidente" and "Congresso em busca do tempo perdido," *Visão,* November 7, 1969, pp. 19–25; and Murilo Melo Filho, "Mudaram os Tempos ou Mudou a Oposição?" *Fatos e Fotos,* November 27, 1969, pp. 24–27.

General Garrastazú Médici bore less impressive career credentials for the presidency than had his military predecessors. Born in December, 1905, the son of Basque and Italian immigrants, he was a member of the 1927 military academy class (which also contained Juracy Magalhães, Jurandir Mamede, Idálio Sardenberg, José Canavarro Pereira, Alvaro da Silva Braga, Carvalho Lisboa, and Adalberto Pereira dos Santos). He graduated from the General Staff and Command School in 1941 and was promoted to major in 1943, lieutenant colonel in 1948, and colonel in 1953. He was Costa e Silva's Chief of Staff when the latter commanded the Third Military Region; in 1961 he received his first stars, subsequently serving during the Goulart years with a Cavalry division in Matto Grosso and as Commandant of the Military Academy at Agulas Negras. Sent by Castelo as Military Attaché in Washington and Brazil's representative on the Inter-American Defense Board, he was promoted to divisional general in July, 1965, and assigned to the Third Military Region, based in Pôrto Alegre. After an assignment as subchief of the Army General Staff, he was selected by Costa e Silva to head the SNI. Promoted to four-star rank in early 1969, he was named to command the powerful Third Army.

The government organized by Garrastazú Médici was, on the civilian side, essentially one of technicians rather than politicians, but military political considerations were given due weight. Thus, Justice Minister Alfredo Buzaid was a São Paulo lawyer and university administrator; Agricultural Minister Luiz Fernando Cirne Lima was a young Rio Grande do Sul agronomist (and son of the 1966 MDB gubernatorial candidate); Labor Minister Julio de Carvalho Barata, an ESG graduate, had been president of the Superior Labor Tribunal; Minister of Industry and Commerce Fabio Riodi Yassuda had headed the highly successful Cotia Agricultural Cooperative in São Paulo; Health Minister Francisco de Paula da Rocha Lagoa was a medical researcher and member of the ESG class of 1963. Career diplomat Mario Gibson Barbosa, a 1951 ESG graduate, returned from his post as Ambassador in Washington to become Foreign Minister. João Paulo dos Reis Veloso, a thirty-eight-year-old economist, educated in the United States, who had headed the Social and Economic Planning Institute of the Ministry of Planning under both Campos and Beltrão, moved up to be Minister.

These seven civilian technical experts joined two similar holdovers from the Costa e Silva cabinet, Finance Minister Antônio Delfim Netto and Minister of Mines and Energy Antônio Dias Leite.

On the military side, Senator Jarbas Passarinho moved from the Labor ministry to Education, José Costa Cavalcante remained as Minister of Interior, and Mario David Andreazza was held over as Transportation Minister. Orlando Geisel, second to the new President on the High Command's preference list, became Army Minister, and Admiral Adalberto de Barros Nunes moved up from Chief of Naval Operations to replace the Vice President-elect as Navy Minister. Márcio de Souza e Mello remained as Air Minister. Garrastazú Médici selected Colonel Higino Corsetti, a former instructor at the Military Academy, to take over the least important of the ministries, that of Communications. João Leitão de Abreu, a Pôrto Alegre lawyer and brother-in-law of General Lyra Tavares, was named Chief of the Civil Cabinet, with fifty-one-year old Brigadier General João Batista de Oliveira Figueiredo, who had been Garrastazú Médici's Chief of Staff in both the SNI and Third Army, as Chief of the Military Cabinet and Secretary General of the National Security Council. General Carlos Alberto da Fontoura was retained as head of the SNI.[30] A young economic planning technician, Marcos Vinicius Pratini de Morais, was appointed to head a new Office of General Coordination attached to the presidency, with special responsibility for watching over the new administration's plan for mobilizing popular support behind a dramatic development program (a feat which Kubitschek had accomplished quite successfully during the late 1950's).

In the two months before this blueprint for development, baptized "Project Brazil: Great Power," or even a preliminary set of impact projects could be readied, two deaths captured the attention of the Brazilian public, that of revolutionary terrorist leader Carlos Marighela and that of Costa e Silva. The former all but eclipsed the national party conventions finally held in November, while the ex-President's fatal heart attack —which called for a period of official mourning—undercut his successor's efforts to quickly follow up on his inaugural eve declaration which

[30] Biographies of the cabinet can be found in *O Estado de S. Paulo* and *Jornal do Brasil,* October 28, 1969.

reiterated the theme that "the people cannot be spectators in the process of development, but must be among the actors." [31]

On November 4, police in São Paulo caught Marighela in an ambush and shot to death the leader of the violence-inclined wing of the Communist movement. This was part of a general crackdown on suspected urban terrorists, which was even more severe than the wave of arrests following the Elbrick affair two months earlier. Arrests of a number of clergy and seminary students accused of aiding radical leaders to escape from the security forces' manhunt led to renewed conflict between the government and the Catholic Church.[32] Accusations of torture of suspected terrorists brought a tightening of press censorship, but finally elicited pledges from the Justice Minister and President to curb such abuses.[33]

With public attention still focused on terrorism and repression, the national conventions of ARENA and the MDB met in Brasília on November 20.[34] Garrastazú Médici's hand-picked candidate, ex-Civil

[31] The speech is summarized in *O Estado de S. Paulo,* October 28, 1969.

[32] See "Estratégia para Matar o Terrorismo," *Veja,* November 12, 1969, pp. 22–30; Ivan Alves, "Marighela: A Ultima Batalha do Terror," *Fatos e Fotos,* November 20, 1969, pp. 8–13; and Murilo Melo Filho, "Como Morreu Marighela," *Manchete,* November 22, 1969, pp. 12–18. "O Igreja mais perto do Govêrno," *Visão,* August 15, 1969, pp. 58–61, portrays the relatively conciliatory attitude of the Catholic hierarchy on the eve of the succession crisis (as by a vote of 70–120 the National Commission of Brazilian Bishops disapproved a document on "The Church versus the Government" prepared by its progressive wing). "Brazil: entre la cruz e la espada," *The Economist para América Latina,* November 26–December 12, 1969, pp. 11–12, places total arrests at nearly 5,000. See also articles on the clergy and subversion in *Veja,* November 19, 1969, pp. 29–33 and November 26, 1969, pp. 34–35.

[33] "A Violência Fora da Lei," *Veja,* December 3, 1969, pp. 18–24. A convenient source on events of 1969 is the Center for Inter-American Relations, *Brazil: 1969* (New York, 1970).

[34] Pesquisa JB/Marplan, published in *Jornal do Brasil,* August 31, 1969, indicated that in politically sophisticated Guanabara only 3 per cent of the sample surveyed could correctly identify the national president of ARENA and 4 per cent his MDB counterpart. A similar opinion poll, published in *Jornal do Brasil* on September 7, showed that 26 per cent viewed the old-line politicians in a favorable light as the most experienced leadership available, while 25 per cent felt that a turnover in party leadership was important in bringing about redemocratization. Some 11 per cent went on record as viewing the question as unimportant, given the artificial nature of the parties. A clear majority (55 per cent) expressed no interest

Cabinet chief Rondon Pacheco, was ratified as the president of the government party, with Deputy Batista Ramos, Senator Wilson Gonçalves, and Deputy João Calmon as vice presidents. Arnaldo Prieto was chosen as ARENA secretary general, Deputies Raimundo Padilha (once again the majority leader in the Chamber) and Virgílio Távora as secretaries, and João Cleofas (indicated by the President to preside over the Senate) as treasurer. In his speech to the convention, Garrastazú Médici made it clear that he would actively command the party and expected its loyal support.

At the relatively subdued MDB convention, Senator Oscar Passos was reconfirmed as party president, with Deputies Ulisses Guimarães and Pedro Faria and Senator Nogueira da Gama as vice presidents. Deputy Adolfo de Oliveira remained as secretary general, along with Deputy Franco Montoro as first secretary and Senator José Ermirio de Morais (probably the richest man in the Congress) as treasurer. The MDB adopted a position of constructive and constitutional opposition, in keeping with the President's declaration that criticism of the government and its policies would be accepted but not attacks upon the revolution or the political system that had subsequently emerged. Although the party was divided into an intransigent wing, realists, moderates, and advocates of collaboration with the regime, the MDB leadership came predominantly from the second and third of these groups, in large part because the party's more militant elements had been turned into political nonpersons through cancellation of their political rights during the period of congressional recess.

Municipal elections on November 30 in ten states and three territories neither significantly reinforced nor undercut Garrastazú Médici's plans to transform ARENA into a disciplined mechanism for building government majorities in the more important 1970 elections. The MDB, victorious in the larger provincial centers, was deprived of the opportunity for any major gains, since the state capitals and other major cities as "national security areas" had their mayors appointed. In the smaller towns and rural areas ARENA, relying upon the alliance of established

in the scheduled elections of regional party directorates, while only 28 per cent replied that they were interested (and 9 per cent stated that they had no interest in politics whatsoever). Thus, public interest in the conventions was quite limited.

UDN and PSD machines, generally emerged on top. (ARENA claimed some 500,000 inscribed members at this stage, as compared to about half that number for the MDB.) [35]

Although terrorism and party politics drew the most public attention, there were also potentially important developments in the military sphere during the initial shakedown period of the new government. Following the assumption of the Army Ministry by Orlando Geisel (with Lyra Tavares offered the ambassadorial post in Paris which he assumed after election to the Brazilian Academy of Letters), a number of significant shifts occurred with respect to Army commands. Arturo Duarte Candal da Fonseca had already taken charge of the Fourth Army during the succession crisis, and Breno Borges Fortes replaced Garrastazú Médici at the head of the Third Army. A Department of Education was established within the Army Ministry to provide a position for the rehabilitated Moniz de Aragão. Ernesto Geisel, sixty-two-year-old brother of the new Army Minister, was given the presidency of Petrobrás. (The younger Geisel, who was experienced in the petroleum field where he had been superintendent of the President Bernardes Refinery in 1955–1956, and the War Minister's representative on the National Petroleum Council in 1957–1958 and 1959–1961, gave the Sorbonne group control over the most important governmental agency in the field of fuels and energy.) His place on the Superior Military Tribunal was taken by General Jurandir Mamede.

Promoted to four-star rank along with Candal da Fonseca and Breno Borges Fortes, were Rodrigo Otavio Jordão Ramos (who replaced Mamede in the Department of Production and Works) and Idálio Sardenberg (named to head the Brasil-U.S. Joint Military Commission). João Bina Machado became Vice Chief of the Army General Staff (replacing newly promoted Borges Fortes), while fellow three-star general Newton Fontoura de Oliveira Reis took over as Chief of the Army Minister's Cabinet (a job he would leave in March, 1970, after a heart attack). At the end of the year, Fritz de Azevedo Manso, a three-star general with a reputation as a legalist and strong disciplinarian, assumed

---

[35] The views of several major political figures on the viability and future directions of the political system as it emerged from the succession crisis are contained in "Confronto revela dilemas políticos," *Visão*, February 14, 1970, pp. 55–102.

command of Rio de Janeiro's strategic Vila Militar and its 1st Infantry Division, replacing hard-liner João Dutra de Castilhos (one of the chief articulators of the December 1969 coup within the coup). Aware of some dissatisfaction within the ranks of the officer corps with the course of events, the junta had promulgated Institutional Act No. 17 on October 14, which provided a variety of sanctions against officers found to be "acting against the cohesion of the Armed Forces." Designed to silence critics of the selection of Garrastazú Médici, its provisions for temporary forced retirement provided the new President with a more flexible instrument for dealing with military dissidence.[36]

Although the term "relative continuity" was repeatedly used by Garrastazú Médici to describe the relationship of his policies to those of the preceding government, the President also manifested the intention to avoid the mistakes of Castelo and Costa. The field where this ambiguity seemed to be most rapidly dissolving was education, a major problem since 1964.

During the first months of the Garrastazú Médici administration, Education Minister Jarbas Passarinho frequently made the headlines and generally attracted more favorable public attention than any other member of the cabinet. Upon taking over this cumbersome and traditionally inefficient ministry, the hard-driving Passarinho pledged a sweeping reorganization (which became a reality within six months) and declared that he would put an end to the situation in which "different bands are accustomed to play different music."[37] In mid-November, he announced preliminary plans to attack the problem of adult illiteracy and instituted a new university pay scale designed to make it possible for professors to devote full time to their academic responsibilities. The top was set at NCr 3,000 per month (roughly U.S. $750) for full professors, with full time assistant professors beginning at NCr 2,300.)[38] Aware of the fact that nearly 70 per cent of the 360,000 university students viewed the government as hostile, Passarinho strove to project

[36] *O Estado de S. Paulo,* October 15, 1970, contains the text of AI 17. A biography and character sketch of General Azevedo Manso appeared in *ibid.,* January 11, 1970.

[37] See *O Estado de S. Paulo,* November 1, 1969.

[38] *O Estado de S. Paulo,* November 19 and December 10, 1969. See also Lauro de Oliveira Lima, *O Impasse na Educação* (Petrópolis, 1969) and "Analfabetismo, um problema de mobilização nacional," *Visão,* February 14, 1970, 124–32.

a relatively progressive image (as he had frequently been able to do as Costa e Silva's Labor Minister). He plugged away at the theme that the government should view education as an investment rather than an expense.[39]

On December 2, Passarinho won a major victory as the President canceled plans to hold Expo 72 in Brazil and announced that the funds already appropriated would be used instead to complete the long unfinished suburban campus of the Federal University of Rio de Janeiro. The regular Ministry of Education budget for 1970 was announced as NCr 1.36 billion(roughly US $330 million), substantially higher than in preceding years (9.6 per cent of the federal budget, with total educational expenditures to exceed 1969's 5 per cent of GNP, itself more than double the proportion for the mid-1960's). In January, Passarinho unveiled a new university salary scale including a category of "exclusive dedication" to teaching which reached nearly NCr 4,000 for associate professors and NCr 4,600 for full professors (or approximately US $1,000 and $1,150 per month, very respectable pay by Brazilian standards).[40]

Although Passarinho still enjoyed the President's confidence and backing, his favorable references to the Cuban approach to the illiteracy problem and his advocacy of academic freedom even for Marxist professors, as well as for substantial educational reforms, brought him under fire from conservative civilian groups and the hard-line military. (He had repeatedly weathered similar attacks while serving as Costa's labor minister, and each attack by such right-wing press organs as *O Globo* probably gained him a good deal of sympathy among the student-labor constituency whose support he was seeking to win.) Trimming his sails a bit to conform more closely to the ESG-advocated labor market

[39] "A Calmaria das Universidades," *Veja,* November 12, 1969, pp. 56–64, and "1970: A Prova Mais Difícil de Passarinho," *Fatos e Fotos,* January 22, 1970, pp. 32–35, are useful sources on Passarinho's policies and pronouncements. A meanful symposium on the educational system at this juncture is *A Educação que Nos Convém* (Rio de Janeiro, 1969).

[40] According to a Rio de Janeiro opinion poll published in the *Jornal do Brasil,* December 21–22, 1969, 45 per cent supported the abandonment of Expo 72, while 25 per cent were opposed. A year after the December, 1968, crisis, only 22 per cent favored an end to the provisions of Institutional Act No. 5, while 28 per cent were opposed and nearly half had no opinion.

or "manpower" approach to education, in February and March, 1970, Passarinho came to focus upon secondary education as the country's priority bottleneck.[41]

Planning Minister João Paulo Reis Velloso provided the government with a link between such internationally oriented *Castelista* economists as Roberto Campos and the more nationalistic technocrats —military and civilian—concerned with growth of the internal market, improvement of the position of Brazilian enterprise relative to foreign investment, and regional imbalances (if not in all cases national integration, income redistribution, and basic reforms). Along with education, he had early singled out agricultural productivity, housing, and scientific technology as priority areas. With the President desiring to develop a central thrust to domestic policies and avoid any appearance of drift, Velloso was ready by mid-December to unveil the basic outlines of "Project Brazil: Great Power." But just as he began his maiden presentation to the cabinet on December 17, word was received of Costa e Silva's fatal heart attack. This initial collective gathering of Garrastazú Médici's minsters was immediately adjourned, and, with the proper observance of a period of official mourning, could not be resumed until after the Christmas holidays.[42]

[41] His address to Brazil's university rectors is analyzed in *Correio da Manhã,* January 28, 1970, with Garrastazú Médici's remarks to the same group analyzed in *O Globo,* January 29, 1970.

[42] On Costa's death, see the final article by Carlos Chagas on "113 Dias de Angustia," *O Estado de S. Paulo,* February 7, 1970, and "Costa e Silva, 1964–1969: As lições da política," *Veja,* December 24, 1969, pp. 22–31. In "Tempo de balanço," *O Estado de S. Paulo,* January 6, 1970, Roberto Campos compared the Castelo Branco and Costa e Silva governments. In his view, Costa had been accepted by the bureaucracy without enthusiasm, and lacked "reformist innovation and programatic imagination." Under the slogan of "humanization," the money in circulation was allowed to increase until "inflation rather than prices was stabilized." On the positive side, a high rate of economic growth followed from export incentives and rationalized agricultural production. Transportation, tax collection, reform of the capital market, and increased investment in education were other pluses of Costa's 30 months in office. Communication with the political class deteriorated as the President sought to command ARENA, not cultivate its support. "Intuitive and spontaneous," rather than "analytical and objective" (as was his predecessor), Costa let coordination of economic planning and financial policy break down under pressure from "nationalist and paternalistic" elements within his government.

4. 1970, ESCALATION OF VIOLENCE OR LEGITIMACY
THROUGH PERFORMANCE

In welcoming the New Year, Garrastazú Médici outlined "four horizons for the near future" in which priorities, policies, and programs should be viewed: (1) the year 1970, (2) the four years of his administration, (3) the decade of the 1970's, and (4) the remainder of the century.[43] On January 6 the cabinet finally met to consider the presentation of "Project Brazil: Great Power" interrupted three weeks earlier. Predicting a 7 to 9 per cent annual increase in GNP over the next four years (in light of an estimated 9 per cent for 1969), the Planning Minister implicitly rejected the more dramatic developmental goals espoused by some ESG graduates on the presidential staff in favor of a series of feasible impact projects while maintaining a steady pace of economic growth.[44]

In keeping with the administration's desire for a disciplined policy behind the development program being worked out by the planning and finance ministries, Minister of Commerce and Industry Fabio Yassuda left the cabinet at the end of February. His replacement was Marcos Vinicius Pratini de Morais, a thirty-one-year-old technocrat who had been serving as economic planning coordinator in the presidential staff. Associated with Velloso from their days as aides of Roberto Campos

[43] "As Novas Palavras de Paz," *Veja,* January 7, 1970, pp. 22–26. Other useful articles discussing the government's position as it moved into the 1970's include "O Saldo do Ministro Delfim," *Veja,* January 7, 1970, pp. 42–51; Fernando Pedreira, "A cadeira de rodas," *O Estado de S. Paulo,* December 14, 1969; Murilo Melo Filho, "O Estilo Médici," *Manchete,* December 13, 1970, pp. 26–29; and "Uma década decisiva à consolidação da democracia no Brasil," *Visão,* February 14, 1970, pp. 37–52.

[44] "Velloso e seus 'Grandes Impactos,'" *Veja,* January 14, 1970, pp. 18–25. In his report GNP growth rates over the past 15 years were officially calculated as follows:

1954—10.1%	1959— 5.6%	1964—2.9%
1955— 6.9%	1960— 9.7%	1965—2.7%
1956— 3.2%	1961—10.3%	1966—5.1%
1957— 8.7%	1962— 5.3%	1967—4.8%
1958— 7.7%	1963— 1.5%	1968—8.4%

Press coverage of this project also includes "Os cem días do presidente," *Veja,* February 18, 1970, pp. 20–22 and "Eles planejam uma Grande Poténcia para o Brasil," *Fatos e Fotos,* February 5, 1970, pp. 24–26.

during the Castelo government, Pratini's appointment signified that this ministry would no longer function primarily as an influence channel for business and industrial interests. Delfim Netto and Velloso would be free to pursue economic and financial rationality without interference from a politically oriented Minister of Commerce and Industry (as had been the case with General Edmundo Macedo Soares during the Costa e Silva government).[45]

The orientation of the regime became increasingly clear in a series of major policy pronouncements during March. On the 10th in a speech opening the new academic year at the War College, Garrastazú Médici propounded the concept of the "revolutionary state" in which the President retains extraordinary emergency powers as the leader of the revolutionary movement alongside his constitutional authority as chief executive. The duration of this "Estado Revolucionário" would be determined by the time necessary to "implant the political, administrative, juridical, social, and economic structures capable of promoting the integration of all Brazilians to minimum levels of well-being." Less than two weeks earlier the President had stated in a televised press conference that his October, 1969, pledge to leave democracy firmly installed in Brazil was an expression of hope rather than a definite commitment, and that it would depend on the actions of the opposition as well as of the government. (He might well have added that it had also been a calculated move to calm public opinion and ensure a political honeymoon period at the inception of his administration.) Now addressing an important segment of the regime's in-group, the military-technocratic alliance, this "harder" speech was Garrastazú Médici's way of assuring them that economic development and internal stability continued to have precedence over a return to a competitive political order. Its timing also suggested a none-too-gentle reminder to the Congress, preparing to

---

[45] Yassuda had sought a greater role for his ministry in economic policy making. Having first received a setback at the hands of Passarinho with the cancellation of Expo 72, he decided to quit when Pratini was imposed upon him as a director of the Brazilian Coffee Institute (IBC) after Delfim Netto and the SNI had obstructed several of his appointments to this important agency. Pratini had been staff chief for Castelo's Ministers of Commerce and Industry. See "Mudança no ministério," *Veja*, February 25, 1970, pp. 22–23 and a follow-up article in the issue of March 4, 1970, pp. 22–25, as well as an earlier profile of Yassuda in *Veja*, November 19, 1969, pp. 29–33.

open a new session after the December-February recess, that it was in effect on probation, functioning at the sufferance of the military.

Elaborating upon his earlier observation that "juridical formulas" with regard to democracy are not as important as "means of its effective implementation," the President pointed out that no country had managed to emerge from underdevelopment without "the total sacrifice of liberties." The Brazilian Revolution, he asserted, was determined to prove that this could be accomplished. To this end he called upon the ESG to concern itself more with "real and objective projects" directed to the government's policy makers and focusing on the problems involved in seeking accelerated economic development with internal stability as well as a "politically open society."

The President's address to the nation on the anniversary of the 1964 revolution stressed more heavily the fight against subversion while rejecting any escalation of repression. Viewing the resort to urban terrorism as an indication of the radical opposition's failure to win mass student or rural support, he pledged that repression against the perpetrators of violence would be "implacable," but that his government would not "confuse the innocent with the guilty in the same suspicions and same restrictions."

The outlines of the National Development Plan foreshadowed on March 10 and 31 were more fully defined in the presidential message to Congress on April 1. Replete with references to a "government of social communication" and the "search for social cohesion," this address proclaimed that

the new center of gravity of our political order rests in a democratic model which rendering obsolete the molds of classic or liberal democracy guarantees man his new rights, without prejudice to the values under whose invocation, within the horizons of the western world, Brazilian culture was formed.[46]

Rather than resorting to the populist redistributive policies of the pre-1964 era, characterized by substantial increases in the minimum wage, the Garrastazú Médici government opted for a gradual extension of the benefits of economic development to the masses through increased pub-

---

[46] This speech was carried in the Brazilian daily press and analyzed in "A Democracia: Um Regime pôsto a prova," *Veja*, April 8, 1970, pp. 18–25.

lic investment in education, health measures, housing, and cheaper and more readily available foodstuffs. The former was again singled out by the President as the priority aim of his administration.

A somewhat discordant note was sounded by Marshal Cordeiro de Farias in his March 31 speech to the War College in which he advised a policy of conciliation to isolate the terrorists from other groups. From the platform of the institution he had founded a quarter of a century before, he called upon the government to "reaffirm the democratic commitment of 1964 in order to regain a union of classes behind the Revolution." On the same day, however, Army Minister Geisel reminded the Armed Forces that "representative democracy is founded in love of liberty with responsibility" rather than "romantic democracy" as espoused by the regime's liberal critics. General Meira Matos, striking a balance on the first six years of the "Revolution" stressed national integration and prosperity as the critical objectives of the government, with social peace, democracy, and preservation of national values largely dependent on the success of development efforts. Forecasting more than a doubling of per capita GNP during the 1970's, he held out the prospect of an integrated mass consumption economy by the end of the century—sufficient to underpin a Brazilian capacity to play the role of a major power in the world rather than hemispheric arena. To bring this about, however, the nation would need to follow the leadership of a strategic elite dedicated to such principles as austerity, administrative efficiency, productivity, free enterprise, and liberty with responsibilities as well as social peace and respect for human dignity.[47]

The President's promise to limit repression to the perpetrators of violence and to distinguish between opposition to his administration and challenges to the revolution itself came at a time when relations with the Church were strained over the issue of torture. In late 1969 prominent European Churchmen and Catholic intellectuals had submitted a dossier on such abuse of authority and violations of human rights to Pope Paul VI, who on January 26, 1970, personally received Dom Helder Câmara with a public acknowledgement of his dismay over atrocities in Brazil. The Pope communicated his displeasure to the

[47] General de Brigada Carlos de Meira Mattos, *Doutrina Política de Potência* (Bahia, 1970).

Brazilian government through diplomatic channels while also canceling a tentatively scheduled visit to Brasília.[48]

The Garrastazú Médici government, in keeping with its emphasis on intelligence and communications techniques, dealt more skillfully with this problem than had either of its predecessors. Colonel Miguel Pereira Manso Neto, who had succeeded Pratini as chief of the special advisory staff within the presidential office, flew over to Rome with a confidential message from Garrastazú Médici designed to correct "distortions" in the Vatican's perception of the Brazilian situation. More significantly, when the XI General Assembly of the National Conference of Brazilian Bishops met in Brasília on May 17, the participants were assiduously cultivated by top government officials including the President himself. (Education Minister Jarbas Passarinho and Colonel Manso Neto were particularly effective in this respect, and Justice Minister Buzaid addressed a plenary session and answered questions relating to torture.)

The communique issued by the prelates after ten days of discussion and debate reflected the success of this effort to gain "comprehension" for the regime's position. While criticizing torture and police abuses, the bishops also condemned terrorism and recognized the developmental progress made under the military governments. Even their call for a policy of human valorization did not sound too different from the relevant passages of the presidential state of the union message or recent pronouncements of the Education Minister.[49] The vote of 159 to 21 for a document which expressed confidence that torture was not condoned by the government and termed political terrorism by the radicals "a form of torture of the people" in the context of the moment clearly constituted a net gain for the regime.

Although the National Eucharistic Congress, which opened on

[48] The most comprehensive discussion of these matters is Ralph della Cava, "Torture in Brazil," *Commonweal,* XCII, No. 6 (April 24, 1970), 135–41. The dossier presented to the Pope was published as "Livre Noir: Terreur et Torture au Brésil," *Croissance des Jeunes Nations,* No. 94 (Paris, December, 1969), pp. 19–34. Additional materials and reprints of relevant newspaper articles are included in the American Committee for Information on Brazil, *Terror in Brazil* (New York, 1970).

[49] The full text of the communique is found in *Jornal do Brasil,* May 28, 1970, with an analysis of the meetings in *Veja,* June 3, 1970, pp. 24–26.

May 27, was not favored by the participation of the Pope as had been hoped by its organizers, the presence of nearly one hundred bishops at a presidential reception and attendance of Vatican representatives along with Brazil's five Cardinals at an official lunch with Garrastazú Médici's cabinet and military aides marked a significant rapprochément between Church and state.[50]

Terrorism, relatively quiescent since the death of Carlos Marighela, was manifested during the first half of 1970 by two diplomatic kidnapings which followed quite closely the style of the Elbrick affair. Just after the President's War College address, a band of São Paulo terrorists abducted Japanese Consul General Nobuo Okuchi, releasing him on March 14 in exchange for five political prisoners including Mother Superior Maurina Borges da Silveira (allegedly a victim of police torture), Damaris Lucena (widow of a Lamarca associate killed by the authorities in a raid several weeks earlier), and three young revolutionaries connected to the VPR apparatus. Plans for an ambassadorial abduction in Rio de Janeiro were disrupted on April 21 by the arrest of a group of young conspirators, but on June 11 elements linked to Lamarca seized the West German Ambassador, killing one of his Brazilian security guards in the process, and held him for over five days. The fact that another West German Ambassador had recently been killed in Guatemala when that country's government refused to exchange political prisoners for him strengthened the hands of the Brazilian revolutionaries in their dealings with the authorities. Yet in spite of the fact that the ransom was raised in this case to 40 "subversives" under arrest, the kidnaping had substantially less impact upon Brazilian public opinion than that of Elbrick or even of the Japanese Consul. For throughout the Von Hollenben affair, public attention remained focused upon the World Cup soccer competition taking place in Mexico.[51]

Indeed, for the entire first quarter of the revolution's seventh year

[50] The Tradition, Family and Property group of Catholic laymen had been able to gather 1.5 million signatures in 1968 for a manifesto against "Communist infiltration of the Church." Since that time the TFP was reported to have grown substantially in membership and to enjoy the support of significant numbers of conservative clergy. See "Cavaleiros da Tradição," *Veja,* May 20, 1970, pp. 30–37.

[51] This episode is heavily treated in the press and weekly newsmagazines of the period, but with only a fraction of the coverage given to the activities, care, and even feeding of the Brazilian team in Mexico.

the interest of the Brazilian populace turned massively away from the frustrations of the political situation toward *futebol,* while the second quarter opened with an atmosphere of widespread euphoria as a result of Brazil's unbroken string of international soccer triumphs during June. Victors in 1958 and 1962 in this quadrennial competition (which means much more to most Brazilians than the Olympics, the World Series, and the Superbowl combined to sports-minded elements of the United States public) but upset by England's win in 1966, Brazil during 1969 became caught up in a national crusade to reestablish preeminence in this most international of competitive team sports. (Readers who question the relevance of this matter to politics might do well to consider the effect of the New York Mets' pennant and World Series victories upon the 1969 mayorality race in New York City. And our "World Series" of baseball is only a national championship with no overtones of international competition, much less the element of a young, developing nation defeating the major powers of the world.)

During the first three weeks of June some 30 million Brazilians viewed game after game on television while an even greater number paid rapt attention at their radios. Finally on June 21, led by the incomparable Pelé (Edson Arantes do Nascimento, at 29 the first player in the history of the game to score over 1,000 career goals) along with São Paulo's Gérson de Oliveira Nunes, Minas Gerais' Tostão (twenty-three-year-old Eduardo Gonçalves de Andrade), and Rio de Janeiro's Jairzinho (twenty-five-year-old Jair Ventura Filho), the unstoppable Brazilian attack swept over Italy's vaunted defense like a tidal wave. The 4–1 victory brought an unprecedented third world championship to Brazil and with it permanent possession of the Jules Rimet trophy.[52]

For President Garrastazú Médici and his government, the national triumph meant much more than just patriotic pride and days of carnival-

[52] There is some reason to believe that the very strong possibility of a Brazil-West Germany final in the World Cup was both a factor in the terrorist selection of Ehrenfreid von Hollenben as their target and the government's willingness to ransom him with little evidence of significant internal dissention. Nothing could be allowed to mar the favorable impact of the soccer triumph. It may be worth speculating that the emotional drain (and financial loss on the part of the millions of small bettors) occasioned by England's failure to defend her title successfully may have contributed to the apathy of many Labor voters at the end of the British election campaign and thus to Harold Wilson's upset defeat.

like celebration. Indirect propaganda for the revolution was linked to the accomplishments of the Brazilian team through insertion of skillfully done films featuring the developmental gains of the regime before and after each of the thirty-two game telecasts from Mexico. Then, speaking as "a common man, as a Brazilian who, above all things, has an immense love of Brazil and an unsinkable faith in this country and this people," the President hastened to turn the World Cup into political capital for his administration. Identifying teamwork and collective will as the principles which had most made possible Brazil's victories on the soccer fields, he called for their application to the "struggle for national development."

While the World Cup competition and the prolonged celebrations which ensued helped many Brazilians view the contemporary situation through rose-colored glasses and see the future more optimistically, the government took full advantage of the breathing space to move ahead with its political consolidation. The Military Club elections of May had passed quietly with retired General Walter Menezes Paes defeating General Manoel Mendes Pereira—the candidate backed by such dissatisfied elements as those represented by Albuquerque Lima, Moniz de Aragão, and Marshal Mourão Filho—by a margin of roughly 700 in a total of slightly over 5,000 votes cast. This near stand-off accentuated the question of promotions at the end of July and again in late November. With Albuquerque Lima at or near the top of the seniority list for four-star rank and several hard-line colonels in analogous positions with regard to advancement to brigadier general, close attention was guaranteed.

Although the new governors would not be elected formally until the existing legislatures acted on October 3, by mid-year little doubt remained as to their identities. Following a strategy of controlled renovation basically similar to that adopted by Castelo Branco in 1966, the President handpicked the candidates for succession at the state level. First the SNI explored the possible alternatives and "vetted" the candidates while the presidential staff studied the problems, needs, and priorities of each state to decide which qualities would be most required in a new chief executive. Then ARENA head Rondon Pacheco paid a flying visit to consult in the state capital with the leaders of the several ruling party factions and to talk with the would-be governors. Finally

Garrastazú Médici made his choice, often picking a political newcomer who had proven his executive ability in an administrative position or a military figure out of active duty and associated with civilian affairs. Such new faces were favored particularly when there seemed to be an impass looming between the ex-UDN and ex-PSD leaders within the government party.

Highly cognizant of Castelo's difficulties with the Rio Grande do Sul succession in 1966, the President moved quickly to resolve the deep ARENA split there. Both ex-Education Minister Tarso Dutra and the rival aspirant endorsed by Governor Peracchi Barcelos were passed over in favor of Congressman Euclides Triches, a fifty-one-year-old retired colonel and experienced ARENA legislator who had been a classmate of Ministers Andreazza and Corsetti. Defeated by Leonel Brizola in the 1955 election for mayor of Pôrto Alegre, Triches subsequently saw service as Secretary of Public Works in the 1962–1966 state administration which collaborated in the overthrow of Goulart. In Bahia the presidential nod went to Salvador's Mayor Antônio Carlos Magalhães, long the favorite of Governor Luiz Vianna Filho. At age 42 already a proven administrator and ex-federal deputy, Magalhães benefited from hard-line military reservations concerning his chief rival, ex-governor Lomanto Júnior. São Paulo was the third major state situation to be resolved, with forty-nine-year-old Laudo Natel, who had governed the state in 1966 during the eight months from the cassation of Adhemar de Barros to the inauguration of Abreu Sodré, selected. (Since Delfim Neto had served as Natel's Secretary of Finance in that interim administration, Natel was a natural choice for the governorship once the President decided that he could not spare his Finance Minister for the job.)

Filling out the numbers from South, forty-five-year-old Colombo Machado Salles, an experienced engineer of the Transportation Ministry, was indicated by the President to govern Santa Catarina, where the ancient rivalry between the Ramos (PSD) and Bornhausen (UDN) family machines could not directly be accommodated. For Paraná the power struggle within ARENA involving Governor Paulo Pimentel and ex-governor Ney Braga was resolved by the selection of Congressman Harold Leon Peres.

Leaving the states of the central region for later disposition, the President undertook to decide the succession question in the North and

Northeast during April and May. In Ceará the desire of Virgílio Távora to return to the office he had held in 1962–1966 was overridden by the naming of Colonel César Cals de Oliveira Filho, an engineer who had been serving as head of the region's major hydroelectric power company. Pernambuco presented the administration with a particularly delicate situation involving a pair of ex-governors within ARENA wishing to return to the statehouse. After imposing Eraldo Gueiros, a judge of the Superior Military Tribunal in Rio de Janeiro, as a compromise candidate, the federal government strove to convince both Cid Sampaio (1958–1962) and Paulo Guerra (1964–1966) to forget their gubernatorial disappointment and run for the Senate. In Maranhão, Piauí, and Sergipe the relatively young incumbent governors chose to step down by April 3 in order to be eligible for election to the Senate. In the first of these states Pedro Neives, Finance Secretary in the cabinet of forty-year-old José Sarney, was indicated as ARENA's candidate for the governorship. In Piauí the nod went to Alberto Silva, head of the state's electric power company, but only after the President reluctantly decided that active duty military status ruled out his initial choice, Colonel Stanley Fortes Batista, who at forty-two had already been chief of the National Department of Anti-Drought Works and an instructor at the military academy. Sergipe's official candidate was Paulo Barreto de Menezes, while for Rio Grand do Norte the President selected Cortez Pereira, ex-director of the Bank of the Northeast. Paraíba's new governor was to be Ernani Sátiro, once national chairman of the UDN and presently serving on the Superior Military Tribunal.

The governing of Alagoas was entrusted to Afrânio Lages, at fifty-five experienced in the politics of that state. Fernando José Guilhon, a forty-nine-year-old engineer who had been Secretary of Public Works under Jarbas Passarinho during the 1964–1967 period, received the presidential preference in Pará, while in Amazonas the recipient was reserve Colonel João Walter de Andrade and in Acré Wanderlei Dantas, a thirty-seven-year-old congressman and education ministry official.

With sixteen governorships decided more than four months before the scheduled ratification by ARENA majorities in the state assemblies, the government could concentrate its attention upon the remaining six states in the central-eastern region of the country. For Minas Gerais, where problems of finance and inadequate planning vied for attention with a pressing need for renovation of political leadership (to replace the entrenched ARENA gerontocracy with its continuing feuds between UDN and PSD patriarchs), the President chose Rondon Pacheco himself. Rio de Janeiro posed the thorny problem of rivalry between aging Deputy Raimundo Padilha and Marshal Paulo Tôrres, who had governed the state during the Castelo Branco administration. With the substantial strength of the MDB, the absence of younger ARENA leaders, and the residual prestige of the many *cassados* weighing heavily in his decision, the President opted for Padilha. In Espírito Santo the choice fell upon development bank director Gerhardt dos Santos and in Mato Grosso on ARENA president José Fragelli, at 46 an experienced legislator (as well as nephew of Senator Correia da Costa. Faced with a multiplicity of feasible candidates in Goiás the President ultimately chose thirty-six-year-old Leoníno Caiado.

A unique situation prevailed in Guanabara, where the MDB held a comfortable majority in the legislative assembly. Aware of the disproportionate attention paid by foreign observers to this metropolitan area, Garrastazú Médici accepted the prospect of an opposition victory as long as the candidate was one who accepted the 1964 revolution and would prove agreeable to a *modus vivendi* as had Negrão de Lima since 1967. With the MDB machinery in the hands of newspaper publisher Antônio Chagas Freitas, whose long service in Congress had shown him to be far from a radical and who enjoyed good personal relations with a number of military figures, such a solution appeared eminently viable. The government concentrated upon obtaining re-election of Gilberto Marinho to one of the three Senate vacancies in the November balloting by persuading the MDB to run only two strong candidates as a concession to the ARENA forbearance in accepting a Chagas Freitas victory in the governorship race. Although the selection of the new governors went off without a hitch on October 3, as the recently chastized state legislatures ratified the presidential choices more routinely than in 1966, the government was at least partially disappointed in its hopes for the November congressional balloting. ARENA gains were substantial in some states, but the opposition retained its hold on voter loyalties in major urban centers, particularly Guanabara, minimizing the chance that these carefully staged elections would be perceived as a significant step toward redemocratization.

As compared with 409 congressmen elected in 1966, the new Chamber of Deputies chosen on November 15 by the more than 27 million registered voters would contain only 310 members. (São Paulo, Minas Gerais, Rio Grande do Sul, Paraná, Bahia, Guanabara, Rio de Janeiro, and Pernambuco retained their dominant position with 6.2 million, 3.5 million, 2.3 million, 2.0 million, 1.8 million, 1.7 million, 1.5 million, and 1.3 million registered voters respectively or three-fourths of the national total.) While ARENA captured over 70 per cent of the Chamber seats and was successful in all but six of the 46 senatorial races, they failed to elect even one of three senators from Guanabara and saw MDB leaders Franco Montoro and Amaral Peixoto victorious in São Paulo and Rio de Janeiro State. Instead of achieving significant renovation, the elections returned mostly old style politicians to office. Such new stellar vote-getters as appeared on the scene turned out to be the sons of Adhemar de Barros, Faria Lima, and Aluísio Alves, trading upon the popularity of their deceased or purged fathers. Moreover, the total number of abstentions, null, and blank votes reached nearly 50 per cent in many areas, indicating a potentially serious degree of alienation from the electoral process, which had been semi-rigged by the elimination of most popular opposition figures by the repeated purges under Institutional Acts nos. 1, 2, and 5. (The ESG alumni association immediately launched a study of the null and blank votes in an effort to assess the broader political implications of this phenomenon.)

If the elections were less than a rousing endorsement of the government, they did constitute a step toward its objective of a Mexican-style dominant one-party system. Most MDB leaders were defeated in their bids for reelection, the casualty list including party president Oscar Passos, vice-presidents Ulisses Guimarães and Nogueira da Gama, treasurer José Ermírio de Morais, Senate floor leader Aurélio Viana, and Chamber minority leader Mário Covas. Although the MDB held on to the Guanabara legislature, it was in a decidedly weak position in the other major states (where its urban votes had been outweighed by the government's supporters in the interior), having only token representation in some of the Northern states. Then, too, as reported in *Veja* of

November 18, a Marplan survey focused on the 2 million voters who had reached the age of eighteen since 1966 indicated that a slim plurality of youth favored the government party over the MDB.

The administration's activity at the end of its first year in office was not limited to the electoral arena. In late August the government announced its Program of Social Integration, an uniquely Brazilian alternative to profit sharing designed to give the workers a direct stake in productivity and in the expansion of the private sector. A gradually increasing proportion of the gross receipts of each enterprise was to be credited to the individual accounts of its employees with the federal savings bank and invested for them by the government in the stock market. This "participation fund" was expected to reach US $1 billion by 1974, easing the shortage of risk capital as well as, hopefully, leading the workers to identify their future with the regime. Then in early October Garrastazú Médici revealed ambitious plans for the crash construction of a Trans-Amazon highway stretching nearly 2500 miles from the coast to the Peruvian border, 1600 miles of which were to be ready by January 1972 and the rest by the end of that year to mark a century and a half of Brazilian independence. Intended to provide work for the victims of the Northeast's periodic drought, the worse since 1958, the project called for homesteading tens of thousands of the construction workers along the route opening up the lower part of the vast Amazon region.

Shortly after the elections, Generals Muricy and Souza Aguiar reached the limit for retirement. Although he was second in seniority among the three-star officers, Albuquerque Lima was pointedly passed over for promotion, which went instead to João Bina Machado and Humberto da Souza Mello. Like almost all the others advanced to four-star rank since 1967, they had not been promoted during the Kubitschek-Quadros-Goulart period. The next two on the list of eligibles for advancement to the top grade were reportedly Itiberê Gouvêa do Amaral and João Dutra de Castilho. One of these should replace Sizeno Sarmento upon his retirement in March, 1971, and the other should succeed Souto Malan, Moniz de Aragão, or Augusto Fragoso later in the year. (Retirement ages are 59 for colonels, 62 for brigadier generals, 64 for divisional generals, and 66 for four-star generals. If, however, age or time in grade does not open up at least two vacancies a year at the top level, seven at the three-star rank, and twelve for colonels to move up to the lowest rung of the general officer ladder, then the Army High Command decides who will be retired prematurely to provide for this degree of mobility.) The subsequent reshuffle of the Army's key assignments saw Alfredo Souto Malan become Chief of Staff, with Candal da Fonseca taking his place as head of the Department of General Provisions. Souza Mello went to the Second Army and Bina Machado was given command of the Fourth Army. (Sarmento retained the First Army and Breno Borges Fortes the Third Army.) Rodrigo Otávio (Production and Works), Isaac Nahon (Personnel), Canavarro Pereira (Munitions), and Moniz de Aragão (Training and Research) rounded out the *Alto Commando*. Idálio Sardenberg remained as Chief of the Joint U.S.-Brazil Military Commission and Fragoso as ESG commandant. Muricy was immediately chosen as the president of the ADESG; he indicated that his organization would launch a full-scale extension course in São Paulo, chiefly for industrialists and state officials, as well as inaugurating a continuing national security seminar in Brasília for congressmen and higher-level bureaucrats.

The early months of the administration's second year in office were marked by considerable activity on the internal security front. In November as many as 4000 suspects were taken into custody in an effort to frustrate supposed plans of the National Liberating Alliance (ALN) to commemorate the anniversary of Marighella's death with a series of abductions. (Marighella's successor, Joaquim Câmara Ferreira, had died in jail after his arrest in October.) This escalation of repression, which involved members of the Young Catholic Workers (JOC) and tightening of press censorship, had led the Central Committee of the National Conference of Bishops to criticize the government. Now, to underscore the continued existence of intransigent revolutionary opposition, even after the elections, Swiss Ambassador Giovannia Enrico Bucher was kidnapped in Rio de Janeiro on December 7. This time, in contrast to the three previous analogous episodes, negotiations dragged on as the regime refused to give publicity to the terrorists' manifesto or to furnish free rides to workers on the commuter railroads in the interim. Apparently satisfied that the adbuctors had more to lose than to gain by killing the bachelor diplomat, the government accepted the idea of releasing 70 prisoners as his ransom, but refused to include those who had been sentenced to long terms or who had possible death penalties hanging over their heads. Moreover, a number of the persons on the original list of December 18 preferred to take their chances in the courts rather than to be subject to perpetual banishment as the price of their exchange for Ambassador Bucher. Thus over five weeks passed before final agreement could be reached on the twenty-two replacement names and the exchange could take place.

Meanwhile, the President continued to project an image of concern with more significant matters, proclaiming 1971 to be the "great year of industrial development" and announcing plans to quadruple steel production by 1980 (to a total of 20 million metric tons). As 1971 opened, evident signs of increasing prosperity and governmental confidence did not, however, guarantee the continued positive psychological predisposition required to begin transforming "Project Brazil: Great Power" into an effective integrating and mobilizational myth.

Yet the government has already been able to channel the energies of a substantial minority of university students into "Project Rondon," a program which during the vacation periods takes them into frontier areas of the country to study at first hand the socio-economic conditions prevailing there. Inaugurated in 1967 by then Interior Minister Albuquerque Lima and focusing upon the Amazon region, Project Rondon took advantage of the students' nationalistic concern over alleged United States designs on that area to arouse initial interest in the program (originally proposed by a group of younger military officers and MUDES, the University Movement for Economic and Social Development, a nearly still-born proregime student organization from the Castelo Branco period.[53] Carried on twice a year, in January-February and again in July, this rapidly growing program now involves more than 10,000 students a year and has been extended to nearly all of Brazil's frontier areas as well as the interior of major rural states. Its purpose is to acquant students with the Brazilian "reality" and to gain their support for a program of "less talk and more action"; in short, it is a challenge to students to work for the country's modernization and development

[53] H. Jon Rosenbaum, "El Projecto Rondon: un experimento brasileño de desarrollo económico y político," *Foro Internacional,* 38 (October-December, 1969), pp. 136–48, provides a useful account of the origins and evolution of the project, which was named after the late Marshal Cândido da Silva Rondon, founder and long-time director of the Indian Protection Service.

rather than to denounce the present system and call for its violent demise. Along these lines measures under consideration during the second half of 1970 would make all Brazilians of draft age subject to service in some activity linked to national development and security, with many of them to be employed in massive literacy campaigns.

Thus, nearly seven years after stepping in to oust Goulart from office, the Brazilian Armed Forces manifested an intention to retain power for a substantially longer period than they themselves had heretofore deemed necessary. While the President defined the authoritarian regime's tenure in terms of tasks to be completed rather than a fixed period of time, the War College's association of graduates announced plans to disseminate its doctrine of national security and development on an even more ambitious scale than had been the case during 1970 as part of an effort to broaden the civilian elite of bureaucratic, entrepreneurial, and professional elements sharing in the military's doctrine of national security and their blueprint for Brazilian development.

Only time will tell if Garrastazú Médici and his advisors have correctly judged the consequences of their programs and priorities, but a note of cautious skepticism seems warranted, particularly in light of Huntington's views. Brazil has known stability chiefly when the rate of social mobilization has been low, since political institutionalization has generally been lacking (with rigidity, subordination, and disunity, if not necessarily simplicity, more characteristic than adaptability, autonomy, coherence, and complexity). The present regime's relative stress upon education, particularly if combined with significant beginnings of agrarian reform, should give impetus to social mobilization. Huntington views rapid economic growth more as politically destabilizing than as a factor making for political order, although he does recognize that if economic development keeps ahead of social mobilization social frustration may be minimized.[54] Then, too, over the short run at least, Huntington admits restriction of political participation as a substitute for increased institutionalization as a means of keeping the ratio balanced.

The main thrust of Huntington's analysis, however, concerns the necessity, in order to achieve validated stability, for a regime to organize the countryside before its opponents do so. Agrarian reform and institutionalized political parties provide the most effective vehicles for

[54] *Political Order in Changing Societies,* pp. 49–55.

reaching this goal, one which the Garrastazú Médici government has set for itself. It does not appear that the present administration or its possible successors from within the military institution realize that "the key to political stability is the extent to which the rural masses are mobilized into politics within the existing political system rather than against the system." [55] Even if they are aware of this need "to mobilize the peasantry into politics as a stabilizing force to contain urban disorder," most of the Brazilian military and their technocratic allies seem prone to underestimate the importance of political parties in this process and are inclined to "attempt to modernize the society politically without establishing the institution that will make their society politically stable." [56] This denigration of parties by the military, analyzed by Huntington as a general phenomenon of the military mentality, may be accentuated in the Brazilian case by the woeful inadequacy of parties in the past and their consequent image in the eyes of the bureaucratic elites as obstacles to rationality and progress.

Although the Brazilian Armed Forces view their March 31, 1964, intervention as a true revolution, it was in fact largely a "veto coup." In this regard, Brazil conformed closely to Huntington's dictum: "If, however, a society moves into the phase of mass participation without developing effective political institutions, the military become engaged in a conservative effort to protect the existing system against the incursions of the lower classes, particularly the urban lower classes." [57] Brazil's recent experience also bears out his contention that veto coups frequently "come in pairs, the initial coup followed by a consolidating coup in which the hard-liners attempt to overthrow the moderates and prevent the return of power to the civilians." [58] In light of the consistently close fit of Huntington's broadly comparative propositions to Brazilian reality, his assertion that the military can develop stable political institutions only to the degree that they can "identify their rule with the masses of the peasantry" and capture their support merits careful attention.[59]

[55] *Ibid.*, pp. 74–75.
[56] *Ibid.*, pp. 78 and 92.
[57] *Ibid.*, p. 222.
[58] *Ibid.*, p. 232.
[59] *Ibid.*, p. 241.

Perhaps even more crucial is the question of political parties. For if there are some among the "bishops' of the Brazilian Armed Forces (although perhaps not among its "cardinals" and rarely among the "archbishops") who may appreciate the need for attention to the rural masses, they have manifested no awareness of the complementary aspect of Huntington's prescription, that of the primacy of party. In his view of world experience,

The support of rural elements is, however, only a precondition to the development of political institutions by a military regime. Initially, the legitimacy of a modernizing military regime comes from the promise it offers for the future. But eventually this declines as a source of legitimacy. If the regime does not develop a political structure which institutionalizes some principle of legitimacy, the result can only be a military oligarchy in which power is passed among the oligarchs by means of *coups de état,* and which also stands in danger of revolutionary overthrow by new social forces which it does not possess the institutional mechanisms for assimilating.[60]

Modernization of Brazil under the aegis of the Brazilian Armed Forces might become a possibility if military leadership came to accept the need for political institutions which are capable of integrating emerging groups, effectively articulating and aggregating interests (and thus mediating group conflict while building consensus), and fostering a sense of community. After nearly seven years of military rule, this prospect still appeared remote, albeit not unattainable. Divisions with the Armed Forces accentuated by differences over how to deal with kidnapings and other terrorist activities will largely determine whether eighth and ninth years of the military's stay in power will witness liberalization, increasing authoritarianism, or yet another coup-within-the-coup. The findings of this analysis of the experience of the 1960's will be focused more systematically on such considerations in the following chapter. While in many respects Brazil remains the land of the future, the 1970's will be critical in defining what that future will be and the road by which Brazil may attain its destiny.

[60] *Ibid.,* p. 242.

CHAPTER NINE

Institutionalization of a New Authoritarian Order

A SIGNIFICANT NUMBER of recurrent themes have been observed in the course of our analysis of trends and events in Brazil during the past several political and military generations, from the political decadence of the Empire through the emergence in recent years of a technocratic military regime of an increasingly authoritarian bent. Many of these were previewed in Chapter 1, where attention was focused on some of the hypotheses and theoretical propositions to be found in the rapidly growing body of relevant literature. In the concluding chapter of this study, the procedure of the introduction will be reversed and an effort will be made to present a more adequate analytical model of the present Brazilian political system than put forth at the beginning of this work. While built upon ideas and interpretations introduced in Chapter 1, this model will be more highly conceptualized in terms relating closely to recent work on contemporary authoritarian regimes.

The final section will strive to redeem the promises made in Chapter 1 to reassess and reformulate a number of the comparative propositions present in the literature on civil-military relations and political modernization in light of the most significant findings from the contemporary Brazilian developmental experience. The emphasis in this endeavor is on refinement and greater precision with respect to limiting conditions. As one of the major features of the initial section is to be filling in of the gap in Gabriel Almond's array of prototype political systems, the final section will center upon operationalization of Samuel Huntington's approach to *Political Order in Changing Societies.*

1. ELEMENTS OF AN ANALYTIC MODEL

In the initial chapter of this book a limited amount of theoretical material was introduced concerning the comparative analysis of political systems. Subsequently a good deal of historical interpretation and empirical data was added. The organization of this mass of material and its ordered interpretation have already provided the reader with a substantial understanding not only of what has taken place in Brazil, but also of how it has come about and why. Nonetheless, rather than a clear conceptualization of the system, the bulk and detail of the data provided may well have left a more lasting impression of Brazilian politics as who does what to whom, how long, in which ways, to what ends, with what result, and for whose benefit. Indeed, at one level this has been the author's objective in view of the absence of any significant analytical literature in English on the post-1964 regime. But to a substantial degree the purpose of this exhaustive enterprise has been instrumental: to furnish the necessary elements for elaboration of a reasonably meaningful and valid model of the contemporary political system and analysis of the dynamics of change during the 1964–1970 period.

No effort will be made here to summarize the main features of the Brazilian polity, as such a resumé has been provided in Chapter 1, particularly pages 2–7 and 21–29. A brief recapitulation of the discussion of "Obstacles to Modernization" (which will be expanded in *Modernization and the Military in Brazil*) is, however, appropriate in order to link these considerations to the analysis of the post-coup polity found in the introduction to Chapter 4 and the opening pages of Chapter 6. This should then provide the requisite foundation for a more refined and systematic conceptualization of the emergence of a modernizing authoritarian regime. Although neither United States models nor Brazilian formulations are fully adequate to the task in hand, both will be drawn upon, in the belief that a synthesis of the frameworks and insights of observers both within and outside the system promises in the long run to yield the greatest possible understanding of its processes and institutions.

In the traditional cartorial-clientelistic polity, the dominant land-owning-mercantilist elite provided employment to the "prematurely" expanding middle class in return for its political support.[1] When the absorptive capacity of this system reached its limits, the middle class acquiesced in Vargas' semi-fascist regime under which they were guaranteed a major role in an expanding bureaucracy. But as Vargas turned toward a new political strategy based on an industrialist-working class alliance, the middle class suddenly recalled its "liberal" precepts and supported, along with the old provincial landed oligarchies and the mercantilist elite, the ouster of the dictator and the "re-establishment of democracy" under military supervision.

With Vargas' return to power in 1951, Brazil entered a period of instability in which traditional elements controlled Congress, while the presidency was decidedly more subject to influence by the emerging populist groups. Within the context of this "structural crisis," the Armed Forces came to play an increasingly decisive role. They generally supported the threatened groups when the processes of change were perceived as possibly escaping the bounds of control, and "radical" elements were perceived as carrying populism beyond the limits of elite manipulation to a point where the internal dynamics of the movement might become self-sustaining. As economic and social development progressed, a plethora of new associational interest groups made their appearance. These intermediary organizations gave the political scene the outward appearance of an increasingly pluralistic representative system, although in reality most of them functioned at least partially as corporatist extensions of the state, enjoying only limited autonomy. With industrialization taking place under conditions of borrowed modern capital-intensive technology, the expansion of employment in the cities was chiefly in the tertiary sector rather than in manufacturing. The development of a large unemployed, or seriously underemployed, urban population contributed both to the relatively low political militancy of the employed and organized working class and to a middle class fear of proletarization. (The ramifications and interrelations of these are developed more fully on pages 30–34.)

[1] Consult Raymundo Faoro's *Os Donos do Poder: Formação do Patronato Político Brasileiro* (Rio de Janeiro, 1958), particularly pp. 183–271.

Populism, a blend of personalism and urban machine politics, was the ascending trend in Brazilian politics in the 1950's and early 1960's. It arose in the great metropolitan centers to fill the vacuum left when the old fashioned form of clientelism proved unable to adapt fully to the socio-economic changes of the postwar period. Its several distinct strands included (1) Vargas' labor-oriented nationalism during his 1953–1954 drift to the left; (2) Adhemar de Barros's overhaul of the patronial-patronage system to fit the needs and opportunities of São Paulo's rapid growth; (3) Jânio Quadros' moralistic exploitation of anti-Vargas and anti-Adhemar sentiment among the middle sectors, combined with demagogic appeals to the masses; (4) the cult and mistique of *Lacerdismo* with emphasis on intransigent opposition in a culture where "realism" often meant opportunism; (5) Goulart's efforts to become the new Vargas; (6) Brizola's more ideologically leftist and nationalist stress upon basic reforms; and (7) Miguel Arraes' emergence as the spokesman of the forgotten masses of the "neglected" Northeast and the under-developed interior.[2] Whatever its failings, populism in Brazil was something which socialism, articulate but ineffective, could not break through or free itself from. Even to the end of the Goulart period, essentially manipulative forms of populism had a stronger hold on the urban masses than did radical leftism, although Brizola was striving to fuse the two.

What existed in 1964, then, was a polity in which the elite was composed of several sedimentary layers which varied greatly in influence from metropolis, to provincial capital, to the rural areas and with a recent history of repeated realignments and shifting coalitions of interests. Replete with contradictions, it defied easy or neat categorization. Although not in the analytical meaning of modern social science, the "system" ("o sistema" in Brazilian discourse) had a meaning both substantially broader and more concrete than, for example, the term "establishment" has in the United States. In a partial and imprecise manner, it conditioned the expectations of major political actors and defined their mutual perceptions of institutional arrangements and structural interrelationships. As described by its most assiduous observer and inter-

[2] Arraes remains the least understood of the major political leaders of the early 1960's and the one who most requires more careful study. His prolonged exile in Algeria has made this quite difficult, as has his refraining from contributing to the unwieldly body of writings by those politically dispossessed in 1964.

preter, Oliveiros S. Ferreira, the Brazilian system is not something in which its components are explicitly aware of membership, but rather an organism that responds as a whole, in an almost reflex manner, "when one of its vital parts is threatened." [3] While this construct of the system falls far short of providing the framework for an adequate conceptualization of the Brazilian polity, it has the merit of underscoring the fact that there has been a notable stability of structures and roles persisting in the face of substantial economic transformation and social change. Indeed, any useful analytic model of the Brazilian political system must emphasize its position as a substantially independent, albeit intermediate, type, and not necessarily a way station to pluralist democracy, a modern mobilization system, or any other particular type of polity on an evolutionary scale. Such a model must be capable of explaining the Brazilian system substantially in terms of its own characteristics (as Ferreira does) while at the same time meaningfully relating it to more inclusive conceptualizations (as we are attempting to do).

From the perspective of early 1964, David Apter's "neo-mercantilist" and "reconciliation" types, discussed in Appendix A, appeared to offer a possibly productive avenue for approaching the construction of a model of the Brazilian system, although significant elements of his "modernizing autocracy" were also present, if this could be freed from its excessive and essentially unnecessary ties to monarchy. With the permanence of authoritarian features underscored by the October, 1965, "coup within the coup," adaptation of Apter appeared increasingly less feasible, in spite of the refinements he was concurrently making which removed Ghana and Uganda from behind some of the verbal underbrush

[3] A heavily jargonistic explanation of the system is contained in Ferreira's articles on "Uma caracterização do Sistema," in *O Estado de S. Paulo,* October 17 and 24, 1965. Other pertinent analytical articles by this scholar in *O Estado* bearing on the theme of the system and its replacement include: "Representação Revolucionária," April 18, 1965; "Organizar o Povo e Salvar a Nação," May 2, 1965; "Revolução Institucional," May 23, 1965; "A Nôva Crise no Bojo da Revolução," June 20, 1965; "O Estado Nôvo e a CLT," November 14, 1965; and "A Nação sem Projeto," November 21, 1965. His most significant essays, from May through September, 1966, are reprinted in *O Fim do Poder Civil.* He also provided a new constitutional framework for the nation (differing from the old and that put forth by Castelo Branco) in a series of *O Estado* articles during late 1966 and early 1967. The concept of "o sistema" was made familiar to United States scholars in a number of unpublished news letters from the Reverend Brady Tyson during 1964 and 1965, when he was working in São Paulo.

and brought Argentina and Chile at least partially into the picture. Apter himself subsequently tentatively classed Brazil as a hybrid between a "modernizing reconciliation system" and an "industrializing reconciliation system." But in light of the trends and developments of the past several years, Brazil could more appropriately be called a "bureaucratic" system blending elements of the "neo-mercantilist" and "military oligarchy" subtypes. Thus Apter's conceptualization is useful chiefly to distinguish Brazil (in relatively imprecise terms) from most of the other countries in the developing world, particularly the Afro-Asian nations, and (even less precisely) to facilitate comparison with other Latin American states. Readers who find Apter's scheme intellectually congenial can encounter in the more theoretical sections of this volume and its companion study the requisite elements for a fuller and more detailed Apterian formulation of the Brazilian system. (This stimulating if frustrating intellectual exercise will not be pursued further in this book in light of its decreasing utility as recent developments in Brazil have accentuated the salience of factors to which Apter's analytical approach is least suited.)

Two young Brazilian scholars have conceptualized their country's structural crisis as rooted in a contradiction between adaptation (equated chiefly with economic development) and integration (defined largely as maintenance of the political system).[4] Working with a relatively early version of Apter's classification of polities, Cintra and Reis describe Brazil as a "limited scope consociational system." While amply lubricated by a steadily growing economy, this system could accommodate the basic interests of the diverse politically participant social sectors, but with the slowdown in the development conciliation as the basis for renegotiating the boundaries and rules of the political game was no longer viable. Legitimacy based largely upon efficacy and performance wore perilously thin, and conflicts had been postponed and accumulated more than resolved. Marginal adjustments and incremental adaptations were not sufficient when politics began to be viewed as a zero-sum game by a significant proportion of the players.

[4] Antônio Octávio Cintra and Fábio Wanderley Reis, "Política e Desenvolvimento: o Caso Brasileiro," *América Latina,* IX, No. 3 (July-September, 1966), 52–74. Both have subsequently pursued doctoral studies at M.I.T. and should soon be in a position to refine their preliminary model.

Many conclusions regarding the post-revolutionary regime belong to the treatment of civil-military relations in the final section of this chapter. It is appropriate here, however, to recall the multistage process by which Brazil passed from a crisis junta to a government striving to reconcile the imperatives of the revolution with a renovated, but functioning representative system, then through a period of more sweeping extraordinary powers to the inauguration of a "constitutional" successor in March, 1967. The story of the subsequent decline into dictatorship has been told in the preceding chapters. Leadership composition, political style, and policy content changed during the immediate post-revolution years, but enough of the system remained intact that well-informed observers could view the polity as not having undergone a system transformation. The strengthening of the state and its implications were quite clearly seen by Jaguaribe, and Cândido Mendes brilliantly analyzed the emergence of a new type of mixed military and civilian technocracy. (See pages 111–115 for an analysis of their analyses.)

The very real authority dilemma that has contributed to the undermining of representative government and to the present regime of military authoritarianism has been touched upon by Robert Daland.[5] Within the broader context of Brazil as a prismatic political system characterized by elite dissensions and a tradition of systemic instability, Daland seeks answers to "why the Brazilian bureaucracy has been unable to plan, to order, and to implement economic development, which is the manifest goal of all Brazilian governments in the last two decades or more." [6] Writing during the early days of the Costa e Silva government (when Brazil appeared to be operating as a system of substantial, albeit limited, competition and military tutelage), he saw the bureaucracy as functioning "in a minor way as a patronage system for the rulers of Brazil, more importantly as a support system for the incumbent regime, and as an inferior mechanism of interest aggregation." [7] Viewing the bureaucracy as "a congeries of agencies with their own value systems and support systems resting on informal regional groups," Daland argued that imposition of controls could come only from "a military

[5] "Development Administration and the Brazilian Political System," *Western Political Quarterly*, XXI, No. 2 (June, 1968), 325–39.

[6] *Ibid.*, p. 328.

[7] *Ibid.*, p. 333.

dictatorship much more totalitarian than any regime in Brazilian history." [8] Considering this undesirable, he advocated decentralization of development-oriented programs. Intellectually appealing in terms of the fact that "very many and potentially powerful elements of the modernizing elite of Brazil are scattered through the society and the governmental institutions to the extent that no self-conscious modernizing elite can dominate," the feasibility of Daland's prescription rested upon an assumption, since proved erroneous, that the regime's removal of opponents had ceased and the purges of the Castelo Branco period were a thing of the past.[9]

Rather than highly critical of the changes imposed by the Castelo Branco regime, Daland rather generously interprets them in an optimistic light:

The cold fact is that every Brazilian president, including Vargas the "dictator," has found it necessary to assemble more power than that with which he was anointed in order merely to remain in office, to say nothing of achieving positive developmental goals. Thus it might well be viewed as a sign of positive political development that the military regime in Brazil has for the first time defined its intervention in political affairs in terms broader than merely removing threats to the constitutional order by controlling the incumbent president and his coterie. The revolutionary regime retained the reins of power pending the time when it could change the political structure to fit its conception of the appropriate constitutional system. . . . A greatly strengthened Presidency might conceivably shift the political struggle from the assembling of power to matters of policy and implementation and reduce the relative autonomy of the bureaucracy. The two parties might develop into aggregative instrumentalities. The one critical point is the degree to which the Military-as-supreme-court would exercise self-restraint and permit all political interests to enter the political battle. Should it be able to do this, the "Revolution" would prove to have been genuine, and significant political development would have occurred. The bureaucracy could then be made "responsible" to the Presidency and ultimately to party.[10]

This has not been the direction of change since 1967, and in doubting the military's capacity for following instead an authoritarian and cen-

[8] *Ibid.,* p. 335.
[9] Daland draws on the careful study of Kleber Nascimento, "Change Strategy and Client System: Administrative Reform in Brazil," an unpublished Ph.D. dissertation in the Department of Public Administration (University of Southern California, 1966).
[10] "Development Administration and the Brazilian Political System," p. 339.

tralizing line, Daland overlooks the existence of the "national security" (*segurança nacional*) doctrine, which has been spread to civilian bureaucrats other than the United States-trained or influenced public administrators associated with the Getúlio Vargas Foundation who emerge as the protagonists of his scenario. The April, 1969, establishment of a "Course of Brazilian Studies" at the Federal University of Rio de Janeiro, patterned after the War College program of studies, indicates the direction in which the regime is moving in developing a "technocratic" elite, rather than relying more heavily on the parties. The concurrent purges of the University of São Paulo were in part designed to pave the way for a similar innovation there. In justice to Daland, as well as to the Brazilians responsible for the policies involved, it must be admitted that although the costs have been very high indeed—particularly in terms of emasculation of representative processes and restrictions upon individual freedoms—the governmental system has been renovated or at least rationalized in a number of significant respects. Extractive and regulatory capabilities have been increased as a result, while responsive and symbolic capabilities have lagged behind or regressed.

The post-1964 military regime has been generally developmentalist in the narrow economic sense of the term, but it has sought to brake the process of social mobilization and has severely restricted political participation. Thus it has not been a modernizing regime in the broader sense of the term. In a more limited sense, it is "modernizing" rather than "traditional," in large part owing to the circumstances of the times. Having come to power in a country well embarked on the road to industrialization, the military could hardly have reversed this trend, especially since their concept of national security called for reinforcing it. This continuation of development ensures that some attitudinal changes will continue independent of the regime's desires, as side effects of industrialization.

With Castelo, Cordeiro de Farias, Juarez Távora, Golbery, Juracy Magalhães, Leitão da Cunha, the Geisels, and Roberto Campos all closely associated with the War College, ESG doctrine was at the heart of the first military government's program and tactics. Yet these views, although widely disseminated, were not accepted in their entirety by many officers, particularly in the lower ranks including those lieutenant colonels and colonels who had not yet been systematically initiated into the "national security" doctrine through attendance at the Command and General Staff School. Together with the generals who had not become part of the ESG circle that constituted the core of the Castelo Branco team, these officers, as has previously been demonstrated, opposed and undermined key elements of the regime's programs.[11] The key military figures of the Costa e Silva administration demonstrated a nearly complete absence of the career characteristics of Castelo's associates. As a result, their views on economic nationalism and relations with the United States differed sharply from those of their predecessors.

The Castelistas' self-criticism centers around an admitted overestimation of the political maturity of the professional political class if not the electorate as a whole. Castelo's struggle to institutionalize the revolution so as to avoid both discretionary regimes and chaotic excesses of power in the future were not "understood" by the politicians and consequently were undercut if not aborted by the 1965 "coup within the coup." Thus nothing permanent in the socio-political field was gained by an inherently coherent and dedicated administration, whose accomplishments were instead limited to the area of economic recovery.[12] Many of the civilian backers of the 1964 movement and the Castelo government hold that the entire political class should have been dismantled in 1964 and the groups actively backing the coup utilized as the nucleus for a new political force.

[11] Alfred Stepan, "Patterns of Civil-Military Relations in the Brazilian Political System," chap. xi, analyzes the "atypical" career experiences of the Castelista group. His most salient findings are that 60 per cent were veterans of FEB (compared to less than 30 per cent for the rest of the 1964 generals and only 25 per cent of the pro-Goulart minority); 90 per cent had graduated from the ESG (as against 62 per cent and 50 per cent); 70 per cent had served on the ESG staff (compared with 13 per cent and 18 per cent); all had graduated first in their class from at least one of the major courses (against 33 per cent and 20 per cent); all had attended military schools abroad, chiefly in the United States (contrasted to 24 per cent and 20 per cent). Stepan perceptively interprets the significance of this "cluster" of career experiences of Castelo's collaborators for their inability to guarantee continuity of policies through control of the presidential succession in 1966–1967.

[12] In relatively embittered hindsight, one of the leading Castelistas maintained in conversations with the author that in his desire to preserve as much of democracy as possible, Castelo "improved his place in history at the cost of sacrificing chances for more thorough-going changes in the old system."

The political system of the Brazilian subcontinent, perhaps more than that of any other country, bears out Juan Linz's contention that "in some cases, particularly in Latin America, much of the difficulty lies in the further diffusion of modern elements from some regions to others, the modernization of some sectors while others are already highly modernized." [13] The sources of heterogeneity in Brazilian society are fundamentally similar to those he identifies for Spain, except that variations in ethnic composition, traceable to differential patterns of immigration, replace Spain's older differences in linguistic and cultural tradition. Clearly the emphasis on "the two Brazils," dominant in so much of the literature on Brazil, is most inadequate in this respect, as are the traditional studies of regionalism that concentrate on the distinctive characteristics of key areas.[14] While André Gunder Frank's model of the "capitalist development of underdevelopment in Brazil" points out a number of the shortcomings of the dualist approach, its construct of "constellations of metropolises and satellites" is useful more as a corrective to the dual society view than as an essentially satisfactory alternative frame of reference for analyzing political development.[15]

Fernando Henrique Cardoso also demonstrates the inadequacies of the simplified modern versus traditional confrontation of sectors. Beyond this, he analyzes the political comportment of the Brazilian entrepre-

[13] Juan J. Linz and Amando de Miguel, "Within National Differences and Comparisons: The Eight Spains," in Richard L. Merritt and Stein Rokkan (eds.), *Comparing Nations* (New Haven, 1966), pp. 267–319. The quote is from p. 271. The findings of this study also support Linz's assertion that in place of the developed-underdeveloped dichotomy "We need a distinctive intellectual approach to those Western societies—in the Mediterranean and Latin America—that share many key institutions closely associated with the modern industrial society . . . but whose countries have failed in economic development and in accepting certain values that go with the methods of an advanced industrial society." (p. 282n)

[14] Among the more useful studies of this type are Jacques Lambert, *Os Dois Brasís* (Rio de Janeiro, 1953), and Moisés Vellinho, *Brazil South* (New York, 1969). Most systematic in terms of modern political sociology is Gláucio Dillon Soares, "The Politics of Uneven Development in Brazil," but here, too, the analysis is still essentially dichotomous, between the "underdeveloped" Northeast and the "developed" Center-South, and relies too heavily on simplified distinctions between political parties, which can be maintained only as relative differentiations and variations in degree.

[15] André Gunder Frank, *Capitalism and Underdevelopment in Latin America* (New York, 1967), pp. 145–218.

neurial class in a manner congruent both with its origins and its behavior in the crucial 1963–1965 period.

> . . . populist policies during the Goulart government became nonviable when
> they passed the tacit limits of the "developmentalist alliance" and tried to
> mobilize rural popular sectors (unionization of peasants, peasant leagues,
> etc.) and to favor, within the urban sector, the tendency toward an expansion-
> ist wage policy at a time of low foreign investments. The "developmentalist"
> front rapidly disintegrated in favor of strengthening the party of "order-
> property-prosperity" to which the industrial bourgeoisie rapidly adhered. . . .[16]

The accommodation of the national bourgeoisie with the "traditional"
agrarian and mercantilist sectors, when faced by radical pressures for
change which threatened to escape the bonds of manipulative populism,
was one side of the coin; the other was the result of the economic stagnation of 1963–1964. For the "developmentalist alliance" rested on the
willingness of the entrepreneurial interests to tolerate support by the
nationalist popular group of expansion of the public sector of the economy in exchange for their acceptance of substantial foreign investment
in industry.[17]

The breakdown of the developmentalist alliance and the subsequent
realignment of propertied classes behind the military movement of 1964
opened the way for an authoritarian regime under Army leadership. The
political marginalization of the populace facilitated the shift to a developmentalist model based on heavy foreign investment, while close
association with international enterprises and sources of capital largely
replaced the idea of public quasi-monopolies as the chief complementary
vehicle to private enterprise in the process of economic development.
But with the progressive alienation of the middle class, as well as increasing discontent from the politically downgraded populist groups,
only an essentially authoritarian regime could maintain a controlled
political situation in which development through interdependence could

[16] Fernando Henrique Cardoso, "Hegemonia Burguesa e Independência Econômica: Raízes Estruturais da Crise Política Brasileira," *Revista Civilização
Brasileira,* No. 17 (January-February, 1968), p. 74. An earlier and more general
analysis by the same author is available in English as "The Industrial Elite," in
Seymour Martin Lipset and Aldo Solari (eds.), *Elites in Latin America* (New
York, 1967), pp. 94–114.
[17] Cardoso, "Hegemonia . . .," p. 92.

flourish. As a result, repeated efforts toward political normalization since 1964 have been aborted by the government itself in order to preserve the revolution's gains in the field of economic rationality and modernization of the capitalist system.

2. A "MODERNIZING AUTHORITARIAN" REGIME

For Gabriel Almond and G. Bingham Powell, writing in 1966, Brazil represented a "modernizing authoritarian" system as distinct from the "conservative authoritarian" system of Spain, a "premobilized authoritarian" system (Ghana), or a "democratic" system with "low subsystem autonomy" (Mexico). Admitting that "some measure of real pluralism and competitive process" still exists in authoritarian systems, Almond stresses the "traditionalist" elements of the Spanish regime, while failing to articulate any significant interpretation of the "modernizing" aspects of Brazil's political experience.[18] As his discussion of authoritarianism borrows almost entirely from the fecund works of Juan Linz, it may be useful here to elaborate a parallel model of the Brazilian system. While Linz too refrains from commenting on the possibly modernizing facets of an authoritarian system in a relatively young and aggressively developmentalist country such as Brazil, his conceptualization and comparative generalizations provide the foundation for such theorizing.[19]

Enough highly qualified analysts have made the point in recent years that authoritarianism is distinct from both totalitarianism and

[18] Almond and Powell, *Comparative Politics*, p. 274.

[19] Linz's model is found in "An Authoritarian Regime: Spain," in E. Allardt and Y. Littunen (eds.), *Cleavages, Ideologies and Party Systems. Contributions to Comparative Political Sociology* (Helsinki, 1964), pp. 291–341. His brilliant conceptualization of the Spanish political system is given additional content on the dimension of electoral behavior in "The Party System of Spain: Past and Future," in Lipset and Rokkan, *Party Systems and Voter Alignments*, pp. 197–282. On a number of points the concept of the "syncratic" political system as developed by A. F. K. Organski in *The Stages of Political Development* (New York, 1965), pp. 122–56, might be used as an alternative model. Based heavily on the Italian, Spanish, and Argentine (Peronist) experiences, it is a substantial improvement over the loose use of "fascist." But it does not provide for distinctions among different types of authoritarian regimes. In stressing the anti-modernizing accommodation between agricultural and industrial elites and generally assuming civilian dominance, Organski skirts the question of the developmentalist orientation of the military so critical in the Brazilian case.

pluralist democracy that it is unnecessary to sum up or continue the argument here.[20] Linz's definition is fundamentally adequate and sufficiently broad to cover a modernizing authoritarian regime such as Brazil, as well as the more traditional Spanish regime.

Authoritarian regimes are political systems with limited, not responsible, political pluralism: without elaborate and guiding ideology (but with distinctive mentalities); without intensive nor extensive political mobilization (except some points in their development); and in which a leader (or occasionally a small group) exercises power within formally ill-defined limits but actually quite predictable ones.[21]

With respect to pluralism, the young military-run modernizing authoritarian regime in Brazil is in a position of curbing and disciplining groups and interests accustomed for over twenty years to operating within a system in which the government was relatively weak and conciliatory, while that in Spain is more concerned with the problem of slowly loosening controls after more than three decades in power. Representing the military institution, or at least its leadership, rather than an entrenched *caudilho* or personalist clique, the Brazilian regime has not proceeded nearly so far as Spain's with the cooptation of leadership nor are the several elites yet fully under its consolidated control. As considerable work remains in the field of bringing existing associations under the new order, little has been done to date about establishing supplantive or supplementary ones under regime sponsorship. Crucial as the government's response to the existence and activity of associational interests is in defining the exact nature of the regime, in the case of Brazil there are only clues to the emerging pattern of interrelationships between the state and society. Pluralism is certainly to be limited, but substantial experimentation is likely with regard to both manner and degree in a system where significant vestiges of a functioning representative system remain from nearly a quarter century of liberal democracy since the previous experiment with authoritarianism under the *Estado Nôvo*.

One of the most important examples of limitation of pluralism

---

[20] In addition to Linz, the main points are made by Louis Coser in his essay, "Prospects for the New Nations: Totalitarianism, Authoritarianism or Democracy?," in Louis Coser (ed.), *Political Sociology* (New York, 1966), pp. 247–71.

[21] "An Authoritarian Regime: Spain," p. 297.

under the regime is the relationship of industrial and commercial groups to the government. As analyzed by successful private sector figures who had occupied high bureaucratic offices during the Castelo Branco regime, the entrepreneurial class is subject to intimidation if not control by the government, particularly through control of credit and selective enforcement of regulations. The traditional "accommodationist" elements of the self-styled "producing classes" seek a system in which profits are privatized while risks and losses are socialized. This conflicts with a puritanical tendency among the military to favor capitalism and private initiative in principle, but to be suspicious of sizable profits. In a situation where the great weight of economic power is no longer made effective through the electoral arena (owing to the absence of competitive elections), the entrepreneurial elite finds its political influence fragile and dependent upon the government's wishes, rather than weak (in terms of rival interests having greater influence).

The work of Phillipe Schmitter on the development of associational interest groups in Brazil confirms the view that development does not necessarily lead directly or immediately to substantial pluralism. Moreover, it demonstrates that the relative proliferation of associational interest groups has not resulted in a substantial increase in their influence upon the shaping of public policy.[22] The survey data on political culture in Schmitter's study of associational interest groups substantiate the view that the attitudes of their representatives are not in sharp conflict with a system in which there are substantial controls, a relatively high degree of cooptation, and a great deal of manipulation of groups by the authorities.

The main adjustment for many such particularistic interests is not that of decreased autonomy in the positive sense—since most function primarily to defend their acquired privileges from the threats inherent in change—but to the modernizing regime's increasingly enforceable demand that these vested interests be subordinated to its view of the national good and the imperatives of "national security." In this respect

---

[22] Schmitter's University of California dissertation on this subject will be published by Stanford University Press in 1971. While his study covers the 1930–1965 period, and field work was completed at the end of that time, his conceptualization also draws upon much of the Brazilian social science literature published in 1966–1967.

some of the greatest curbs and sacrifices are being placed on the political class that enjoyed such a high degree of autonomy and influence under the old *Sistema*. It is in this regard that Schmitter's discussion of what he terms a "populist, semi-competitive authoritarian regime" is most dated, since his stress throughout is on the persistence of the political class-dominated *sistema,* a view that enjoyed substantial viability prior to the turn toward dictatorship in December, 1968. The professional politicians have borne much of the brunt of the ensuing hardening of military authoritarianism, paradoxically in the company of progressive intellectuals who were among the leading critics of this class and its "corrupt" *sistema.* (Thus much of Schmitter's conceptualization, like Leff's stimulating theoretical propositions concerning economic policy making, dwells on features of a largely superseded system. Neither deals at all comprehensively with post-1964 developments.)

Hence Schmitter's model of "populist, semi-competitive" authoritarianism is most useful as providing insight into the authoritarian elements present even during the "experiment with democracy" of 1946–1964 rather than for analyzing the evolving system of the post-revolution years. The *dictablanda* or *democradura* (literally, "soft dictatorship" and "hard democracy") of 1964–1968 appears in retrospect to have been transitional as the military modernizers coexisted with the old *sistema* and its political class until the influence of the traditional liberal democrats within the Army's ranks was diluted, opening the way for a more authoritarian regime relatively untrammeled by the populist requirements of even a tutelary representative democracy. Clientelism, capitalism, and control have all been present to varying degrees in the political strategies of all Brazilian governments in the republican era. As in the period from 1937 on, the stress on control is presently much higher than usual, with the mixture of patronage and paternalism so characteristic of most previous regimes now discredited and in large part discarded.

Linz has suggested that the degree of political mobilization might be the most meaningful criteria for distinguishing among subtypes of authoritarian regimes. Admitting that this may in large part be a function of the stage of development of the system, he maintains that such variations with regard to mobilization result more from "the opportunities offered by the social structure, the political context and the international situation for a mobilization in support of those in power, than on the outlook of the rulers." [23] While low mobilization is characteristic of stabilized authoritarian regimes, newer ones may temporarily carry over substantial political participation from the crises in which they emerged.

Thus on the one side we have regimes coming to power after periods of considerable organized political strife, lack of consensus under democratic governments and aborted revolutions: all these will tend to use apathy to consolidate their power, at least the apathy of those not likely to be won over to their policies. The depolitization in these cases would be one way to reduce the tension in the society and achieve a minimum of re-integration, which otherwise could probably be reached only by totalitarian suppression of the dissidents. . . .

On the other side we have regimes trying to gain control of societies in which the masses have never been mobilized by any political force, particularly if the preceding regime had been one of colonial rule, or a traditional monarchy, or even an oligarchic democracy. These situations are likely to coincide with underdeveloped rather than semi-developed societies, where the underprivileged masses have not given their loyalty to any organized movement, and consequently their manipulation is easy, at least initially.[24]

Although historically the Brazilian system has differed from the Hispanic authoritarian model quite sharply on the dimension of mobilization, this divergence has been greatly reduced since 1965 and particularly since December, 1968. With respect to such considerations as organization and popular participation, Brazilian-style authoritarianism remains in a phase of pronounced depolitization. However, given the developmentalist orientation of important elements of its leadership, and the mobilizational as well as elitist components of the military's evolving political doctrine, this may be a transitory tendency and a successor to Garrastazú might well follow a significantly populist line, particularly if the Peruvian populist-nationalist model continues to prove effective.

The sharpest differentiation between the Brazilian model and that of Spain (as well as most other authoritarian regimes) concerns the party system. If, as Linz points out, the authoritarian party frequently plays a "second-rate role," in Brazil it is several rungs farther down the ladder, albeit in part owing to the yet incomplete transition from a competitive system. Party identification is substantially lower than in Spain, member-

---

[23] "An Authoritarian Regime: Spain," pp. 304–307.
[24] *Ibid.*, p. 307.

ship less meaningful (and all but non-existent in a cadre sense), ideological indoctrination absent rather than minimal, and organization less than skeletal. Indeed, when Congress was closed, as in 1969, the executive ignored the governing party, except to purge it of elements considered unreliable. The ARENA presidency was left unfilled for months, and its leader in the Chamber of Deputies was "elevated" to the Superior Military Tribunal, where he would have a more influential and satisfying function to fulfill.

The Armed Forces in Brazil seem likely to retain a role and influence exceeding that ascribed to them in Linz's model. As a result of both its more substantial ideology and the insignificance of the party, the military in Brazil is in a much more dominant position than in Spain. In many respects the Armed Forces are more deeply entrenched in the political and governmental institutions than is the case even in Egypt. (Although it would be most illuminating, sufficient data is not presently available for a meaningful comparison with the Greek military regime.)

The dominance of the military at this relatively early juncture in the evolution of Brazil's authoritarian system leads to an apparent departure from Linz's model in terms of the composition of the top elite. Even so, his basic conclusion remains applicable.

. . . a significant part of the authtoritarian regime's leadership had already participated actively in the country's political life as parliamentarians, and through seniority in the army, civil service, or academic world would have been assured a respectable position in the society under any regime. Given the non-ideological character of much authoritarian politics, the emphasis on respectability of expertise, and the desire to co-opt elements of established society, a number of those assuming power will have little previous involvement in politics. Occasionally, particularly at the second level, we find people who define themselves publicly as apolitical, just experts, The old fighters of the extremist groups which contributed to the crisis of the previous regime, who participated in the take-over, who hoped to take power, may find their claims rejected, and will have to content themselves with secondary positions. In some cases their political style, their ideological commitments, their exclusivism, may lead them to break away and retire to private life.[25]

The newness of the Brazilian regime precludes any valid conclusions concerning recruitment and renewal patterns. Similarly, it is far too early to essay any evaluation in light of Brazilian experience of Linz's proposi-

[25] *Ibid.*, p. 325.

tions concerning the dynamics of authoritarian regimes. He has already pointed out that Vargas' Estado Nôvo experience, particularly its non-violent demise, deserves careful study as an apparent exception to his rule that there are few examples of transitions from authoritarianism to democracy or totalitarianism without "serious crises or revolutionary changes." [26] (This has been done in Chapter 5 of *Modernization and the Military in Brazil.*) Developments during 1974 and 1975, when the Garrastazú government is slated to give way to an elected successor, if the military regime proves viable to that point, may be of substantial significance in providing elements for the refining of propositions in this field as well as for the evaluation of the efficiency of authoritarian regimes along the dimensions proposed by Linz.

The Brazilian model of an authoritarian regime also differs significantly from that put forth by Linz in terms of its distinctive "mentality" or ideological content. In the case of Spain, Linz may be correct in accepting Janowitz's conclusions regarding military ideology and terming it "little related to any intellectual elaboration." [27] But in Brazil the pervasiveness within the Armed Forces and the allied civilian technocrats of an inclusive and relatively elaborate national security doctrine adds a distinctive element to the model. It also brings into question Linz's association of a large or decisive role for the military with a higher degree of traditionalism. Then, too, in general, the prominent role of bureaucratic elites in the ongoing functioning of the political system is perhaps more accentuated in Brazil's very active "modernizing" authoritarian regime than in the stable, traditional type represented by Spain, particularly since it is the mechanism for much of interest aggregation in the absence of a significant party structure.[28]

[26] *Ibid.,* p. 337.

[27] *Ibid.,* p. 301n.

[28] James L. Busey, "The Old and the New in the Politics of Modern Brazil," in Eric W. Baklanoff (ed.), *The Shaping of Modern Brazil* (Baton Rouge, 1969), pp. 58–85, considers the post-1964 regime as closely approximating "quasi-democratic, paternalistic semi-authoritarianism," with the representative aspects somewhat muted. The Castelo Branco and Costa e Silva administrations fall into his multi-dimensional diagrammatic typology of governments at almost the identical point as those of Marshals Deodoro and Floriano three-quarters of a century earlier. His broadest interpretation of Brazil's political development can be found in "Brazil's Reputation for Political Stability," *Western Political Quarterly,* XVIII, No. 4 (December, 1965), 866–80.

In many important respects, the accommodationist pattern of political life prior to 1964 closely followed the model for Hispanic-American countries constructed by Charles Anderson.[29] The bargaining nature of politics and the tentative and shifting nature of the governing coalitions were evident in the pre-1964 Brazilian polity. That elections are not the only means of manifesting a power capability is obvious from the series of military interventions, as well as from the strikes and demonstrations that have been mentioned in several chapters of this study. New power contenders have been admitted to more than symbolic participation without threatening the existence of the established forces. By and large, the new players accepted the existing rules of the game as the price of admission. The result was, however, not so much pluralism in the accepted United States-Western European sense as a bureaucratic state in which major policy decisions were avoided or postponed in the absence of meaningful parties or effective mechanisms for conflict resolution. Moreover, many of the policy decisions essential to the functioning of the system were largely determined by factors outside the control of domestic Brazilian political forces. Then, too, to a degree which throws Anderson's scheme out of balance, the Armed Forces in Brazil have functioned as the cutting edge for new power contenders, although their role in helping block admission of the rural masses in 1964 supports one of his major (if all but self-evident) points. Thus, while for comparative purposes it might be useful to formulate a model of Brazil's political processes in an Andersonian vocabulary, such an exercise would not significantly further an understanding of the post-1964 system. Given the wide use and pervasive influence of Almond's work in the field of comparative politics, there might also be utility in recasting the model more explicitly in terms of Almond's categories, but to do so here would do little to advance the central purposes of this work.

More pertinent to our purposes here in the attempt of Von Lazar to do some theory building in the area of the "dynamics of authoritarian political control in transition." [30] Assuming that "modern" authoritarian

[29] See his *Politics and Economic Change in Latin America* (Princeton, 1967), particularly chap. iv, pp. 87–114. Anderson based his theoretical propositions chiefly upon the experience of Central America and the Andean countries.

[30] Arpad Von Lazar, "Latin America and the Politics of Post-Authoritarianism: A Model for Decompression," *Comparative Political Studies,* I, No. 3 (October, 1968), 419–29.

political systems, such as those of the contemporary Brazilian and Argentine military regimes, seek to introduce policies that induce popular support for the system and lead civilians to identify with the values and authority pattern of the government, he hypothesizes a process in which "evolution within society induces the power wielders to adjust their policies to relative or imagined fulfillment of the popular demands, while the actual execution of these policies will perpetuate and often increase the demand for further 'liberalization.' " [31] The regime must then seek a means for responding to and channeling this feedback process without seeing the authoritarian system "invaded" by challenging influences. For in the view of Von Lazar, "the very process of decompression activates a dialectic of strengthening the position of the power wielders in some ways and weakening their position in other ways." [32]

According to this imaginative analysis, the regime may respond to discontent with force, by resorting to a very limited and carefully controlled decompression or by permitting a substantial liberalization. These two courses of action can get out of hand, leading to a "temporary deluge" that can be brought back under control by coercive measures or, escaping control, can result in a breakdown of the authoritarian system. Given the context of Brazilian politics six years after the 1964 coup, the detailed "timetable of dynamism" presented by Von Lazar as a synthesis of the experience of all recent Latin American military regimes warrants continuing attention as a possible, indeed perhaps plausible scenario for future political development. Efforts by such governments to win popular support through limited concessions are more likely to give rise to serious crises than to ease tensions.

A. Socioeconomic or political situation is unsatisfactory and the power wielders deem the granting of some concessions as imperative. These concessions are thought to be the source of further support for the system.

B. Few concessions are made on a limited scale. This is still essentially a stage of the process when mass involvements are minimal.

C. There is slowness and reluctance on the part of the masses to take the developments seriously and a reaction to the concessions is weak. At this point, there are the first signs of emergence and crystallization of new social *groups* into influence, i.e., intellectuals, students, etc.

[31] *Ibid.*, p. 420.
[32] *Ibid.*, p. 423.

D. Tentative probings of the masses, channeled through the actions of the new groups of influence. At this stage, the power wielders' role as the initiators of change is, step by step, overtaken by the challengers. The gap between the possibility for granting further substantial concessions and the growing demand for these is increasing.

E. The flood of popular demands, manipulated by the challengers, penetrates the entire system. The irony of the situation is that the course of events is, by this time, becoming popular with the public. The popularity of the program depends largely upon its continuance. The power wielders are inclined to go along with this development but naturally at a much slower rate of speed than demanded by the public. . . .

F. Emergence and consolidation of groups that are the most outspoken in their demands. The effectiveness of the control apparatus of the system is by this time seriously weakened. The new groups of influence attempt to transplant issues of political and ideological nature into economic terms, thereby mobilizing public opinion. . . .

G. Increased concern among the power wielders resulting in possible rifts within their ranks. As the process of decompression accelerates, the power wielders' reluctance to go along becomes more evident.

H. Efforts to slow down the process, to persuade the public and to coerce the challengers not to "go too far." This already reveals the weaknesses of the power wielders and their concern about public attitudes.

I. Failure of these efforts. Attempts for the re-imposition of control only generate further demands for concessions.

J. Reluctant re-imposition of controls which ensues in ideological and/or physical conflicts. The cycle is ended through the use of force which brings about the temporary control of the process (or alternatively, total disintegration of control and thus the system).[33]

Admittedly an empirical gap remains between the tentative model of the emerging authoritarian political system presented above and this conceptualization of the process of decompression. Yet the fundamental outlines of Von Lazar's scheme appear congruent with the course of events in Brazil since 1964, in which each effort toward "normalization" has instead brought the country another step closer to a more purely authoritarian regime. Since none of the transitory regimes involved— Castelo's rennovative phase and his 1966 controlled competition, Costa's experiment with constitutional government and "humanization," and his mid-1969 moves toward reopening of Congress—was a fully elaborated, entrenched authoritarian system corresponding exactly to Von Lazar's

[33] *Ibid.,* p. 427.

ideal type, the cycle in each case was less profound and complex than in his scenario. Rather than new social groups emerging at point *c,* the existing representative political strata, particularly the national Congress, played the role of "challenger." With the Garrastazú Médici government corresponding more closely to a full-fledged authoritarianism, the possibility is increased of a more profound decompression dilemma in the future.

3. POLITICAL DEVELOPMENT AND CIVIL-MILITARY RELATIONS

The Brazilian version of an authoritarian political system has been analyzed in terms designed to facilitate meaningful comparison with other polities. It remains to reassess, if not refine, some of the theoretical propositions examined in Chapter 1 in the light of Brazilian experience. Many of the most systematic comparisons over time are left for the companion study, in which substantial attention has been devoted to the structural, contextual, and configurational features of each crisis as well as the mix of motivations and the effects of the outcome both upon the country's political development and the historical memory of the Armed Forces at it conditioned their behavior in subsequent crises. Yet the basic outlines of this analysis are relevent here as they bear on the existing military institution.

On the first order of importance, three fundamental crises of regime have been experienced during Brazil's nearly 150 years of life as an independent nation. That of the 1880's resulted in the replacement of the Empire by a presidential republic; that of the 1920's led to the 1930 revolution and a subsequent period of experimentation, which included an eight-year authoritarian regime (the Estado Nôvo), as well as a subsequent eighteen-year experience with representative democracy; and that of the late 1950s and early 1960's paved the way for the 1964 revolution and its unfolding authoritarian system. In each of these three periods of instability, which resulted in a system change rather than just a replacement of a government, a common factor was the existence of a significant gap between the substantial rate of social change and mobilization of new groups into politics and the much slower development of adequate political organization and institutionalization. This was most noticeable with regard to parties, which have never functioned effectively as vehicles for integration and modernization in Brazil.

In Huntington's terms, Brazil—a praetorian rather than a civic polity for most of its existence—may have reached the civic threshold under the Empire in the 1850's and 1860's and again with the Old Republic around the time of World War I. It may have come close again the late 1940's. In each case, however, the inability to handle the incorporation of new groups—first the middle class, then the urban working class, and finally the peasantry—resulted in an institutional crisis and return to praetorianism in terms of "the absence of effective political institutions capable of mediating, refining, and moderating group political action. . . . Equally important, no agreement exists among the groups as to the legitimate and authoritative methods for resolving conflict." [34] Within limits, conceptualizing the course of political development and decay in Brazil as one of crossing and recrossing the boundary between civic and praetorian at generational intervals has its utility. But it may be more meaningful to view Brazil as being most frequently in an intermediate category, characterized by a medium ratio of institutionalization to participation. In this view, by 1964 Brazil reached the point at which the participation crisis involved was that of moving from medium toward high by incorporation of the rural population. (As suggested on pages 15–16, a three by three typology rather than his present three by two matrix would help Huntington deal more effectively with the analytical challenges presented by the modernizing Latin American nations.)

Leaving aside for the moment participation and institutionalization per se, the three great crises of regime (or system) possessed a comparable socio-economic dimension in which the common element was the impact of industrialization. The number of industrial establishments in Brazil in 1881 was only 200, but by the death throes of the Empire in 1889 this figure had more than trebled to over 600. Between 1880 and 1884, some 150 industrial firms with a capital of 58,000 contos were established, while from 1885 to 1889 the increment was 248 firms with over 200,000 contos of capital.[35] This period also witnessed much of the adjustment from slave to wage-earning labor in the agricultural sector. Again while nearly 7,000 industrial firms were established in Brazil during the first twenty-five years of the Old Republic (or an

[34] *Political Order in Changing Societies,* p. 196.
[35] Basbaum, *História Sincera da República,* Vol. I, p. 149.

average of under 300 per year), almost 6,000 (or 1,200 per year) were founded during the 1915–1919 surge that accompanied World War I. Since the series of crises which culminated in the 1930 Revolution began during the early 1920's, it is clear that intensive spurts of rapid industrialization preceded each of the great crises of regime, and it appears that the inability of the political system to accommodate to the societal changes stemming from these waves of industrialization is one of the major constants. In the postwar period, the parallel phenomenon lies in the forced-draft industrialization of the Kubitschek era which, combined with the failure of Quadros to deal adequately with the resulting socio-economic tensions, led to an accumulation of problems beyond the capabilities of the competitive semi-democratic system.

It has been evident in the course of my larger research that the timing of the three crises resulting in systems changes appears to coincide with the expiration of the influence span of a leadership generation. Closer examination of the material on the orientation toward political activity on the part of the officer corps strongly indicates that at about forty-year intervals, a new military generation has emerged to replace one which has been dominant for an impressively long period of time. This took place in the 1880's as the young positivists became politically active on behalf of republicanism and, behind the figure of Deodoro, pushed through a decisive action on the part of the military establishment that was alien to the views of the generals whose dominance dated back to the Paraguayan War. Rising over the years to general officer rank themselves, the lieutenants of the 1880's became a major prop of the Old Republic, only to have their authority challenged by the *tenentes* of the 1920's, first behind the figure of Marshal Hermes, and then (following his death) on their own. As in the 1880's, the young, discontented officers raised the standard of reform and modernization, attacking a system they perceived as decadent and outmoded. The ex-*tenentes* remained for decades the politically dominant military group; they rose rapidly in the 1930's, controlled military education in the 1940's, and became generals in the 1950's.

The stage was thus set for the dual challenge to this generation during the 1960's, first by a relatively small group of "nationalist" officers endorsing a shift from a patronial to a populist system, and subsequently by the younger officers of the *linha dura* reacting against the survival of many basic features of the *sistema*. The greatly increased indoctrination of the lower ranks of officers into the "national security" mentality through the Army's increasingly elaborate system of schools and courses has tied the older leadership and the emerging groups within the officer corps more closely together than in the 1880's or 1920's, but the hold of the extraordinary *tenentismo*-Brazilian Expeditionary Force generation cannot carry over into the 1970's. (The influence span of the *tenentes* of the 1920's was extended both by their leadership over a newer group of lieutenants and captains during the Italian campaign, and subsequently through their establishment and control of the War College.)

Although reliable empirical data on this point is still scarce, especially for the earlier period, it appears that changes in the social origins and recruitment patterns of the officer corps has been a major factor in these three generational renovations of the Army's dominant strata. This study has, however, adduced strong evidence for the hypothesis that shifts in the general political environment, changes in the political socialization of the young officers, and evidence of serious political decay with respect to the political system have been more important explanatory factors. In two cases, 1889 and 1930, the younger military elements aided the bourgeoisie and middle sectors to make their effective entrance into national political life. In these instances of "breakthrough coups," the civilian elements involved were from essentially the same social strata as the officers themselves. But in the 1960's, the groups seeking participation and influence have been the urban and rural working classes, viewed by the military as potential competitors rather than prospective allies. While Huntington's general formulations with respect to this phenomenon are adequate, Nun's more detailed and elaborate analysis (discussed on pages 18–21) more closely fits the Brazilian case.[36]

---

[36] Stepan, "Patterns of Civil-Military Relations . . .," pp. 52–53, demonstrates that since World War II the proportion of new officers from families of upper class occupational categories decreased from nearly 20 per cent to only 6 per cent. (Based upon a comparison of cadets entering the Military Academy in 1941–1943 and 1962–1966.) This was not, however, accompanied by any substantial increase in lower-class representation, largely because of the high school graduation requirement for entry to AMAN. Some three-quarters of the Brazilian Army officer corps through the 1940's, 1950's, and 1960's have been of middle-class social origins as classified on both objective and subjective (self-assessment) measures.

The coincidence on the one hand of political decay (participation-institutional crises with parties worn out and discredited) in the aftermath of a surge of industrialization with the emergence on the other of a young military counterelite and its first political stirrings goes far toward explaining the three crises of regime (1889, 1930, 1964), but leaves a good deal unanswered with regard to the several lesser crises that entailed significant military interventions into politics without resulting in a transformation of the political system. Although Huntington's concept of a "veto coup" is of some utility, it has been shown in the detailed analysis of each of these episodes that important factors not discussed by Huntington are also involved. The more salient feature is of course the Brazilian military's concept of the "moderating power" and the substantial legitimacy accorded by other groups to its exercise of this function.

Throughout the period of some eighty years covered by this study, embracing several generations of political and military leadership, it is clear that significant civilian groups did not wish the military to stay out of politics—at least when its intervention could be useful to their aims and strategies. During the latter stages of the Empire, Republicans and abolitionists sought support within the military and strove to turn them against the monarchy, while the government also contributed to the politization of the Armed Forces. At the state level, contending elite groups in the Old Republic formed frequent alliances with military elements. The civilian leadership of the 1930 Revolution had been working for nearly two years to build an alliance with military elements, and the early 1930's witnessed competition by contending political forces for military support very reminiscent of that around the turn of the century. The early Estado Nôvo years were one of the few periods when no significant opposition groups sought military support against the regime. But this had changed by 1943–1944, and the military's ouster of Vargas and tutelage over the establishment of the new republic was greater than that after 1930 if not as complete as in the 1889–1893 period.

Before each instance in which the Armed Forces exercised their function of "guardian" or moderating power, significant civilian groups and major press organs had been reminding them of their responsibility and calling upon them to act. At the same time, the legitimacy of the government had been publicly called into question, generally in terms of its alleged plans to subvert "democratic" institutions and perpetuate itself in office. In the one unsuccessful effort, that of 1961, the unexpected nature of Quadros' resignation and the fact that Goulart, never having been in power, could not be attacked effectively on these grounds, deprived his military opponents of this crucial legitimacy factor. The 1955 situation was complicated in this respect, with support for the "preventive coup" justified by belief (backed by what appeared to many a plausible coincidence) that the caretaker government—whose legitimacy was questioned by those important groups which had backed Vargas—was planning to thwart the popular will as expressed at the polls the preceding month. In 1955, as in 1961, there was strong sentiment that it was not within the rules of the game for the military to veto an individual and bar him from the presidency, that incapacity or unfitness must be proved by his actions in office.

By the postwar period, the military's continuing role as guardian of "democratic" institutions and as umpire of the political game had received substantial legitimacy through acceptance by civilian groups. Rather than a meddling outsider, the Armed Forces constituted an integral part of the political system; at times, they reacted more as an essentially dependent sub-system than as an alien, interventionist force. In this regard the Brazilian Army bears out Schmitt's contention that "the military will not be and cannot be distracted from politics whenever its major interests are affected or whenever serious disorders arise among the politically active sectors of the civilian community." [37]

Although the ebb and flow, along with the impinging factors involved, is too complex and intricate a story to be summarized here, this study and its complementary volume have abundamently documented the fact that from the birth of the Republic to the present there has always been a current within the military advocating an active political involvement, a large ambivalent middle mass, and intransigently legalist elements. At each decisive moment, the numerically largest group within the officer corps has been that characterized by ambivalent attitudes and has based its decisions on a variety of factors, including a concept of the military as the arbiter of crises and moderator of conflicts that

[37] Karl M. Schmitt, in a review of Edwin Lieuwen's *Mexican Militarism: The Political Rise and Fall of the Revolutionary Army, 1910–1940,* in *The Annals of the American Academy of Political Science,* CCCLXXXIII (May, 1969), p. 193.

threaten the fabric of society, as well as regard for the institutional interests of the military establishment. When in power, these officers often exhibit deep concern over the developments of internal divisions and loss of credit and popularity with civilian opinion groups; out of power, however, they tended to chafe over the government's lack of attention to military needs.

The demise of the old pattern of civil-military relations became clear from the course of events after 1964, as the Armed Forces were clearly prepared to remain in power as long as necessary to implement their plans for "renovating" the nation and to forestall the return to power of the forces supporting the radicalization of the Goulart regime. This abandonment of the traditional attitude toward politics, or rather the emergence as dominant of a strain of thought which had long been held in check by civilist and legalist scruples, can be properly understood only in the perspective of the prolonged instability of 1954–1964, in which the anti-Goulart move appeared to most of its military participants as an unfortunately necessary replay of the Vargas succession crisis.

The presidential military *dispositivo* in 1954, and again a decade later, disintegrated when opponents within the Armed Forces were given an issue on which even the legalists were hard-pressed to support an "erring" chief executive. Beyond all the reasons those inclined to oppose Vargas and Goulart had for suspicion of their intentions and the dissatisfaction of conservative elements over "radical" innovations and groups, it was the assassination attempt against Lacerda in 1954 and the naval indiscipline issue in March, 1964, that swung the nonpolitical mass of the officer corps against the government and enabled the Armed Forces to act against it with overwhelming unity. Disregard for the life of a fellow officer by the regime in 1954 turned an essentially partisan or factional issue into an institutional question in the eyes of the Armed Forces. The clearer issue of institutional interest in 1964 catalyzed nearly instant military unity.

Given the military divisions and cleavages resulting from the ambiguous nature of the 1955 and 1961 crises, the build-up of the triumphant military coalition of 1964 was the most complex and many-layer interaction of Armed Forces' mobilization against the regime. To the historical plotters were added first the original articulators from the War College side, then what might be termed the "second thoughts" group (those disturbed by the leftward trend of Goulart's government), in late March those dedicated to maintenance of discipline, and finally at the last moment the bandwagon joiners. Moreover, the neutral onlookers of March 31 comprised three distinct strata: those essentially unconcerned with the issues at stake; some conscientiously apolitical to the end; and a large number paralyzed by ambivalence. There were also the constitutionalists with reservations concerning Goulart, who followed orders but took no initiative to defend the regime; a small number of loyalist officers who stood by the President to the end; and an even smaller group of "nationalist" officers who were among the forces pulling Jango toward the left. Thus at least ten significant groups can be identified within the military at that juncture rather than the oversimplified for-against-bystander trichotomy resorted to by some observers.

The prolongation of Castelo's term and the imposition of Costa e Silva take on greater meaning if viewed in their proper perspective as a reaction to the 1954–1955 experience and the rapid comeback of the Vargas political heirs. In 1964, the military was determined not to hold elections that might let the old group back in after the revolutionary regime had had time only for politically unpopular economic stabilization and administrative house-cleaning measures. The politically active strata of the officer corps had come to believe that not only was the "moderating power" role insufficient for the depth of the present crisis but that the Armed Forces had perhaps themselves contributed to the problem by not controlling the situation in the Estado Nôvo period and by failure to act decisively enough in 1954–1955 and 1961.

Each decisive military intervention in the political life of the nation has been linked to the question of presidential succession. But other factors should not be lost in the shadow of this salient fact. In each political crisis of the postwar period, for example, greater ingenuity was required on the part of civilian leadership to find even a temporary "solution" that might preserve the appearances of constitutionality. As a result, fewer were satisfied with the outcome each time, the military was drawn in even more deeply, and the institutional outcome increasingly did violence to the spirit if not the strict letter of the Constitution (which could always be modified). Having personally experienced all the crises and attempts at reconciliation from the 1920's on, the top military leadership after 1964 drew on elements of each experiment of the preceding forty years in what might harshly be termed a mixture of ossified *tenentismo* with *segurança nacional*. Thus the political purges, institutional acts, and so forth of the Vargas era were blended with efforts to develop a highly sanitized, technocratic approach to the nation's problems. The result of the contradictions of this outlook and the frustrations encountered in efforts to put it into practice has not unexpectedly been an authoritarian dictatorship.

The road to "re-democratization" or "normalcy" is complicated by the military's realization that the type of leadership it strongly feels essential for the nation would have little chance of victory in even a very restricted and "controlled" direct election. This is accentuated by their lack of a reliable political party as an electoral vehicle in light of the 1965 and 1966 elections and subsequent developments. Hermes da Fonseca's victory in 1909 notwithstanding, no Brazilian military candidate has proved an effective campaigner. Dutra won because of Vargas' support and against another military figure who was little more at home on the speaking platform than he. Juarez Távora was decisively out-campaigned by Kubitschek and in most respects by Adhemar de Barros, who lacked national party machinery for his presidential bid yet fell only 390,000 votes behind the UDN military candidate. Lott, with the benefit of PSD and PTB support, could hold on to only 33 per cent of the national total while finishing nearly 1.8 million votes behind Jânio Quadros. On the other hand, in the postwar period the UDN, political backbone of the post-1964 regime, never found a civilian candidate for the presidency within its ranks. After nominating Brigadier Gomes in 1945 and 1950, it backed General Juarez Távora in 1955 and reached far outside the party in 1960 to get on the Quadros bandwagon.

Composed essentially of a majority of the old UDN (but minus most of its modernizing minority) plus a major segment of the PSD and most of the minor party accommodationists, the regime's congressional support was not sufficiently cohesive or disciplined to hold together when the government directed a body blow at Congress or strongly attacked the political class itself. The result was parliamentary revolts—really little more than symbolic manifestations of independence—in late 1965, 1966, 1967 (in a less accentuated form), and finally 1968 with the regime's ultimate solution to the problem lying in closing Congress and purging nearly one-fourth of its membership. Thus throughout

1969, three military governments—Costa e Silva's, the junta, and that of Garrastazú Médici—were paralyzed by the political impasse that had led Brazil into a dictatorial cul-de-sac.

The lessons brought home to the military in their exercise of power have involved more than their relationships with civilian political structures. Indeed, one of the most salient lessons of the 1964–1970 experience has been the degree to which military unity and discipline itself have difficulty withstanding the strains placed upon it not only by control of the governmental apparatus but by responsibility for direction of the political system as well. Rather than any evidence of a growing consensus, deeper cleavages appear to be developing within the officer corps on both questions of fundamental policy and who should occupy the seats of power and prestige. The apparent disaggregation of the revolutionary movement in 1964 did not necessarily reflect a falling out of elements that had previously demonstrated any positive cohesion. The heterogeneity of the groups opposed to Goulart's continuance in office all but ruled out any extremely broad coalition behind a coherent and focused governmental program. Thus from the viewpoint of leading strategists of the Castelo Branco regime, the revolution did not devour any of its "legitimate" children, but only the strange bedfellows who had been accepted as participants in the ouster of the old regime. The Sorbonne–*linha dura* differences within the heart of the military institution were far more important and lasting in their impact than the angry attacks by "leaders" of the March, 1964, conspiracy whose ambitions for subsequent influence and aclaim had been disappointed.[38] From December, 1968, on, the decay of military unity has been painfully evident; the papering over of differences among the senior generals in the composition of the Garrastazú Médici government cannot hide the extent of dissidence within the Armed Forces, nor is time likely to strengthen the older generals against the challenge from a newer generation moving up the ladder of rank and seniority. Emílio Garrastazú Médici's prospects for serving out his full presidential term would seem to be no better

---

[38] The complexity of military politics and factionalism is underscored by the view of key aides of Castelo that the *linha dura* was in a limited sense his Brizola, most often an inconvenient complication, but useful at other times as both a lightning rod and a bogeyman which could be used to gain support for the administration as a lesser evil when compared to the military extremists.

than the average for the Brazilian Republic—less than a fifty-fifty proposition. For in abandoning the role of an institutional "moderator" for that of directors, the Brazilian generals have also removed the most important restraints upon a "colonels' coup."

From the perspective of early 1971, the outlook for Brazil in the years immediately ahead appears, in the political realm at least, one of continued instability within the context of military rule. While the role of militant opposition groups might certainly affect the course of events to a significant degree, the most important developments are likely, as in the past, to come from within the Armed Forces. Based upon an uneasy reapproximation of the dominant elements of the two preceding governments—the remaining Castelistas and the late Costa e Silva's collaborators—the present regime is rooted in a military generation already in relative decline as retirement takes its steady toll of those who had decisive voices in the resolution of the September-November, 1969, succession crisis. Unlike its clerical counterpart, the Army "college of cardinals" that was able to impose its solution will have a distinctly different complexion within another two or three years, and its composition will have changed all but completely by 1974. Whether this will entail a change of faces in the executive or bring in its wake a significant policy reorientation is much more problematical. Not only Brazil's domestic experience but also the relative success of military regimes in its two largest neighbors—Argentina and Peru—will be one of the factors in this equation.

APPENDIX A

⟨∾≫∾⟩

Comparative Formulations

THE MOST IMMEDIATELY relevant theoretical propositions from the burgeoning literature on political development and civil-military relations in modernizing polities have been discussed in Chapter 1, section 2. Many of the other comparative formulations can be appropriately left for discussion in *Modernization and the Military in Brazil*. Nonetheless, there is one analytical approach in each of these conceptual areas that might well contribute sufficiently to the needs and interests of the reader concerned with systematic cross-national comparisons to merit attention in this work. Hence, the basic concepts of David Apter on political development and of Martin Needler on the military's role in Latin American political processes—both widely influential among scholars in this field—are briefly discussed in this appendix in relationship to Huntington's propositions as operationalized in the text.

Although no specific consideration and very little incidental mention of Brazil is included in his several works, the seminal value of Apter's models is such that their applicability to Brazil merits careful consideration.[1] Apter's classification of political systems is fourfold, with significant subtypes or variations recognized for his major categories. It is chiefly to the degree that he finds most modernizing nations

[1] David E. Apter, *The Politics of Modernization* (Chicago, 1965) and *Some Conceptual Approaches to the Study of Modernization* (Englewood Cliffs, N.J., 1968).

to be hybrids that Apter's models are of use in gaining a clearer understanding of Brazil relative to other developing countries.

For Apter, modernization is a special case of development in which the social system is able to innovate without disintegrating, owing to belief in the acceptability of change and the existence of differentiated and flexible social structures. It involves the adoption of industrial-type roles and has as its central consequence the expansion of choice.[2] Like Huntington, Apter holds that political parties are "such a critical force for modernization in contemporary societies that the particular pattern of modernization adopted by each is quite often determined by its parties."[3] The function he postulates for parties is beyond that which they have ever effectively fulfilled in Brazil.

The political parties of a modernizing society play an active entrepreneural role in the formation of new ideas, in the establishment of a network of communication for those ideas, and in the linking of the public and the leadership in such a way that power is generated, mobilized, and directed.[4]

In elaborating his set of political systems models, Apter begins with a distinction concerning values. Normative ends in application with empirical means and generally in association with an intense ideological content are defined as "consummatory values" (preferences) in contradistinction to the "instrumental values" (interests) that arise through the routine competition among political groups and involve empirical ends as well as means.[5] These two value types, which can for the sake of convenience be thought of as those of a moral significance versus those of a developmental nature, are combined by Apter with a dichotomy in kinds of authority structures to produce his four basic models of political systems. "Hierarchical authority" (low governmental accountability to the public) combines with consummatory values to yield a "mobilization" system, but linked to instrumental values results in a "bureaucratic" type. A high degree of governmental accountability, termed

[2] *The Politics of Modernization,* p. 67, and *Some Conceptual Approaches . . .,* pp. 330–34.

[3] *The Politics of Modernization,* p. 179.

[4] *Ibid.,* p. 186. In his own efforts to adapt his models to the industrializing states of South America, Apter and his associates have concentrated on Argentina, Chile, and Peru.

[5] *Some Conceptual Approaches . . .,* p. 337.

"pyramidal" authority, in conjunction with consummatory values leads to a "theocracy"; combined with instrumental values it constitutes a "reconciliation" system.

Apter defines representation as the link between government and society and discriminates between its "popular," "interest," and "functional" forms in terms of the basis of claims for a voice in decision-making. Thus, popular representation rests on the presumed individual rights of citizenship; interest representation on the social significance or special contribution of occupational groups; and functional representation on professional expertise and the need of government for particular technical skills.[6] Goal specification, institutional coherence, and central control are the fundamental functions of representation in Apter's formulation.

Categories for stratification are important to Apter's analysis and include: (1) caste-like primordial and exclusivist groupings; (2) class based on subjective awareness and largely determined by occupation; (3) class membership and identification rooted in multiple factors, including income, education, life style, and family background; and (4) status differentiation based primarily on skills, functional roles in industrialization, and professionalization. Relating these to the differing claims for representation, Apter hypothesizes that "the greater the degree of modernization, the greater the possibility of multiple claims to representation, and the greater the possibility of restrictive and authoritarian political solutions."[7] He also maintains that during the transition to industrialization a class structure similar to that of urban life in industrial societies emerges and that this "embourgoisiement" results in a low level of working-class radicalism and the translation of differences of values into interest issues.

With progress in modernization toward industrialization comes the beginning of pluralism, to which bureaucratic systems respond by "manipulating interest group representation and functional representation while restricting popular representation."[8] In the case of modernizing reconciliation systems: "central control tends to become more organized around a bureaucracy. Goal specification is shared by competing class

[6] *Ibid.*, pp. 295–96.
[7] *Ibid.*, p. 303.
[8] *Ibid.*, pp. 308–309.

and status groupings, while institutional coherence is sustained through multiple and overlapping institutional groupings." [9] Conflict occurs in this situation between popular representation in the electoral process and the functional influence of the bureaucracy, army, and other organized interest groups. Apter agrees with Nun that the middle class-type elites may then tend to call for military intervention. Political and social stalemate and repeated crises are the likely result. Brazil, according to Apter, falls between this and an "industrializing" reconciliation system, being distinguished from the latter by its military regime and somewhat lower level of industrialization. What this apparently also means is that Brazil is too far along the road to industrialization to fit the model of a modernizing reconciliation system.

Brazil, along with Argentina, Chile, and Venezuela, exemplifies for Apter the countries "approaching the change from modernization to industrialization," a transition during which "governments are less stable and quite often more autocratic. Choices are uncertain, and uncertainty leads to non-rational acts of decision-making." [10] In fact, he postulates "the closer a modernizing country comes to the stage of industrialization, the greater the political problem of controlling and integrating the process." [11]

Apter holds that mobilization systems can prove optimum for the transition from a high degree of modernization to early industrialization but very quickly reach their limits as vehicles for carrying traditional societies through the early stages of modernization. Reconciliation systems are posited as common in Latin America during modernization, but subject to stagnation through their high degree of accountability and lack of control over the major competing interest groups. Inequality and corruption contribute to a low commitment to the society unless the country is fortunate enough to enjoy an exceptionally high rate of economic growth. Movement between reconciliation and bureaucratic systems is frequent in Latin America. While the former involves a process of mediating and reconciling interests, the latter, based on a powerful organization such as the military, represents a "more immediate and

[9] *Ibid.*, p. 321.

[10] *The Politics of Modernization*, p. 235n, the only discussion pertaining directly to Brazil in all of Apter's work.

[11] *Some Conceptual Approaches* . . ., p. 336.

direct balance of forces." [12] It is held to be optional for intermediate modernization, where the widening range of choice as mediated through a "normative, structural, and behavioral imbalance" has resulted in a relatively high degree of uncertainty. Weakened by competition among diverse groups over which governmental employment of centralized coercion is limited by its accountability, reconciliation systems tend to break down, with the military apt to take over, converting the system to a bureaucratic one as authority becomes hierarchical.[13]

In terms of Apter's categories, then, it might be argued that Brazil was an essentially reconciliation-type system moving toward some form of mobilization in the early 1960's, with the regime's emphasis upon nationalism and "basic reforms" taking on the nature of consummatory values. The military intervention of 1964 aborted this process and installed instead a modified type of bureaucratic system characterized by a neomercantilist concern with a "presidential monarchy" and a stable one-party government.[14] Yet as Apter draws his models, Brazil's 1967–1969 regime under President Artur da Costa e Silva partook somewhat more of the "military oligarchy" variant of the bureaucratic type of system than did that under his immediate predecessor, Marshal Humberto Castelo Branco.

Martin Needler, in a recently published book, as well as two articles (in *The American Political Science Review*) spun off from the same study, presents an analysis of political development in Latin America essentially congruent with Huntington, whose sponsorship he enjoyed during the research for this project.[15] Needler sees the definite tendency in Latin America with regard to coups and the regimes that ensue as one in which

A military group has made itself master of the country, yet it undertakes to relinquish power almost immediately. The striking thing about this pattern of behavior is not that the results of the ensuing elections may sometimes not be respected, or that they may be conducted in a partial manner, but that the hold of the norms of democratic ideology is so great, even on the

[12] *Ibid.*, p. 340.

[13] *Ibid.*, p. 345.

[14] *The Politics of Modernizaton*, pp. 397 and 408–416, discusses the neomercantilist subtype.

[15] Martin C. Needler, *Political Development in Latin America: Instability, Violence, and Evolutionary Change* (New York, 1968).

perpetrators of a successful *coup d'état,* that any situation other than the restoration of a formally constitutional government issuing from free elections is simply not thinkable.[16]

While he admits that Argentina constitutes an exception to this rule, he is strangely silent concerning Brazil. With more than three-fifths of South America's population living under governments that do not conform to Needler's proposition, and most of the others in countries where the military has not intervened in politics during the period of his consideration, it appears of limited utility as a key to comprehension of political-military phenomena. (Indeed, its validity would seem limited to the minor countries of the region, with relatively few cases clearly congruent with his thesis, even in Central America and the Caribbean.)

This pervasive lack of knowledge concerning the Brazilian experience is reflected again when Needler, in illustrating a point he holds to be of equal validity for all the major Latin American nations, devotes two pages each to Mexico and Argentina, one to Chile, and a rather incidental four-and-a-half lines to Brazil as a tail on the discussion of Mexico.[17] Yet this concept of a "participation crisis within a participation crisis" has a substantial applicability to Brazil, which provides a case in which the military rather a political party played the key role in breaking the resultant impasse.

Needler reintroduces the concept of legitimacy, which is relegated to oblivion by Huntington. He also places stress on democratic values in contrast to Huntington's concern with effectiveness. In large part this results from Needler's regional focus, which excludes the problems and experience of the "non-Western" and "new" states as compared to the global range of Huntington, in which Latin America frequently takes a back seat to the Afro-Asian nations. Elaborating a typology of uses of violence in Latin America's political life that runs from anomic and representational through "supplantive" to a variety of revolutions ("good government," modernizing, democratizing, and socializing), Needler also draws quite careful distinctions among the corresponding kinds of counterrevolution.[18] The "civilian-military revolt" of 1964 in Brazil is classified as a "particularly natural and effective composite counterrevolution

---

[16] *Ibid.,* p. 28.
[17] *Ibid.,* pp. 33–38.
[18] *Ibid.,* pp. 46–52.

. . . which combines the characteristics of a counterrevolution against democratizing and socializing tendencies with those of a revolution in favor of good government and modernization."

Needler is in substantial agreement with Huntington when he asserts that "the frequency of military intervention in politics is related primarily not to internal characteristics of the military forces but to the requirements of the political system as a whole." [19] In keeping with his focus on political development, Needler examines changes in the frequency of coups over time and emerges with the proposition that coups are more likely when economic conditions worsen. During the 1935–1964 period, he finds the proportion of "reformist" coups has fallen off sharply, the number with armed conflict involved has risen markedly relative to the bloodless coup, constitutional regimes are now the target more than de facto governments, and that military intervention occurs more frequently during the time when presidential succession is an active issue.[20] These propositions are congruent with Brazil's experience, and Needler's concept of differential thresholds for intervention and the role of the "swing-man" also fit.[21]

While much of Needler's interesting effort to relate political development in Latin America to social and economic development is only tangentially relevant to the central focus of this study, it is appropriate to note that Brazil emerges as one of only two countries in the region in which the relative standing on his constitutionality index correlates perfectly with rank in GNP.[22] At the same time, Needler's hypothesis that "if participation increases greatly, constitutional integrity will tend to deteriorate unless the country's economy develops at the same time," while imprecise, does correspond to observable reality in the case of Brazil, at least to the degree that no coup occurred during the years of rapid economic growth under Juscelino Kubitschek (1956–1961), while the ouster of Goulart coincided with a severe recession in terms of a stagnant GNP.

[19] *Ibid.,* p. 60.
[20] *Ibid.,* p. 65.
[21] *Ibid.,* pp. 66–75.
[22] *Ibid.,* p. 87.

◠◠◡◠◡◠◡

Biographic Data
on 1964 Army Leaders

THE CAREERS of the two most important military figures in Brazil after the successful coup of March 31, 1964, have been discussed in the text: Humberto Castelo Branco in Chapter 4, and Arthur da Costa e Silva at the beginning of Chapter 6. Examination of the careers of other key generals of the 1964–1969 period can also add significantly to a comprehension of relationships and motivations at the heart of the complex pattern of military politics since the revolution. In addition to those senior officers most closely associated with Castelo and Costa e Silva, those chosen for discussion here include the chief protagonists of the 1968–1969 crises. Several of those who faded from the political scene at the end of Castelo's administration have subsequently returned to prominence under the Garrastazú Médici government.

General Justino Alves Bastos, chosen to command the crucial Third Army after the revolution, was known by his colleagues to harbor political ambitions. Son of a general who became Army Chief of Staff in 1922, he was born in 1900. An active *tenente* by 1930, he sided with the São Paulo rebels in 1932. Like Costa e Silva, he achieved promotion to brigadier general in 1952. Close to General Denys, he occupied a series of key posts under the latter in the Rio de Janeiro area: the Vila Militar's artillery, Chief of Staff of the First Army (1956), coast artillery

(1957–1959), and the 1st Military Region (1960–1961). Elected president of the Military Club in 1958 and re-elected in 1960 (having been promoted to major general at the end of 1958), he was named Ambassador to Paraguay by Quadros. Returning to active military duty in February, 1963, he commanded the 5th Military Region until promoted to full general and given Command of the Fourth Army late in the year. Unlike most of the top ranking officers, he had not been part of the Expeditionary Force during World War II.

General Oswaldo Cordeiro de Farias, who was senior to Castelo, Costa, and Alves Bastos, and had a much more prominent political background, lay claim to major influence within the triumphant revolution. A very important figure among the *tenentes,* Cordeiro had commanded part of the Prestes Column and became São Paulo police chief in 1931. Active in combatting the *Paulista* revolt, he served from 1938 to 1943 as Interventor in Rio Grande do Sul. After a series of troop commands and a term as the first Commandant of the National War College, he was elected Governor of Pernambuco in 1954, returning to active duty as head of the Joint Brazil-United States Military Commission at the end of 1958. Chief of the Armed Forces General Staff in 1961, Cordeiro was in the front ranks of the effort to block Goulart's accession to power. A very active plotter during 1962–1963, he was named Minister for Coordination of Regional Agencies in the Castelo Branco government and was most often referred to as Minister of Interior. In keeping with his distinguished career, Cordeiro soon showed signs that he considered himself superior as a potential president to Costa e Silva, who he felt had joined the revolution at the last moment. He resigned his post rather than accept Costa as the administration's candidate.

General Ernesto Geisel, chosen by Castelo to head his Casa Militar and thus serve as secretary of the National Security Council, was known to be one of the Brazilian military's most intelligent officers. Born in 1908, he served in the early 1950's on the staff of the National Security Council and in 1955 as a military aide to the President. In 1957, he was named to represent the War Ministry on the National Petroleum Council. He subsequently headed the intelligence section of the Army general staff, at a time when his brother Orlando was First Army Chief of Staff. Chief Military Aide to Ranieri Mazzilli during the latter's brief administration in August–September, 1961, he came to work closely with Castelo prior to the 1964 coup.

General Golbery do Couto e Silva, selected by Castelo to head the National Intelligence Service (SNI)—a rough combination of the functions of the FBI, Secret Service, and CIA that functioned as the intelligence arm of the presidency—was known as one of the most scholarly of senior Brazilian officers. First student in his Academy class, he was the only officer to pass the special competitive examination for the Command and General Staff College opened to captains in 1941. After study in the United States, service with the FEB in Italy, and a training mission in Paraguay, he began his intelligence career within the Army General Staff in 1950. From March, 1952, to November, 1955, Lieutenant Colonel Golbery served on the staff of the Escola Superior de Guerra, being transferred to a troop command following the military crisis and the Lott-Denys preventive coup. Returning to the General Staff the next year as a full colonel, he headed the staff of the National Security Council during the Quadros period, at which time he worked closely with General Geisel. He retired from active service rather than accept Goulart as President. Subsequently, he provided the link between the War College group and civilian opponents in the business sector as head of IPES's research office. One of Brazil's leading geopoliticians, a field in which he published important books in 1955 and 1957, he was a leading spokesman of the Sorbonne group as well as one of Castelo's most trusted aides. A chief architect of the Castelo Branco regime's political strategy, Golbery represented those military elements within the government most opposed to Costa e Silva's election as Castelo's successor.[1]

General Carlos Amaury Kruel, born in 1900, had been a boyhood schoolmate of Castelo Branco, who retained him as Commander of the Second Army. Having served as Chief Presidential Military Aide and Minister of War under Goulart, he was considered the most centrist of the major military figures after the revolution. Breaking with Castelo, he

---

[1] Golbery's most influential publications, and those on which his reputation as a leading geopolitician rest, include *Planejamento Estratégico* (Rio de Janeiro, 1955) and *Aspectos Geopolíticos do Brasil* (Rio de Janeiro, 1957). An number of his more important articles and conferences have been brought together in *Geopolítica do Brasil* (Rio de Janeiro, 1967).

ran for Congress in 1966. His brother, General Riograndino Kruel, who had also been a classmate of the President, was named by Castelo Branco as Chief of the Federal Department of Public Security (DFSP). For the preceding nine years, the older Kruel had been an official of the Guanabara state police, and he sought to expand the DFSP into a true national police force.

Pery Constant Bevilaqua remained Chief of the Armed Forces General Staff under Castelo Branco. A year older than the President, he had been a strict legalist in the 1961 crisis and nationalist standardbearer in the 1962 Military Club elections. Appointed to command the Third Army by Goulart, he later opposed leftist labor agitation as Second Army commander in 1963 and was transferred to the prestigious but largely powerless desk job by Goulart. He alone of the generals in Rio de Janeiro objected to Costa e Silva's assuming control of the Army during the March 31–April 1 revolution. After becoming a Minister of the Superior Military Tribunal in March, 1965, he became an articulate opponent of militarism and critic of moves toward dictatorship and was removed from that position after the coup-within-the-coup of December, 1968. Bevilaqua was the brother-in-law of General Décio Escobar, who at the end of a long career rose to be Army Chief of Staff replacing Castelo Branco in April, 1964.

Marshal Adhemar de Queiroz, retired from active duty at the end of 1963 and one of the most effective organizers of the 1964 revolution, was appointed by Castelo Branco to head Petrobrás, but in mid-1966 he moved over to the War Ministry as Costa's replacement. Like most of those close to Castelo, he was a veteran of the Italian campaign.

Olympio Mourão Filho, who had first been indicated for the Petrobrás post, was instead retired (reaching the compulsory age limit in May) and named Chief Minister of the Superior Military Tribunal. From the beginning he was treated by the Castelo Branco government more as a potential critic than as architect of the military movement of March. He became a vocal critic of the regime and advocate of a variety of institutional reforms including a third legislative chamber.

General Aurélio de Lyra Tavares, appointed to succeed Alves Bastos as commander of the Fourth Army, was one of the group of rising generals who, born in 1905, were several years younger than Castelo Branco, Costa e Silva, Cordeiro de Farias, Bevilacqua, Adhemar de Queiroz, Mourão Filho, and the Kruels. Son of a Senator and brother of two noted academician-jurists, Lyra Tavares, with law and engineering degrees as well as a score of publications to his credit, was one of the Army's outstanding intellectuals. Having served as an observer in North Africa in 1943, Lyra Tavares was on the staff of the Brazilian Expeditionary Force and subsequently represented Brazil in the occupation of Germany, where he remained until the time of the Berlin blockade. After stints as an instructor at the Army Staff and Command School and mid-career courses, he held positions on the staff of the Minister of War and as a section chief in the Armed Forces General Staff, and as principal aide to the Army Chief of Staff. Assignments as Director of Communications, First Army Chief of Staff, and the War Ministry's Director of Basic Training (under Castelo as Director General of Education) preceded key positions as Commander of the Second Military Region (1962) and First Subchief of the Army General Staff just prior to the 1964 revolution. Command of the Fourth Army, one of the major departments of the War Ministry, and the War College completed his ample preparation for the job of Army Minister that he assumed in March, 1967, and held through October, 1969. (Interestingly, he had been a member of the twelve-man Brazilian contingent at Ft. Leavenworth in 1943. Six of this group attained the rank of marshal— Estillac Leal, Lott, Castelo, Kruel, Augusto Magessi, and Floriano Lima Brayner—while Lyra himself rose to the top Army position at age 61.) [2]

Others among this group of influential "younger" generals included Orlando Geisel, who would take over the Third Army in 1965 and subsequently become Chief of the Armed Forces General Staff; Rafael de Souza Aguiar, an "apolitical" engineer, medical doctor, and lawyer named to command the 11th Military Region and Brasília garrison, but given the crucial First Military Region in late 1965 and appointed Fourth Army Commander a year later; and Alvaro Alves da Silva

[2] The several books of Lyra Tavares reflect the evolution of his thought from strictly military topics toward broad-gauged consideration of national problems which brought him election to the Brazilian Academy of Letters in 1970. A brief character sketch is contained in Murilo Melo Filho, "Lira Tavares: Não Somos Militaristas," *Manchete,* May 27, 1967, pp. 122–23. A number of his more academic writings covering a quarter century are collected in *Além dos Temas da Caserna* (Fortaleza, 1968).

Braga, Director General of Ordinance and Material, who subsequently headed the Inter-American Peace Force in the Dominican Republic before receiving command of the Third Army in September, 1966.

A special case among this group was General Jurandir de Bizarria Mamede. Born in 1906 and active as a *tenente* in the 1930 Revolution at the side of Juracy Magalhães, he earned the lasting enmity of War Minister Lott as the detonator of the November, 1955, crisis. Passed up for promotion to brigadier despite a brilliant record until Denys succeeded to the War Ministry in 1960, Mamede was subsequently named Commandant of the Army Command and General Staff School. After playing a major role in the actions of March 31, he was promoted and put in charge of the autonomous Amazon region command, the only field position in which as a major general he would not be under the jurisdiction of one of the Army commanders. After presiding over the ouster of the corrupt governments of Pará and Amazonas, Mamede was appointed in late 1965 to command the strategic Vila Militar in Rio de Janeiro. Subsequently he became head of the Second Army, but having been frequently mentioned as a possible alternative presidential candidate to Costa e Silva, this ranking leader of the Sorbonne group was transferred in 1967 to head a department of the War Ministry.

Also a very special case was Carlos Luís Guedes, who after seconding Mourão in the initial march against Rio de Janeiro on March 31, was returned to the Fourth Military Region until transfer to the Second Military Region in 1965. Although serving as interim Commander of the Second Army from August to October, 1966, he would subsequently be shifted to the post of Director of the Department of Supplies rather than given one of the top troop commands. Passed over for promotion to full general, he retired in July, 1969. General António Carlos Muricy, another leader of the "Tiradentes Column," was given command of the Seventh Military Region in the Northeast, but in 1966 had his ambitions to become Governor of Pernambuco thwarted by Castelo Branco. As Army Chief of Staff in 1969 he became one of the country's most powerful individuals.

Although not enjoying politically influential assignments during the Castelo Branco administration, two generals who emerged as major power contenders during the early stages of the Costa e Silva government did all they could to strengthen their positions within the military.

General Sizeno Sarmento was sent off by Castelo Branco to command the Brazilian detachment in the U.N. peace-keeping force in the Gaza strip, but was Costa e Silva's first choice for promotion to four-star rank in 1967, and was given command of the Second Army and subsequently the Rio-based First Army. Afonso Augusto de Albuquerque Lima, born in 1909 and the younger brother of a ranking *tenente,* Stenio Caio de Albuquerque Lima, headed the National Department of Anti-drought Works during the Quadros government, then spent the Goulart years at the War College. In April, 1964, Albuquerque Lima was named Interventor of the National Railroad System. As First Army Chief of Staff he was to play a key role in the October, 1965, crisis and was subsequently sent by Castelo to Rio Grande do Sul to command the Second Cavalry Division before being named Director of Military Engineering. Costa e Silva named him Minister of Interior, and he quickly became one of the most frequently mentioned presidential possibilities. Involved as was Sarmento, as a key figure in the December, 1968, crisis, Albuquerque Lima became the candidate of the hard-liners in the intramural succession crisis of September-October, 1969. Youngest of the senior three-star generals, he was passed over for promotion in November, 1970, ending his active military career.

Essay on Sources

BECAUSE THE ANALYTICAL and interpretive literature on the post-1964 Brazilian system is still quite limited, I have relied heavily on the daily and periodical press in reconstructing the course of events. Interviews with participants and qualified observers have also been very important in trying to probe behind the façade of developments and ascertain intentions, tactics, and motivations. Indeed, since the imposition of press censorship in mid-December, 1968, personal contact with individuals close to the Brazilian political scene has been indispensable.

All Brazilian press organs reflect definite economic-interest orientations and related political viewpoints. The daily press in Brazil is not dominated by one or two major newspapers. Indeed, there are a rather large number of papers with significant circulation or major influence on strategic readership groups. No papers are truly national in scope and range, although the declining *Diarios Associados* chain is represented in nearly all major cities, and the rising *Jornal do Brasil* has a network of correspondents in most state capitals. The close linkage between newspapers and radio and television stations (a great many of which are owned by the major newspapers) amplifies the impact of these papers on public opinion.

Although it does not have the largest circulation, Rio de Janeiro's *Jornal do Brasil* is probably the best balanced and most informative if not the most widely influential Brazilian newspaper. Roughly speaking, it is Brazil's equivalent of *The New York Times*. Owned and managed by the Dunshee de Abranches family, it has attained a hemispheric position as a progressive innovator in the field of journalism. Moderately conservative in its political orientation, with its classic liberalism tempered by a realization of the magnitude of the nation's problems, it maintains a relatively internationalist line on foreign affairs and frequently has appeared most closely attuned of all Brazilian newspapers to the desires and policies of the Foreign Ministry. (Indeed, its co-director has been ranking diplomat on leave.) It generally supports free enterprise as represented by the modernizing elements of the private sector. Its editor-in-chief, Alberto Dines, is one of the most sagacious observers of national life, and the head of its Brasília bureau, Carlos Castelo Branco, who doubles as its leading political columnist and pundit, is widely regarded as the best-informed political analyst in Brazil. By United States as well as by Brazilian standards, the *Jornal do Brasil* avoids sensationalism and combines a high regard for accuracy with a considerable degree of objectivity in its treatment of the news. It is highly responsible in its selective criticism of the government.

O Estado de S. Paulo is one of Brazil's most influential journals. Strongly conservative in orientation, in recent years it has departed from its classical liberalism to call for stringent measures against leftists who in its eyes are "subversives" and enemies of the 1964 revolution. Owned and operated by the Mesquita family, *O Estado* has excellent coverage of economic affairs, including both industry and agriculture. It is invaluable for detailed treatment of the activities and views of powerful *Paulista* interests. Its analysis of national politics is done largely by its Rio de Janeiro bureau, headed by Fernando Pedreira, a keen analyst of political affairs who operates with a good deal of independence and follows a moderate centrist interpretation that at times injects a surprisingly progressive note contrasting with the often hard-line conservatism of the paper's editorial page.

Rio de Janeiro conservatism finds its most expressive voice in *O Globo,* published by the Marinho family. (Publisher Roberto Marinho is a personal friend of President Garrastazú Médici.) It is influential among the upper classes, and widely read on Mondays, when many of its competitors do not publish (*Globo* has no Sunday edition). Its radio and television outlets also give it significant influence among *Carioca* public opinion. *Globo* is the weakest of the major papers in its coverage of political and economic matters, tending to sacrifice depth for black-and-white interpretations. It is the most consistently pro-United States of Brazil's major press organs.

O Jornal, Rio de Janeiro-published leader of the *Diarios Associados* chain, has been declining in influence in recent years. Strongly pro-private enterprise (as is its *Paulista* sister, *Diário de São Paulo*), its editorial page and key features merit attention chiefly insofar as they are duplicated in affiliated papers that may be very influential in their own region (as is the case in Recife, Belo Horizonte, Brasília, Pôrto Alegre, and Belem.) *O Jornal's* line is also broadcast over the large number of radio and television outlets controlled by the chain. (At its peak, a few years ago, the DA empire included thirty-one newspapers, fifteen television stations, and twenty-two radio stations throughout the country, in addition to four magazines and a news agency.) The *Diarios Associados* are still a formidable, if declining, power in the public opinion arena, and not only the chairman, João Calmon, but also the chain's São Paulo chief, Edmundo Monteiro, are influential congressmen.

Correio da Manhã, a serious morning paper, has generally surpassed *O Jornal* and *O Globo* in terms of journalistic quality. Its opposition role has appeared most strongly on the editorial page, where several of its regularly featured columnists were strong to virulent critics of the Castelo and Costa e Silva regimes. (Two of its young writers, Márcio Moreira Alves and Hermano Alves, won election to Congress in 1966 as a result of their outspoken attacks on the government. The former triggered the December, 1968 crisis.) Financial difficulties and heavy political pressures by the regime since December, 1968, have forced *Correio* to adopt a reduced size and restricted format, and it has been leased to a group of Brazilian businessmen for the 1970–1973 period.

The most important organ of leftist-nationalist views in Brazil is *Ultima Hora,* which prior to April, 1964, was well on its way to becoming a national journal (with regional editions in São Paulo, Pôrto Alegre, Recife, and Curitiba, as well as in Rio de Janeiro). With its founder-publisher Samuel Wainer stripped of his political rights and living in exile, and a number of its other personnel also banned from active participation in its direction, *Ultima Hora* still enjoys a wide readership among labor, student, and nationalistic middle sector groups. It also publishes a Monday edition (unlike *Jornal do Brasil, Correio da Manhã,* and most other Brazilian papers), which is read by many of those who find *O Globo's* arch-conservative views unacceptable. In sum, *Ultima Hora* reflects the views of the majority of the elements that made up the Brazilian Labor Party and today constitute the backbone of the MDB. Its managing editor, Danton Jobim, head of the important Brazilian Press Association (ABI), was the most radical of the three Guanabara MDB Senate candidates in 1966, receiving 167,000 votes to trail *Jornal do Brasil* columnist Mario Martins, and in 1970 was elected Senator.

These are six newspapers I have read most closely throughout the 1960's. In addition, however, several other papers have been consulted at important junctures for particular content. *Tribuna da Imprensa,* closely linked to Carlos Lacerda, has frequently carried front-page declarations, open letters, or editorials by the Guanabara ex-Governor. Changes in its attitude on any particular subject may tenatively be taken as an indication of a possible shift by Lacerda, who remains close to its editor-publisher and leading columnist, Hélio Fernandes. *Jornal do Comércio* is important on financial and economic affairs, albeit not quite Brazil's *Wall Street Journal. Diário de Noticias* retains a substantial readership, particularly on Sundays, and has some high quality special features and occasional in-depth analyses. *O Dia* and *A Notícia* are both published by Guanabara Federal Deputy Chagas Freitas (elected as governor by the MDB in 1970). Aimed at the lower-class mass readership, they are highly sensationalist. (The biggest vote-getter among all congressional candidates in Guanabara in 1966, Chagas Freitas' nearly 160,000 votes came largely from the readership of his papers, a following that includes many civil servants and other white collar workers.) For matters concerning São Paulo, the *Folhas* (*Folha da Manhã,* its afternoon counterpart *Folha da Tarde,* and the evening *Folha da Noite*) are useful, and while generally centrist frequently diverge from the favorite causes and interpretations of *O Estado de S. Paulo.*

The fortnightly *Visão,* a relatively high quality newsmagazine, has a generally adequate treatment of political developments, highlighted by the commentary of Luíz Alberto Bahia, as well as a fairly strong economic section and occasional informative cover articles. It is read by many business and professional men. Since its inception in late 1968, the weekly *Veja* has provided strong competition for *Visão* and perceptive political analysis. The pictorial weekly *Manchete* often contains useful features, such as the 1967 series of interviews with all the ministers and key agency heads of the Costa e Silva government, or its serialization of Lacerda's memoirs. Its rise has coincided with the decline of *O Cruzeiro,* which has carried little material of political significance since 1966. The bimonthly *Revista de Civilização Brasileira* has become a major vehicle for intellectuals critical of the Brazilian establishment and often carries interpretive articles of considerable interest. *Cadernos Brasileiros* and *Tempo Brasileiro* also provide, although with less regularity, articles on politics and national problems. The semestral *Dados,* put out by Candido Mendes' Instituto Universitário de Pesquisas, and the quarterly *Síntese,* published by the social science institute of the Catholic University in Rio de Janeiro, also publish analyses of interest on political-economic matters and public policy. The more academic *Revista Brasileira de Estudos Políticos* (University of Minas Gerais) and *Revista de Ciências Políticas* (Getúlio Vargas Foundation) are other important sources of relevant political analysis.

A detailed discussion of bibliography on pre-1964 developments will be

included in *Modernization and the Military in Brazil.* The most complete
treatment to date is contained in the notes to Thomas Skidmore's *Politics in
Brazil, 1930–1964: An Experiment with Democracy* (New York: Oxford
University Press, 1967). Also useful is the bibliography of John F. W. Dulles,
Unrest in Brazil: Political-Military Crises, 1955–1964 (Austin: University
of Texas Press, 1970). These two books are the most comprehensive works
in English on Brazilian politics in the pre-1964 period, with Skidmore beginning his account in 1930 and Dulles, in 1954, having treated the earlier period
in his *Vargas of Brazil* (Austin: University of Texas Press, 1967). Vladimir
Reisky de Dubnic, *Political Trends in Brazil* (Washington, D.C.: Public Affairs Press, 1968), is a less comprehensive work emphasizing political parties
and foreign policy.

The discussion in this study draws selectively from the burgeoning field
of civil-military relations. The most complete and useful bibliographic introduction to the literature is Kurt Lang's *Sociology of the Military: A Selected
and Annotated Bibliography* (Chicago: Inter-University Seminar on Armed
Forces and Society, 1969). Jacques Van Doorn (ed.), *Armed Forces and
Society* (The Hague: Mouton, 1968), is comprised of papers from the September, 1966, Sixth World Congress of Sociology, while J. Van Doorn (ed.),
Military Progression and Military Regimes (The Hague: Mouton, 1969),
contains papers from the 1967 meeting of the International Sociological
Association's Research Group on Armed Forces and Society. With regard
to the studies bearing on Latin America, John J. Johnson's *The Military and
Society in Latin America* (Palo Alto: Stanford University Press, 1964),
represents the "revisionist" ("realist" or "pragmatic" are equally appropriate
labels) school, with Edwin Lieuwen's *Generals vs. Presidents: Neo-Militarism
in Latin America* (New York: Praeger Publishers, 1964), reflecting the influential "traditional" ("idealist," or "liberal") school. Lyle McAlister has helped
bring some degree of synthesis out of this dialectic in his "Changing Concepts of the Role of the Military in Latin America," *The Annals of the American Academy of Political and Social Science,* CCCLX (July, 1965), 85–98,
and his more comprehensive "Recent Research and Writings on the Role of
the Military in Latin America," *Latin American Research Review,* II, No. 1
(Fall, 1966), 5–36. The latter is the logical starting point for anyone interested in pursuing further the state of the literature and research trends in this
field.

Samuel P. Huntington, *Political Order in Changing Societies* (New
Haven: Yale University Press, 1968), provides the most useful integration of
theory on civil-military relations with a systematic conceptualization of political development. Dankwart A. Rustow, "The Organization Triumphs over

Its Function: Huntington on Modernization," *Journal of International Affairs,* XXIII, No. 1 (1969), 119–32, should be read as an intelligent assessment of Huntington's contribution. Two important papers by José Nun are helpful for relating civil-military relations in Brazil to patterns in Argentina and other relatively developed Latin American countries: "A Latin American Phenomenon: The Middle Class Military Coup," University of California, *Trends in Social Science Research in Latin American Studies* (Berkeley: Institute of International Studies, 1965), pp. 55–99, and "The Middle-Class Military Coup," in Claudio Véliz (ed.), *The Politics of Conformity in Latin America* (New York: Oxford University Press, 1967), pp. 66–118. Also worth consulting is Irving Louis Horowitz, "The Military Elites," in Seymour Martin Lipset and Aldo Solari (eds.), *Elites in Latin America* (New York: Oxford University Press, 1967), pp. 146–89.

Gabriel A. Almond and G. Bingham Powell, *Comparative Politics: A Developmental Approach* (Boston: Little, Brown, 1966), is the most widely influential formulation of a system-functional approach to political development but should be read in light of Almond's subsequent article on "Political Development: Analytical and Narrative Perspectives," *Comparative Political Studies,* I, No. 4 (January, 1969), 447–70. David E. Apter, in *The Politics of Modernization* (Chicago: The University of Chicago Press, 1965) and *Some Conceptual Approaches to the Study of Modernization* (Englewood Cliffs, N.J.: Prentice-Hall, 1968), provides an alternative approach to the comparative study of political systems. Martin C. Needler, *Political Development in Latin America: Instability, Violence, and Evolutionary Change* (New York: Random House, 1968), applies a loosely Huntingtonian approach to Latin America in general. For a comparative perspective on Brazil in relation to other Latin American Nations consult Jacques Lambert, *Latin America: Social Structures and Political Institutions* (Berkeley: University of California Press, 1967) and Luis Mercier Vega, *Roads to Power in Latin America* (New York: Praeger Publishers, 1969). For relevant propositions concerning other developing nations, one can fruitfully peruse W. Howard Wriggins, *The Ruler's Imperative: Strategies for Political Survival in Asia and Africa* (New York: Columbia University Press, 1969). On basic conceptualization, Dankwart A. Rustow, *A World of Nations* (Washington, D.C.: The Brookings Institution, 1967); Samuel N. Eisenstadt, *Modernization: Protest and Change* (Englewood Cliffs, N.J.: Prentice-Hall, 1966); and Lucien W. Pye, *Aspects of Political Development* (Boston: Little, Brown, 1966) are also of value. Cyril E. Black, *The Dynamics of Modernization: A Study in Comparative History* (New York: Harper & Row, 1967) presents a global, across-time comparative analysis of modernization experiences. Karl W. Deutsch, "Social Mobilization and Political Development," *American Political Science Review*, LV (September, 1961), 493–514 is the seminal work on this topic. Sidney Verba, "Some Dilemmas in Comparative Research," *World Politics*, XX, No. 1 (October, 1967), 112–28 provides a discussion of the requisites of comparative political studies.

In the forefront of Brazilian scholarship on political development are found the numerous works of Hélio Jaguaribe, beginning with "Política de Clientela e Política Ideológica," *Digesto Econômico*, VI, No. 68 (July, 1950), 41–62, and continuing during the first half of the 1950's in his frequent analytical articles for *Cadernos do Nosso Tempo*. His ideas are further refined in *O Problema do Desenvolvimento Econômico e a Burguesia Nacional* (São Paulo: Forum Roberto Simonsen, 1956); *Condições Institucionais do Desenvolvimento* (Rio de Janeiro: Instituto Superior dos Estudos Brasileiros, 1958); *O Nacionalismo na Atualidade Brasileira* (Rio de Janeiro: Instituto Superior dos Estudos Brasileiros, 1958); and *Desenvolvimento Econômico e Desenvolvimento Político* (Rio de Janeiro: Editôra Fundo de Cultura, 1962). A substantially rewritten and updated version of this latter work has been published in English as *Economic and Political Development: A Theoretical Approach and a Brazilian Case Study* (Cambridge, Mass.: Harvard University Press, 1968). A number of papers written during his post-1964 stay at Harvard and Stanford Universities are collected in *Problemas do Desenvolvimento Latino Americano: Estudos de Política* (Rio de Janeiro: Editôra Civilização Brasileira, 1967). His English-language writings also include *Brazilian Nationalism and the Dynamics of its Political Development* (Washington University, St. Louis), *Studies in Comparative International Development*, II, No. 4 (1966); "The Dynamics of Brazilian Nationalism," in Claudio Véliz (ed.), *Obstacles to Change in Latin America* (New York: Oxford University Press, 1965), pp. 162–87; and *Political Strategies of National Development in Brazil* (Washington University, St. Louis), *Studies in Comparative International Development*, III, No. 2 (1967–1968). This latter essay is reprinted in Irving Louis Horowitz, Josué de Castro, and John Gerassi (eds.), *Latin American Radicalism* (New York: Random House, 1969).

Also of substantial importance in relating Brazilian development to the mainstream of comparative political analysis are two works by Gláucio Ary Dillon Soares, "The Politics of Uneven Development: The Case of Brazil," in Seymour M. Lipset and Stein Rokkan (eds.), *Party Systems and Voter Alignments* (New York: The Free Press, 1967), pp. 467–96; and "The New Industrialization and the Brazilian Political System," in James Petras and Maurice Zeitlin (eds.), *Latin America: Reform or Revolution?* (New York: Fawcett, 1968), pp. 186–201. The largely neglected concept of Populism is treated by Francisco Weffort in *State and Mass in Brazil* (Washington University, St. Louis), *Studies in Comparative International Development,* II, No. 12 (1966) and "Política de Masses" in Octavio Ianni et al., *Politica e Revolução Social no Brasil* (Rio de Janeiro: Editôra Civilização Brasileira, 1965). It is touched upon in Juarez R. B. Lopes, "Some Basic Developments in Brazilian Politics and Society," in Eric N. Baklanoff (ed.), *New Perspectives of Brazil* (Nashville: Vanderbilt University Press, 1966), pp. 59–77. Very little work has been done analyzing Brazil's political culture. José Honório Rodrigues, a distinguished Brazilian historian who in recent years has served as a visiting professor at the University of Texas and Columbia University, has explored the national character aspects of this phenomenon in his *The Brazilians: Their Character and Aspirations* (Austin: University of Texas Press, 1968), originally published as *Aspirações Nacionais: Interpretação Histórico-Político* (São Paulo: Editôra Fulgor, 1963). Rodrigues carries this interpretation of political life further in his *Conciliação e Reforma no Brasil: Um Desafio Histórico-Cultural* (Rio de Janeiro: Editôra Civilização Brasileira, 1965) and *Interêsse Nacional e Política Externa* (Rio de Janeiro: Editôra Civilização Brasileira, 1966).

Conceptualization of the post-1964 Brazilian political system is all but totally lacking in the English-language literature. Although treating the earlier period, four books published in recent years do furnish useful insights into the more permanent characteristics of Brazil's governmental processes. Nathaniel Leff, *Economic Policy-Making and Development in Brazil, 1947–1964* (New York: John Wiley, 1968) provides a systematic study of decision-making in several areas of national economic policy and theorizes concerning the weakness of interest group influence, the relative antonomy of executive officials, and the nature and role of "elite public opinion." Robert T. Daland, *Brazilian Planning: Development Politics and Administration* (Chapel Hill: The University of North Carolina Press, 1967) carries his analysis of national planning and development agencies into the Castelo Branco period, with some updating in his "Development Administration and the Brazilian Political System," *Western Political Quarterly,* XII, No. 2 (June, 1968), 25–39.

The crucial role of the Brazilian bureaucracy in the process of political modernization can perhaps be best comprehended through application of Fred A. Riggs' model of the "prismatic" society as elaborated in his *Administration in Developing Countries: The Theory of Prismatic Society* (Boston: Houghton Mifflin, 1964). Certainly Brazil represents a situation of "wide variation between its still predominantly traditional hinterland and its 'modernized' urban centers." There is a significant overlapping and interaction of the relatively diffuse structures of the former with the highly differentiated institutions of the latter. The major attempt to apply this conceptualization to Brazil is Lawrence S. Graham, *Civil Service Reform in Brazil* (Austin: University of Texas Press, 1968). Graham demonstrates that government employment provides both security and at least acceptable social standing for established middle-class elements at the same time that it has been highly coveted as a means of modest upward mobility for urban working class individuals seeking to achieve white collar status. With the parties functioning very imperfectly as vehicles for access to elite status for the politically ambitious, the bureaucracy remains a major channel for achieving political influence and elite recruitment. Frank P. Sherwood, *Institutionalizing the Grass Roots in Brazil* (San Francisco: Chandler Publishing, 1967), provides a picture of local government just before the centralizing impact of the late Castelo period and the Costa e Silva administration sharply undermined municipal autonomy.

James L. Busey's interpretation of Brazil's political development is contained in two essays, "The Old and the New in the Politics of Modern Brazil," in Eric W. Baklanoff (ed.), *The Shaping of Modern Brazil* (Baton Rouge: Louisiana State University Press, 1969) and "Brazil's Reputation for Political Stability," *Western Political Quarterly,* XVIII, No. 4 (December, 1965), 866–80.

James W. Rowe has written several essays on the Castelo Branco period including "Revolution or Counterrevolution in Brazil? Part I: The Diverse Background" and "Part II: From Black Tuesday to the New Reform," *American Universities Field Staff Reports,* East Coast South America Series, XI, Nos. 4 and 5 (June, 1964); "The 'Revolution' and the 'System': Notes on Brazilian Politics, Part I: Seeds of the System," "Part II: The 'System'— Full Flower and Crisis," and "Part III: The 'Revolution'—Generals and Technocrats," *American Universities Field Staff Reports,* East Coast South America Series, XII, Nos. 3, 4, and 5 (July-August, 1966); and "Brazil Stops the Clock, Part I: 'Democratic Formalism' before 1964 and in the Election of 1966," and "Part II: The New Constitution and the New Model," *American Universities Field Staff Reports,* East Coast South America Series, XIII, Nos. 1 and 2 (March, 1967).

Two recent unpublished doctoral dissertations treat the Brazilian military. Alfred C. Stepan, "Patterns of Civil-Military Relations in the Brazilian Political System" (Columbia University, Department of Political Science, 1969) analyses the "moderating pattern" of civil-military relations as it functioned after World War II and its breakdown during the 1961–1964 crisis period, including an analysis of the 1964 coup. Rooting his highly comparative study in a revision of the extant literature on military involvement in politics, Stepan combines sophisticated conceptualization with systematic empirical data concerning the civilian tendency to attribute legitimacy to military intervention under particular circumstances. He devotes relatively little attention to the post-1964 system (pp. 340–423), with emphasis in this treatment on the Castelo Branco period. Max G. Manwaring, "The Military in Brazilian Politics" (University of Illinois, Department of Political Science, 1968) is an essentially descriptive study of the Brazilian Army in power during the Castelo Branco period. With only the sketchiest background treatment of the Brazilian political system and a highly stereotyped and telescoped discussion of the military's earlier political involvement (two pages for 1894–1930, three for 1930–1945, and ten for the 1945–1955 period), Manwaring provides a relatively superficial view of the 1964 crisis and developments up to 1966. A series of important manifestoes and documents are included as appendices, a boon to those who do not read Portuguese.

Octávio Ianni's *O Colapso do Populismo no Brasil* (Rio de Janeiro: Civilização Brasileira, 1968), or *Crisis in Brazil* (New York: Columbia University Press, 1970) is less a systematic analysis of populism as a political phenomenon than an examination of strategies of development. Defined by the São Paulo sociologist as "the political form assumed by the mass society" as well as "a political 'model' for development," populism is used in both a narrower and a broader sense; sometimes to cover all non-elitist political movements (p. 218) and at other times restricted to a shorthand term for the political style of Jânio Quadros, as distinct from Goulart's "labor" style (p. 71) or the "left." Ianni views the post-1964 regime as substituting an "ideology of modernization" for an "ideology of development" (p. 187). The English translation is a useful work for those who do not read Portuguese, since well over one-third of the book is made up of lengthy extracts from pronouncements of leading figures and relevant documents. While Ianni provides a very basic bibliography, a much more comprehensive "Bibliografia Sôbre a Modernização do Brasil, Principalmente Depois de 1930" is contained in Florestan Fernandes, *Sociedade de Classes e Subdesenvolvimento* (Rio de Janeiro: Zahar, 1968), pp. 205–56. Also of considerable use to the reader concerned with this field is Lucia Maria Gaspar Gomes and Fernando José Leite Costa, "Contribuição ao estudo da sociedade tradicional: bibliografia comentada (1)," *Dados*, No. 5 (1968), pp. 167–80, which, although considerably narrower in scope, is more selective and discusses each item in some detail. On the working class and the labor movement, the most complete bibliography is that in José Albertino Rodrigues, *Sindicato e Desenvol-*

vimento no Brasil (São Paulo: Difusão Europeia do Livro, 1968), pp. 191–215.

The most systematic conceptualization of the Castelo Branco regime is contained in two articles by Cândido Mendes de Almeida, "Sistema Político e modelos de poder no Brasil," *Dados,* No. 1 (Second Semester, 1966), pp. 7–41, and "O govêrno Castelo Branco: paradigma e prognose," *Dados,* No. 2/3 (1967), pp. 63–112. See also his "Elites de Poder, Democracia, e Desenvolvimento," *Dados,* No. 6 (1969), pp. 57–90 and "Prospectiva do comportamento ideológico," *Dados,* No. 4 (1968), pp. 95–132. A generally congruent analysis of the orientation of entrepreneurial sectors is Luciano Martins, *Industrialização, Burguesia Nacional, e Desenvolvimento* (Rio de Janeiro: Editôra Saga, 1968). Other relevant writings of Martins include "Formação do Empresariado Industrial no Brazil," *Revista do Instituto de Ciências Sociais,* II, No. 1 (1966), 91–138, and "Aspectos Políticos da Revolução Brasileira," *Revista Civilização Brasileira,* No. 2 (May, 1965), pp. 15–37. On Brazil's political system also consult Antônio Octávio Cintra and Fabio Wanderley Reis, "Política e desenvolvimento: O Caso Brasileiro," *America Latina,* IX, No. 3 (July-September, 1966), 52–74.

The very substantial constitutional changes of the 1964–1969 period are adequately covered in specialized Brazilian publications. Amendments 9 and 10 to the 1946 Constitution are published in the *Revista de Direito Público e Ciência Política,* VIII, No. 2 (May-August, 1965), 216–23. Institutional Acts Nos. 2 and 3 as well as Complementary Acts 1 through 9 were printed in *ibid,* IX, No. 2 (April-June, 1966), 168–99. The exceptional acts and constitutional decrees of the Castelo Branco era are brought together in Osny Duarte Pereira, *A Constitução Federal e Suas Modificações Incorporadas ao Texto* (Rio de Janeiro: Editôra Civilização Brasileira, 1966) and *A Constitução do Brasil 1967* (Rio de Janeiro: Editôra Civilização Brasileira, 1967). The Castelo Branco constitution is included in *Revista de Ciência Política,* I, No. 1 (March, 1967), 195–238. Critical treatments by distinguished constitutional experts and congressional leaders are Afonso Arinos, *A Reforma Constitucional de 1966* (Brasília: Imprensa do Congresso, 1966) and Oscar Dias Correia, *A Constituição de 1967* (Rio de Janeiro: Editôra Forense, 1968). Paulo Bonavides, *A Crise Política Brasileira* (Rio de Janerio: Editôra Forense, 1969) contains discussion of its innovations in the fields of political rights and the party system. The fundamental revisions of October, 1969, are included along with the unaltered provisions of the 1967 constitution in *Constituição da República Federativa do Brasil,* Emenda No. 1 (Brasília: Imprensa Nacional, 1969). Major judicial decisions of the Castelo period are discussed in Edgard Costa, *Os Grandes Julgamentos do*

Supremo Tribunal Federal, Quinto Volume, 1963–1966 (Rio de Janeiro: Editôra Civilização Brasileira, 1967).

On electoral legislation and practice the only English-language studies are Ronald M. Schneider, James W. Rowe, and Charles Dougherty, *Brazil Election Factbook,* Number 2 (Washington, D.C.: Institute for the Comparative Study of Political Systems, 1965) and Ronald M. Schneider, *Brazil Election Factbook Supplement* (Washington, D.C.: Institute for the Comparative Study of Political Systems, 1966). Basic works include Edgard Costa, *A Legislação Eleitoral Brasileira* (Rio de Janeiro: Imprensa Nacional, 1964); Arnoldo Malheiros and Geraldo da Costa Manso, *Legislação Eleitoral e Organização Partidária* (São Paulo: Editôra Revista dos Tribunais, 1956); Benedito Evanes Dantas and Yolanda Ramos de Costa, *Ementário de Legislação Político-Eleitoral Brasileiro 1821–1966* (Rio de Janeiro: Livraria Brasiliana Editôra, 1966); *Anteprojecto de Código Eleitoral e de Estatuto Nacional dos Partidos* (Brasília: Imprensa Nacional, 1965); *Revista de Direito Público e Ciências Políticas,* VIII, No. 1 (January-April, 1965), 91–145 and VIII, No. 3 (September-December, 1965), 131–209 and 217–26; and *Revista Brasileira de Estudos Políticos,* No. 23/24 (July, 1967–January, 1968). Also relevant are two articles by Maria Terezinha V. Moreira, "A Renovação dos Quadros no Guanabara," *Revista de Ciência Política,* I, No. 1 (March, 1967), 127–48, and "Composição do Poder Legislativo na Guanabara," *Ibid.,* I, No. 3 (September, 1967), 47–74.

Debate over economic and development policy has been heavy since 1964, with the most intense controversy during the Castelo Branco administration. The basic document on that government's financial policy and economic planning is *Program de Ação Econômica do Govêrno 1964–1966* (Rio de Janeiro: Imprensa Nacional, 1964). Roberto Campos' fundamental pre-1964 views on socio-political as well as economic matters can be found in the various papers gathered together in his *Reflections on Latin American Development* (Austin: University of Texas Press, 1968). Among his extensive writings on policy questions and governmental actions the following are of greatest utility: *Economia, Planejamento e Nacionalismo* (Rio de Janeiro: APEC Editôra, 1963); *Ensaios de História Económica e Sociologia* (2d ed.; Rio de Janeiro: APEC Editôra, 1964); *A Moeda, O Govêrno e o Tempo* Rio de Janeiro: APEC Editôra, 1964); *Política Econômica e Mitos Políticos* (Rio de Janeiro: APEC Editôra, 1965); *A Técnica e o Riso* (Rio de Janeiro: APEC Editôra, 1967); *Do Outro Lado da Cêrca* (Rio de Janeiro: APEC Editôra, 1968); and *Ensaios contra a Maré* (Rio de Janeiro: APEC Editôra, 1969). The last three volumes contain his speeches and writings for the periods March, 1964–March, 1967, April-November, 1967, and December,

1967–September, 1968, respectively. Campos still writes frequently for *O Estado de São Paulo* and *O Globo*. Ex-Finance Minister Octávio Bulhões' outlook, with its concentration upon fiscal matters and tax policy, can be found in his *Dois Conceitos de Lucro* (Rio de Janeiro: APEC Editôra, 1969) in which he differentiates between speculative and technical or efficient profits. His successor's views are contained in Antônio Delfim Netto, *Planejamento para o Desenvolvimento Econômico* (São Paulo: Livraria Editora Pioneira, 1966). Antônio Dias Leite's generally critical views on economic policy are expressed in his *Caminhos do Desenvolvimento* (Rio de Janeiro: Zahar, 1966), which brings together a series of articles published chiefly in *Journal do Brasil* between 1964 and 1966. A moderately strong critic of Campos' PAEG who subsequently reached ministerial rank in the Costa e Silva and Garrastazú Médici governments, Dias Leite wished to combine what was valid in the pre-1964 experience with important elements of the post-1964 political economy. As Dias Leite saw it, the Campos-Bulhões program not only "courageously repudiated many false and inadequate concepts" but also broke "with what was valid in the previous experience. In their anxiety to renovate, the authors of the Program constructed a new and artificial model of the Brazilian economy, disconnected from national reality, adopting some slogans as extreme as those previously preached by the negative left." (Pp. 194–95 and 225.) A number of specialists contributed to "Debate Sôbre a Política Econômica do Govêrno CB," *Revista Civilização Brasileira,* No. 15 (September, 1967) pp. 147–89. Paul Singer, *Desenvolvimento e Crise* (São Paulo: Difusão Européia do Livro, 1968), pp. 159–81 provides a synthesis of the economic policy debate from a coherent socialist viewpoint. Howard S. Ellis, ed., *The Economy of Brazil* (University of California Press, 1969) contains a series of essays by United States advisors to the Castelo Branco government and their Brazilian collaborators such as Campos, Bulhões, Simonsen, and Chacel.

Fernando Gasparian *Em Defesa da Econômia Nacional* (Rio de Janeiro: Editôra Saga, 1966), contains much of the debate within the National Economic Council over the PAEG, including both the author's criticism (basically compatible with those of Dias Leite) as well as rebuttal. Rui Gomes de Almeida, *Ideías e Atitudes* (Rio de Janeiro: Livraria José Olympio, 1965) furnishes insight into the views of the long-time leading figure of the Rio de Janeiro Commercial Association. Its Vice President from 1946 to 1955, he served as President of that class organ through most of the Kubitschek, Quadros, and Goulart years; replaced in 1965 after his second four-year stint in office, he was reelected to head the AC in 1969. This collection of his speeches and public declarations from 1952 through 1964 contains in its final pages a number of criticisms of the Castelo Branco regime, but no word of complaint directed against the Armed Forces, which are repeatedly viewed as a legitimate spokesman for the nation's interests. More recent pronouncements of Gomes de Almeida are contained in his *Empresariado e Renovação Nacional* (Rio de Janeiro: Associação Comercial, 1969), which brings together in pamphlet form speeches published in the *Revista das Classes Productoras*, XXXII, No. 1020 (June, 1969), 6-21. A 1970 perspective on all sectors of the economy is provided in *O Brasil Cresce,* a massive supplement to *Realidade* of July, 1970.

Luiz Carlos Bresser Pereira, *Desenvolvimento e Crise no Brasil, Entre 1930–1967* (Rio de Janeiro: Zahar, 1968), contains little discussion of post-1964 developments. Celso Furtado's production since the fall of the Goulart regime includes three books as well as a variety of articles. His *Subdesenvolvimento e Estagnação na América Latina* (Rio de Janeiro: Editôra Civilização Brasileira, 1966) and *Teoria e Política do Desenvolvimento Econômico* (São Paulo: Difusão Européia do Livro, 1967) contain relatively little new on Brazil, especially when compared to his widely read *Um Projecto para o Brasil* (Rio de Janeiro: Editôra Saga, 1968). A more pointed political analysis in his "Brasil: De la Republica Oligárquica al Estado Militar," *Política* (Caracas), VI, No. 68 (December, 1967), 93–116. On a more systematic basis of political sociology, a very relevant approach improving upon this type of economically-oriented analysis can be found in Fernando Henrique Cardoso, "Hegemonia Burguesa e Independência Econômica: Raízes Estructurais da Crise Política Brasileira," *Revista Civilização Brasileira,* No. 17 (January-February, 1968), pp. 67–95, also contained in his *Mudanças Sociais na América Latina* (São Paulo: Difusão Européia do Livro, 1969). Carlos Lacerda's views as they bear upon the revolution and Castelo regime can be found in *O Poder das Idéias* (Rio de Janeiro: Distribuidora Record, 1963); *Reforma e Revolução* (Rio de Janeiro: Distribuidora Record, 1964); *Palavras e Ação* (Rio de Janeiro: Distribuidora Record, 1965); *Brasil entre a Verdade e a Mentira* (Rio de Janeiro: Bloch Editôres, 1965); and *Crítica e Autocritica* (Rio de Janeiro: Editôra Nova Fronteira, 1966).

The abundant literature on the events leading up to the 1964 revolution will be discussed in my *Modernization and the Military in Brazil.* Brazilian writings concerning the coup itself and the early months of the succeeding government are numerous, although generally journalistic rather than systematically analytical. A large number of books are primarily collections of newspaper columns written by the authors during 1964 and subsequently published in book form. Among the more significant works of this type are Márcio Moreira Alves, *A velha classe* (Rio de Janeiro: Editôra Arte Nova,

1964); João Carlos Alvim, *A revolução sem rumo* (Rio de Janeiro: Edições do Val, 1964); Alceu Amoroso Lima, *Revolução, reação ou reforma?* (Rio de Janeiro: Editôra Tempo Brasileiro, 1964); Otto Maria Carpeaux, *O Brasil no espelho do mundo* (Rio de Janeiro: Editôra Civilização Brasileira, 1965); Mário Martins, *Em nossos dias de intolerância* (Rio de Janeiro: Editôra Tempo Brasileiro, 1965); Afonso Arinos de Mello Franco, *Evolução da crise Brasileira* (São Paulo: Companhia Editôra Nacional, 1965); Edmundo Moniz, *O golpe de Abril* (Rio de Janeiro: Editôra Civilização Brasileira, 1965); Beneval de Oliveira, *Odio destrói o Brasil* (Rio de Janeiro: Editôra Tempo Brasileiro, 1965); João Camilo de Oliveira Torres, *Razão e Destino da Revolução* (Petropolis: Editôra Vozes, 1964); and Augusto Frederico Schmidt, *Prelúdio a revolução* (Rio de Janeiro: Edições do Val, 1964). Miguel Reale, *Imperativos da Revolução de Março* (São Paulo: Livraria Martins Editôra, 1965) and Goffredo Telles Júnior, *A Democracia e o Brasil* (São Paulo: Editôra Revista dos Tribunais, 1965) represent the first wave of literature justifying the revolution in semi-ideological terms. Popular columnist David Nasser has brought together his weekly magazine articles in *A Revolução que se perdeu a si mesma* (Rio de Janeiro: Edições O Cruzeiro, 1965); and *João Sem Mêdo* (Rio de Janeiro: Edições O Cruzeiro, 1965).

A number of the works published in 1964 reflect serious scholarship more than political positions and are crucial to an understanding of subsequent developments. Fernando Pedreira, *Março 31: Civis e Militares no Processo de Crise Brasileira* (Rio de Janeiro: José Alvaro Editor, 1964) is of substantial analytical as well as interpretative value. Two selections of essays by Oliveiros S. Ferreira, *As Forças Armadas e o Desafio da Revolução* (Rio de Janeiro: Edição GRD, 1964) and *O Fim do Poder Civil* (São Paulo: Editôra Convívio, 1966), should be consulted along with Pedreira's book.

The military movement of 1964 has been described less systematically but with greater detail in Alberto Dines et al., *Os Idos de Março e a Queda em Abril* (Rio de Janeiro: José Alvaro Editor, 1964), and José Stacchini, *Março 1964: Mobilização da Audacia* (São Paulo: Companhia Editôra Nacional, 1965). Araken Távora, *Brasil, 1 de Abril* (Rio de Janeiro: Branco Buccini Editor, 1964) is a much weaker reportorial effort which has been unduly influential owing to its simulaneous publication in English by the Brazilian publisher as *How Brazil Stopped Communism*. Background detail is rich in the journalistic chronological treatment of Mário Victor, *5 Anos que Abalaram o Brasil: de Jânio Quadros ao Marechal Castello Branco* (Rio de Janeiro: Editôra Civilização Brasileira, 1965). A more critical treatment is contained in Nelson Werneck Sodré, *História Militar do Brasil* (Rio de

Janeiro: Editôra Civilização Brasileira, 1965) as supplemented by his *Memorias de um Soldado* (Rio de Janeiro: Editôra Civilização Brasileira, 1967). Glauco Carneiro, *História das Revoluções Brasileiras,* Vol. II (Rio de Janeiro: Edições O Cruzeiro, 1965), also covers the fall of Goulart and the early stages of the military regime. Most valuable of the books by members of the Goulart government is Abelardo Jurema, *Sexta-Feira, 13: os últimos dias do govêrno Goulart* (Rio de Janeiro: Editôra O Cruzeiro, 1964); his *Entre os Andes e a Revolução* (Rio de Janeiro: Editôra Leitura, 1965) adds some additional details.

Materials on repression and punishment during the early stages of the military regime include Alceu Amoroso Lima, *Pelo Humanismo Ameaçado* (Rio de Janeiro: Editôra Tempo Brasileiro, 1965); Carlos Heitor Cony, *O Ato e o Fato: Crônicos Políticos* (Rio de Janeiro: Editôra Civilização Brasileira, 1964); Cid Franco, *Anotações de um Cassado* (São Paulo: Livraria Martins Editôra, 1965); Mario Lago, *1° de Abril: Estórias para a História* (Rio de Janeiro: Editôra Civilização Brasileira, 1964); Carlos Marighella, *Porque resistí a prisão* (Rio de Janeiro: Edições Contemporâneas, 1965); Márcio Moreira Alves, *Torturas e Torturados* (Rio de Janeiro: Editôra Idade Nôva, 1966); and Saldanha Coelho, *Um Deputado no Exílio* (Rio de Janeiro: Editôra Leitura, 1965). Enio Silveira, "Primer Epístola ao Marechal: Sôbre o 'Delito de Opinião,' " *Revista Civilização Brasileira,* No. 3 (July, 1965), pp. 3–11 and "Segunda Epístola: Sôbre a vara de marmelo," *Ibid,* No. 4 (September, 1965), pp. 3–8 are open letters from a leftist publisher to Castelo Branco complaining of the regime's harsh and insensitive treatment of intellectuals. Subsequently, Silveira elicited generally critical comment on the administration's policies through a questionnaire addressed to a number of public figures and published as "Questionário proposto pela Revista Civilização Brasileira a personalidades da vida pública nacional," *ibid,* No. 7 (May, 1966), pp. 15–73. The administration's foreign policy was severely attacked by another of Silveira's reviews, *Política Externa Independente,* during its short life in 1965–1966.

"O terrorismo cultural," *Revista Civilização Brasileira,* No. 1 (March, 1965), pp. 239–97 brings together a large number of stories of repression directed against students and intellectuals. The flavor of zealous, if not fanatic, military investigations directed against supposed "subversives" can be found in books by two governors victimized by the hard-line military. Mauro Borges, *O Golpe em Goiás: História de uma Grande Traição* (Rio de Janeiro: Editôra Civilização Brasileira, 1965) carries this story further into the Castelo Branco administration than João de Seixas Doria, *Eu, Réu Sem Crime* (Rio de Janeiro: Editôra Equador, 1965). João Cândido Maia Neto,

Brasil, Guerra Quente na América Latina (Rio de Janeiro: Editôra Civilização Brasileira, 1965), presents a perspective of developments corresponding closely to that of Leonel Brizola, whose press aide the author had been. Edmar Morel, *O Golpe Começou em Washington* (Rio de Janeiro: Editôra Civilização Brasileira, 1965), is the most coherent treatment of the early post-coup period from a strongly anti-United States point of view. A series of relevant articles include "História de 'Historia Nova,' " *Revista Civilização Brasileira,* No. 3 (July, 1965), pp. 27–40 and 321–65, continued in No. 4 (September, 1965), pp. 71–84; " 'História Nova': Denúncia do Procurador-Geral," *Revista Civilização Brasileira,* No. 11–12 (December, 1966-March, 1967), pp. 208–12; and "Discurso Pronunciado Pelo Deputado Mata Machado e Publico no DCN de 30-3-67," *Paz e Terra,* No. 4 (August, 1967), pp. 229–42. "Abril, Documentario Extra," *Paz e Terra,* No. 6 (April, 1968), pp. 281–97 recounts subsequent difficulties between the regime and students. Ralph della Cava, "Torture in Brazil," *Commonweal,* XCII, No. 6 (April 24, 1970), 135–41 is the most competent study of this darker side of the post-1964 scene. Hélio Fernandes, *Recordações de um Desterrado em Fernando de Noronha* (Rio de Janeiro: Editôra de Tribunal da Imprensa, 1967) represents the attitude of intransigent critics of the military regime. The anti-communist military's views on intellectuals as subversives is demonstrated in Col. Ferdinando de Carvalho, *Inquérito Policial Militar No. 709, O Comunismo no Brasil* (4 vols.; Rio de Janeiro: Biblioteca do Exército, 1966–1967). Márcio Moreira Alves, *O Cristo do Povo* (Rio de Janeiro: Editôra Sabiá, 1968) stresses regime repression against Catholic youth leaders and progressive churchman. "Congresso da UNE Aguça a Crise Igreja-Govêrno," *Paz e Terra,* No. 6 (April, 1968), pp. 181–97; and Frei Francisco de Araújo, "O Cristão e a Violência," *Paz e Terra,* No. 7 (1968), pp. 99–112 are also indicative of intensification of Catholic opponents of the regime. Perhaps the most penetrating analysis of the radicalization of Brazilian Catholic youth is contained in Cândido Mendes de Almeida, *Memento dos Vivos: A esquerda Católica no Brasil* (Rio de Janeiro: Edições Tempo Brasileiro, 1966), particularly pp. 173–215. The most comprehensive treatment of the MEB and various related movements can be found in Emanuel de Kadt, *Catholic Radicals in Brazil* (New York: Oxford University Press, 1970), pp. 102–274; Manoel Cardoso, "The Brazilian Church and the New Left," *Journal of Inter-American Studies,* VI, No. 3 (July, 1964), 313–21; Thomas G. Sanders, "Catholicism and Development: The Catholic Left in Brazil" in Kalman Silvert (ed.), *Churches and States* (New York: American Universities Field Staff, 1967), pp. 81–100; and David E. Mutchler, *Roman Catholicism in Brazil* (Washington University, St. Louis), *Studies in Comparative Inter-*

national Development, Vol. I, No. 8 (1965) are also of use in this respect. The historical political role of the Church is portrayed in a dissertation by Margaret Todaro, "Pastors, Prophets and Politicians: A Study of the Political Development of the Brazilian Church, 1916–1945" (Columbia University, Department of History, 1971). A more recent period is covered by Thomas Bruneau, "Conflict and Change in the Brazilian Catholic Church" (University of California, Department of Political Science, 1970). These should be supplemented by three Institute of Current World Affairs Newsletters by Thomas G. Sanders, "The Regional Seminar of the Northeast," "Catholics and UNE," and "The Evolution of a Catholic Intellectual," dated, respectively, August, September, and October, 1967. The relevant Brazilian literature includes João Camilo de Oliveira Torres, *História das ideas religiosas no Brasil* (São Paulo: Editorial Grijalbo, 1968) and Padre Raimundo Caramuru de Barros, *Brasil, uma Igreja em Renovação* (Petropolis: Editôra Vozes, 1967). The views of the conservative Tradition, Family, and Property movement have evolved from Antônio de Castro Mayer, Geraldo de Proença Segaud, Plínio Corrêa de Oliveira, and Luiz Mendonça de Freitas, *Reforma Agraria: Questão de Consciência* (São Paulo: Editôra Vera Cruz, 1960). The evolution of reformist Archbishop Helder Câmara's views during the period under examination can be seen in his "Evangelização e Humanização num Mundo em Desenvolvimento," *Paz e Terra,* No. 1 (July, 1966), pp. 235–42; "Imposições da Solidariedade Universal," *Paz e Terra,* No. 5 (October, 1967), pp. 159–68; and "O Violência—Unica Opção," *Paz e Terra,* No. 7 (1968), pp. 89–97. More comprehensive in his *Revolução dentro de Paz* (Rio de Janeiro: Editôra Sabiá, 1968). A number of documents bearing on the inception of Church-military differences in the Northeast can be found in "Nova questão religiosa?" *Paz e Terra,* No. 2 (September, 1966), pp. 240–87. An eloquent defense of the Church's progressive wing against military and conservative criticism is Edgar G. de Mata Machado, "A Igreja Voltada para o Futuro, o Govêrno Apegado ao que Passou," *Paz e Terra,* No. 7 (1968), pp. 301–15.

The most important work in English on the Brazilian student movement is that of Robert Myhr, beginning with his Ph.D. dissertation, "The Political Role of University Students in Brazil" (Columbia University, Department of Political Science, 1968). A summary version can be found in Donald K. Emmerson (ed.) *Students and Politics in Developing Nations* (New York: Praeger Publishers, 1968), pp. 249–85. See also his "The University Student Tradition in Brazil," *Journal of Inter-American Studies and World Affairs,* XII, No. 1 (January, 1970), 126–140; and "Nationalism in the Brazilian Student Movement," *Inter-American Economic Affairs,* XXII, No. 4 (Spring,

1969), 81–94. The most comprehensive history of political activity by Brazilian students is Arthur José Poerner, *O Poder Jovem: História da Participação Política dos Estudantes Brasileiros* (Rio de Janeiro: Editôra Civilização Brasileira, 1968). Articles of value include Sulamita de Britto, "A Juventude Universitária e a Política," *Cadernos Brasileiros*, No. 48 (July-August, 1968), pp. 5–19; her "A Crise entre Estudantes e Govêrno no Brasil," *Paz e Terra*, No. 3 (1967), pp. 191–24 and "O Radicalismo Estudantil," *Cadernos Brasileiros*, No. 35 (May-June, 1966), pp. 71–77; José Maria Mayrink, "A Inquietude Universitaria, *Cadernos Brasileiros*, No. 39 (January-February, 1967), pp. 44–54; A. L. Machado Neto, "A Ex-Univeresidade de Brasília: Significação e Crise," *Revista Civilização Brasileira*, No. 14 (July, 1967), pp. 139–58; Sérgio Guerra Duarte, "A Presença Americana na Educação Nacional," *Cadernos Brasileiros*, No. 46 (March-April, 1968), pp. 35–59, and his "Uma Frustração Nacional: A Educação," *Cadernos Brasileiros*, No. 42 (July-August, 1967), pp. 27–35; and Ted Goertzel, "MEC-USAID: Ideologia de Desenvolvimento Americano Aplicado a Educação Superior Brasileira," *Revista Civilização Brasileira*, No. 14 (July, 1967), pp. 23–37. H. Jon Rosenbaum, "El Projecto Rondon: um experimento Brasileño de desarrollo econômico y político," *Foro Internacional*, 38 (October-December, 1969), pp. 136–48, provides an analysis of the government's efforts to gain student support through enlisting their energies in developmental programs.

Although far from adequate, the literature on education in Brazil contains several particularly useful items. Robert J. Havighurst and Aparecida Joly Gouveia, *Brazilian Secondary Education and Socio-Economic Development* (New York: Praeger Publishers, 1969); Robert J. Havighurst and J. Roberto Moreira, *Society and Education in Brazil* (Pittsburgh: University of Pittsburgh Press, 1965); and Marialice M. Foracchi, *O Estudante e a Transformação da Sociedade Brasileira* (São Paulo: Companhia Editôra Nacional, 1965) are basic sources. "Bibliografia Sôbre Reforma Universitária no Brasil, 1966–1968," *América Latina*, XII, No. 1 (January-March, 1969), 116–127, provides additional leads. General Meira Mattos' study of the educational system and student problems is contained in *Paz e Terra*, No. 9 (October, 1969), pp. 199–241. This issue also contains the reports of other groups studying reform of the university system. The most recent assessments are Fernando Bastos D'Avila et al., *A Educação que Nos Convém* (Rio de Janeiro: APEC Editôra, 1969) and Lauro de Oliveira Lima, *O Impasse na Educação* (Petrópolis: Editôra Vozes, 1969).

The relatively sparce sources on the agrarian situation include Armin K. Ludwig and Harry W. Taylor, *Brazil's New Agrarian Reform: An Evaluation of Its Property Classification and Tax System* (New York: Praeger Publishers, 1969); James W. Rowe, "The 'Week of the Land' in the Brazilian Sertão," *American Universities Field Staff Reports,* East Coast South America Series, XII, No. 1 (February, 1966); Robert E. Price, "The Brazilian Land Reform Statute" (mimeo; Land Tenure Center, University of Wisconsin, April, 1965); Sílvia Loreto, "Reforma Agraria no Brasil—Implicações Sociológicas," *Revista Brasileira de Estudos Políticos,* No. 27 (July, 1969), pp. 95–150; José de Souza Martins, "Modernização e Problema Agrário no Estado de São Paulo," *Revista do Instituto de Estudos Brasileiros,* No. 6 (1969), pp. 121–145. Miss Marta Cehelsky of Columbia University's Department of Political Science is completing a Ph.D. dissertation on agrarian reform (as a case study in decision-making) in Brazil. On the political organition of rural populations, the most comprehensive work is the doctoral dissertation by Neale Pearson, "Small Farmer and Rural Worker Pressure Groups in Brazil" (University of Florida, Department of Political Science, 1968), a thorough study ranging from Rio Grande do Sul to the Northeast based upon field research carried out in Brazil during 1964–1965. A condensed version of this work is available as "Small Farmer and Rural Worker Characteristics in the Emergence of Brazilian Peasant Pressure Groups, 1955–1968" in Merrill Rippy, ed., *Cultural Change in Brazil* (Muncie, Indiana: Ball State University, 1970). *A Reforma Agraria: Problemas—Bases—Solução* (Rio de Janeiro: Instituto de Pesquisas e Estudos Sociais, 1964) is a basic study of the problem which heavily influenced the agricultural policy of the Castelo Branco government. The best source on the trade union movement is the doctoral dissertation of Kenneth P. Erickson, "Labor in the Political Process in Brazil: Corporatism in a Modernizing Nation" (Columbia University, Department of Political Science, 1969). Also of considerable value is Howard J. Wiarda, *The Brazilian Catholic Labor Movement* (Amherst, Mass.: University of Massachusetts Labor Relations and Research Center, 1969).

The political orientation of the Armed Forces is discussed by several authors in a special issue of *Cadernos Brasileiros,* No. 38 (November-December, 1966). National security doctrine is treated in an entire number of the *Revista Brasileira de Estudos Políticos,* No. 21 (July, 1966). Other sources in this field are more of an official nature. The War College Graduates' Association (ADESG) was founded in 1951 to propagate "doctrinary concepts related to the Security and Development of Brazil, in accord with the work methods and studies of the ESG" and to provide its associates with the current doctrine of the ESG.' In addition to *Segurança e Desenvolvimento,* the ADESG journal which publishes non-classified ESG conferences, two useful sources for accompanying Brazilian military thought are *A Defesa*

Nacional and the *Revista Militar Brasileira,* with the *Revista do Instituto de Geografía e História Militar do Brasil* valuable more on historical topics than on current doctrine or controversies. Both the *Mensario de Cultura Militar* and *Revista do Clube Militar* contain relevant articles on current issues of concern to the officer corps. For example, the issue of *Mensario* . . . , No. 183–184 (January-February, 1964), pp. 5–12 and 13–21, is particularly interesting for its inclusion of two conferences by then Army Chief of Staff Castelo Branco preparing military opinion for possible action against the President. The dissemination of basic "National Security" concepts to civilian elite groups is exemplified by Major Fernando Guimarães de Cerqueira Lima, *Os Diferentes Aspectos da Guerra Moderna* (São Paulo: Forum Roberto Simonsen, 1961). This pamphlet by the Second Military Region's intelligence officer, published by the Forum Roberto Simonsen (an organ of the Center and Federation of Industries) served to introduce the concept of irregular warfare to the businessmen and industrialists of São Paulo. See also, for example, Antônio Carlos Pacheco e Silva, "Guerra Psicológica," *Convivium,* III, No. 2 (1964), 3–31. That the roots of this civilian-military collaboration on politically significant matters goes back well before 1964 is evidenced by the fact that the Federation of Commerce of the State of São Paulo more than a decade earlier had established an Instituto de Sociología e Política, which in 1954 undertook a series of studies of Brazilian "reality" within the ESG framework of "Segurança Nacional." Eventually published as *Estudo Socio-Político da Vida* (São Paulo: Federação do Comêrcio do Estado de São Paulo, SESC e SENAC, 1958), the conclusions of this entrepreneurial group were quite pessimistic concerning the trends they saw emerging in the country and essentially congruent with eventual acceptance of a military movement such as that of 1964. Brigadier Lysias A. Rodrigues, *Geopolítica do Brasil* (Rio de Janeiro: Biblioteca Militar, 1947), exemplifies the unrefined geopolitical concepts prevalent within the Brazilian military prior to the institution of the ESG. A somewhat broader perspective of stock taking in light of the post-war world is provided by Colonel Adalardo Fialho, *Problemas do Brasil* (Rio de Janeiro: Biblioteca do Exército, 1952). Also representative of currents of military thought are Carlos Maul, *O Exército e a Nacionalidade* (Rio de Janeiro: Biblioteca do Exército, 1950); Samuel Guimarães da Costa, *Formação democrática do exército Brasileiro* (Rio de Janeiro: Biblioteca do Exército, 1957); Hermes de Araújo Oliveria, *Guerra Revolucionária* (Rio de Janeiro: Biblioteca do Exército, 1965); and Sérgio Marinho, *Aspectos de Sociología* (Rio de Janeiro: Biblioteca do Exército, 1958).

The "Sorbonne" outlook as of the Castelo period can be seen most clearly in the works of General Golbery do Couto e Silva, particularly *Planejamento Estratégico* (Rio de Janeiro: Biblioteca do Exército, 1955); *Aspectos Geopolíticos do Brasil* (Rio de Janeiro: Biblioteca de Exército, 1957); and *Geopolítica do Brasil* (Rio de Janeiro: Livraria José Olympio, 1967). Oliveiros S. Ferreira, "La geopolítica y el Ejército brasileño," *Aportes,* No. 12 (April, 1969), pp. 111–332, contains a critical review of Golbery's works. Castelo Branco's own speeches have been compiled in a series of official volumes. See Humberto de Alencar Castelo Branco, *Discursos 1964* (Brasília: Imprensa Nacional, 1965); *Discursos 1965* (Brasília: Imprensa Nacional, 1966); and *Discursos 1966* (Brasília: Imprensa Nacional, 1967). Many of his writings on military matters have been brought together in Colonel Francisco Ruas Santos, *Marechal Castelo Branco: Seu Pensamento Militar* (Rio de Janeiro: Imprensa do Exército, 1968). The evolution of the views of General Carlos de Meira Mattos, one of the intellectual heirs of Castelo Branco, can be seen by a comparison of his *Projecão Mundial do Brasil* (São Paulo: Grafica Leal, 1961) with his *Ensaio Sôbre a Doutrina Política da Revolução* (Bahia: Imprensa Official, 1969) and *Doutrina Política de Potência* (Bahia: Imprensa Oficial, 1970).

The most prolific writer among the high military figures of the 1964–1969 period was General Aurélio de Lyra Tavares with his *Território Nacional: Soberania e Domínio do Estados* (Rio de Janeiro: Biblioteca do Exército, 1955); *Segurança Nacional: Antagonismos e Vulnerabilidades* (Rio de Janeiro: Biblioteca do Exército, 1958); *Exército e Nação* (Recife: Imprensa Universitária, 1965); *Segurança Nacional: Problemas Atuais* (Rio de Janeiro: Biblioteca do Exército, 1965); *O Exército Brasileiro visto pelo seu Ministro* (Recife: Imprensa Universitária, 1968); and *Além dos Temas da Caserna* (Fortaleza: Imprensa Universitária do Ceará, 1968). More revealing of his political views are *Orações Cívicas e Militares* (Joaô Pessoa: *Universidade Federal da Paraíba,* 1967) and *Por Dever do Ofício* (Rio de Janeiro: Imprensa de Exército, 1969). Gilberto Freyre's favorable views on the military were published as "Fôrças Armadas e Outras Fôrças," *A Defesa Nacional,* LII, No. 605 (January-February, 1966), 7–22. José Américo de Almeida et al., *A Revolução de 31 de Março: 2° Aniversario. Colaboração do Exército* (Rio de Janeiro: Biblioteca do Exército, 1966), contains speeches by a variety of regime spokesmen.

Relations among the senior officers of the post-1964 period were often influenced by their experience during World War II. Thus in 1968–1969 major controversy arose with the publication by Marshal Floriano Lima Brayner of *A Verdade Sôbre a FEB: Memórias de um Chefe de Estado-Maior na Campanha da Itália* (Rio de Janeiro: Editôra Civilização Brasileira,

1968). Holding that this volume attempted to down grade the role of Castelo Branco, the latter's admirers rushed into print Marshal João Baptista Mascarenhas de Moraes' two-volume *Memórias* (Rio de Janeiro: Livraria José Olympio, 1969) complete with a preface by General Meira Mattos emphasizing the FEB commanding general's reliance upon Castelo's advice (as head of the Operations Section) in preference to that of his Chief of Staff (Lima Brayner). The standard sources on FEB prior to publication of these two studies were Mascarenhas de Moraes, *A FEB Pelo Seu Commandante* (São Paulo: Instituto Progresso Editorial, 1947) and Manoel Thomaz Castelo Branco, *O Brasil na II Grande Guerra* (Rio de Janeiro: Biblioteca do Exército, 1960).

Brazilian sensitivity concerning possible U.S. designs upon the Amazon region is reflected in General Tácito Lívio Reis de Freitas, "A Amazônia em Foco: O Caso do Instituto da Hiléia," *Revista Civilização Brasileira,* No. 17 (January-February, 1968), pp. 36–48 and Arthur Cezar Ferreira Reis, *A Amazônia e a Cobiça Internacional* (3d ed.; Rio de Janeiro: Gráfica Record Editôra, 1968). An optimistic view of Brazil's future is contained in Mário Henrique Simonsen, *Brasil 2001* (Rio de Janeiro: APEC Editôra 1969), with José Itamar de Freitas, *Brasil Ano 2000: O Futuro sem Fantasia* (Rio de Janeiro: Editôra Monterrey, 1969) taking a pessimistic attitude. The foreign policy outlook of the military regime is reflected in Ministério das Relações Exteriores, Secretaria Geral Adjunta para Planejamento Político, *Documentos de Política Externa de 15 de Março a 15 de Outubro de 1967* (Rio de Janeiro: Imprensa Nacional, 1968) with the basic tenor of military-technocratic views embodied in J.O. de Meira Penna, *Política Externa Segurança e Desenvolvimento* (Rio de Janeiro: Livraria AGIR Editôra, 1967).

Lúcia Maria Gaspar Gomes, "Cronologia do Govêrno Castelo Branco," *Dados* 2/3 (1967), pp. 112–232 and "Cronologia do 1° ano do Govêrno Costa e Silva," *Dados,* 4 (1968), pp. 199–220 provide convenient aids to students seeking to establish the time relationship among events in the political and economic realms. Analytical works covering the last part of the Costa e Silva government and the Garrastazú Médici regime do not yet exist. In addition to the Brazilian journals and newspapers, which operated under substantial restraint and "self-censureship" after December, 1968, there are very limited English-language sources. *Brazil 1969* (New York: Center for Inter-American Relations, 1970) brings together frequently insightful articles on Brazil originally published in *Latin America,* a weekly newsletter published in England.

The most useful model of an authoritarian political system is that contained in Juan Linz's "An Authoritarian Regime: Spain," in E. Allardt and Y. Littunen (Eds.), *Cleavages, Ideologies and Party Systems: Contributions to Comparative Political Sociology* (Helsinki: Transactions of the Westermarck Society, 1964), with some further development of content in his "The Party System of Spain: Past and Future," in Lipset and Rokkan, *Party Systems and Voter Alignments,* pp. 197–282. See also Juan J. Linz and Amando de Miguel, "Within National Differences and Comparisons: The Eight Spains," in Richard L. Merritt and Stein Rokkan (eds.), *Comparing Nations* (New Haven: Yale University Press, 1966). A very relevant theoretical work on the political dynamics of dictatorial military regimes is that of Arpad Von Lazar, "Latin America and the Politics of Post-Authoritarianism: A Model for Decompression," *Comparative Political Studies,* I, No. 3 (October, 1968), 419–29. Useful for broader comparison are Louis Coser, "Prospects for the New Nations: Totalitarianism, Authoritarianism or Demorcacy?," in Louis Coser (ed.), *Political Sociology* (New York: Harper & Row, 1966), and A.F.K. Organski, *The Stages of Political Development* (New York: Alfred Knopf, 1965). There remains a temptation to apply the masterful analysis by Barrington Moore, Jr. of the "capitalist and reactionary" road to modernity to contemporary Brazil, but upon reflection its relevance is primarily to the experience of the Old Republic and secondarily to the Vargas era rather than to the postwar period. It provides more the backdrop of the *sistema* than it illuminates the emergence of the present brand of authoritarian regime. See Barrington Moore, Jr., *Social Origins of Dictatorship and Democracy: Lord and Peasant in the Making of the Modern World* (Boston: Beacon Press, 1966), particularly pp. 433–53. The analytical literature on authoritarian regimes in Latin America is very weak, although descriptive-interpretative studies of dictators and dictatorship abound. The most useful work is on the Dominican Republic, a small Hispanic Caribbean country which differs substantially from Brazil in many (if not most) significant respects. It would appear to represent a sub-type distinct from both the Spanish and the Brazilian models of authoritarianism. See particularly the several works of Howard J. Wiarda, including *Dictatorship and Development: The Methods of Control in Trujillo's Dominican Republic* (Gainsville: University of Florida Press, 1968) and his Ph.D. dissertation on "The Aftermath of the Trujillo Dictatorship: The Emergence of a Pluralist Political System in the Dominican Republic" (University of Florida, Department of Political Science, 1967), as well as a series of articles spun off from the latter work during 1965–67. Consult also Robert D. Crassweller's fascinating and informative *Trujillo: the Life and Times of a Caribbean Dictator* (New York: Macmillan, 1966). The Dominican model, which could quite feasibly be generated into a broader Caribbean type of authoritarianism, necessarily involves the sophisticated analysis of the complex pattern of *caudillismo,* a phenomenon quite far removed from the realities of the Brazilian system. As a central feature it must stress personalism even significantly beyond the extent to which this is a factor in the Spanish case. In his insistence upon linking modern dictatorships with totalitarianism and traditional dictators with authoritarianism, Wiarda has, for the present at least, foregone the opportunity to achieve or approximate what he himself recognizes as necessary: "that a conceptual framework which relates typologies of dictatorships to theories of political development and modernization, and which thus allows for numerous transitional kinds of regimes, would be a more useful theoretical tool . . ." (*Dictatorship and Development,* p. 12). Instead he ends up with a formulation which minimizes the possibilities for meaningful comparative analysis, with the Trujillo regime considered as "a blend of traditional, nineteenth-century caudillo dictatorship, transitional authoritarianism (in the sense this term is used by Linz), and modern, twentieth-century totalitarianism." Wiarda and his wife, Ieda S. Wiarda (a Brazilian), have written an article on "Revolution or Counter-Revolution in Brazil?" *The Massachusetts Review,* VIII, No. 1 (Winter, 1967), 149–65; it is, however, essentially reportorial rather than analytical. Their future work on Brazil, along with that by a number of scholars on contemporary Argentine and Peruvian politics may facilitate meaningful comparison among Latin American systems of an authoritarian character.

Index of Names

Index of Subjects